AIR POWER
AND
NATIONAL SECURITY

Indian Air Force: Evolution, Growth and Future

AIR POWER
AND
NATIONAL SECURITY

Indian Air Force: Evolution, Growth and Future

Air Commodore Ramesh V. Phadke (Retd.)

INSTITUTE FOR DEFENCE STUDIES & ANALYSES
NEW DELHI

PENTAGON PRESS

Air Power and National Security: Indian Air Force: Evolution, Growth and Future
Air Commodore Ramesh V. Phadke (Retd.)

First Published in 2015

ISBN 978-81-8274-840-8

Published by
PENTAGON PRESS
206, Peacock Lane, Shahpur Jat,
New Delhi-110049
Phones: 011-64706243, 26491568
Telefax: 011-26490600
email: rajan@pentagonpress.in
website: www.pentagonpress.in

Branch
Flat No.213, Athena-2,
Clover Acropolis,
Viman Nagar,
Pune-411014
Email: pentagonpresspune@gmail.com

In association with
Institute for Defence Studies and Analyses
No. 1, Development Enclave,
New Delhi-110010
Phone: +91-11-26717983
Website: www.idsa.in

Printed at Aegean Offset Printers, Greater Noida, U.P.

This book is dedicated to the memory of my parents,

Shri V.V. Phadke and Shrimati Vimal Phadke,

My in-laws, Brig. G.S. Sidhu, AVSM and Mrs. Pritam Sidhu,

Late Flg. Offr. Harita Deol, my niece, who died in an Avro accident on December 24, 1996,

Late Flt. Lt. Sandeep Jain, another niece's husband, who was shot down by a Pakistani missile in Siachen on August 26, 1996,

To all the past and future air warriors of the Indian Air Force.

Contents

Acknowledgements

This book has been in the works for considerable time, delayed due to family ill health, bereavements, my own indifferent health and other domestic issues.

Many friends, colleagues and mentors, in and outside the Indian Air Force, have given me guidance and support. Late Air Cmde. Jasjit Singh, former Director of Institute for Defence Studies and Analyses (IDSA) and Centre for Air Power Studies (CAPS); late Professor Matin Zuberi and my school teacher Shri Manohar Parnerkar continue to inspire me in the pursuit of my study of India's security.

Late Brig. G.S. Sidhu, AVSM, my father-in-law, the Brigade Major of the 7th Brigade, from 1959 when it moved from Ambala to Bomdi La until early 1962, and an active participant in the 1965 and 1971 Indo-Pak wars, gave me immense first-hand information about the real state of affairs in the army during his long service.

AVM Kapil Kak, former Deputy Director, IDSA, Dr. Arvind Gupta, former Director General, IDSA, Brig. Rumel Dahiya (Retd.), Deputy Director General, IDSA and Lt. Gen. V.R. Raghavan (Retd.) have played an important role in the publication of this book through their patience, advice and encouragement.

Air Marshals Randhir Singh, P. Rajkumar, S.G. Inamdar, Narayan Menon, Raghu Rajan, B.K. Pande and AVM H.S. Ahluwalia provided me with valuable guidance and information. Air Marshal M. Matheswaran assisted in enhancing my understanding of recent developments in the Indian Air Force. Gp. Capt. Ajit Agtey (Retd.), a friend of over four decades and a passionate flyer, continues to be a veritable treasure trove of information and knowledge and has always readily and generously shared it with me.

I also thank Professors Rajaram Nagappa, Chandrashekhar and Nabil Mancheri of the National Institute of Advanced Studies, Bangalore for their valuable advice.

Professor K.R. Singh, Dr. Rajaram Panda and senior colleagues and friends at IDSA, now professors at JNU, Drs. Rajesh Rajagopalan, Swaran Singh, and P.R. Kumaraswamy, deserve my sincere thanks.

I thank my friends at IDSA, Gp. Capt. Vivek Kapur, Brigs. Raj Shukla, Harinder Singh and Col. Deepak Sharma who have since returned to active duty and Drs. Rajiv Nayan, S. Kalyanaraman, Ashok Behuria, Smruti Pattanaik, Laxman Behera and Uttam Sinha, and many others from whom I learnt a lot during my second stint at IDSA. Gp. Capt. (Dr.) Ajey Lele and Dr. Prashant Kumar Singh of the IDSA took time to read through the draft and gave me very valuable suggestions. A word of special thanks to Ms. Sumita Kumar and Mr. Vivek Kaushik of IDSA for their editorial assistance and insightful comments that have helped reduce inaccuracies.

I am indeed grateful to Shri Mukesh Kumar, Shri Pitamber Datt, and other staff members of the IDSA library for their timely and cheerful assistance.

Finally, I owe an enormous debt of gratitude to my family: my son Akshay, himself a fighter pilot; daughter Aarohi an artist and an MA in History from Hindu College; and my wife Dr. P. Sidhu Phadke, a graduate of the Lady Harding Medical College, New Delhi, a true healer and author of four books for their unstinted and selfless support and encouragement.

While I have made every effort to be as accurate and impartial as possible, I am responsible for any errors or omissions.

Ramesh V. Phadke

1

Introduction

Air power has been around for over a century and is not new to India. India's first experience with aviation was when a flying display was staged at Allahabad Polo Grounds on December 10, 1910,[1] just seven years after the first flight of the Wright Brothers' heavier-than-air machine, at Kitty Hawk on the eastcoast of the United States (US) on December 17, 1903.

In response to the nationalist demands for 'Indianisation' of the military, the Indian Air Force (IAF) came into being on October 8, 1932 with a single flight of eight Westland Wapiti bi-planes. It slowly but steadily grew to become the fourth largest air force in the world in terms of number of personnel and aircraft. Yet, the IAF is in no way as advanced as many of the smaller yet more potent air forces of the Western world. In fact, until the 1990s, it remained largely tactical, with limited range armaments equipped only with the first and second generation aircraft. As a result, its capabilities were at best modest and yet it proved to be a decisive factor in the wars that were *imposed* on India.[2]

The very limited assets of the fledgling IAF were successfully used within weeks of India becoming independent to help evict the *mujahideen* (tribal raiders) that Pakistan sent to 'liberate' the Indian state of Jammu and Kashmir (J&K). Undoubtedly the high watermark of the IAF was when, in a mere 72 hours in December 1971, it established total command of the skies over erstwhile East Pakistan, helping in its liberation and the creation of a new nation-state of Bangladesh.

The IAF has also been used on numerous other occasions for providing relief and succour when natural calamities, such as floods and cyclones hit parts of India and its neighbourhood. It has also been used to aid civil power and for limited intervention in situations outside India. For over a decade, the IAF has been in the process of a comprehensive modernisation programme, the results of which will take another decade to reach fruition. It has already obtained a formidable array of aircraft and weapons and a variety of force multipliers and is today poised to play a much larger, even strategic role in the Indian Ocean Region (IOR) in concert with the fast-modernising Indian Navy's Fleet Air Arm. Given India's continued dependence on foreign countries for high-technology aircraft, missiles and other armaments, the modernisation process is, however, fraught with many uncertainties and unpredictable delays. In the meantime, parts of the IAF fighter fleet have been showing signs of ageing and obsolescence. The IAF leadership is thus faced with the challenge of safeguarding the nation's air space with rapidly dwindling combat assets.

The stark reality that characterises India's national security scenario is the long-running dispute it has with two major neighbours: the Islamic Republic of Pakistan and the People's Republic of China (PRC). India shares a 4,000 km long disputed border with the PRC in the high Himalayas where China illegally occupies some 38,000 sq km of the Indian state of J&K and in addition claims some 93,000 sq km of Indian territory in the state of Arunachal Pradesh. Pakistan, on the other hand, occupies some 86,023 sq km of Indian territory in Pakistan-occupied Kashmir which includes Gilgit-Baltistan (earlier referred to as Northern Areas by the Government of Pakistan). There are reports of Chinese People's Liberation Army (PLA) soldiers and technicians working on the Karakoram highway in this region. Right from its inception, Pakistan has shown its hostility by constantly and consistently challenging and undermining India's very existence as a secular democratic state. "India and Pakistan are locked not in a geographical dispute but in an ideological war over the present and future of the Indian sub-continent. Pakistan believes in the two-nation theory conceived in the conviction that Hindus and Muslims cannot cooperate as equals."[3] This twin challenge, if not an existential threat from its two major neighbours, demands that India does everything in its power to deter or at least dissuade these implacable and aggressive neighbours from harming its core national interests of sovereignty and territorial integrity.

Just as human beings are creatures of their circumstances, so are nation states. India gained its hard-fought independence from the British colonial masters largely through peaceful and non-violent methods. Due to its vast geographic expanse, large population and unique and strategically important location at the head of the Indian Ocean, India was considered the pivot of the then British Empire but faced few external threats. The so-called threat of imperial Russia, later the Soviet Union, was more in the minds of the British imperialists and hence the large British Indian Army was used mainly to secure the interests of the empire in distant North Africa, the Middle East and even China. All decisions regarding the defence and security of India, were made by the British Government. As a result, until World War II, India only had a Department of Defence, that was staffed and run exclusively by British civil servants and military officers under the guidance of the Secretary of State for India in London, and the Viceroy and the Commander-in-Chief in India. Indians played no part in the formulation of its defence policies.

The Indian leadership at the time of independence was therefore, relatively inexperienced in dealing with the myriad security problems that emerged soon after independence. The integration of the 565 small and large princely states, some like Hyderabad and J&K being as large as some sovereign countries of Europe, into the Indian Union; the many challenges of an exceedingly bloody partition; communal clashes in the north and east; and above all administering an infant sovereign country of continental proportions, put to test the political and administrative acumen and sagacity of the founding fathers. Mahatma Gandhi, Jawaharlal Nehru, Vallabhbhai Patel, and other stalwarts of the Indian National Congress were of the view that the most pressing and vital task for the leadership was to ensure the welfare of the vast multitudes of poverty-stricken Indians. The transformation of the Indian Union into a viable, pluralistic and progressive nation-state followed its own unique model of development based on the principles of freedom, equality and justice, in a constitutional democracy; and a foreign policy based on Panchsheel, the five principles of peaceful coexistence and non-interference.

In the aftermath of the six-year long World War II, that witnessed millions of casualties and worldwide destruction and only ended with the dropping of atom bombs on Hiroshima and Nagasaki in Japan, the whole world was looking to Gandhi's India to provide a peaceful alternative. The period, however, also saw the beginning of the Cold War that was to soon divide the world into two rival blocs led by the US and the Union of Soviet Socialist Republics (USSR). It was thus only natural that Nehru, the first Prime Minister, wanted to steer India clear of this superpower rivalry and instead stand shoulder-to-shoulder with the oppressed peoples of other European colonies in their fight for freedom.

Even though India reluctantly used force to save the princely state of J&K from Pakistan-assisted and inspired tribal raiders, the threat was not seen as insurmountable or long term. In the vain hope that the conflict would be resolved peacefully, India took the dispute to the United Nations (UN) as soon as the Kashmir Valley was cleared of the tribal raiders in January 1948. That was to prove a costly mistake as the dispute continued to fester and soon got embroiled in the larger Cold War calculus, with Pakistan effectively remaining in control of a sizeable portion of the erstwhile princely state of J&K. As Gandhi had prophesied, partition of British India had given rise to two new states in perpetual enmity with each other.[4]

China was just emerging from a long, bloody civil war with the victory of the Communists over the Nationalists and the Kuomintang fleeing to Taiwan. Nehru had earlier visited China and enjoyed excellent rapport with General Chiang Kai-shek, the leader of the Kuomintang. He had met Chiang Kai-shek when the latter had visited India during World War II. Chiang had fled with his followers to the nearby island of Formosa (now Taiwan) and Mao Zedong had become the new leader of Communist China. Nehru was quite aware of China's claims on Tibet and Sardar Patel had cautioned him of the new threat that Communist China might pose to India by occupying Tibet, but Nehru had also calculated that it would take the PRC at least 20 years to build its strength and in the meantime it was preferable to develop friendly relations with that country. Nehru had also organised an Asian Relations Conference to forge Asian solidarity, at New Delhi on March 23, 1947 and had hoped that building friendly relations with all Asian states would help to promote the cause of freedom throughout Asia and indeed the world. India thus was one of the first few powers to recognise Communist China. At its founding on October 1, 1949, Mao, the 'Supreme Leader' declared that, "China had stood up"[5] and would work towards its long cherished goals of national reunification and fight the forces of imperialism and colonialism. Within months, China not only attacked Tibet in October 1950, but also entered the Korean War on the side of the North Koreans, when it sent large numbers of Chinese National Volunteers – in reality PLA soldiers – to Korea in November 1950 to stem the advance of the US-led UN forces.

In April 1954, India signed a trade agreement with the PRC giving up its rights in Tibet and acknowledged Chinese suzerainty there, in the hope that the slogan 'Hindi Chini Bhai Bhai' or 'India-China are Brothers' would actually translate into reality. This hope proved to be false and by 1957, unknown to India, the PRC had constructed a road linking Xinjiang with Tibet through the Aksai Chin area of Ladakh in the high mountains of Himalayas and in fact occupied a large chunk of Indian territory. Although there had been some minor border incidents at Bara Hoti (in Uttar Pradesh) in the central sector of the border in the mid-fifties, it was generally believed that these could be peacefully resolved through negotiations. India, it seems, failed to assess China's long-term strategic objectives and hence also failed to read Chinese signals and the dispute finally resulted in a short but intense border war in October-November 1962 that ended in a crushing defeat of the Indian army in North East Frontier Agency (NEFA), now Arunachal Pradesh. Fifty years on, there are no signs of an early resolution of the dispute even after 16 rounds of parleys between the special representatives of the two countries. As a matter of fact, while speaking at the Council for Foreign Relations in Washington DC, on November 23, 2009, the former Indian Prime Minister Manmohan Singh said, "in the recent past, the PRC has become more assertive", possibly alluding to Chinese PLA troops repeatedly intruding into

Indian territory in parts of Ladakh.[6] Although the border or the Line of Actual Control (LAC) has remained peaceful, repeated intrusions show the fragile nature of the situation on the border.

In the early 1990s, Pakistan, as is its wont, began to fan the flames of what it called an insurgency in J&K and has since launched trans-border terrorism from terror training camps in Pakistan, first in J&K and later in many other parts of India as an instrument of state policy. It hopes to get away with it because it believes that it has effectively neutralised India's conventional superiority by declaring a 'first or early use' doctrine of nuclear weapons. Worse still, for some years, both Pakistan and the PRC have worked in concert to constrain India's options while simultaneously enhancing Pakistan's conventional military capabilities. Following the 9/11 terrorist strikes in the US, Pakistan not only regained its importance as a frontline state in America's 'Global War on Terror' (GWOT), but also succeeded in obtaining both financial and military assistance from the US, in return for the use of its territory as the main transit route for military supplies to the US-led International Security Assistance Force (ISAF) fighting the Taliban and remnants of Al Qaeda in Afghanistan. With the departure of ISAF from Afghanistan in 2014-15, Pakistan is poised to play a bigger role in Afghan affairs. This may further enhance its capability to pose a potent sub-conventional or even a conventional threat to India.

In all probability, India will be forced to expend a much greater effort in financial and material terms to meet this combined challenge from the north-west and the north. In addition to the threat of cross-border terrorism, Maoists and other separatist forces have also been posing an increasingly more potent and lethal threat to India's internal security. Given its rising economic profile and rapidly increasing foreign trade, India must work to ensure a peaceful Indian Ocean Region (IOR). In the past, India has provided timely assistance to its neighbours in times of need (Maldives in 1988, Indonesia and Sri Lanka during the tsunami in December 2004). The IAF and its sister services will thus have to train for 'stabilisation' and 'out-of-area' operations on their own or in concert with other friendly powers.

This study is aimed at assessing India's extant security policy/strategy of meeting these threats and the role that air power, mainly the IAF, plays in the larger scheme of things. A caveat is, however, necessary here. While dealing with the subjects of air power and national security, the context and emphasis is on India and hence theories of International Relations and Western approaches to air power deployment are discussed only when these are germane to Indian conditions. Although the book traces the evolution and growth of the IAF, it is not intended to be a definitive history of the IAF nor a theoretical treatise on air power but an enquiry into the increasing relevance of air power in India's security.

The chapter on the *Nature of Air Power* briefly deals with the evolution of air power; its attributes, limitations and the all-important concept of 'command of the air'; and the nature of air warfare with particular stress on its employment in Indian conditions. It also examines if employment of air power is really escalatory.

The chapter, *Evolution of India's National Security Practice*, attempts to study the evolution of and reasons for Indian security practice, its successes and failures and the likely future course. India's grand strategy, non-alignment, strategic restraint and other features by which it is characterised are discussed. It also deals with issues such as strategic autonomy, the evolution and management of India's Higher Defence Control Organisation (HDCO), the impact of Pakistan's nuclear doctrine on India's security and related questions.

Having discussed the evolution and major lessons of air power employment during both the world wars, an attempt is made in the chapter on *Air Power Employment: Lessons from the Past* to briefly list relevant air power-related lessons of the wars India has fought with Pakistan and the PRC and against the Liberation Tigers of Tamil Eelam (LTTE) in Sri Lanka. This chapter also brings out important lessons related to air power deployment in numerous other wars and conflicts across the world.

The chapter dealing with the *Development of IAF Force Structures* traces the history of India's attempts to build and expand the IAF's capabilities with the aim of establishing a balanced air force. It discusses Force Posture and doctrinal influences.

The chapter on *The Indian Air Force Today*, examines the present threats that the IAF is required to prepare for, taking into account the relative strengths of the Pakistan Air Force (PAF) and the People's Liberation Army Air Force (PLAAF). Why has it reached this stage? This includes human resources, maintenance, flight safety, exercises with other air forces and the lessons learnt.

The chapter on *The Future of Air Power in India* is devoted to the likely course that the IAF's ongoing modernisation programme might take on a 2030 timeline. What is the IAF aiming for? Is it sustainable? Where is the nascent Indian defence industry headed?

The next chapter discusses a number of important issues such as civil military relations, the nuclear dimension and military doctrine.

The concluding chapter presents main findings and recommendations.

NOTES

1. K.A.V. Pandalai, *Fifty Golden Years of the Aeronautical Society of India (1948-1998)*, Aeronautical Society of India, Bangalore, 1998, p. 10.
2. The Indian leadership has built an elaborate mythology that all wars were thrust upon India. While largely true, it is perhaps due to India's apparent reluctance to use force that its rivals have taken liberties with its security.

3. M.J. Akbar, "Obama and Manmohan: A Tale of Two Second Terms", *Sunday Times of India*, Bangalore, November 23, 2013, p. 14.
4. Durga Das, *India from Curzon to Nehru and After*, Rupa & Co., New Delhi, 1969, (Reprinted 1974), p. 239.
5. Wu Xinbo, "China: Security Practice of a Modernizing and Ascending Power", in Muthiah Algappa (ed.), *Asian Security Practice: Material and Ideational Influences*, Stanford University Press, Stanford, 1998, p. 115.
6. See http://www.cfr.org/india/conversation-prime-minister-dr-manmohan-singh/p20840 (Accessed February 2, 2010).

2

Nature of Air Power

In the century of aircraft as an instrument of war, the capabilities of air power have grown exponentially. And we have expanded the way in which we think of air power to include several new aspects. Today the very instruments of power are undergoing change as a result of technological development.

—**Shivshankar Menon**[1]

The advent of the aeroplane on December 17, 1903 opened up new vistas for human adventure in the third dimension, viz. air. These ideas gave rise to its employment in different roles in war and peace. Although a few early air power visionaries such as the American Brigadier General William (Billy) Mitchel, the Italian General Giulio Douhet and the Royal Air Force (RAF) Chief, Sir (later-Lord) Trenchard had put forward revolutionary ideas about the use of the third dimension during the inter-war years, it was only in the post-World War II period that scholars actually began formulating theories and doctrines based on the long, varied and extensive experience of the previous four decades.

At least in the initial period, it was seen that airmen by nature were inclined to action rather than to devoting time and energy to conceptual thinking. According to Winston Churchill:

> Air power is the most difficult of all forms of military force to measure or even to express in precise terms. The problem is compounded by the fact that aviation tends to attract adventurous souls, physically adept, mentally alert and pragmatically rather than philosophically inclined.[2]

Even so, air power thought progressed and relevant doctrines crystallised in due time.

Air Power Definitions

Early air power visionaries did not really know what to make of this refreshingly new dimension of war fighting. Some simply called it 'the ability to do something in the air'. 'Anything that flies' was the shortest description of air power by one of its early protagonists, Brigadier General Mitchel of the US Army, who was court-martialled for propagating radical views on air power in the early decades of the 20th century.

As early as the 1940s, General Carl Spaatz of the US Army Air Force (USAAF)[3] defined it "as the capacity of a nation to impose its will on others through the medium of air." He went on to say, "Further, air power is not simply the military component but includes all aviation assets and activity, extant or potential, civil or military; public or private."

In its official doctrine, the RAF describes air power as the nation's "ability to project power from the air and space to influence the behaviour of people and the course of events."[4]

Understanding of air power grew with the gradual development of aviation to include a more comprehensive form of explanation. According to the 1995 IAF Doctrine duly amended in 1997, air power in the military sense is "the ability to project military force by or from a platform in the third dimension above the surface of the earth." It goes on to add that air power has the capacity to "deliver cargo, people, destructive missiles and war making potential through the air to a desired destination to accomplish a desired purpose" and further that it is the "ability of a nation to assert its will through the medium of the air."[5] Air power thus includes all the military aviation assets of a nation's air force, army and navy, its fleets of commercial and private aircraft, and also the aviation and armament industry that together feed all elements of air power. In other words, air power is the use of fighter and transport aircraft, scout, attack, utility and heavy lift helicopters and missiles and in recent times, Unmanned Aerial Vehicles (UAVs) and Unmanned Combat Aerial Vehicles (UCAVs). Infrastructure such as airfields, runways, air force bases, radar stations and other allied facilities including firing ranges and space-based assets such as the Global Positioning System (GPS), navigation and reconnaissance satellites and above all 'Command and Control' systems form part of the gigantic structure that normally comprises a nation's air power apparatus.

Air power is thus not restricted to, or circumscribed by, the colour of the uniform or the current ownership of these resources. Air power needs a mechanism that readily lends itself to seamless use of all its assets, not least the nation's air space to project the nation's air power. It should not, and usually, does not matter who owns or controls a specific facility or instrument. The Department of Meteorology and Air Traffic Services are national assets usually controlled by different civilian ministries in peacetime but are also available for the use of military aviation in peace and war and are regularly exercised to ensure proper understanding of the requirements of the nation's armed forces, especially the air force.

Air power, depending on national resources and needs, will have a role in different situations including coercion, compellence, out-of-area contingencies, intervention and for power projection operations.

Although national air forces are the primary air power operators, air power is inherently joint and combined or, in other words, indivisible. Experience has shown that it must be controlled at as high a level as possible while its execution may be decentralised and delegated to lower levels of command or control authority. Air power clearly belongs to and comes from all three services; it includes commercial and private aviation resources of the nation as was so brilliantly demonstrated by the airlift of troops to Srinagar so early in India's independence history. The RAF Manual AP 3000 says:

> It influences and is in turn influenced by land and maritime environments and is unconstrained by national boundaries and terrain and is uniquely pervasive and offers the prospect of access to any point on or above the earth with the opportunity to observe and decisively influence operations in the other environments, (that is on land and at sea).[6]

Control of air also therefore means control over ground or sea. If, for example, we have our aircraft in, or over a particular area, we can easily control or at least have the potential to control the events on the ground or sea below or keep a discrete watch over events. *This is perhaps air power's biggest advantage and hence makes allocation and control of air power resources so contentious across the globe.*

Air Power Attributes

The first and the most remarkable attribute of air power is its ability to exploit the third dimension. Although speed is a more easily discernible feature of air power, it was its ability to exploit the third dimension or 'elevation' that initially attracted the early thinkers and this is what so clearly distinguishes aviation forces from their land and maritime counterparts. As aviation developed, speed and range conferred the third attribute, namely 'reach'. The unique ability to quickly 'reach' a desired destination became an important feature of air power and made it so appealing to military commanders and national leaders.

Height, speed and reach are attributes that together give it complete freedom of action. As would be evident from the examples cited above, the first and perhaps the most crucial attribute of modern air power is its ability to respond instantaneously to an emerging situation; whether in peace or war. Speed allows for rapid projection of force; reach, the ability to strike distant targets; and height, the unique ability to observe and dominate the activities on the surface of the earth below. Air power, can thus also control battle-space and shape the battlefield. National leaders or administrators often undertake aerial surveys of flood, drought, or cyclone-affected areas at the very first opportunity as such observation gives them a far better idea of the extent of damage and the likely effort needed to bring succour to affected people, than if they were to travel by surface means to the affected area. During war, aerial reconnaissance gives the military leader vital information about the enemy.

From about the late 1970s, modern air power has developed the unique ability to deliver Precision Guided Munitions (PGMs) against a wide range of targets. Continuous developments in target identification and acquisition, delivery techniques and small diameter bombs, often from stand-off distances, have conferred upon the modern aeroplane/helicopter and now also the UCAV, the ability to reduce and many times totally avoid collateral damage. Even so, stray incidents of civilian and non-combatant casualties invite severe criticism and place further restrictions on the use of air power.[7]

Advances in aviation technology such as more efficient jet engines, improved avionics and enhanced load-carrying capacity today allow decision-makers to employ air power without undue delay and with greater assurance of success. For example, India's fledgling air force provided much-needed relief to the troops fighting the tribesmen in the North West Frontier Province (NWFP), now Khyber Pakhtunkhwa, in the 1930s. Those aircraft were, however, not equipped with instruments and means to operate in bad weather. Sometime later, when IAF's No. 7 Squadron was asked to move to Gwalior from Campbellpore, it met with unexpected bad weather in the form of thunderstorms and lost as many as three aircraft because they had no reliable instrumentation to fly in strong winds and severe turbulence.[8] On the other hand, in 2008, eight Su-30 MKI multi-role fighters of the IAF, successfully flew all the way across the seas to the US Air Force (USAF) base at Nellis, with just two Il-78 tankers and two Il-76 support aircraft that carried the men and material for the maintenance of the Su-30 MKI.[9] It was an amazing achievement, considering it was the first such deployment.

Ability to Overfly Natural Obstacles

Being an airborne platform, aircraft can very easily negotiate natural terrain, mountains and wooded/forested areas, and deliver firepower or essential supplies without much difficulty. Such operations are of course restricted by the range and payload of the aircraft. In 1947, India employed a large number of Dakota transports of the IAF and commercial/private operators to fly in troops to Srinagar when it was threatened by Pakistani forces. Similarly, the An-12, a far bigger and commodious cargo plane with rear ramp doors, flew in three AMX-13 tanks to

Ladakh in 1962. Today the Il-76 can perform the same task with considerable ease. The C-17 Globemaster, recently inducted into the IAF, can transport 77 tonnes of payload, or more than 134 fully combat-ready troops, over a distance of 4,400 km in one sortie, in a matter of few hours, even if the runway at the other end is not paved.[10]

Modern air power can strike targets deep inside enemy territory, without having to first engage or neutralise the enemy's ground or naval forces, and it is this capability that makes air power an attractive instrument for national leaders. According to Elliot Cohen of Johns Hopkins University, "Air power is an unusually seductive form of military strength, in part because like modern courtship, it appears to offer gratification without commitment."[11] Herein also lies the risk of indiscriminate employment of air power. As in any other case of use of force, the air power option is certainly fraught with the risk of retaliation by the enemy's air forces, and the aggressor has to be prepared to fight his way in and out and perhaps, also incur some losses. As we shall see later, enemy air defences have to first be neutralised or at least degraded through a Suppression of Enemy Air Defences (SEAD) campaign. It will be instructive to remember that since the end of the Vietnam War in 1975, the USAF has not engaged in a single air campaign without first undertaking SEAD operations.

Flexibility/Agility

Air power by its very nature is immensely flexible. Modern multi-role aircraft, both fighter and transport, are capable of undertaking a variety of missions with little extra effort or change in configuration. In some cases, it is possible to redirect/reallocate an already airborne aircraft or even a UAV without changing its armament configuration. Transport aircraft and helicopters have routinely answered such emergency calls in mid-air, and provided the much needed relief to victims of natural disasters, and/or evacuated casualties from all corners of the country.

Ubiquity

In simple terms, ubiquity means the ability to be everywhere almost simultaneously. Ubiquity is a combination of reach and persistence. At first somewhat difficult to visualise, this is a unique characteristic of air power. Due to its speed and reach, air power can appear out of 'nowhere and be everywhere'. As Winston Churchill had said, "Air power is the most difficult of all forms of military force to measure or even express in precise terms."[12] This attribute becomes easy to appreciate when with aerial refuelling, almost intercontinental ranges can be achieved. Modern fighter and transport aircraft are routinely called upon to deliver effects at phenomenal distances. Recent application of air power in Libya in 2011 is a good example of how fighters based in the UK operated 3,000-km return flights, until bases in Italy became available. Three decades earlier, British V-bombers had successfully bombed targets in distant Falklands, operating from Ascension Island on the equator. Today, High Altitude Long Endurance (HALE) UAVs, such as the Global Hawk, have an endurance stretching to several weeks and can remain on '*station*', usually at heights of around 60,000-65,000 feet at great distances from their launch bases.

Concentration of Firepower

Air power can deliver concentrated firepower at a point of one's choice without having to physically group together or deploy the delivery platforms at a single location on the ground. This also makes it difficult for the enemy to respond, as attacking aircraft simply evaporate into thin air after delivering their armament. The enemy can thus be punished, his offensive capability degraded, and his will or behaviour influenced without having to resort to physical mobilisation of large bodies of troops, which is usually time-consuming, expensive and cumbersome. This is especially true when one wants to avoid unnecessary escalation, as such missions can be launched in a measured response, and called off the moment the primary political aim is achieved. The American bombing of Libyan targets in Operation El Dorado Canyon in 1986, the US Navy's Tomahawk cruise missile strikes against suspected Al Qaeda camps in Afghanistan in 1998, and air dropping of the much-needed foodgrains from An-32 aircraft to the Tamil population in Northern Jaffna in 1987, are some examples of these missions. Further, simply announcing a change in the alert status of air assets at their home bases can send a strong political signal.

Revolution in Military Affairs (RMA) is yet another development that has substantially enhanced the effectiveness of modern air power. In simple terms, RMA comprises Stealth, Reach or Range, PGMs and now 'super cruise', the last being the ability to fly at supersonic speeds without using 'reheat or after burner' or in other words, burning too much fuel. This has added a new dimension to air power capabilities. Stealth or low observable characteristics denote the ability of a platform to avoid radar detection. Super cruise and enhanced 'situational awareness' further add to the overall performance, versatility and invulnerability of the platform.

Shock Effect

Combat air power by its sudden appearance from the skies, with little or no warning, tends to cause a temporary deterioration or slowdown, sometimes even a shutdown, of all human faculties, thus affecting a kind of paralysis amongst the enemy or people on the ground. This is termed as shock effect. Depending on the scale and damage, the nature of the effect can be strategic or tactical. During the second Iraq War in 2003, the USAF deliberately designed its air operations to achieve what it termed 'shock and awe' on the Iraqi government and people. This effect is further enhanced with the use of PGMs and the inherent accuracy of such air-delivered weapons, to strike at the heart of the enemy target with little collateral damage. Shock effect is, however temporary, and the general population, depending on its culture, confidence in its leadership and the country's overall response, may get inured to aerial bombing. It is, therefore, imperative that to be decisive, air action is concentrated and yet carefully calibrated, or else indiscriminate bombing of the enemy, especially its civilian population, would become counterproductive and may even help reinforce its national resolve. When used judiciously, air power can exploit this effect to obtain speedy political and tactical outcomes.

Limitations

Along with the many advantages, air power also has some limitations such as: impermanence; fragility; limited weapon and other loads; relatively high unit costs and; dependence on basing facilities which even the Short Take Off and Landing (STOL) aircraft are subjected to.

Impermanence

Unlike ground forces, air power cannot hold ground and its presence is ephemeral. In order to increase its staying power, it will have to be based at an air base with at least the necessary minimum facilities for operations. Helicopters, however, are relatively less affected by this limitation and it is possible to support the operations of a sizeable number of helicopters from an unpaved open ground of modest dimensions.

It is relatively expensive to keep air power in theatre without basing facilities. For example, the US and British air forces enforced a 'no fly zone' south and north of Iraq for 11 years, from the end of the Gulf War in 1991 until the beginning of the second Gulf War in March 2003, effectively boxing in Iraq's Air Force. This operation proved effective, but costly, as a large number of fighters were used to routinely and continuously fly at medium levels to deter Iraqi aircraft from breaking the cordon, and engage them, if they did. Since such long tenures disrupted the training schedules of the aircrews and used up precious flying hours, both aircraft and aircrews had to be frequently rotated for rest and recuperation and for routine aircraft servicing. Shorter duration Combat Air Patrol (CAP) missions can and are, however, flown for the arrival and departure of VVIPs, induction of fresh troops or emergency evacuation in the face of enemy interference and situations where it is difficult to assure total security from ground and air attacks.

Limited Weapons Load

Compared to a regiment of tanks, field/mountain guns, or a ship's armoury, a modern fighter carries a limited load. Yet, aircraft of the Su-30/Rafale/Jaguar class can carry a heavy load of up to 8,000 kg of high explosive and incendiary laser-guided bombs, missiles, rockets and external fuel tanks. Speed, reach and high sortie rates can make up for this limitation – to some extent.

Fragility

Modern aircraft depend largely on avionics and micro-miniaturisation for their performance. Modern avionics and most other airborne equipment are relatively fragile and vulnerable to dust, air pollution, extreme temperature conditions and hence need constant care, maintenance and even replacement. Inclement weather, rain, sleet, snow, dust and thunderstorms can severely restrict air operations. These factors also add to difficulties in aircraft maintenance. Since modern multi-role combat aircraft pack a variety of delicate avionics components per unit volume, these become extremely vulnerable to even small arms fire, especially when on low-level strikes. The IAF lost a large number of its fighter-bombers to small arms fire in such attacks in the 1971 war.

Weather

Although most modern aircraft are capable of operating by night and in all-weather and low light conditions, their performance is invariably affected. Blind flying instruments only help the crews to fly from one base to another, provided that the destination also has the requisite navigation and landing facilities. Operations like accurately delivering weapons in poor light or night conditions can still pose some difficulty, especially when engaging moving targets in a rapidly changing ground situation. In peacetime too, bad weather, especially over mountainous terrain, can severely restrict air operations, as was evident during the rescue missions launched following the cloudburst in Uttarakhand in June 2013.[13]

Dependence on Basing Facilities

As emphasised above, aircraft cannot operate without base facilities. It is the air base that houses all maintenance facilities, spare parts, instrument calibration laboratories, living accommodation for air and ground crews and hence plays a vital role in keeping the aircraft airborne. Bases therefore, also need elaborate ground and air defence protection. Earlier, when air forces operated relatively less advanced aircraft, the facilities provided were minimal. In the IAF too, base facilities were not very sophisticated until the arrival of the Jaguar, Mirage-2000, Su-30 and Il-76 aircraft. One of the more expensive but inescapable facilities at every forward base is a series of bomb-proof aircraft shelters also known as 'blast pens'. Due mainly to 'short legs' or limited range of the IAF fighters, many of the air bases are located close to the border. This proximity makes the aircraft even more vulnerable to enemy attacks, when not parked in these 'blast pens'.

High Acquisition and Life Cycle Costs

Air power was and continues to remain capital-and technology-intensive. High technology raises the unit cost of aircraft, engines, radars, precision weapons and air defence systems, satellites and communication infrastructure. Until the 1970s, a Gnat fighter aircraft cost a mere Rs. 20-25 lakh; with Mystere IVA, Toofani costing about the same and the Hunter a little more. When the BAe Hawk was first offered in the mid-1980s, the cost was believed to be around $4.5-5 million, whereas it finally cost $25 million in 2004. The Medium Multi-Role Combat Aircraft (MMRCA), Rafale is to cost upwards of $65 million and the C-17 Globemaster much more. It is obvious that no country can thus afford to acquire large numbers of modern aircraft.

"Between 1960 and 1990, the nominal cost of RAF combat aircraft grew by a factor of ten, but the size of the service's front line fell by only one-third."[14] Operators have tried to extend the life of combat aircraft by resorting to mid-life upgrades. C-130 Hercules, B-52 and even the F-16 have now been in frontline service with the USAF for over four decades. The IAF too has learnt this lesson and operates many old fighters such as the MiG-21 and Jaguar. The Mirage-2000, its frontline fighter, is now 25 years old and is being upgraded so that its life can be extended by another 20 years. High unit costs, however, are not the problem of aircraft alone. Frontline tanks such as the T-90 cost around $4-5 million and the army's total tank inventory is more than 3,500. The cost of *INS Vikramaditya*, the Indian Navy's new aircraft carrier, has escalated from around $1.3 bn to nearly $3bn.[15] Andrew G.B. Vallance says, "What counts is value for money in the broadest sense. The apparent growth in air power cost in recent decades has been dramatic, but so has been the growth in capabilities."[16]

Terrain

Mountainous terrain, especially for high altitude air operations, poses a major challenge as the lack of oxygen places severe limitations on the fighting ability of aircraft. The reason for low oxygen concentration in the atmosphere is the reduced air density at higher altitudes. This also adversely affects the performance of the piston, turboprop and turbojet engine; the first more so, than the other two. In addition to reducing the thrust of a jet engine, low density also affects aircraft manoeuvrability as its control surfaces do not respond the way they do at sea level. Air-launched weapons such as rockets, bombs and missiles also behave unpredictably at high altitudes.

During the 1999 Kargil War, for example, the shoulder-fired Stinger missile used by the Pakistani forces proved lethal as its heat-seeking warhead could more easily home onto the heat of a jet engine in the very cold ambient atmosphere. High altitude is normally not an impediment to simple 'route' flying as most fixed wing aircraft routinely fly at heights of 30-40,000 feet; but undertaking offensive operations requiring the launching of air weapons or combat manoeuvring is a different matter. Helicopters, on the other hand, are usually restricted to lower altitudes. This is because reduced engine performance and aerodynamic forces severely restrict manoeuvrability of the aircraft; its flying controls become less effective with altitude, and the height lost in recovering from a dive increases and so does the turn radius.[17] All of these aerodynamic and performance penalties make it difficult to negotiate the narrow and steep valleys and gullies in the high mountains.

High altitude adversely affects all air breathing platforms. It is mistakenly believed by some that dedicated ground attack aircraft like the Russian Su-25/39 or American Fairchild A-10, and attack helicopters such as Mi-25/35 would overcome these difficulties. With altitude, the payloads of aircraft and helicopters stand reduced. Artillery guns and even mortars have to be dismantled and carried piecemeal to high altitude areas such as Siachen.

Historical Background

The evolution of air power since the first manned flight in December 1903, makes a fascinating study because unlike land and maritime warfare, air power development was far more rapid and opened many new vistas in modern warfare.

The 2011 Libyan air campaign lasted for seven and a half months from the launch of the first weapon against the Gaddafi Government targets on March 19 to October 31. Today, few remember that it also marked the end of the first century of air power employment. On November 1, 1911 an Italian Air Force bi-plane had bombed Turkish positions at Ain Zara during the Tripolitan War. The outcome of that conflict was that the three North African provinces then ruled by the Ottoman Empire were ceded to Italy and on gaining independence in 1951 became the nation of Libya.[18]

Soon after the successful first flight of the aircraft by the Wright brothers, aviation enthusiasts began to apply their minds to the military use of the aircraft. The most remarkable feature of the aircraft was its ability to exploit the third dimension. Until its advent, the military leaders' most vital requirement was to occupy high ground, so that they could get a better view of the enemy's dispositions from this elevated position. As a result, the first role for infant air power was reconnaissance of the enemy. "Early air power visionaries such as Major Fullerton and Captain Burke and eminent engineer F.W. Lancaster argued that air vehicles could revolutionise warfare."[19] As early as 1907, Lancaster also suggested that "under the conditions of the near future, the command of the air must become at least as important to the safety of the [British] Empire as will be our continued supremacy of the high seas."[20] On the European continent, the Italians were at the forefront with their aircraft being used in the Balkan Wars of 1912. By the time World War I broke out, most European armies and many navies had built significant fleets of military aircraft.

World War I (1914-18)

The rate of progress during the war was astonishing with aircraft capabilities advancing enormously. Between 1914 and 1918 the speed of military aircraft doubled, their payload increased ten-fold and their airworthiness grew beyond compare. In 1914, the Royal Flying Corps had less than 180 aircraft on its books. Yet, "just four years later, Britain had a true air force with nearly 300,000 men, two hundred squadrons and over 22,000 aircraft."[21]

From simple aerial reconnaissance, pilots and observers began to carry rifles, handguns and later integral machine guns which they used against enemy aircraft and also to harass enemy troops on the ground. In September 1914, British aircraft bombed the Zeppelin sheds at Dusseldorf and Cologne; subsequently factories, power stations and ammunition dumps were raided. The first air attacks against enemy supply lines took place in early 1915. In June 1917, air power played a decisive part in the capture of the key port of Jeddah, near Mecca, from the Turks. Naval aircraft made an early contribution to overland operations but had little impact on operations at sea. However, during the last two years of the war, the use of air power at sea began to gather pace. German Zeppelins continued to do useful scouting work, and the Allies developed seaplane carriers into proper aircraft carriers. Allied aircraft also helped to counter the U-boat menace, and by 1918 there were over 3,000 aircraft in service with the Royal Navy alone.[22]

With the proliferation of own and enemy aircraft over the battlefield, "control of the air itself came to be seen as something of great potential importance." According to Vallance, the first direct attacks against air bases date from August 1914, and the first air-to-air combats took place between opposing scout aircraft soon afterwards. Both sides began to enhance their counter-air efforts dramatically. By 1915 the first true 'fighter' aircraft (the Fokker Eindecker) made its appearance.[23]

By the time Italy abandoned its pre-war alliance and declared war on Austria-Hungary on May 23, 1915, several German aircraft had already been shot down by British and French two-seaters, in which the observer was armed with a machinegun, and the French pilot, Roland Garros[24] had notable success in a single-seater Morane monoplane, equipped with a machinegun fixed to fire through the arc of the propeller.[25]

As the fledgling aircraft operators gained experience, (there were no true air forces as yet) tactical experiments began with numerical superiority, cross-cover and mutual support and tight formations, to get the better of the enemy in the air while protecting own members of the fighter formations.

The final key air power capability – strategic bombing – emerged slightly later in World War I, than other types of combat operations. On January 19, 1915 two German Zeppelins bombed the Norfolk coast in Britain and by the standards of the time caused insignificant physical destruction but shook civilian morale and damaged Britain's sense of invulnerability. Twenty more raids were launched against Britain during 1915, but by 1916, countermeasures had been developed. Only six raids were launched against Britain in 1917 and four in 1918. Even so, some 17,340 anti-aircraft artillery troops and 12 squadrons of fighters were tied down permanently to countering the threat, an early example of the strategic diversion which strategic bombing can generate. Thus, within little more than two years after the outbreak of World War I, three basic operational applications of air power had emerged. The first was the 'auxiliary', 'air support', or more accurately anti-surface force operations: the use of air power against the enemy army and navy; second, 'counter-air' operations: the use of air power to deter, contain or defeat the enemy air forces; and third, 'independent' or strategic bombing operations: the autonomous use of air power to bomb deep in the enemy's heartland and undermine his will and ability to wage war. Even then, expert opinion was divided over which of these three types of operations should be considered the primary function of air power. All the experts felt that counter-air was essentially an enabling operation; not an end in itself, but a means by which either anti-surface force or strategic bombing operations could be carried out effectively. But few experts saw the latter two types of operations as compatible, let alone complementary. Instead, most military men – including aviators – continued to believe that aviation forces should be used directly in support of the surface forces. In their view, strategic bombing could only be a distraction from the real business of war, that of defeating the enemy army and navy. The opposing lobby argued that strategic bombing offered a short cut to victory, a way of avoiding the costly and apparently futile trench warfare stalemate which dominated contemporary land warfare.

The debate was brought to a critical phase when 21 Gotha bombers attacked Folkestone on May 25, 1917, inflicting nearly 300 casualties in just 10 minutes. During the next month, the Gotha raids were extended to London, which thereafter was raided regularly. The Gotha bombers never numbered more than 40; often suffered heavy damage and the physical damage inflicted by them was hardly more than that of the Zeppelins. Nevertheless, the Gotha raids induced widespread fear and panic and war production fell.

As a result, the British government withdrew a substantial force of fighters from France to defend London; it also formed the Smuts Committee to review not only "the defence arrangement for Home Defence against air raids" but also "the air organisation generally and the directions of air operations". The Smuts Committee had only two members, Lieutenant General Jan Christian Smuts and the British Prime Minister David Lloyd George, with the former doing most of the work. Smuts produced two reports, the second of which proved most important as it unequivocally recommended the formation of an independent air force.

"As far as can at present be foreseen there is absolutely no limit to the scale of the air service's independent war use. And the time may not be far off when aerial operations with their devastation of enemy lands and destruction of industrial and population centres on a vast scale may become the principal operation of war, to which the older forms of military and naval operations may become secondary and subordinate."

The report was accepted by the British War Cabinet and on April 1, 1918 the RAF was born as the world's first independent air service.[26]

In Europe too, air services of Austria-Hungary, France and Italy were increasingly resorting to use of their fledgling air power assets. Both sides used their unwieldy aircraft to bomb enemy targets such as railway lines, docks, industry and other targets.

> On February 14, 1916, 10 (Austro-Hungarian) aircraft armed with 80 kg of bombs flew from a base in Trento to attack Milan. This was 15 months before the first raid on a town in Britain by German heavier-than-air-machines...though the Germans had already attacked London with airships. 'Navigating' by the white shimmering 'cathedral' of Milan, two of the attacking aircraft unloaded their bombs in the general direction of a power station, killing 12 people and injuring 70. The other eight aircraft apparently became lost and scattered their bombs elsewhere...On August 9, 1916, 17 Austro-Hungarian aircraft bombed Venice killing seven civilians and sinking a British submarine docked at the arsenal, probably the first submarine ever to be sunk by air bombing...On November 16, 1916 a single Austro-Hungarian bomb killed 93 civilians sheltering in a casemate in the old fortification of Padua. It was the worst incident involving civilians taking shelter from an air raid during the entire course of World War I although there had been an even greater toll when a French reprisal raid on Karlsruhe (across the border in south-west Germany) had destroyed a circus during a matinee, along with killing most of the children in the audience...Altogether, more than 400 civilians were killed in Austro-Hungarian raids on towns in northern Italy, 1,414 civilians were killed in German raids on England and 746 were killed in British-French raids on industrial centres in Western Germany.[27]

Inter War-Years (1918-39)

While these years saw some advances in civil and commercial aviation such as mail and passenger services, the use of military aircraft was largely restricted to 'police action' or air control operations of remote and thinly populated areas in North Africa, Iraq and NWFP in India. Air transport was used less during World War I, but soon began to develop with the RAF, in 1921, reinforcing the British garrison in Kirkuk (Iraq). Nearer home, in the winter of 1928-29, the RAF evacuated nearly 600 British citizens from the besieged city of Kabul in Afghanistan.[28]

The period also saw air power visionaries such Douhet, Mitchel and Trenchard advocating the theory of strategic bombing, in which they saw large formations of bombers overflying enemy armies and devastating the enemy's heartland, without having to first defeat enemy armies and navies. Brigadier General William Mitchel, an early proponent of flexibility of air power in different roles, later became an advocate of strategic bombing. All three had grossly over-estimated the capabilities of the 'bomber' and effective air defence was judged to be impossible. Bombers flying in close self-supporting formations protected by defensive fire would (it was thought) break through the defences, no matter how strong they were.[29]

In 1932 the British Prime Minister Stanley Baldwin stated in Parliament:

> I think it well also for the man in the street to realise that there is no power on earth that can protect him from bombing, whatever people may tell him. The bomber will always get through.[30]

The reality, however, was quite different. While some bombers always managed to get through, bomber losses were prohibitively high in World War I. Given the fast-improving performance of the contemporary fighter aircraft, bombers became more and more vulnerable. During the Spanish Civil War, the German Condor Legion, supporting the nationalist forces, found that it needed fighter escorts to protect its bombers. The fighters also found that the increasing pace and complexity of the air battle demanded larger and more flexible fighter formations, as lone fighters were more vulnerable to the defensive fire of the bomber, as also to the bomber escorts. All these developments led to new tactical doctrines which profoundly challenged Douhet's conclusions. Yet, the implications were widely ignored. Instead, the destruction by bombing of Shanghai by the Japanese and of Guernica by the Germans in 1937 – although unique in each war – were cited as validation of the strategic bombing doctrine and proof of bomber invincibility. In March 1939, the threat of an aerial 'knock-out blow' against Prague induced the Czechs to concede to Hitler's demands. The British of the time also believed that the only way to thwart the potent threat posed by German bombers was an immediate and overwhelming counter-attack, prompting Harold

Macmillan (later British Prime Minister) to admit later: "we thought of air warfare in 1938 rather as people think of nuclear warfare today."[31]

The debate over the relative merits of 'air defence' and 'offensive fighter or fighter-bomber' or even the 'strategic bomber' has often depended on the level and credibility of current technology of the aircraft and the destructive capability of the armament delivered. Hence, no country can take a chance with a fighter-bomber/ bomber carrying nuclear weapons, whereas the threat of conventional weapons, however accurate, would not give any one sleepless nights.

In the absence of 'proper trials', 'controlled exercises' or serious operational analysis to assess the actual destructive capacity of the bomber in terms of technology and more importantly, the strength of the civilian population to withstand and adapt to the shock of aerial bombing, the claims of the 'prophets' of strategic bombing met with mixed results during World War II.

World War II (1939-45)

Although many of the early air power theorists tended to over-estimate the capabilities of aircraft, there is no gainsaying the fact that, by the end of World War II air power had become an essential part of modern warfare. In fact, it had acquired a central position in military strategy. No modern army or navy could contemplate any worthwhile surface operation without first neutralising, or at the very least, significantly degrading enemy air power. Every tank, gun or ship was vulnerable to enemy air power.

Wars tend to spur technological development, and in that sense World War II proved to be no different. Aircraft speeds, performance, all-up weight, armament, and overall weapon delivery accuracy showed remarkable progress. The advent of the jet engine, ground-based and later airborne radar and high-precision navigation aids, increased the overall capabilities, and as the war progressed, new air platforms such as ballistic missiles (V1), cruise missiles (V2) and helicopters, added to air power efficiency and efficacy.

In Europe, air power proved to be a key element in the success of the German invasion of Poland (1939), Norway, the Benelux Countries, France (1940), the Balkans and Russia in 1941. The first check on Nazi aggression came from air power during the Battle of Britain in 1940. From 1942 onwards, German weakness in the air proved to be its Achilles heel. It must however, be remembered that relentless German aerial bombing during the Battle of Britain had at one time brought England to the brink of defeat. It was the stupendous effort of the RAF Fighter Command, under the able guidance of Air Marshal Sir Hugh Dowding, which saved the situation. It was also the fickle and changing targeting strategy of the German Luftwaffe, switching from bombing aircraft factories and industry to the bombing of cities, and the diversion of its air power resources to the Eastern Front that helped Britain to successfully defeat the threat of German invasion.

British Prime Minister Winston Churchill paid a memorable, and now famous, tribute to these young men: "Never in the history of human conflict has so much been owed by so many to so few."[32] Examples of success in purely defensive counter-air operations have been relatively few, with the Battle of Britain being the only exception in the long history of air power deployment.[33]

In the North African campaign, it was again the British superiority in air power, with close coordination between its army and its Desert Air Force that ultimately defeated Rommel's armies. According to Rommel,

> As a result of the British command of the air and hence of the seas in the Central Mediterranean, the army's supplies were hardly sufficient to enable it to eke out a bare existence even on quiet days...There were days when the British flew 800 bomber sorties and 2,500 sorties of fighters, fighter-bombers and low-flying fighter aircraft. We, on the other hand could at the most fly 60 dive-bomber and 100 fighter sorties. This number moreover continually became smaller.[34]

Further commenting on British air superiority, Rommel said:

> Anyone who has to fight, even with the most modern weapons, against an enemy with complete air superiority, fights like a savage against modern European troops, under the same operational and tactical handicaps and with the same chances of success.[35]

In the Pacific, the Japanese attack on Pearl Harbour on December 7, 1941 nearly crippled the mighty US Pacific Fleet. It was by sheer luck that many of its aircraft carriers escaped destruction by being away at sea on that fateful morning. In retrospect, some analysts believe that the Japanese attack could have caused more permanent damage to the US Navy, had they chosen to destroy the repair and maintenance facilities at Pearl Harbour instead of targeting individual ships. Japanese advance into the Philippines, Malaya and Singapore and the sinking of three British ships anchored at Singapore was also largely due to air power.

When the US entered the war and launched counter attacks against the Japanese Navy, the naval battles in the Coral Sea, Midway and later Leyte Gulf, were won by naval air power with the opposing fleets never coming into visual contact.

Bomber fleets of both sides suffered very heavy attrition:

> During the Battle of Britain on September 15, 1940, the Germans lost 56 bombers. During the American daylight bombing raids on Schweinfurt and Regensburg on October 17, 1943, 63 of the 280 attacking bombers were shot down. In a night bombing raid by the British on Nuremburg on March 30-31, 1944, 94 of the 710 bombers were lost to German fighters and AA fire. The lessons were clear: either establish control of the air or concede.[36]

The US bombers had for some time, towards the end of the war, been using incendiary bombs against Japanese cities and had successfully razed many of the cities to the ground; but the Japanese surrender came only after the US B-29 bombers dropped atom bombs on Hiroshima and Nagasaki on August 6 and 9, 1945 respectively, killing some 100,000 people and injuring an equal number.

Counter Surface Force Operations (CSFO) were proving increasingly more successful in both the theatres. The German invasion of Greece and Crete employed air power in airborne assault, air transported/landed operations, but they had to discontinue these because of extremely heavy casualties.

"During World War II, more warships were sunk by aircraft and 61 per cent of those were sunk by land-based aircraft." Maritime air power had come of age with surface fleets within the strike range of aircraft proving vulnerable.

The large transport fleets also played a major role in providing strategic and tactical mobility, and air supply. In the Allied campaign in Burma (now Myanmar), during the 1944 siege of Kohima and Imphal, 155,000 Allied troops were entirely supplied by air for three months. Later, during the Allied offensive, 300,000 men received 90 per cent of their supplies from the air.[37]

Control of the air proved to be the war-winning factor, as without it, all air activity was at risk of attrition or at least disruption by opposing air power. The war also proved that the side that paid equal attention to all types of capabilities was better and more versatile. The Germans, for example, suffered because of their emphasis on short-range fighters. In order to make up for the lack of offensive capability, they launched the V1 and V2 'flying bombs' towards the end of the war, the first of which was dropped on Swanscombe, in Kent on June 13, 1944, and the last one on Orpington in Kent on March 27, 1945. A total of 6,725 V1 flying bombs were dropped. Of these, 2,340 struck London and led to 5,475 dead and 16,000 injured. Three lines of defence were used against these bombs/ missiles: RAF fighters along the English Coast; anti-aircraft batteries; and balloon barrages which were successful in downing 3,500 V1s. The V2 'cruise missiles' were launched in September 1944 and in the next few months 1,400 of these struck London. Since they flew at the speed of sound, there was no warning and they could not be intercepted. Although these missiles did not prove very successful, the RAF mounted strikes against their launch sites at Peenemünde in northern Germany in 1944. The missile threat finally ended only when the advancing Allied troops captured the launch sites towards the end of the war.

World War II saw air power come of age. As seen earlier, by the early 1950s, air power had become indispensable to warfare and many countries across the globe had formed independent air arms. The USAAF soon became an independent entity and the demands of the Cold War spurred technological developments in all air power applications. Air power was not, however, always successful in deterring conflict. Although nuclear weapons had proved their amazing destructive capacity, these did not deter the Soviet-aided North Koreans from attacking South Korea in June 1950. The veiled threat of nuclear weapons also did not deter the Chinese from entering the Korean War. In 1948, the Soviet Union was not deterred from imposing a 14 month long blockade on West Berlin, but the American and British transport fleets helped the city brave the blockade by flying in 2,326,000 tons of supplies between July 1948 and September 1949. The relatively slow and unwieldy transport aircraft had to fly in narrow air corridors in appalling weather and were often harassed by Soviet fighters.

The Indian Experience

In just over two months after independence, India used its nascent and very limited air power resources when a few Dakota DC-3 twin-engine transport aircraft of the IAF and many more belonging to the few commercial and private operators, successfully airlifted a battalion (later one full infantry brigade) of the Indian Army to Srinagar on October 27, 1947. Since then, the IAF has seen its employment on numerous occasions, in both combat and non-combat roles. From the early 1950s to date, the IAF continues to supply the army and civilian populations along the country's mountainous borders through air maintenance. Although in a limited way, it was also used during the liberation of Goa in December 1961. During the Sino-Indian border conflict, the IAF did not employ its fighter fleet but its transport aircraft and helicopters flew numerous sorties for logistics support and casualty evacuation (Cas-Evac) operations at considerable risk. The Canberra strategic reconnaissance aircraft flew a number of missions to provide invaluable photographic evidence of Chinese activity, especially the Aksai Chin road and its army positions in the mountains.

Air power was again in the forefront when on September 1, 1965 responding to an SOS from the Army, the IAF launched 12 Vampires and 14 Mystere IVA fighters and helped save the situation in Chhamb, the loss of which would have threatened India's only access to the State of Jammu and Kashmir. The IAF was employed in all its classical roles during this 22 day long war and won high praise and appreciation of the nation. Air power played a decisive role in the 14 day long war for the liberation of East Pakistan and creation of Bangladesh in December 1971, and achieved complete air superiority in the Eastern theatre. The IAF supported the army by attacking Pakistan Army targets and the road and riverine transport system in erstwhile East Pakistan and severely degraded the mobility of the Pakistan Army. It launched a major airborne operation at Tangail in which it dropped a battalion group, and a heliborne operation to lift a battalion across a damaged bridge in the IV Corps sector. Simultaneously, the IAF maintained a dominant posture in the Western Sector and prevented Pakistan from making any forays into Indian territory. In a classical offensive air support operation, IAF Hunters decimated an entire regiment of Pakistani armour in Longewala that was poised to overrun Indian troops on their way to a strategically important town of Jaisalmer in the Rajasthan sector.

On June 4, 1987, the IAF was again used to drop emergency rations to the Tamil population in the Jaffna peninsula in Northern Sri Lanka, an operation that paved the way for the Indo-Sri Lanka Accord signed on July 29, 1987. The IAF helicopter and transport elements were active throughout the three year long Indian Peace Keeping Force (IPKF) operation codenamed 'Operation Pawan'. Again in 1988, when the Government of Maldives requested Indian assistance to thwart a coup attempt, two Il-76 heavy lift transport aircraft of the IAF air transported a battalion of elite paratroopers from Agra across 3,000 km to Male, the capital city and successfully restored calm. The IAF also played a major role during the 1999 Kargil war, and helped the Indian Army to evict the Pakistan Army intruders, and also deterred the enemy from expanding the scope of that border conflict, even though IAF aircraft were not allowed to cross the Line of Control (LoC). It played a major role when a devastating tsunami in the Bay of Bengal hit the Andaman and Nicobar Islands, the coast of Tamil Nadu and Sumatra in Indonesia. Indian air power carried out the evacuation of stranded Indians in Kuwait prior to the 1991 Gulf War, and again from Lebanon in 2006, when war broke out between Israel and the Hezbollah fighters operating from Southern Lebanon.

Air power can send a strong message, sometimes unintended. For instance, in 1988, Bangladesh was struck by a devastating cyclone. An urgent request for six helicopters was received from Dhaka through its High Commission in New Delhi late in the day. After due clearance from the various government agencies in New Delhi, six IAF Mi-8 helicopters were over Dhaka at dawn the next morning. Such was the speed of response that the then President of Bangladesh, General Hussain Muhammad Ershad, expressed his concerns, about the exceptionally high alert status of the IAF in peacetime, to the then Prime Minister of India, Rajiv Gandhi, during the next SAARC Summit.

The helicopter and transport forces of the IAF have on numerous occasions rescued stranded troops and mountaineers in the Himalayas, saved people during floods, earthquakes, tsunamis and other natural and man-made disasters. In addition, the IAF has been called in support of civil administration in all parts of the country, in counter-insurgency operations. The IAF Super Constellation also known as L-1049 aircraft, transferred from Air India after the latter began operating the Boeing 707 airliners, routinely patrolled the long coastline of the country on maritime search and rescue missions until the Indian Navy and Coast Guard took over this responsibility in the 1980s.

In spite of such extensive and continuous employment throughout the last 68 years in India and for over a century elsewhere, and a realisation that air power was destined to play a decisive role in any modern conflict, even well-informed people including civilian and military experts do not truly understand, and readily accept the role, that air power plays in national defence. Karl Mueller of RAND Corporation says:

> Its (air power's) use and effects are an increasingly important matter of study in international security scholarship; although it is fair to say that land and sea power, with their longer histories and somewhat greater stability of characteristics, remain more familiar to most scholarly observers.[38]

Air Power Employment: Roles and Missions

Command of the Air

No military operations are possible without adequate freedom of action. Just as land or sea operations cannot take place if there is interference from the enemy, air activity also requires a degree of freedom, and to achieve that, in a contested airspace, the air force has to first establish control of the medium. Command or control of the air was seen as the primary objective of an air force because without such a condition being achieved *ab initio*, it was impossible to prevent enemy air forces from interfering with own freedom of action on the surface, as well as in the air. Depending on the degree of control, this condition is variously described as Air Supremacy, Air Superiority or a Favourable Air Situation (FAS). In the present context where opposing air forces are evenly matched, it is nearly impossible to attain total air superiority for long periods of time. The three terms are clearly indicative of the relative degree of freedom that own/friendly forces enjoy. Air superiority or command of the air is thus a dynamic concept. An air force has to continuously fight for air superiority, and once attained, it has to be maintained by continuous and consistent offensive action, or else, it is lost once enemy air forces recoup in time. The German Luftwaffe subjected Great Britain to almost round-the-clock bombing in the first half of 1940. In what came to be known as the Battle of Britain, the RAF put up a sustained defensive fight for over three months, until the ability of the Luftwaffe was very significantly reduced. At the time, because of limited radar cover and fighter range, the RAF had little choice but to try to shoot down enemy bombers after these had come close to, or over, Great Britain. Such examples are rarely seen now, as wars are restricted in time and scope. In the 'six-day war' in June 1967, Israel's Air Force carried out surprise pre-emptive attacks on the Arab forces, especially the Egyptian Air Force, and in a matter of hours destroyed it on ground.

Suppression of Enemy Air Defences

SEAD operations involve specifically targeting enemy air defence by attacking its radars, radar-controlled Anti-Aircraft Artillery (AAA) and Surface-to-Air-Missile (SAM) assets. Radar-controlled AAA and SAMs can also be effectively neutralised with electronic warfare (EW) or jamming. The US-led Allied air forces almost totally neutralised Iraq's Air Force in the first few days of the 1991 Gulf War, and achieved almost total air superiority over the Iraqi skies. Iraq's Air Force did not put up a real fight and many of its aircraft even fled to neighbouring Iran, or were trapped in damaged/destroyed bomb shelters, effectively grounding them. The USAF and RAF also imposed a 'no fly zone' over Iraq from 1991 to 2003; which was another effective way to gain air superiority over northern and southern Iraq for 11 years. The IAF too achieved total air superiority over East Pakistan in the first three days of the 1971 Indo-Pakistan War. SEAD operations were also undertaken in Kosovo (1999); Second Gulf War (2003); and in Libya (2011).

Such examples of total air superiority are, however, rare. In most other conflicts where the two warring sides are more evenly matched, as for example in the 1965 Indo-Pak War, it is difficult, time-consuming and costly to achieve total air superiority. Both the IAF and Pakistan Air Force (PAF) managed to create a FAS, at different times, over areas of immediate interest or where ground battles raged, and at times got the better of the opponent. Both sides abandoned counter air attacks on each other's air bases after suffering heavy attrition in the first few daylight raids, and switched to night attacks by the Canberra/B-57 light bombers, since neither side possessed a really effective night air defence. The PAF through better coordination with the ground forces, however, managed to provide better and timely offensive air support to the Pakistan Army.

During the nearly three-month long Kargil War in 1999, the IAF combat operations were restricted to the Indian side of the LoC. The PAF did not enter the fray, and thus the IAF enjoyed a kind of local favourable air situation, that prevailed on own side of the LoC. Even so, PAF F-16 fighters were often seen on high alert on the Pakistan side. To deter the enemy, the IAF also mounted a Combat Air Patrol (CAP) when necessary, and provided air defence escort to most strike aircraft engaged in attacking enemy positions in the high mountains.

Counter Air Operations

The Counter Air Operations (CAO) campaign, as the name suggests, is an offensive mounted to specifically neutralise the enemy air force's ability to 'effectively' interfere with own surface and air operations by attacking enemy air assets, such as, aircraft on the ground, operating surfaces like runways and taxi tracks, fuel dumps and base facilities and is often given primacy[39] in planning. Defensive CAO also known as Air Defence (AD) on the other hand, are operations undertaken to engage enemy aircraft, Surface-to-Surface Missiles and

UCAVs when these are already on their way to their targets in own territory. The central purpose is the same: the destruction or neutralisation of the enemy's offensive air capability.

In limited wars however, local FAS may suffice, as establishing total air superiority may not be desirable to restrict the scope of operations. The choice will naturally depend on the overall military goals and national strategy. It must, however be remembered, that the risk of enemy air forces interfering with own ground and air would remain high. In fact, given that modern wars are essentially limited in scope, time and purpose, air superiority or more correctly a FAS could well be achieved for brief periods over specific areas, on multiple occasions, without launching a full-fledged counter air campaign. AD or Defensive CAO would, however, have to be carried out to protect own valuable assets generally categorised as Vulnerable Areas and Vulnerable Points (VAs and VPs) from enemy attacks.

Air superiority is not an end in itself but merely an enabling condition, without which, other important tasks and missions, such as attacks on the enemy's sinews of war including its ground forces cannot be undertaken safely and successfully. As has been said, "With air superiority anything is possible, without it everything is at risk."[40]

Air power is always in great demand; everyone wants it, or more correctly needs it, and hence CAO are often perceived as the air forces fighting their own 'private wars' at the cost of surface forces. Such charges originate from inadequate understanding of air power and have no basis in fact. The paramount importance of air superiority cannot, however, be wished away as in one form or the other, enemy air forces will have to be neutralised/defeated or at least temporarily disabled from effectively interfering with own air and surface operations. All air force planning would thus have to be based on this understanding. Air superiority or freedom from enemy interference acquires even greater salience with the on-going modernisation of the PAF and People's Liberation Army Air Force (PLAAF). Both China and Pakistan have in the recent past built up their respective air force strength and technological prowess and pose a formidable challenge. Given that future conflicts would in all probability be limited in time and space, and hence confined to local border skirmishes, it would be essential to employ air power with the sole aim of gaining and retaining initiative. This would require meticulous joint planning in peacetime and high levels of readiness.

Air Defence

Although air power is best utilised in offensive mode, AD, or the protection of national air space against enemy attack, during peace and war, is one of the most important missions of the air force in war and peace. The aim is to deter a potential enemy from attacking own, or friendly centres of gravity such as: political leadership; industry; power stations; dams and large irrigation projects; oil refineries; business districts; communication nodes and surface communications; bridges; choke points; ports; railway yards and networks; nuclear weapon sites; own military forces and assets and a host of other targets. Airfields, aircraft, radar sites, army tank harbours, ammunition and fuel depots are some examples of military targets. It is very difficult, if not impossible, for an air force to provide adequate AD protection to each of these targets. A study to determine the *inter se* priority of all important targets is carried out and VAs and VPs selected. The selection depends on the importance of the target system, the effect of its destruction on national morale and war effort, and above all, the degree of vulnerability to enemy air attack, e.g. its proximity to borders. Once this is done, a list of the selected targets requiring air defence protection is made and prioritised and suitable resources allocated. Those in forward areas are deemed more vulnerable and accorded a higher priority and greater resources. AD operations comprise four major steps: Detection; Identification; Interception and Destruction. Each of these is a complex operation and yet vital to successful AD in war and peace.

In peacetime, there are hundreds of aircraft, mostly civilian and commercial, that fly in a nation's air space at any one time, with many foreign commercial and private aircraft transiting and operating by day and night. In India, as elsewhere, the air defence control organisation and civil aviation Air Traffic Control (ATC) networks monitor and control these movements, with the help of static high-powered radar sets and facilitate their operations, while at the same time, ensuring that no hostile air activity takes place. These radar stations and civil ATC control zones called Flight Information Regions (FIR) routinely expect commercial and other scheduled traffic, to report their position over pre-determined reporting points, by means of radio or for some years now through automatic 'transponders'. Thus, all traffic is technically always under radar surveillance or at least their approximate position in the air is always known.

If and when a flying object – commonly referred to as 'track' – is reported by the agencies concerned, as not conforming to known predetermined/assigned routes or movement schedules, the Fighter Controllers at the Air Defence Direction Centre (ADDC) concerned take immediate action to establish if a scheduled airline aircraft has veered off its predetermined route, and make an attempt to identify the 'track' by means of radio or Identification-Friend or Foe (IFF) equipment or any other transponder. It is designated as unknown 'track' until it is identified as friendly, and interception ordered in the event it is declared hostile.

During peacetime, the IAF maintains a number of armed fighter interceptors on AD alert at its forward airfields and other air bases. These are controlled by the local ADDC equipped with surveillance and early warning radar sets that provide cover over the area of their responsibility. If, and when, a hostile 'track' is reported, these AD fighter interceptors on alert, are ordered to get airborne or *scrambled* in a matter of minutes and *vectored* on to the hostile 'track'. The pilots of these aircraft first try to make a visual identification, 'show' themselves by flying in close proximity if the aircraft is obviously a commercial airliner, establish radio contact on a predetermined and internationally known radio frequency and either instruct the offending aircraft to return to its allocated route, or, if it does not follow these instructions, force it to land at the nearest civil or air force airbase. In the event that the 'track' ignores or refuses to follow these instructions, permission is sought to destroy it, if and only if, it is engaged in any *hostile* act. If it is recognised as a friendly, lost, unarmed or commercial aircraft out of radio contact or in an emergency every attempt is made to assist its safe recovery. Very often such *scrambles* are initiated when scheduled traffic inadvertently strays from allocated lanes and is assisted to return to its assigned route.

If and when all attempts to shepherd the 'track' to a nearby airfield fail, the ADDC or higher authority approves its destruction, which in peacetime is a rarity. Even during war, only enemy aircraft, positively identified as such, are cleared for destruction lest own or friendly aircraft are endangered due to navigational error, loss of radio contact or other emergencies. Internationally recognised procedures such as extending landing gear immediately on seeing the interceptor also help ensure aircraft safety. In war, however, AD alert acquires a totally different meaning. Here too the most critical task is selection and allocation of suitable and effective AD elements to meet the incoming threat: AD Interceptors, SAM defences or AAA, depending on the warning time.

Weapon Release Line (WRL)

The steps enumerated above are invariably followed in peace and war but the very purpose of maintaining an elaborate AD network would be lost if the enemy is allowed to cause damage to or destroy own assets with impunity. It is thus essential that a hostile enemy aircraft is intercepted and destroyed as far away as possible from its intended target, but definitely well before it is able to release its weapons. Normally, fighter bombers or ground attack aircraft with first/second generation weapons have to necessarily fly over, or close to the targets before they can release their weapons and would usually provide adequate warning if detected in time. But those with stand-off ranges have to be intercepted at considerable distances from own air bases or international borders.

In the 1960s and 1970s, when aircraft ranges were very short and the IAF had very few radar stations, enemy aircraft were detected very late or not at all and often got away unscathed. Given the far superior ranges and weapon loads of the current generation fighters, more advanced and sophisticated ground and airborne radars (collectively known as Air Defence Ground Environment System or ADGES) and the availability of AWACS (Airborne Warning and Control System) aircraft in the region, forward air defence has become possible. An AWACS aircraft such as the Phalcon-equipped Il-76 can maintain effective surveillance up to 300 km. This provides adequate early warning to own fighters to anticipate and position themselves, so that enemy intruders are destroyed, even before they reach the International Border (IB) or LoC. AWACS also improves detection capabilities at night, in bad weather and to some extent over mountainous border areas, if and when, the terrain does not mask the approaching enemy aircraft. With both Pakistan and the People's Republic of China (PRC) in possession of AWACS aircraft, the next conflict will see a bitter contest for the control of air.

Deep or Strategic Strike

Although strategic bomber operations, as seen above, proved expensive and less effective in undermining the enemy's morale and resulted in wanton destruction of cities and population centres, modern air forces often have to resort to bombing strategic targets in the enemy hinterland. To diminish the enemy's war potential, in the 1971 War, the IAF Canberra medium bombers and Hunter fighter bombers, targeted Pakistan's oil refinery at Attock, Mangla Dam and oil depots at Karachi. Deep or strategic strikes were also undertaken during the two Gulf Wars (1991 and 2003) and in other wars. Compared to the Allied bombers of World War II, the fighter bombers or multi-role aircraft of today carry far heavier and more diverse armament loads of accurate PGM and can also defend themselves against enemy aircraft by using Electronic Counter-Measures (ECM), Electronic Counter Counter-Measures (ECCM), and a variety of other means. Accuracy of bombing also assures destruction of specific targets with little or no collateral damage, except when the enemy takes recourse to human shield tactics.

There is also much criticism about use of airpower against decapitating strikes aimed at enemy leadership. In the 2003 Gulf War, for example, the first few air strikes targeted the building which, according to Allied intelligence, was used by Iraq's President Saddam Hussein. Although the site was accurately hit, he had providentially left the building minutes before the air strike. In the recent past, there has also been a clamour against the use of 'drones' or UAVs by the North Atlantic Treaty Organisation (NATO) forces in Afghanistan and its eastern border areas where the Taliban insurgents have routinely taken shelter. Such strikes have been largely successful and have received tacit approval of the Pakistan government, but have been criticised in public, for these strikes are seen to be violating the sovereignty of Pakistan. Be that as it may, the capability of an air force to strike deep into enemy territory also plays a major deterrent role and is unlikely to be given up in the future. In fact, advances in technology, such as small diameter bombs and GPS-aided navigation attack systems will further improve accuracy, while at the same time severely restricting the area of actual destruction, and in all probability, become more acceptable if collateral damage is further reduced.

Those inclined to view air power only in the narrow sphere of offensive support to surface forces, may not easily accept the need to possess deep strike capability and view such expenditure as wasteful. Today, multi-role combat aircraft, however, confer this capability without having to maintain dedicated bomber forces, and offer far greater flexibility to the national political leadership, which may or may not allow deep strike missions.

Counter Surface Force Operations (CSFO)

Earlier known as Army Cooperation, Close Air Support (CAS) and Offensive Air Support (OAS) but now called Battlefield Air Strike (BAS), these operations are aimed at supporting the ground/surface forces (both Army and Navy) and, therefore, are a vital part of the IAF's role. With improvements in technology, increasingly more sophisticated means of Intelligence, Surveillance and Reconnaissance (ISR), and improvements in target detection and identification, it is now relatively easier to engage enemy ground targets in close proximity to own troops.

World War II, particularly the North African campaign, saw rapid progress in this department. New and innovative ways were found and the reaction time considerably reduced. Own ground forces usually place pre-planned demands on the supporting air force units, the previous evening, for execution the next day. Demands requiring an *immediate* response from the air force could, however, be placed as and when the situation so demands. An elaborate procedure was evolved to vett these demands at the appropriate high levels of army, typically the controlling Corps Headquarters, where an air force representative was/is always available for necessary advice. After due vetting, these demands are prioritised and orders sent to the Army Ground Liaison Officer (GLO) at the air force unit/station and Forward Air Controllers (FACs) for execution. These procedures needed secure and fool proof radio/signal communications and very often much time was lost. When needed, ground attack fighters were maintained on airborne alert, but this being very costly in terms of air effort and often impractical, a system called 'cab rank' was devised during the Korean War, in which air force aircraft remained at cockpit readiness and were launched as soon as army demands were received. Such a system was nonetheless resource intensive and often tied up precious aircraft on the ground.

The army air cooperation was at its zenith during the North African campaign. So impressed was General Lord Montgomery, the famous British military leader (later Field Marshal) with the performance of the RAF that he said, "If we lose the war in the air, we lose the war and we lose it quickly."[41] The RAF and later the USAAF successfully attacked German forces in the field, interdicted their lines of supply and prevented their safe and organised retreat. The spectacular offensive action of the IAF in decimating Pakistan's armour in Longewala in 1971, remains a permanent reminder about how vulnerable tanks or mechanised forces are to air power. Conversely, if these tanks had been supported by the PAF, the outcome of the battle would have been less one-sided. During the Falklands conflict in 1982, of the 24 vessels lost or damaged, all but two were destroyed by aircraft. During the 1991 Gulf War, air-delivered weapons sank all 14 vessels lost by the Iraqis.[42]

Effect on Morale

While it is true that the presence of own fighter aircraft over or in close vicinity to friendly ground forces works as a great morale booster for own troops, employment of air power to achieve this limited objective is very often wasteful. History shows that the morale of own ground forces is far more adversely affected by the presence and activity of enemy air forces over their heads, and it is thus axiomatic that own air forces relentlessly attack the enemy air forces and prevent their effective interference with own ground operations. This is because providing a protective fighter CAP over own troops on a 24-hour basis, would prove uneconomical and often impossible due to limited resources. With thorough prior joint planning, however, it would be possible to execute a successful air-land operation, since every move would be pre-planned and only emergencies arising from an unexpected enemy attack would require immediate remedial action by the air force.

To obtain best results from a CSFO campaign, both the army and air force commanders must carefully plan their operations and regularly review the success or failure of these plans on a daily, if not hourly, basis. Network Enabled Warfare today provides secure and reliable communications between the ground and air component commanders and also an up-to-the-minute battlefield situation assessment, further easing the difficulties of joint operations. There is today a surfeit of sensors and channels for flow of information that sometimes leads to information overload. It is for the air and army commanders to sift the grain from the chaff and take correct and timely decisions. CSFO, OAS or Battlefield Air Strike (BAS) operations will continue to form a vital component of offensive air operations against surface forces.

Some of the important conditions for air power employment in CSFO role are:

(a) The relative importance and priority or urgency to engage the target system. Targets that can easily, and economically, be engaged with integral artillery fire power, should not normally be allotted for BAS by air forces unless there is a strong reason to do so: e.g. to demonstrate the seriousness with which the country views enemy action.

(b) Ease or difficulty of target recognition and identification. A small error resulting in damage or casualties to own troops and equipment can wipe off all the gains of prompt air action and adversely affect the morale of troops.

(c) Availability of assistance on the ground, such as FACs to guide the aircraft on to the target.
(d) Separation from troops, equipment or assets so as to avoid 'friendly fire' incidents or fratricide.
(e) Air defence environment and coordination with organic air defence weapons with the surface forces. History shows that small arms fire can be very lethal to modern fighters and hence repeated 'copy book' attack patterns from predictable directions must be avoided. Presence of enemy fighters must be taken into account and suitable escorts or 'top cover' provided, even when AWACS are available to give early warning. This is essential to minimise attrition to air power resources from own and enemy small arms and AD weapons in the tactical battle area.
(f) Weather, light and visibility conditions prevailing in the vicinity of the target area would continue to impinge on the success of BAS/CSFO. Where possible, recce-pods and electro-optical sensors must be used to locate and identify enemy targets. A wide variety of multi-purpose missiles and small diameter bombs and PGMs, such as Joint Direct Attack Munitions (JDAM), are now available to improve accuracy without coming within the envelope of Man Portable Air Defence Systems (MANPADS), such as the lethal Stinger missile that the Pakistani intruders used in the Kargil war.
(g) Political Direction or Rules of Engagement will finally decide the exact tactics and weapons of air power employment.
(h) To the extent possible, air power employment should conform to a broad strategy and knee-jerk reactions or frequent changes in target priorities must be avoided.

Post-strike damage assessment is vital for assured success and the effect on the enemy's plan of operation must also be assessed at all times. Such assessments must become routine, even during peacetime joint army-air exercises, to correctly validate own procedures and priorities to further refine doctrine.

Regardless of the scale of conflict, national objectives and security policy/strategy will naturally play an important role in deciding the level and scale of air power employment in any future war. The likely enemy response, escalation control, likely duration and the proposed end state or exit point would decide the employment of air power. To obtain the maximum dividend, air power employment strategy must always be aimed at creating asymmetry at the time and place of own choosing.

The successful employment of American UAVs in what is popularly known as 'Drone Attacks' against insurgents and Taliban fighters along the Afghanistan-Pakistan border, has in recent times added a new and efficient dimension to BAS.

Even so drone strikes have invited close scrutiny from the legal and ethical viewpoint. In November 2011, around 24 Pakistani soldiers were killed in an errant drone attack. Such mistakes proved extremely costly as the clamour for banning these attacks forced the Pakistan Government to close the NATO supply route for nearly eight months, until the then US Secretary of State Hillary Clinton, finally rendered a public apology and the supply route opened in July 2012.[43]

Availability of Forces

At first glance, this might appear self-explanatory, but given the demand for air power resources in war and peace, the availability and allocation of air effort often becomes a contentious issue. In a vast country such as India, that regularly faces natural calamities, civil unrest and incidents along the volatile borders with its neighbours, the air force is always in demand. In war too, the tasks of providing air defence, achieving at least a reasonably benign or favourable air situation and undertaking effective CSFO can often stretch air resources to the limit. It is, therefore, imperative that the control of air power resources is kept at the highest practical level. Notwithstanding the pressure under which airmen may have to work, they understand and relate to soldiers and sailors and indeed paramilitary forces and empathise with the difficulties they face and hence are always prepared and eager to provide all kinds of support. Be it fire power or food, heliborne support or search and rescue, airmen will always find ways to provide it, in time, every time and right till the job is done. Airmen inherently understand joint warfare and always are an important and integral part of it.

Battlefield Air Interdiction (BAI)

This operation is primarily aimed at cutting or disrupting the enemy's lines of supply, by directly targeting the transport systems such as railway lines, trains, loco-sheds, road and rail bridges and military convoys. An essentially tactical operation, its effectiveness depends on accurate intelligence and timely execution and requires a close understanding of the army's operational plans.

Air Space Management

In a conventional war scenario, the airspace over the battlefield is likely to be cluttered with a variety of flying objects including army and air force helicopters, low-flying high-speed fighters going to and returning from targets in enemy territory, a dense barrage of long-range artillery shells, and above all, enemy fighter bombers attacking own/friendly targets. Such dense traffic will inevitably make the task of providing air defence and identifying hostile aircraft extremely difficult, necessitating a highly reliable air space management system with dependable fail-safe communications.

For effective employment, modern air power is increasingly dependent on Space-based assets such as navigation, reconnaissance and communication satellites and is now inseparable from Space. The current nomenclature 'aerospace power' is thus more appropriate. In this study, the subject is discussed in a separate chapter.

Air Transport Operations

These involve the carriage of ground troops from one theatre to another and sometimes also within theatre. Both fixed wing transport aircraft and medium or heavy lift helicopters are used for this task. With the recent induction of the Hercules C-130J and Globemaster C-17 aircraft, the IAF can provide strategic mobility over considerable distances when required. The Mi-17 V5 and the soon-to-be-inducted Chinook troop lift helicopters will further enhance the IAF capability to airlift troops and equipment to less accessible areas in the mountains. The IAF has for over 50 years regularly air maintained troops and civilians deployed/resident in the forward areas, an operation unique in its scope and reach.

Airborne Assault

These operations involve the air dropping of assault troops on the intended target by means of parachutes. The Indian Army maintains a Parachute Brigade trained for this task which regularly exercises with IAF transport aircrews. It is available on call even during peacetime, in a matter of hours, as demonstrated in 1988, when India sent a battalion plus of the assault troops, to help the Maldivian President Maumoon Abdul Gayoom, when his government was threatened by a coup.

Special Heliborne Operations (SHBO)

Heliborne assault falls in the same category except that in this case troops are transported by helicopters and either land on, or near the target, or slither down a rope with the helicopter hovering above the landing site. This type of operation is usually resorted to when commandos or Special Operation Forces are employed to raid or capture enemy hideouts and similar targets.

Casualty Evacuation (Cas-Evac)

As the name suggests, helicopters are very frequently employed in this role in peacetime and have on numerous occasions saved precious lives. Combat Search and Rescue (CSAR) operations, are aimed at rescuing downed pilots and other personnel from enemy territory, or high threat areas. The USAF has routinely mounted these operations, usually under fighter cover, and successfully retrieved many downed aircrews from enemy territory. These operations are obviously very risky and demand thorough planning and close coordination with fighter and other elements.

Air Power in Perspective

For all its ubiquity, flexibility and reach, air power should never be seen as a panacea for every situation. Air power assets will always be in great demand and therefore, the tendency to employ them simply because these are idling on ground must be checked. As we have seen, gaining control of the air is undoubtedly a vital task, but it is only an enabling condition. Once achieved, the condition must be quickly used to prosecute other military tasks and missions, or else the effort would be wasted. Simply carrying out medium- or high-level offensive sweeps to entice the enemy to give fight might prove, though temporarily, that the enemy is reluctant to fight, but he may in fact, be waiting for a more opportune moment to strike at more important and vulnerable targets.

Full Spectrum Dominance

As the name suggests, this concept aims to achieve total superiority over the enemy in land, air, maritime, space, cyber, economic, political and strategic domains – a somewhat ambitious objective for even the lone superpower. Most modern air forces, including the IAF, have been trying to achieve Full Spectrum Dominance, or are at least hoping to achieve a very high level of dominance in all spheres. China's 2004 Defence White Paper also specifically mentions Command of the Air as an important objective of future wars. Galloping technological advances are perhaps driving such thinking. While this concept, first propounded by the USAF in the immediate aftermath of the 1991 Gulf War (Operation Desert Storm), is essentially aimed at achieving such dominance, using all the three branches of the military, air power is seen as being a vital enabler, if not the most decisive player.

Air power is attractive because it can be launched, called off or withdrawn, its intensity calibrated in order to punish, show resolve or intention, deter and reassure allies, or quickly achieve the immediate objective. Cohesion and clarity of thought are necessary for effective employment of air power. Its inherent offensive nature requires that it be used with relative freedom of action. A purely defensive approach to air power employment does not pay dividends. To derive the maximum shock effect, it must be unleashed like a torrent and not in small doses. In the 1999 Kargil war, IAF aircraft were not allowed to cross the LoC. While this gave India some diplomatic dividends, it constrained air power employment, as it was not easy to manoeuvre high-speed fighters at high altitudes, while carrying out precision attacks. Pakistani Stingers near the targets, and PAF F-16 fighters waiting on the other side, made the task even more difficult. In the future too, air power might have to be used with such strict Rules of Engagement, but in that case less than optimum results will have to be accepted.

Relentless offensive action is designed to put the enemy on the defensive and any signs of the offensive action slowing down, will allow the enemy to recoup. War is a contest of will between the opposing sides. It is only this will to fight that sustains a nation's war effort. Even when a country follows a defensive strategy, if war becomes unavoidable, the only way an aggressor can be checked in his tracks is by immediately going on the 'offensive,' without which the enemy cannot be deterred, or prevented from launching more damaging offensive strikes by land, sea or air. In sum, a purely defensive approach aimed at minimising the effects of the enemy's attacks, can never be successful, even if defensive measures cause some attrition to enemy forces. This is simply because the initiative remains with the enemy.

Air power is essentially offensive. Its special attributes can only be fully exploited when used as an offensive weapon. Even in defence, the spirit of its employment must always remain offensive. Since no air force, however powerful, can guarantee total and complete safety and security from enemy air forces, own VAs/VPs including ground forces in the field have to be protected. Effective air defence thus becomes equally important. Depending on the state of its technological capability enemy air force can in a single attack cause catastrophic damage. It is, therefore, imperative that while strengthening air defence, our air force mounts an offensive against enemy air forces at the first available opportunity, and compels them to gradually go on the defensive.

NOTES

1. P.C. Lal Memorial Lecture, delivered at the Air Force Association, New Delhi on April 2, 2012.
2. RAF AP 3000 Fourth Edition, HMG, 2008, p. 13.
3. US Army Air Force (USAAF) was, at that time, not an independent service.
4. See no. 2, p. 7. As we shall see later, 'air and space power' or 'aerospace power' are more appropriate terms to describe current and future air power thinking.
5. *Doctrine of the Indian Air Force*, Air HQ New Delhi, 1995, (amended 1997), p. 28.
6. See no. 2, p. 15.
7. For example, at Kunduz in Afghanistan, a marriage party was wrongly targeted by a NATO fighter, killing a large number of innocent civilians.
8. Air Chief Marshal P.C. Lal, *My Years with the IAF*, Lancer International, New Delhi, 1986, p. 32.
9. "Red Flag at Nellis: The Indian Air Force in the Big League", *Vayu*, New Delhi, (5), 2008, pp. 40-47. The Indian contingent also maintained aircraft serviceability of 95 per cent.
10. The IAF is slated to induct some ten C-17 heavy transport aircraft for strategic mobility. Gareth Jennings, "India receives its first C-17", *IHS Jane's Defence Weekly*, Vol. 50, Issue 25, p. 17.
11. Elliot A. Cohen, "The Mystique of US Air Power", *Foreign Affairs*, January-February 1994, at http://www.foreignaffairs.com/articles/49442/eliot-a-cohen/the-mystique-of-us-air-power(Accessed September 10, 2014).
12. Winston Churchill as quoted in, Andrew G.B. Vallance, *The Air Weapon: Doctrines of Air Power Strategy and Operational Art,* St. Martin's Press, London, 1996, p. 23.
13. 'Uttarakhand faces flood fury', *Times of India*, June 16, 2013 and other news reports.
14. Andrew G.B. Vallance, no. 12, p. 36.
15. Due to delivery delays and cost of refurbishing the Gorshkov, costs have escalated.
16. Andrew G.B. Vallance, no. 12. This comment was made in 1995. Costs of air power have further climbed in the last two decades and in India's case the rise is likely to be much steeper due to the falling rupee.

17. For those mathematically inclined, the formula for airplane lift L produced by its movement through the air is given as $L = c_l \frac{1}{2}\rho v^2 s$, where c_l is the coefficient of Lift, the Greek letter ρ (rho) denotes air density, v the true air speed and s the surface area of the aerofoil.
18. The Royal Aeronautical Society Air Power Group Paper on the issues and lessons arising from the 2011 Libyan Air Campaign, at http://aerosociety.com/Assets/Docs/Publications/SpecialistPapers/LibyaSpecialistPaperFinal.pdf (Accessed June 25, 2012).
19. Andrew G.B. Vallance, no.12, p. 2.
20. Ibid., p. 2.
21. Andrew G.B. Vallance, no. 12, p. 3.
22. Ibid., pp. 3-4.
23. Andrew G.B. Vallance, no. 12, p. 4.
24. After whom the famous French Open Tennis tournament and tennis courts near Paris are named.
25. A.D. Harvey, "Air Power History", Fall 2000, at http://weaponsandwarfare.com/?p=2126#chitika_close_button, (Accessed July 19, 2013).
26. Andrew G.B. Vallance, no. 12, pp. 6-7. Information in this and the previous paragraphs is from Andrew G.B. Vallance. The long quote is given intentionally to show that the debate over the primary role of air power is nearly century old, but even today both sides seem to stick to their stated stands with equal enthusiasm, if not ferocity. As we shall see later, most air forces including the IAF have opted for a balance that confers on them the ability to conduct all types of aerial operations with equal ease, depending on the situation.
27. A.D. Harvey, no. 25.
28. Andrew G.B. Vallance, no.12, p. 7.
29. Ibid., p. 11.
30. Quoted in Ibid., p. 9.
31. Ibid., p. 10.
32. Churchill's historic address to the House of Commons on August 20, 1940.
33. Andrew G.B. Vallance, no. 12, p. 67.
34. Desmond Young, *Rommel: The Desert Fox*, William Collins and Sons, London, 1950, p. 303.
35. Ibid., p. 281.
36. Andrew G.B. Vallance, no. 12, p. 12.
37. Ibid., pp. 11-15. Most of the statistics provided here are from Andrew G.B. Vallance.
38. Karl Mueller, "Air Power", RAND Corporation Report, at http://www.rand.org/content/dam/rand/pubs/reprints/2010/RAND_RP1412.pdf, (Accessed November 15, 2011)
39. Andrew G.B. Vallance, no.12, pp. 62-85. He gives CAO the status of *primus inter pares* or 'first among equals'.
40. Maj. Gen. Charles D. Link, USAF, "The Role of the US Air Force in the Employment of Air Power", in Richard H. Shultz Jr. and Robert L. Pfaltzgraff, Jr. (eds.), *The Future of Air Power in the Aftermath of the Gulf War*, Air University Press, Maxwell Air Force Base, Alabama, 1992, p. 83.
41. Andrew G.B. Vallance, no. 12, p. 15.
42. Andrew G.B. Vallance, no. 12, p. 87.
43. "Pakistan ends dispute over NATO supply routes after Hillary Clinton apology" at http://www.the guardian.com/world/2012/jul/03/Pakistan-dispute-nato-hillary-clinton. (Accessed October 4, 2012).

3

Evolution of India's National Security Practice

Two events that occurred almost immediately after India became independent on August 15, 1947 – the Pakistani invasion of India in the northern state of Jammu and Kashmir (J&K) and the Chinese invasion of Tibet in 1950 – have shaped India's national security discourse for over 68 years. The tragedy is, that after all these years and all our efforts, the two problems remain unresolved. In addition, India has also been facing challenges to its internal security in the form of separatist movements, terrorism, insurgencies and Left-Wing Extremism (LWE) for nearly the same length of time, and our exertions to lessen their impact have so far met with only mixed results. The long colonial experience, the over half a century long freedom struggle, the six year long World War II and the atomic bombing of Japan were the other major influences that shaped India's view of the world and hence its security and foreign policy.

Since independence, India has fought five wars and except the 1971 Bangladesh liberation war, none was decisive. In the one with China, India was roundly defeated. While Indian leaders have constantly made attempts to make peace with neighbours, these have been largely unsuccessful. Despite this, India has successfully fought many challenges to its democracy, through largely free and fair elections and has preserved its national unity and integrity. The stark reality of India's security situation is that even today, there is no guarantee that peace will prevail.

By virtue of its long civilisational history, size, geo-strategic location at the head of the Indian Ocean, natural resources, vast population, industrial capacity ably aided by a large pool of highly educated and experienced technologists, engineers and other professionals, India has always been an important country, even when weak. It was for its immense potential that the British colonial masters called India the 'jewel in the crown' and used its attributes and strengths to rule and even extend their sway over large parts of Asia. Even if it did not always enjoy a major place in the comity of nations, it could never be ignored and hence India is not 'recently important' as some observers would have us believe.[1]

Lord Curzon, the British Viceroy of India at the turn of the 20th century, had no doubts about its importance and vital place in the British Empire when he said:

> India is the pivot of Empire, by which I mean that outside the British Isles we could, I believe, lose any portion of the Dominions of the Queen and yet survive as an Empire; while if we lost India, I maintain that our sun would sink to its setting.[2]

Addressing the Constituent Assembly on March 8, 1949, Nehru echoed similar sentiments when he said:

> Look at the map. If you have to consider any question affecting the Middle East, India inevitably comes into the picture. If you have to consider any question concerning South East Asia, you cannot do without India. So also with the Far East...whatever regions you may have in mind, the importance of India cannot be ignored...
>
> ...So the point I wish the House to remember is this: First of all, the emergence of India in world affairs is something of a major consequence in world history. We...in the Government are men of relatively small stature. But it has been given to us to work at a time when India is growing into a great giant again. So, because of that, in spite of our smallness, we have to work for great causes and perhaps elevate ourselves in the process.[3]

K. Shankar Bajpai strategic thinker and foreign policy expert also holds similar views:

> Given that India is endowed with many advantages: We had one of the world's five largest armies, ranked tenth in industrial capacity, despite the terrors and strains of partition we had a strong administrative structure, a pool of exceptional talent – and incidentally – no foreign exchange shortages, we were more powerful than is even now realised.[4]

India also had a plethora of dedicated and sagacious leaders moulded in the crucible of the long and arduous freedom struggle. In view of this, it is perhaps natural for us to wonder why India was not able to address its security challenges in a more robust and decisive manner. Has India done the best that it could in the circumstances? Could it have done better? Has it lost some opportunities? Could things have been done differently? These are some of the questions that this chapter attempts to answer. Here we will also try to glean possible lessons that may help guide future generations to avoid the pitfalls of the past. Before tracing the evolution of India's national security narrative, however, a very brief overview of some relevant definitions and theories related to International Relations (IR) and security is considered useful.

Definitions

The term security can be defined in many ways. The more commonly cited definition by Walter Lippmann is: "A nation has security when it does not have to sacrifice its legitimate interests to avoid war, and is able, if challenged, to maintain them by war."[5] Stephen M. Walt believed that, "the main focus of security studies…is the phenomenon of war...Accordingly, security studies may be defined as the study of the threat, use and control of military force." According to Patrick Morgan, "it is important to confine the concept of security to physical safety from deliberate physical harm inflicted intentionally, i.e., across national boundaries. Barry Buzan opined that: "[Security is] primarily about the fate of human collectivities...about the pursuit of freedom from threat. [The] bottom line is about survival, but it also includes a substantial range of concerns about the conditions of existence...Security...is affected by factors in five major sectors: military, political, economic, societal and environmental." To Ken Booth, "the key concept in talking about security is emancipation. Emancipation means freeing people from those constraints that stop them carrying out what freely they would choose to do, of which, war, poverty, oppression and poor education are a few."[6]

Of the definitions included above, the ones by Lippmann and Walt focus on war and military force, whereas those by Buzan and Booth are more inclusive and all-encompassing. In the case of a developing country like India, which was economically weak, and even today has a large portion of population living in poverty, Buzan's view seems more appropriate.

Another scholar, Pierre Jacquet says: "[T]he relationship between international economics and political and military affairs is a major determinant of the international order" and is thus linked to the concept of security. "Security is most commonly defined in a negative way, as a state of freedom from danger, damage and injury (can we include want?). It represents a state or a sense of safety." He adds: "Many actions and policies can be justified in the name of security. An important aspect is its double meaning semantically: the objective sense refers to the absence of threat or the ability to successfully resist a threat; the subjective or speculative sense refers to the degree of fear. From both these meanings, it appears that security as a concept is linked intricately to interdependence: both threat and fear are related to the behaviour of others, which may itself be influenced." Further: "National security can be defined as the protection and preservation of national core values against predatory behaviour of other nations either by deterring aggression or by war; without having to sacrifice one's values or by victory should aggression occur...Security rises and falls with the ability of a nation to deter an attack or to defeat it. Pre-emptive wars can also be engaged for security reasons. Hence, from a national point of view, security cannot be defined by the absence of war or by commitment to peace. Clearly, given this definition, national security can be threatened by international inter-interdependence. Dependency is a source of vulnerability – oil, food, strategic commodity; dependencies always have a national security dimension. Sanctions, embargoes, blockades are designed to exploit these vulnerabilities to punish or influence behaviour."[7]

In the early post-independence period in India, the terms defence and security were often used interchangeably.[8] These terms in a sense focus on the three main objectives of a nation-state (since despite many threats to its primacy, the nation-state has been and will continue to be the main entity to regulate the affairs of mankind), the safeguarding of national sovereignty; protecting territorial integrity and economic and political independence to pursue the national goals of social and economic development; and in India's case, promoting values of non-violence, peace, equality, justice and fraternity for the well-being of all.

In fact, all these goals form part of the Preamble of the Indian Constitution and hence K. Subrahmanyam called it the tenet of India's 'grand strategy' when he quoted the oath taken by the Members of the Constituent Assembly on August 15, 1947:

> At this solemn moment when people of India, through suffering and sacrifice have assured freedom, I, a member of the Constituent Assembly of India, dedicate myself in all humility to the service of India and all her people to the end that this ancient land attains her righteous place in the world and makes her full and willing contribution to the promotion of world peace and welfare of mankind.

This oath, he goes on to say, implied that India would work for [the] promotion of world peace not for its own glory and aggrandisement; India would work for the welfare of mankind, including the welfare of its own population and it would attempt to take its rightful place in the world, by developing itself to the standards of advanced nations of the rest of the world.[9]

In fact, India as a result of the success of its mostly non-violent freedom struggle, became a beacon of hope for other colonies in the immediate aftermath of World War II; and Nehru's policy of remaining equidistant from the two emerging power blocs, or non-alignment, that aimed at friendship with all countries without joining either of the two blocs that were then coming into being, helped India play a significant role in world affairs.

As Shivshankar Menon, former National Security Adviser (NSA), stated during his address at the Cariappa Memorial Lecture:

> There is no question that in Nehru's time we were punching above our weight, measured strictly in realist balance of power terms. This was possible because of the strategic space that the Cold War opened up for us, and because of the eminent good sense and reasonableness of what Nehru was doing and advocating. During the fifties, India stood higher in the world's (and her own) estimation than her strength warranted. During the sixties, the reverse was the case. After 1971, there has been a greater correlation between India's strength and prestige, and this seems likely to continue for the foreseeable future.[10]

Political realists believe that the world is an anarchy where each individual nation-state is by design always jockeying for power, in order to maximise its interests and hence conflict is inevitable. Muthiah Alagappa citing Kenneth Waltz also says:

> Realists depict international policies as a realm of power struggle, and of accommodation. This pessimistic view flows from another of neorealism's[11] core assumptions, 'anarchy', and the logic that it is deemed to imply. In the neorealist view, the international system, populated by sovereign states, must necessarily be decentralised and anarchic. In the absence of a central authority, each state retains the right to judge 'its grievances and ambitions according to its own dictates or desire', and to decide on the use of force.[12]

Security is, however, not absolute because one state's security can be another's insecurity or danger. It is therefore, incumbent on each state to ensure that in trying to guarantee its own security, it does not jeopardise its neighbour's. The reality of international politics is, however, very different. Without entering the quagmire of numerous IR theories,[13] for our purpose, it suffices to say that power politics is inevitable and unavoidable. The norms of behaviour and cultural and civilisational values no doubt play an important role in international relations, but a nation-state cannot overlook its own well-being and interests while trying to work with others.

Evolution of India's National Security Thinking

Shivshankar Menon said:

> Realists believe that in an anarchic international system power rules the day. They also assume that states, like individuals, are self-interested rational maximisers. Uncertainty is rampant, information is always incomplete, and opportunism is always possible in international society. As a result, states have little choice but to defend themselves...

He went on to add:

> [T]he only effective sanction is force or the threat of its use, and the willingness of those who possess it to use it. In other words, while domestic societies have evolved or are evolving towards rule of law, international society is still much closer to primeval anarchy, where to a very great extent 'the strong do as they will and the weak do as they must'.[14]

This public and candid articulation by a high ranking Indian government functionary, on the role of force in international affairs, is a relatively new development and a refreshingly welcome change, since in the past, Indian officials have generally avoided such candour.

After lauding the role that India played in world affairs, for instance, Korea (1953), Vietnam and Laos (1954), Gaza (1956) and Congo (1961), K. Shankar Bajpai, alluding to Nehru's views of India's role cited above, says:

> India was constantly in the lead both to reduce the possibilities of world war and structuring of a world order. Yet, without belittling in the slightest what we tried for and what we contributed, we must acknowledge that we did not become of that 'major consequence in world history', much less the 'great giant' which we expected and which our size, situation, resources and talent ought to have made us. And the reason lies in our difficulty in coming to terms with the role of power in world affairs.

He goes on to blame our 'inwardness'. "Both as a people and as a state, we have throughout history been a world unto ourselves."[15] He highlights how the world has always sought us out, but we have hardly ever looked outwards.

> From being an object of power, our British rulers made us a base of power, which enabled them to exercise their control from Suez to Singapore, which we opposed; and as we assumed charge of our destinies, our historic isolationism resumed charge of our approach to the world.

He substantiates this seemingly harsh charge by recounting the story:

> In the late fifties, as Britain withdrew from the Persian Gulf area, they relinquished Gwadar which though on the coast of Baluchistan, was for some reason administered from Muscat and Oman. The latter enquired if we (India) would like to buy the place. We would not even think of the possibility. We also, more famously, agreed to withdraw the Rupee as the currency of the region; with the Gulf region's oil development, it was probably only a matter of time before the rupee would cease to be relevant there, but the strategic advantage of acquiring Gwadar simply would not enter our thinking.
>
> Two other formative influences, reinforcing this inwardness arose from our freedom movement: anti-imperialism and pacifism, meaning both

> non-violence and an innate inclination to work for peace. I do not think we should ever claim to be holier than others in these respects; the needs of the state drove us to the use of force soon enough-Junagadh, Hyderabad, Kashmir and later Goa, were cited gleefully by our critics as mocking what we professed, but apart from justification of necessity, these cases in no way lessened the very profound belief that power, especially military power, was the cause of evil.[16]

In another case of missed opportunity, when the British withdrew from the Indian Ocean in 1976, India also did not try to get access to the fully developed airfield, from where Royal Air Force (RAF) V-bombers routinely operated, at Gan situated at the extreme southern tip of the Maldives archipelago, something India could have easily done in the more benign circumstances of the period. India now has some kind of a security cooperation arrangement with Maldives and has gifted the island nation a ship and a few helicopters to fight terrorism and piracy, but it is not known if India has plans to request Maldives for the emergency use of Gan airfield. Being situated at the southern end of the Maldivian archipelago, Gan is like a veritable large aircraft carrier some 800 km in the Indian Ocean; a major strategic asset.

The Security Discourse

Right from India's independence, its political leaders and other decision-makers have clung to the belief that India is somehow different from the rest of the world and hence, can strike out on its own unique path. In reality, India was every now and then, forced to accept the reality that without the willingness to use its power, its options were severely restricted. India tried to maintain friendly relations with established powers and even looked for their assistance when the need arose, mostly without discarding these shibboleths of India's eternal quest for global peace, disarmament and non-violence – and often invited derisive comments. Even so, because of its unique security practices, no country, barring a few of its immediate neighbours, considers its rise as a threat to regional or world peace.

The habit of tolerance, developed by Indian philosophy and tradition was, and is, one such important factor that has played a major role in its security practice. By tradition, the Indian outlook is pluralistic. Indian thought has never insisted on one particular form of the truth. This tradition explains India's stress on non-alignment and peaceful negotiations. According to A. Appadorai, "This tradition has made the Indian people react instinctively against the claim of Communism to embody the sole truth, and likewise prevented them from regarding Communism with as much disfavour as the anti-communists do."[17] Another belief stemming from history was the importance of means to achieve ends. Although Kautilya, the well-known political thinker of the fourth century

BC, did recommend that a policy be judged by the results it produced (he was an early Realist!), Indians do not seem to have accepted it as a norm. Suffice it to say that traditional ancient Hindu thought substantially influenced Indian policy-makers. The desire to get world opinion in India's favour is also rooted in Indian history. Appadorai narrates a story from *Mahabharata* in which he attributes a statement to Lord Krishna who said, "Even if he (Lord Krishna) did not succeed in his mission to avert war between the warring Kauravas and Pandavas, it would b useful to show the world that they were right and Kauravas wrong."[18] Throughout India diplomacy of the last six-and-a-half decades, the influence of Indian thought is clearly discernible even if it is not always acknowledged.

India's security edifice, it seems, was built on lofty ideals, and a misplaced notion, that its intentions to peacefully coexist with its neighbours would automatically be reciprocated in full measure. There is thus a strong tendency to delay the consideration of use of force until the very last moment. This has been an enduring feature of India's security management. Such procrastination on moral and ethical grounds has often cost India dear, both in men and material. What were the other reasons for India to strongly oppose the resort to force in international relations? The experience of the two long and devastating World Wars no doubt weighed heavily on the makers of modern India. To be fair, they attempted to maintain peace at almost any cost and did not, and even today, do not care if the world reads this as hypocrisy or even timidity. Nehru's unshakeable faith in Asian solidarity and 'Third Worldism' also played a role in his preference for a pacific resolution of disputes.[19]

Mahatma Gandhi's belief in finding a solution to conflict in which neither party suffered significant lss, was also instrumental in shaping India's policy in Korea and later, in Indo-China. Indianleaders saw a great opportunity for a non-aligned India to play such a mediatory role in the then developing conflict of the Cold War situation. India might nt have always got the credit that was due to its diplomacy and mediation because of its moral attitude, but there is no doubt that India consistently believed that,unless an attempt was made to see that neither party suffered a significant loss, the results of any negotiation would not be stable.[20]

Grand Strategy and National Power

A *grand strategy* and articulations of a nation's values are not sufficient to safeguard the country's interests; for that the country has to formulate a national security policy. Further, a well thouht out and formulated security strategy and the willingness to build and use national power are also equally essential.

National Power can be termed as the capacity of a nation to use its tangible and intangible resources, which normally include its demographic, economic, industrial, geo-strategic, ideational and miltary strength, to influence the behaviour of other nations, whether friendly or hostile, and to protect its own interests when the need arises. National Power, however, is not merely the sum of its capabilities, but becomes manifest only with strategic purpose, national will and resolve to actually utilise these strengths to safeguard its national interests. The nation's self-image, often decides its behaviour and responses to different situations inside and outside the country. It is only in recent years that Indian officials and political leaders have begun to stress the desirability of striving for Comprehensive National Power (CNP).[21] *National interests* are normally categorised as the safeguarding of the core values of a nation and include the physical security of its people, its territory, economic and industrial sinews and the eneral well-being of society against both internal and external threats. *National security policy* is the laying down of norms, guidelines and the framework within which the nation-state will endeavour to safeguard its national interests. *National strategy*, on the other and, is the process of harmonising ends with means. In other words, strategy would include the 'how' of national security policy. National strategy can be defined asthe art and science of developing and using the political, economic, military and ideational power of the state to secure its national objectives. National strategy directs the national effort in the attainment of national goals and from it flow political, economic and military strategies, each distinct and deliberate, yet fully synergised. Perhaps, for good reasons and despite the recommendations of the Kargil Review Committee, India has not found the need for a declaratory security policy or 'red lines'.

In its absence, it is through the statements in and outside the Parliament and pronouncementsof national leaders, that an ordinary citizen can get some idea of the general direction of the nation's progress, principles and decisions regarding the use or threat of use of force, defence budgets and the size and state of the armed forces. For instance, according to statements made by the former Prime Minister Dr. Manmohan Singh: "India is interested in maintaining a peaceful periphery; her strategic frontiers extending from the Horn of Africa in the West to the Straits of Malacca in the East give an indication of India's intent". India's accommodative stance was indicated by him when he also said that, "there is enough space in Asia for both China and India to grow." In the wake of border incursions in 2010 he said, "China has, of late, become more assertive and...wants to maintain a low level of equilibrium with India." India has also on many occasions voiced concern about China's continued support and assistance to Pakistan in developing its nuclear, missile and defence capabilities. The former Prime Minister has said that the major if not the sole "aim of his life was to normalise relations with Pakistan" and also reiterated that the "destinies of the nations of South Asia are interlinked and the future should bring common prosperity." On internal security, Dr. Manmohan Singh said, "The threat of Left Wing Extremism or that posed by the Maoists/Naxals is the greatest threat to India's internal security."[22]

Shivshankar Menon as NSA, emphasised some aspects of national security. In a sweeping review of independent India's history, he said, "India has weight and influence but needs to develop her power; India's national aim is complete transformation; what is needed is 'jointedness'[23] not only between the three services but also with other organs and departments of the government." He believes that "India is as secure as can be." The establishment of the National Security Architecture, following the Kargil Review Committee (KRC) and the recommendations which included the establishment of the National Security Council Secretariat (NSCS), National Security Advisory Board (NSAB), Integrated Defence Staff (IDS), Defence Intelligence Agency (DIA), National Technical Research Organisation (NTRO), are some recent additions but according to Menon, "this is still work in progress".[24] The question then is what, if any, was the arrangement until the late 1990s.

In the field of self-reliance in defence, some noteworthy statements of the former Defence Minister A.K. Antony include, "We will provide the services with all their needs; it is shameful and dangerous that 70 per cent of India's defence needs are met through imports; we need to maintain absolute transparency in the processes of our defence procurement."[25] He acknowledged that, "there have been some incursions across the Line of Actual Control (LAC) but we have border management mechanisms that effectively take care of these problems which arise essentially because of differing perceptions of the two sides, (of the LAC); we are maintaining peace and tranquility along the borders with China."[26]

While somewhat bold and laudable, these statements do not give any indication about the reality on the ground. These also do not adequately explain India's national security policy and its long-term objectives, vis-à-vis resolution of the outstanding issues with China and Pakistan. India's security philosophy and perhaps even its national objectives are at best vague and undefined.

In the absence of a White Paper or an official document, a rough security narrative can be constructed based on these pronouncements, for further analysis and discussion.

Despite frequent cross-border terror strikes, there is no mention of the steps India is taking to address these threats. It is thus difficult to assess if India is indeed taking any major initiatives or proactive steps, to address the long-term implications of these threats and challenges. It is safe to assume that the government departments charged with defence and security, are in fact taking action to mitigate some or all of these threats, but it is somewhat difficult for an ordinary citizen to find solace in these assumptions, especially when there is little visible evidence of success. It is little wonder then that confusion abounds. Pakistan has steadfastly refused to cooperate with India in bringing the masterminds of the 26/11 Mumbai terror outrage to justice, in spite of the copious evidence that India has provided. As a result, seven years after the event that shook the country, there is little chance of closure. The lone terrorist caught alive, was hanged, while plans to enhance coastal security are caught up in grinding bureaucracy.

While there is nothing intrinsically wrong with being a peace-loving status quo power, inaction cannot be justified. Use of hard power may indeed be considered with extreme caution, but the employment of legal and diplomatic instruments alone, to address terror threats seems grossly inadequate. Such inaction on India's part appears to embolden the adversary to continue to cause pinpricks and launch bigger attacks, as in Kargil, when the Indian leadership was seen to be indecisive or preoccupied with peace overtures. Such inaction and absence of declared red lines or 'limits of Indian patience,' also give rise to widespread belief that India is indeed deterred by Pakistan's putative low nuclear threshold.

After 18 rounds of talks between the Special Representatives of China and India as of February 2015, there is no sign of the two countries coming any closer to the resolution of the vexed border dispute. China has regularly created new problems like issuing of 'stapled' visas to Indians belonging to J&K and Arunachal Pradesh, denial of visas to a high-ranking army officer deputed to visit China on a pre-planned and mutually agreed bilateral meeting, regular incursions across the borders and provocative actions to test Indian resolve. While some believe that such events are bound to happen when the country's borders are unsettled, an ordinary onlooker tends to see Indian inaction as Indian pusillanimity. While both India and China have repeatedly voiced the urgent need to remove mutual mistrust, there is little progress on the ground. This is despite the rapid increase in bilateral trade, that in 2013 reached $73 billion, but India continues to face a huge trade imbalance. Two inferences may be drawn: first, China is in no hurry to resolve the border dispute, as it suits that country to keep India on the back foot; second, India really has few options to address these challenges, due mainly to the huge power asymmetry in China's favour. India's defence and foreign policy options have thus been effectively constrained.

It is highly unrealistic to think that India will find quick and lasting solutions to the inherent internal problems of regional, religious, linguistic, caste/sectarian, urban-rural, political divides that plague Indian society. Ensuring high economic growth is also seemingly difficult. The world is simply moving and changing too fast, and that clearly means India no longer has the luxury of delayed decisions or inaction. In light of the above, the military is required to constantly maintain a very high state of alert, a condition that exacts a heavy price on its morale and efficiency, as training and modernisation suffer.

Several wars and 68 years after independence, there remain some very serious questions about India's security. Late K. Subrahmanyam lists defence policy, nuclear strategy and governance among the three most important strategic challenges facing India.[27] There are two ways in which we can assess India's overall performance in the national security domain. The first, could measure it as reasonably impressive. From a poor, backward country emerging from centuries of foreign rule and colonial oppression, India has made considerable progress in life expectancy – which has more than doubled (from a mere 27 years in 1947 to over 62 years now); indicators of infant mortality; adult literacy; provision of power and potable water to an increasingly large section of the population, that has quadrupled since independence; spreading health and education facilities; increases in industrial and agricultural output; a fast-expanding and confident service sector largely based on Communication and Information Technology (CIT); knowledge and innovative ideas; a steady economic growth of about five to seven per cent in the last two decades and; above all a thriving democracy, with regular and peaceful transfer of power to elected representatives by a process hailed as free and fair; a largely peaceful border, with a strong and modernising military that ranks fourth in the world; and an economy that is third largest in Purchasing Power Parity (PPP) terms today. Widespread famine, which regularly visited colonial India during the nearly 200 year long British rule, has been completely eliminated even during times of severe drought. Self-sufficiency in foodgrains to feed 1.2 billion people, in an exceedingly diverse society spread across a sub-continental sized country, is by any standard, no mean achievement, and hence deserves all praise.

The second, and somewhat more critical and less charitable way of looking at India's performance, gives a different picture. India, it seems, has consistently under performed in various areas. Even after allowing for some fundamental differences in their systems, India and China, as recently as in the 1970s, were categorised as third world countries with generally similar economic indicators, comparable growth rates and Gross Domestic Product (GDP) figures. Today, China's economy, at $7.3 trillion is four times that of India's, which is at $1.85 trillion.[28] China has rapidly modernised its military and possesses a wide variety and range of nuclear capable missiles. China today is the second largest economy in the world and has maintained a spectacular double-digit growth rate for over two decades, built impressive infrastructure across its vast geographical expanse, enjoys unprecedented influence across the globe and is now challenging the established world order, extending its economic, political and strategic reach to the far corners of the world. An emerging superpower, China claims that its rise will be peaceful and non-hegemonic, but its territorial claims in the waters of South China Sea and its 'string of pearls' strategy of establishing outposts at important points of Asian strategic real estate, are already raising concerns, not only amongst its small neighbours, but even in the US, which has had to review and revamp its Pacific security infrastructure, in the face of a rising and increasingly assertive China.

Comparisons, it is said, are odious. To be fair, two totally different systems and societies with different yet long civilisational histories cannot be easily compared.[29] India firmly believes that it follows a unique value system, which lays equal stress on ends and means, is more focused on attaining a just, equitable and peaceful world order (China says almost exactly the same things) and does not wish to enhance its national power with any hegemonic intentions. It has always strongly believed in Panchsheel, the five principles of peaceful coexistence and follows a 'live and let live' philosophy.

Soon after its independence in 1947, by adopting non-alignment, India maintained equal distance with the two blocs during the Cold War confrontation, did not and still does not approve of military alliances, strives for strategic autonomy and eschews the use of force, unless it becomes absolutely unavoidable to safeguard its sovereignty, territorial integrity and socialistic, secular and democratic way of life.[30] While it is one thing to fervently hope for a peaceful world, a country has to also safeguard its interests, build its CNP, while striving to achieve 'just and equitable' peace in a world that has remained largely anarchic. India, it seems, has tended to wish away its problems. Yet, as suggested by Major General Dipankar Banerjee, "Even while acknowledging Nehru's dynamic global influence we could not gloss over the reality of India's many infirmities."[31]

Viewed from this practical perch, the record of independent India's security practice can also be described as a story of lost opportunities, procrastination, a complete absence of initiative and, on occasion, extreme caution bordering on timidity. Grandiloquently founded on principles of righteousness and high-sounding values, India's preference for morality in stark contrast to the hyper-realist approach of its main adversaries, Pakistan and China, appears impractical and even utopian. Shashi Tharoor argues that, "Nehru immolated India's interests at the altar of his ideals: never once was there a mention of India's national interests, or an understanding of how they would be served by this messianic utopianism."[32] These two neighbours have never shied away from stating their ultimate political objectives. For China, the country's reunification is a sacred duty and a core objective. Although directed primarily at preventing Taiwan from taking the path of unilateral declaration of independence, it significantly also includes the safeguarding of Chinese sovereignty over Tibet, Xinjiang and its claims over the island chains of Paracels and Spratly in the South China Sea and Senkaku Islands in the Yellow Sea. China's take-over of Tibet in 1950 brought this military giant on India's doorstep, and its policy of allowing the Dalai Lama and his many supporters to live in India after he fled Tibet in 1959, have together further complicated the security situation in the Himalayas.

Pakistan, on the other hand, has repeatedly declared that Kashmir runs in its blood and that it cannot and will not rest until the Kashmir issue is resolved in its favour. In short, Pakistan wants the whole of Kashmir. With Pakistan occupying a large chunk of J&K, China leasing a significant part and also illegally occupying the Aksai Chin area of Ladakh, India holds just 30 per cent of the original area of the state under its control. India has not only been a status quo power, but has consistently failed to even articulate its claims to territories that continue to remain under illegal occupation of its two neighbours, giving an impression that it is not serious about these issues.

Due perhaps to India's vast geographical expanse, its long history of living under foreign rule and the fact that it has historically faced many major security threats, there is a general tendency to be somewhat complacent about national security. India, like an ageing Sumo wrestler cannot be dislodged easily, but it is agile enough to strike back only when the attacker comes in close proximity. Whatever India's claims, the fact is that it has often failed to prevent its neighbours, especially Pakistan, from incessantly and audaciously staging major invasions, terrorist strikes and other disruptions which include: hijacking aircraft; fomenting separatism; aiding and abating insurgencies in J&K and elsewhere; drugs and human trafficking; circulating counterfeit currency and; actively waging a proxy war for over two decades. Pakistan has also been the cause of flagrant military aggression in 1947, 1965 and again in 1999. China has played an equally negative role by supporting Pakistan, transferring nuclear and missile technology and making every attempt to strategically encircle India. It seems that by its tentative and timid approach and often plain inaction, India has left itself open to these regular and persistent attacks by its neighbours.

In India, the subject of national security regularly creates excitement in the print and electronic media; where informed citizens evince some short-lived interest in the subject. There is no dearth of highly qualified and acclaimed academics and defence experts and analysts in the country and hence national security comes under close scrutiny; but in the face of total silence from the government, and an excessively secretive bureaucracy which does not permit access to official records, there is very little meaningful discussion. Indian universities produce a large crop of IR theorists, but are often ignored by the powers that be simply because the political establishment shows no interest in engaging the public in a security discourse.

The nature of the debate that followed the five nuclear tests in 1998 is illustrative of the prevailing confusion. The Bharatiya Janata Party (BJP) proudly claimed that it had merely followed its declared political manifesto, while the Congress called the tests irresponsible and even reckless, at the same time claiming credit for keeping the nuclear option open and facilitating research and development of nuclear science and technology, throughout the long years when it was in power, from Nehru's time. It thus, becomes very difficult to attribute credit or blame to any particular party. The Congress, having ruled India for over 50 of the 68 years since India's independence, has to take both credit and discredit for the current state of the country's security.

Indians in general, do not take criticism easily and bristle when outsiders, especially Western commentators, criticise India's overly moralistic and self-righteous approach as being hypocritical. India's pathetic pleading to the US to supply a full squadron of modern jet fighters with American pilots, when faced with the Chinese threat in 1962, is often cited as an example of its unrealistic foreign policy. Indians are also loath to find fault with policies of past leaders, and do not readily acknowledge even a minor deviation from the hallowed principles on which India's foreign and security policy is supposedly based, even if it has in fact changed in some respects. Thus, recent attempts by India to form strategic partnerships with multiple states, are also stoutly defended under the same rubric of strategic autonomy and political independence, even when it is evident that in a globalised world, even the sole super power is not really free to do as it wishes.

It is axiomatic that a nation-state has to first clearly understand and carefully lay down what exactly constitutes its legitimate interests. In the case of India, these appear to be met if it is generally allowed reasonable freedom to follow its own chosen path, without too much interference from other powers. Although India has fought four major wars and two relatively limited conflicts (Sri Lanka and Kargil), its unshakeable faith in a live-and-let-live mindset underpins its utmost reluctance to resort to threat or use of force. Critics, however, cite the number of occasions when India, did in fact use force, as in Kashmir, Hyderabad, Goa, Nagaland, Mizoram and Sri Lanka and many times against Pakistan, even if it was to meet an aggression. India has invariably failed to anticipate or initiate conflict and has hurriedly reacted to an emergent threat only when left with no other option. In that sense, it is difficult to describe in precise terms India's legitimate national interests. Even though, today, repeated and regular infiltration attempts by Pakistan-based jihadis into J&K and numerous terrorist strikes claim many innocent lives, India refuses to respond with force.

India's military strategy also appears to be rather naïve. Right from 1947 and again in 1950 when another aggression by Pakistan into J&K became imminent, Prime Minister Nehru declared that any attack on Kashmir would be considered an attack on India and that India would be free to retaliate at a time and place of its choosing.[33] During the 1965 India-Pakistan war, this became Lal Bahadur Shastri's strategy, under which the Indian Army opened a second front in Punjab to relieve the Pakistan Army's pressure on Chhamb which, being in J&K, was a disputed area. In fact, this declaration is the only example of India declaring a 'red line' of sorts. It seems India tacitly and implicitly accepts the status of J&K as *disputed, even while claiming that the accession was legal.* This shows a mentality deeply set in territoriality. Statements such as India's determination to defend every square inch of Indian territory and launching an offensive across the International Border (IB) to grab a piece of Pakistani territory, to compel it to accept negotiations, amply prove such a mindset. Little wonder then that employment of air power to punish the enemy is outside this calculus. This habit has consistently robbed India of initiative and the ability to shape circumstances or choice of 'time and place' when battle was eventually joined. Kargil is the most recent example of India fighting a war on the enemy's terms.

The whole security discourse thus tends to become vague and confusing. During many interactions with citizens of all ages, the author found a sense of helplessness and even indifference when he asked about India's options. "What can we really do: start another war?" was the response. Not only the lay person, even the government and regrettably even the army, fail to accept that actions other than conventional war are possible, even desirable.

On other occasions India has sent its troops, ships and aircraft, on peace-keeping missions, in response to United Nations' (UN) calls. In fact, it has often taken the lead in undertaking UN Peace Keeping Missions in the face of great difficulties. But these engagements have given India little, besides military experience in fighting in distant lands, something that its armies regularly did in colonial times. In the 1950s-60s, the world looked up to India to help resolve conflicts. Use of force or the ability to quickly respond to emergencies has been a specialty of the Indian military. Yet, India has endured with great, and somewhat unnatural stoicism, the almost continuous and increasingly more brazen threats and attacks from Pakistan, and continues to show extreme reluctance to resort to use of force, until it becomes inescapable. In short, India never takes the initiative and is unwilling to chastise its recalcitrant neighbours.

This appropriately portrays the dilemma faced by Nehru. It was thus natural for Nehru to find a path that would help steer India away from the fast developing superpower confrontation, and allow it time to concentrate on nation building. Nehru, however, hedged bets by ensuring at least the support of other countries, notably Britain, while simultaneously extending moral support to countries that were fighting British, Dutch and French colonialism in Asia. His somewhat benign view of the emerging Communist China was also rooted in his strategy of befriending as many potential rivals and opponents as possible. China's invasion of Tibet, so soon after the establishment of the People's Republic, should have warned Nehru of the emerging threat on the Tibet-India border. Sardar Patel had also cautioned him about the Chinese threat on two occasions: first, well before the Communists came to power and second, when they marched into Tibet. Even if he did not show it, Nehru was also wary of China. He thought China would take 20-30 years to fight poverty and acquire the power to become the Asian hegemon and until that happened he was inclined to cultivate China as a friend.[34] Although the following quote refers to a later period, it is still relevant in that it gives an idea of how Nehru's views of China changed with time.

In his memoir the noted journalist and editor, the late B.G. Verghese wrote:

> [T]hough outwardly nothing had changed, Nehru had begun to reassess his position. According to his son Ashok Parthasarathi, his father, the late G. Parthasarathi met Nehru on the evening of March 18, 1958, after all concerned had briefed him prior to his departure for Peking as the new Indian Ambassador to China. G.P. recorded what Nehru said in these terms:
>
> So G.P. what has the Foreign Office told you? Hindi-Chini *bhai-bhai?* Don't you believe it! I don't trust the Chinese one bit. They are a deceitful, opinionated, arrogant and hegemonistic lot. Eternal vigilance should be your watch word. You should send all your Telegrams only to me – not to the Foreign Office. Also, do not mention a word of this instruction of mine to Krishna (Menon). He, you and I all share a common world view and ideological approach. However, Krishna believes – erroneously – that no Communist country can have bad relations with any Non-Aligned country like ours.[35]

In a letter to Sardar Patel dated September 27, 1947, Nehru had also expressed his fears about Pakistan attempting to seize Kashmir by force, and the possibility that the Maharaja's forces would be unable to stop the invaders unless a popular resistance was organised. In a 'perceptive assessment,' Ambassador Chandrashekhar Dasgupta said, Nehru apprehended that Pakistan was making preparations to enter Kashmir in considerable numbers. "It is obvious to me from the many reports that I have received that the situation there (Kashmir) is a dangerous and deteriorating one." Pakistan, he thought, would do so, when winter snows cut off Kashmir from the rest of India. Nehru said, "The Jammu route can hardly be used during winter and air traffic is also suspended. I understand that the Pakistani strategy is to infiltrate into Kashmir now and to take some big action as soon as Kashmir is more or less isolated because of the coming winter." Nehru wanted to secure Sheikh Abdullah's release from prison so that he could build popular support of the Kashmiri people to fight the Pakistani infiltrators.[36]

Despite such premonitions, and intelligence reports, Nehru allowed himself and India to remain ill prepared to face the Pakistani invasion that finally came on October 22 (first in the Poonch area and later in the valley); a fortnight after he wrote the letter to Patel. Some of the major errors of judgment that Nehru made soon after independence were his excessive reliance on the Governor General and the three British chiefs of the armed forces (although on occasion he strongly disagreed with their advice as in the case of the defence of Poonch) who manipulated India's defence policy, and indeed the war fighting strategy, to meet British objectives. All of them enjoyed authority, at least, to render advice based on their vast war experience, but had no responsibility for the consequences, as none of them were involved in actual fighting. This meant that they could put impediments in the path of the Indian Army's offensive plans to throw out the enemy and recover the lost territories in Pakistan-occupied Kashmir (PoK). This not only resulted in India prematurely taking the Kashmir dispute to the UN, but in reality effectively froze the borders of the state, exactly according to British plans.

Nehru had on many occasions suspected British designs to freeze the fighting, when Pakistan was at an advantage and argued and fought with the British senior officers, but could not prevail against the so-called expert military advice. C. Dasgupta cites two studies that were done by the British Indian Chiefs of Staff Committee in Delhi, and by the British Chiefs in London in July 1946. Both reached the same conclusion: that the discovery of oil in the Middle East and the advent of air power had changed the strategic picture. India's vast continental size, its location at the head of the Indian Ocean and on the route to East Asia, its almost 'inexhaustible' manpower and its rapidly growing industrial capacity demanded a re-assessment of its geo-strategic value. This resulted in a notable shift from the naval to the air factor. Britain was thus hoping that India would remain an active member of the Commonwealth at least in the defence field, and allow Britain to use its airfields for any military eventuality. In the event India declined to play an active role, Britain's second option was to maintain a presence in Pakistan, a country the Chiefs believed could play a major role in the Muslim Middle East, and also provide bases to keep a watch on the Union of Soviet Socialist Republics (USSR), and ensure that it was denied air bases in India. The fulfillment of these British objectives would be 'improbable' if India demanded the withdrawal of all British personnel, including those in the service of the Indian Government.[37] The Congress's request that Lord Louis Mountbatten serve as independent India's first Governor General must have been music to his ears, as he wasted no time in recommending that in view of the inexperience of the Indian military officers, India also retain senior British Generals, Admirals and Air Marshals to head the three arms of the Indian Military. Although Mountbatten and the British officers did not perhaps know of Pakistan's plans to send raiders into the Kashmir valley, once that had happened, the British personages tried their utmost, and largely succeeded, in preventing India's borders from abutting the restive North-West Frontier Province (NWFP), Afghanistan, Xinjiang and controlling the Mangla dam on the Jhelum, that would be like the Damocles' sword over the safety of Pakistan, which would now depend on the West for its defence needs.

It is for this reason, and the needs of the larger British strategy, that the British officers obstructed every Indian military move: first, the airlifting of its troops to help the Maharaja; second, stopping the Indian military offensive the moment its troops reached Uri-Tithwal line; third, preventing the 'cordon sanitaire' from being formed for the defence of the Poonch sector; fourth, strongly protesting when a young Air Commodore Subroto Mukherjee, permitted IAF aircraft to chase Pakistani Dakota aircraft transporting supplies to Skardu and Gilgit; and finally, prevailing upon Nehru to take the case to the UN, when the Indian military was on the verge of making a breakthrough into the Western reaches of the state of J&K.

The British Chiefs, gave multiple excuses, India running out of troops being one of them. When the situation in Poonch became desperate, Nehru suggested that India plan attacks on the Pakistani bases in the Sialkot sector, which were supplying the enemy forces opposite Poonch. This suggestion was vetoed by the British Chiefs for fear of wider escalation. The British Governor General and the Chiefs ensured that the war between the two dominions was kept at as low a level as possible and quickly wrapped up, with Pakistan in a distinctly advantageous position.

The Indian Cabinet very often protested and General Robert Lockhart, the first Army Chief, was made to resign when he disobeyed the orders of the Indian leadership, but General Sir Francis Robert Roy Bucher who replaced him stayed on for nearly two years, only retiring as an Officer on Special Duty in 1949, and was largely successful in ensuring fruition of the larger British strategy. Dasgupta says:

> [T]he Permanent Under Secretary at the Foreign Office speculated: If India falls apart we may, I suppose, expect the Moslems to try and enlist British support by offering us all sorts of military and political facilities, to commit ourselves to what would be in effect the defence of one Indian State against another.

Britain was certainly keeping its options open. Later, on Mountbatten's suggestion, Britain even transferred a modern cruiser, the *HMS Achilles* which under its new name *INS Delhi,* joined the Indian Navy to ensure continued Indian dependence on the services of British naval officers.[38] India was thus led up the garden path but could do little to get out of the British clutches. Later Britain, especially Noel Baker, the Secretary of State for the Commonwealth also played a highly negative role in the long drawn out deliberations at the UN.[39]

India's Experience at the UN: Lessons

The first Indo-Pak War lasted over 14 months but ended inconclusively with a large portion of Indian territory remaining in enemy hands. In order to understand our collective mindset about national security, two issues related to this conflict need to be highlighted here.

After many unsuccessful diplomatic attempts to resolve the problem, India took the Kashmir issue to the UN on January 1, 1948. It was a strange situation.

Although fighting raged in many parts of the state of J&K, India and Pakistan were not technically at war. Some Indian army units returned to India post-Partition, well after the attacks on J&K commenced in October 1947. The British Commanders-in-Chief of India and Pakistan as well as the Supreme Commander, Field Marshal Sir Claude Auchinleck, who was appointed to this post and was made responsible to oversee the division of assets between India and Pakistan, remained in regular contact. Talks on division of assets, funds and equipment proceeded apace between the two governments, at different levels, and yet there was no pressure on Pakistan to vacate its aggression in Kashmir. Gandhiji's fast unto death had also ensured payment of Rs. 55 crore to Pakistan and relieved that country to some degree from undue financial hardship. According to K.P. Saksena:

> As early as on December 22, 1947, Nehru had written to Liaquat Ali Khan, the Prime Minister of Pakistan, the details of aid and support that was being given to the raiders by his government and had warned that it amounted to an act of aggression. Requesting the Government of Pakistan to desist from providing bases, training and supplies to the tribal raiders, Nehru warned that if Pakistan did not respond, India would be compelled to take such action, consistent with the provisions of the United Nations' Charter, as might be considered necessary to protect her interest and discharge her obligations to the Government and people of Kashmir.[40]

In reality, however, these actions remained limited to taking the issue to the UN Security Council (UNSC). India never really gave Pakistan any ultimatum nor any threat of full-scale war.

> Having failed to receive any positive response from Pakistan, the Government of India, on January 1, 1948, brought to the notice of the UNSC that due to the operations carried on against the Indian State of J&K by nationals and tribesmen of Pakistan, with the assistance and encouragement of the Government of Pakistan, a situation had arisen which might lead to international conflict. India reported the matter under Articles 34 and 35 of the Charter, so that measures might be taken to end the dangerous situation. The Security Council was requested to ask the Government of Pakistan to prevent all kinds of aid – official and non-official – being given to the invaders.[41]
>
> Pakistan in its reply to UNSC on January 15, 1948 denied that she was giving any aid to the tribal raiders. She stated that the persecuted Muslims in the State of J&K had risen in revolt and declared their independence. It was possible that they had been joined by a number of independent tribesmen from areas beyond NWFP; by persons from the contiguous areas of Pakistan who had close relationships with the Muslims in the State, and by Muslim refugees from East Punjab, who were nationals of the Indian Union.[42]

Pakistan further argued that the invaders were from 'Azad Kashmir' [part of Pakistan-occupied Kashmir] and it did not have control over them. Rather, it accused India of genocide and getting J&K State to accede to it under duress and threatening military action.[43]

On January 6, 1948, the President of the Security Council sent an urgent appeal to India and Pakistan to maintain the status quo in Kashmir. Eleven days later the Security Council reiterated this appeal in a resolution which called the principal parties "to refrain from making any statement or doing...or permitting any acts which might aggravate the situation."[44] In the four-month debate that followed in the Security Council, the issue got lost in the miasma of dialectic, charges and counter-charges. To make its case against India, Pakistan attempted to widen the scope of the issue under UN consideration. In order to achieve this and to divert the attention of the Security Council from the tribal invasion to the communal riots, Pakistan raised many issues of conflict between the two dominions arising from the partition of the subcontinent which, it claimed, required UN mediation. *Kashmir was portrayed merely as one of the numerous points of such conflict.*[45]

India on its part also added to the prevailing confusion by alternately changing its stance. In the first place, it is noteworthy that while India laid charges of *aggression*, it brought its complaint not under Article 39 (Chapter VII) but as a *dispute* under Articles 34 and 35 (Chapter VI) of the Charter. While the Indian representative argued before the Security Council that Kashmir was a part of India, citing the Instrument of Accession as the legal basis for its claim, at the same time, he also drew the attention of the Council to India's 'high-principled statesmanship' in proposing a plebiscite to decide the question of accession. (A direct result of Mountbatten urging Nehru and because plebiscite had also been considered earlier, in the case of Junagarh and Hyderabad).

Without apparently realising the legal implications involved in his statement, the Indian representative reiterated time and again, the principle of plebiscite as the ultimate determinant of the Kashmir issue. The representative stated:

> I would invite the attention of the Members of the Security Council to the high principled statesmanship, characteristic of the Government of India...In accepting accession, they (The Government of India) refused to take advantage of the immediate peril in which the State found itself and informed the Ruler that the accession should finally be settled by a plebiscite as soon as peace had been restored...Plebiscite being conducted, if necessary, under international auspices.

About the scope of the plebiscite the Indian representative stated:

> The question of future status of Kashmir vis-à-vis her neighbours and the world at large, and a further question namely, whether she should

> withdraw her accession to India, and either accede to Pakistan or remain independent, with a right to claim admission as a Member of the United Nations – all this we recognise to be the unfettered decision by the people of Kashmir, after normal life is restored.[46]

India *failed* to draw express attention to the legal character of the accession and to stress the fact that its reference to the will of the people, was a decision of its own government and not part of the acceptance of the ruler of Kashmir's accession offer. Again, while India argued that Pakistan had no *locus standi* vis-à-vis Kashmir, it also stressed the unfettered right of the Kashmiri people to join India or Pakistan or the UN as an independent nation. As will be seen later, India had begun the habit of scoring self-goals. Having made these blunders, India had no option but to finally stress on the point, that it had offered a plebiscite *only after normalcy had been restored and the territories of the State of J&K had been cleared of all invaders and since Pakistan continued to illegally possess parts of Kashmir, India was not obliged to hold a plebiscite* – a much weaker argument.

N. Gopalaswami Ayyangar, a noted lawyer and expert in international law, was then India's representative at the UN. It is indeed amazing that even he did not realise the legal implications of the use of Articles 34 and 35 instead of Article 39. India had itself diluted its case by inadvertently calling the Kashmir issue a *'dispute'* and not an *'armed aggression'*. One wonders if this was done with a purpose or was simply an oversight. Could Nehru, also well versed in law, have done this to take the case to the General Assembly where India could expect a more friendly response compared to that in the Security Council?

This was not all. India made yet another blunder that in effect gave Pakistan the *locus standi* that it did not have earlier. The Security Council never concentrated on the facts of the case, nor made a distinction between the complainant and the defendant. On January 17, 1948, after it had heard both sides, the Security Council, on the initiative of the British delegate, requested its president to hold discussions with the representatives of the two parties in an effort to find some common ground on which the structure of a settlement could be built. Three days later, the president (Belgium) presented a draft resolution providing for a three-member Commission – one member to be chosen by each party and the countries so chosen, selecting the third. The principle significance of this draft resolution lay in the scope of the Commission's activities. In addition to the Kashmir dispute, the commission was called upon to mediate on all other situations raised by the Pakistani representative (note that the initiative came from the British delegate).

Apart from the substance of the resolution, giving the Commission the right to look into Pakistan's complaints, on this occasion, Pakistan scored another victory of considerable significance. The draft resolution presented by the Council President had the title 'Belgian Draft Resolution on the Jammu-Kashmir

Question'. Pakistan's representative Sir Zafarulla Khan suggested that the wording 'Jammu & Kashmir Question' be deleted. When India's Gopalaswami Ayyangar was called upon to express his views, he unsuspectingly, or rather naively, agreed to the deletion. Two days later when the Security Council met again, the agenda, in place of 'Jammu & Kashmir Question' read 'India-Pakistan Question'. It was learnt that the Council President had made the *change at the request of Pakistan.* The Indian representative *objected* to the change of the wording and was supported by the United Kingdom and the USSR but failed to press home the point strongly enough, and the Council was prevailed upon to allow the change. This is how Pakistan managed to become a party to the dispute whereas until then it was only an 'aggressor'. This sorry episode clearly shows the utter ineptitude and thoughtlessness on the part of the Indian representative and more so of the decision makers in New Delhi.[47]

Two other disputes arose at about the same time: Junagarh and Hyderabad. In the first case, Nehru and to some extent Patel too showed reluctance to use force. Patel, however, was in favour of moving troops as a precautionary measure. Here again, the Governor General and the British Chiefs played a negative role. Finally, the Junagarh problem was resolved only when the Nawab of Junagarh fled to Pakistan, and his Dewan, Sir Shah Nawaz Bhutto was unable to run the administration of the small state, in the face of a popular protest by the people. Hyderabad, however, proved a tough nut to crack, with the Nizam trying to buy a piece of land along the Western coast (in Travancore State), to transform his state into an independent and viable country. Congress' K.L. Munshi, who was sent to Hyderabad, feared widespread bloodshed and communal riots. "The Razakars and the Communists were colluding; the Razakars ruled by day while the Communists ruled by night." Delhi reluctantly began contingency planning for possible police action. Once again, Lord Mountbatten and General Bucher, the then Chief of Army Staff, opposed any such move, since in their opinion all the troops were already committed to other equally pressing tasks in riot-hit Punjab. Rajmohan Gandhi's seminal work *Patel: A Life* notes that Patel replied to these objections thus:

> It is not, in the final analysis, the action of an army which maintains law and order-look at the Punjab last August when 55,000 men could not stop the massacres. It is rather the prestige of the Government backed by potential armed action which keeps the people in order. At the moment this prestige is sufficiently high to take action against Hyderabad and maintain order elsewhere at the same time. But if the Government delays action against Hyderabad much longer, then its prestige will fall so greatly that no amount of troops will be sufficient for internal security.

When Patel broached the subject of firm action against the Nizam, Nehru's reply was recorded by Mountbatten:

> Pandit Nehru said openly at the meeting, and subsequently assured me privately that he would not allow any orders to be given for operations to start unless there really was an event, such as a whole scale (sic) massacre of Hindus within the State, which would patently justify, in the eyes of the world, action by the Government of India.

Such response is again indicative of Nehru's and later India's extreme reluctance to resort to use of force for the fear of international reaction.[48] He was obviously concerned about India's reputation in the eyes of the world. In the event, it was only after the departure of Mountbatten, that final preparations to move the army began in earnest, and the so-called 'police action' commenced on September 13, 1948, a full 13 months after independence.

Nehru had at different times accepted the necessity to use force, but in a real-life situation, India was always caught on the back foot. Initially Nehru dithered and later ended up overreacting. Even when recourse to force was reluctantly made, it was withdrawn well before the problem was fully resolved and the consequences are there for all to see even today, especially in J&K.

First, despite a premeditated, blatant and army-supported aggression against J&K in which Pakistan finally fielded three regular brigades, India showed utmost reluctance to continue army operations with the same zest after the raiders had been cleared from the Srinagar Valley, unnecessarily giving rise to speculation that India (Nehru) was never really interested in recovering the Gilgit and Baltistan areas of the State of J&K. Nehru took the issue to the UN on Mountbatten's advice but failed to correctly gauge Pakistan's real intentions not just in Kashmir, but towards India. Mahatma Gandhi was proved right, for he had prophesied that Partition will give rise to two neighbours in perpetual enmity. On the other hand, Jinnah having complained that he had got only a truncated and moth-eaten Pakistan, never forgave India.

Soon Pakistan was again busy plotting against India. During the early 1950s, a serious problem of a mass exodus of Hindus from East Pakistan raised tensions. When India asked Pakistan to take urgent measures as Nehru rightly feared a backlash against Muslims in India, Liaquat Ali Khan flatly denied that his government was responsible, and said such reports were highly exaggerated. Nehru visited Calcutta (now Kolkata) and saw for himself the plight of the fleeing Hindus, and was finally forced to alert the army in the event matters went out of control. It was only after long and tedious rounds of parleys between the two Prime Ministers that the Nehru-Liaquat Pact on the treatment of minorities in the two countries was signed, but that also did not really solve the refugee problem.

No sooner was this matter settled, than Pakistan again raised the bogey of an Indian threat by resorting to rabid propaganda, this time apparently to frustrate India's efforts towards the formation of a separate Constituent Assembly for the State of J&K. It is beyond the scope of this study to go into the details of this episode, except to highlight the need that arose to again alert the Indian army. This time too, Nehru succeeded in avoiding an armed conflict, but was extremely reluctant to move an armoured brigade to the border in Punjab. It was only when senior army officers told him that if the only bridge across the River Beas were to be destroyed by the enemy, Indian armour would be caught on the wrong side and would not be able to move to the border, that Nehru reluctantly agreed; but again cautioned that the troops be kept at a respectable distance from the border to avoid unnecessary provocation. Nehru said he was determined to avoid an 'all-out war' with Pakistan. It is difficult to understand what exactly he meant by the term. India, after all, had only recently fought a 14-month-long war with Pakistan in J&K. Did he fear a war across the border in Punjab and elsewhere? Avoiding undue provocation is understandable, but this caution was based not on military but on moral considerations.

The Sino-Indian Border Conflict

One of the most difficult periods when India's national security policy was put to severe test was in 1962, when hostilities erupted on the disputed India-China border. There were many indications of the likely strong Chinese reaction, but Nehru on the advice of his two very close confidants and advisers – V.K. Krishna Menon, the then Defence Minister, and B.N. Mullick, chief of the Intelligence Bureau – convinced himself, against his own better judgement, that the Chinese would never attack. The ill-equipped, unprepared and poorly supported army posts on the border proved to be no match for the sudden and full-blooded Chinese attack in the North East Frontier Agency (NEFA), but Indian troops in equally difficult conditions of Aksai Chin fought with grim determination, before finally succumbing to superior Chinese military power.

The long confrontation was marked by: a fear of Chinese superiority; inability to decipher Chinese designs; obdurate insistence on India's version of the legality of the border; above all, a monumental neglect of the army's advice and; a lackadaisical approach to the development of infrastructure in the border areas. As a result, the army was unprepared to face the Chinese on the border. India's forward policy of establishing border posts in penny packets to simply show the flag, without concern for mutual support (between the adjacent posts) and logistics backup, proved disastrous. Nehru was also beguiled by his own conviction that in the event of China attacking India, the conflict would inevitably escalate to a 'world' war.

Although there has been much criticism of the army in recent years, not consulting the army was a major failure. Lieutenant General Thorat's plan for the defence of NEFA was never given due consideration, but dismissed out of hand by Krishna Menon. Later the army's plans of fighting the main battle in depth, at Sela, were not accepted, because it was thought that the Chinese troops might enter NEFA and stay put after advancing half-way to the foothills; the dispute after all was about where the actual 'border' lay. While there is some substance in this apprehension, Nehru and his advisors failed to realise that the Chinese army could not indefinitely stay in the mountains, when faced with the constant threat of harassment by the Indian air and ground forces. This aversion to allow the Indian Army to set up defences in depth, was probably rooted in the grand but mistaken or unrealistic belief of the political leadership that it had to defend every square inch of the sacred motherland.

The public declaration to throw the Chinese out of Thagla Ridge probably proved to be the last straw. This area – where the Chinese strongly believed that the Indian posts were sited north of the McMahon Line and hence in Chinese territory – also enjoyed the advantage of height and short lines of supply for the Chinese. The Indian Air Force (IAF) was also not in the loop, even though its Canberra strategic reconnaissance aircraft had carried out a few recce missions and had given much information of Chinese strength and disposition. Once rebuffed, the Indian Army/IAF leadership did not show much keenness to question the thinking of the civilian leaders, due perhaps to the prevailing tension between the military and civilian leadership. P.V.R. Rao, an experienced Defence Secretary, provides a clue to this state of affairs.

> The statements made by the Government on 1962 operations and the sequence of events as unfolded in the *Untold Story* by Lt. Gen. Kaul, a principal participant in those events, suggest that the Chiefs of Staff Committee was rarely in the picture, that the Joint Intelligence Committee and the Joint Planning Committee were either moribund or ineffective and decisions were taken by the Prime Minister with the advice of the Chief of Army Staff (Gen. Thapar); the other two Chiefs seem to have been called in only when it was felt their forces may be involved.[49]

The IAF was not called upon to provide any offensive air support putatively on the advice of B.C. Roy, the then Chief Minister of West Bengal[50] and J.K. Galbraith, the US Ambassador at New Delhi. Since there have been many references to the latter's advice, it would be instructive to briefly summarise the overall import of Galbraith's views on the conflict, to which he devotes nearly three chapters in his diary, the *Ambassador's Journal.*[51]

Galbraith in the above-mentioned book, readily admits to his dislike of Krishna Menon, as he believed that Menon was largely instrumental in single-handedly antagonising the US. Galbraith "was afraid that were we too forthcoming in giving the Indians military aid, he (Menon) would take credit for it." Although an academic and a professor of economics, Galbraith appeared to show a markedly intelligent appreciation of the situation. He says, "In Ladakh, the Indian defenders fought stubbornly but their performance was blanketed by the disastrous collapse in NEFA." Although he was then not entirely sure, in the beginning (on October

23, 1962) he thought that, "this is not more than a border conflict but it seems evident that the Chinese intend to take possession of territory that is anciently their claim and establish themselves before the winter sets in. Then they will negotiate from this position of strength. They are far superior to the Indians in arms, manpower and *possibly also in determination*" (emphasis added).

Galbraith adds, "The Indian Army is without equipment, it is being said, partly because resources have gone into his (Menon's) highly advertised supersonic and transport planes (MiG-21 and An-12) and other gadgets, none of which are available to the soldiers on the frontier." In hindsight an unfair assessment but given the realities of the time, Galbraith can be forgiven for these jibes as he was after all speaking in America's interest.

On the Chinese offer to stop fighting, have a summit between Nehru and Chou En-lai, pull the troops back 20 km from their present position and India's rejection of the offer, he thinks it was "rather cynical of the Chinese to take territory and then negotiate over it." He believes that except the British, "everybody has been ambiguous in their support of the Indians." According to him, "the Canadian High Commissioner thinks that the Chinese can defend their claim to the Aksai Chin Plateau in Ladakh; they occupied it for two years before the Indians seem to have discovered they were there. The Indians might let them have undisturbed possession (of Aksai Chin) in return for the McMahon Line in NEFA" and then in a foot note adds, "This is, in effect, what has happened."

He was also wary "of Pakistan making pro-China noises and the fact that no fewer than three Indian divisions are being kept along this border."

President S. Radhakrishnan tells him that proclaiming a state of emergency is to check rumour-mongering but the actual purpose is to restrain the Communists from peddling 'the Pravda line' to the effect that India and China should agree on Chinese terms.

Radhakrishnan, was also unhappy at the (American) attempts to placate Ayub Khan by "leaning on the Indians when they are under Chinese pressure." (In the end, the Americans got Nehru to open a dialogue with Pakistan on Kashmir.)

Galbraith frankly tells H.M. Patel to tell Nehru that the letter requesting for aid should "come from him as he is loved in the United States as no one else in India. The American people would respond to a request from him as they would not to anyone else." This should partly explain why Nehru had to personally write a letter to President Kennedy. The Indian Communists apparently were carping "[t]hat the US would use the Chinese to attack nonalignment, hitch India to a military alliance and prolong the war."

He also speaks of a possible "Chinese threat from the Chumbi Valley," the obvious implication being that the eastern parts of India beyond North Bengal might be cut off. The Chinese presented a new offer on November 8 to move back 20 km from each side of the McMahon Line, leaving the situation as it is in Ladakh. To Galbraith's mind, this was another indication of the Chinese wanting a swap, but the offer was obviously put forward at such a time that there was little chance of India accepting it.

Galbraith's diary entries of November 20 and 21 are perhaps the most germane to this discussion. This was when the Chinese had reportedly taken over most of NEFA and had on the previous day (November 20) taken Walong in the East and were shelling the airfield at Chushul in Ladakh. Galbraith while referring to the expectations on the Indian side said, "They, (the Indians) want our Air Force to back them up so that they can employ theirs tactically without leaving their cities unprotected. I am not sure that there is any very useful conception at the back of this (*sic*). I would think it would be unwise for them to initiate any air action." "Yesterday (November 20) was the day of ultimate panic in Delhi, the first time I have ever witnessed the disintegration of public morale and for the first time I began to wonder what the powers of resistance might be."[52]

He also tells his staff to arrange a Wing of 12 C-130 Hercules that was needed and wanted these to begin arriving immediately. It is after these developments that he speaks of air power employment. In this context Galbraith says:

> Meanwhile, on the other side, *I affirmed my intention to keep the Indians from using their Air Force with the associated expectation of our support.* Their air arm is not highly effective. The cities of the Gangetic Plain are accessible from the airfields of (*sic*) Tibet. *There is no chance that the Indians could retaliate to China and there is nothing in Tibet.* And there is no technical chance that we could accord them immediately the protection that Nehru asked. The Indian purpose in putting the Air Force was the hope that this would stem the Chinese advance. But the Chinese walk through the woods at night. We learned in Korea that even with complete control of the air we could not keep them from supplying their forces or advancing. These considerations were new to the Indians.

It is in light of this paragraph and especially the italicised text that we need to see Galbraith's advice.

Thus, it can be surmised that, firstly, the US military and more particularly air force assistance was contingent on India not using its own air force. Secondly, Galbraith is right in thinking that the Americans could not have provided any air support immediately. Thirdly, his contention that cities in the north could be reached from airfields in Tibet was correct, but he obviously did not know that the Chinese did not actually have any suitable aircraft in Tibet. Fourthly, he is right about there being no worthwhile targets in Tibet, but not about the IAF's ineffectiveness. It is not known how he formed this opinion, but given that India was desperate to get substantial US air force support, India had to honour its part of the deal by not employing air power. In any case, India should have planned the use of air power well in advancc, and not when the very airfield, at Tezpur, from where it could have been launched was under the threat of imminent enemy occupation. He also had talks with Y.B. Chavan, the new Defence Minister, who he says was in "agreement that Indians keep quiet, win time and be suspicious of the possibilities of air power. However, he (Chavan) was surprised that it would take six months to move in American interceptors and two years to create a modern Indian Air Force." This, also in this author's opinion clearly shows the level of ignorance of the Indian political leadership of military affairs.[53]

Much has already been written about this sad chapter of India's history but it must be reaffirmed that the major, if not the only reason, for so grossly risking and endangering India's security was the unfortunate coming together of important, strong-willed political leadership, Nehru and Menon and an ambitious senior military officer Lieutenant General B.M. Kaul, who completely overshadowed the Army Chief and the Chiefs of the other two Services. Kaul with Menon's help short-circuited the time-tested processes of defence decision-making in the Chiefs of Staff Committee. The mistrust so created has unfortunately not completely evaporated even after five decades and has perhaps got further intensified.

Of all the military actions, the dogged determination to fight the Chinese at Namka Chu (Thagla) was perhaps the biggest miscalculation. Although Nehru wanted the army to evict the Chinese from the Thagla Ridge, he wanted the army to do so only when ready. But since none of the senior army officers except Kaul had actually witnessed the first skirmish on Namka Chu at Tsenjong onOctober 10, it was he who had belatedly advocatcd restraint and withdrawal from Namka Chu which both the Chief of Army Staff (COAS) Thapar and General Officer Commanding-in-Chief (GOC-in-C) Eastern Command, Sen did not approve.[54]

The reluctance of the successive governments to declassify the Henderson-Brooks Inquiry Report is understandable but has unnecessarily aggravated the mutual suspicions between the civil and the military. R.D. Pradhan in his book *Debacle to Revival* clearly states the motives behind the whole exercise (the inquiry). Chavan's appointment of two senior army officers, Lieutenant General Henderson Brooks and Brigadier P.S. Bhagat to conduct an 'in-house' inquiry on the orders of the then Army Chief General J.N. Chaudhuri, was intended to avoid the report being submitted to the Indian Parliament, as it was not a Commission of Inquiry. Chavan also told Parliament, "The enquiry was to carry out a military appraisal of the debacle and was aimed at drawing lessons for the future. Thre would be no witch-hunt. The terms of reference were to find out what was wrong with: our training, our equipment, our system of command, the physical fitness of our troops, and the capacity of our Commanders at all levels to influence the men under them. It was also aimed at learning lessons and not to apportion blame, since the major actors, V.K. Krishna Menon, General P.N. Thapar and Lieutenant General B.M. Kaul had by then left the scene." According to Pradhan, Chavan "was also conscious that his first priority was to put the Indian army back in shape in the shortest time possible and raise its morale. It was not certain when and where the Chinese would resume hostilities. He was also determined to defend the Prime Minister, which he had succeeded in doing. After that debate the NEFA debacle ceased to be a political issue."

Chavan initially did not share the terms of reference with Parliament and despite widespread anger of the parliamentarians, only gave a very cursory overview of the findings of the Inquiry in the Lok Sabha. Pradhan adds, "Contrary to general expectations, te report did not directly indict any political leaders. It was done obliquely." On the lack of proper 'Higher Direction of War', the committee quoted Field Marshal Robert's dictum, "*The art of war teaches us not to rely on the likelihood of the enemy not coming, but on our own readiness to receive him; not on the chance of not attacking but rather on the fact that we have made our position unassailable.*" "There was also a suggestion that political directions were not based on the military means at the military's disposal".[55] For the purpose of this study, however, the most significant thing to note is the unfortunate disconnect between the civilian and military leadership and their failure to even consider the use of IAF combat aircraft already based in the Eastern theatre at Tezpur and Jorhat. The year 1962, it is said, was a turning point in India's military history but the enthusiasm and excitement that it generated to strengthen national security, proved to be short lived. While the government made immediate eforts to increase the strength of the army and the air force it took a long time to procure the necessary aircraft, weapons and equipment. In an effort to improve civil-military relations, Chavan started meeting the three Chiefs and the Defence Secretary every morning and also had records of these meetings maintained; the practice however, soon fell into disuse, or so it seems from the events of 1965. No effort was made to institutionalise and formalise the working of higher defence direction.

Another notable event in the immediate aftermath of 1962 was the signing of the border agreement by Pakistan with China in March 1963 under which, it leased some 5,000 sq km of land in PoK to China. Although the treaty has a clause that the final settlement would be subject to the resolution of the Kashmir dispute between India and Pakistan, for all practical purposes China was gifted another sizeable piece of Indian territory, with India merely sending a protest note to both parties.[56]

China became a nuclear power on October 16, 1964 when it tested the first atomic bomb; in 1966 its tested the thermonuclear bomb and the necessary delivery means. Eventually India lived with this nuclear threat for three and a half decades.

Indo-Pak War, 1965

Soon after the trauma of 1962, India began a major programme to enhance its military capability. The IAF received more An-12 transports and Mi-4 helicopters but it was not before early 1965 that the first batch of 12 MiG-21 supersonic fighters arrived in India, the licence manufacture of which was to commence at Hindustan Aeronautics Limited (HAL) only in 1967. The government announced short and emergency commissions in the army, and the air force began recruiting young candidates to increase the strength of its pilots by a record 1,000. Before India could really complete its military upgrade, Pakistan launched a probing attack in the Rann of Kutch, in March 1965. By early April, two Pakistan Army battalions attacked Sardar Post near Kanjarkot with US-made Patton tanks and heavy artillery. A ceasefire was declared on April 29 with British mediation, but the crisis was resolved only when an agreement was signed on June 30, 1965.

It has been argued that the Indian Army Chief General J.N. Chaudhuri had told the government that the terrain in Kutch did not permit widespread employment of armour, and hence, he favoured a negotiated settlement to this relatively minor skirmish. The IAF had some Vampires based at Jamnagar and used them for photo reconnaissance to confirm the presence of Pakistani tanks in Kanjarkot. This evidence was later used to tell the world that Pakistan was once again the aggressor. The IAF did not have a base in close proximity to the area of operations and did not commit its combat elements. Strangely, there were also rumours of the Pakistan Air Force (PAF) and IAF Air Chiefs having come to some understanding to not use their air forces. These rumours were stoutly denied but the impression, however false – that the IAF was a reluctant onlooker – remained.[57]

Even before the dust had settled on the Kutch skirmish, Pakistan began violating the Ceasefire Line (CFL) in the Kargil sector of J&K and threatened traffic on the Srinagar-Leh road. The Indian Army took these posts on the CFL back after hard fighting, but these were returned when another ceasefire came into effect in less than a month. As expected, Pakistani troops once again began shelling the road from their positions high in the mountains. The Indian Army again took back these posts and also the strategically important Haji Pir Pass in the Pir Panjal mountains west of the Kashmir Valley. But by early August, Pakistan sent in a large number of armed infiltrators into the Valley, with the hope that a general uprising by the Kashmiri people would follow. This attempt also met the same fate as the one in October 1947, and did not succeed.

Pakistan now launched a major thrust across the CFL in the Jammu sector and also began shelling Tithwal, Uri and Poonch areas. With a view to cutting off the lines of communication between Kashmir and the rest of India, Pakistan, on September 1, 1965, attacked Chhamb. By late afternoon, the situation became precarious and the army asked for air support. Details of this conflict are discussed elsewhere, but what is germane here is India's readiness to repeatedly accept hastily brokered ceasefires, and return hard-fought border posts. More astonishingly, India was once again surprised and caught totally unprepared when Pakistan launched this major attack in Chhamb. India, it seems, had failed to learn any lessons from its bitter experience at the hands of the Chinese.

To relieve enemy pressure on Chhamb, India responded with its oft-proclaimed strategy of attacking Pakistan across the International Border in Punjab, but once again failed to make much headway. The 22-day-long war saw fierce fighting along the length of the border; some epic tank battles were fought and won, but the war ended in a stalemate, with both India and Pakistan claiming victory. The Tashkent Agreement was signed in January 1966, and India *once again* agreed to return Haji Pir and other posts that were captured in J&K. This war also brought no peace. Pakistan went on to befriend China, received much military assistance from that country and was once again breathing fire against India.

This brief account of the 22-day war again brings out the persistent disconnect between the army and the air force. The political leaders also did not seem to be mentally prepared for a war, even though Pakistan had shown its hand in Kutch in April and launched its favourite invading force of mujahideen into J&K in August; no offensive action was planned.

The Bangladesh War, 1971

This was undoubtedly a glorious chapter in India's recent history. It saw a resolute Indian Prime Minister in Mrs. Indira Gandhi, deftly using diplomacy to create world opinion in favour of India's position that Pakistan must immediately create conditions in East Pakistan for the 10 million refugees (mostly Hindu) who had fled to India from Pakistani repression, to return to that country. The signing of the Friendship Treaty with the former Soviet Union in August 1971 was a high point of India's diplomatic offensive. Mrs. Gandhi gave the Indian armed forces adequate time to prepare for a military solution in case it became necessary and more importantly, maintained regular consultations with the military without interfering in their plans.

It is believed that India did not initially think that Dhaka would fall so easily, but once the IAF had bombed the government house, it was only a matter of time before General Niazi's forces surrendered. Even so, it was Lieutenant General J.F.R. Jacob who persuaded Niazi to agree to a public surrender, telling him that India had already para-dropped some 5,000 troops, and the latter had little choice but to comply. The Indian Government also ensured that Indian troops left Bangladesh at the earliest and did not place any demands on the newly independent country. Mrs. Gandhi, was however, not quite successful in the negotiations India held at Shimla with Prime Minister Z.A. Bhutto. India tamely gave away 93,000

Prisoners of War (POWs) and managed to get only a verbal assurance from Bhutto, that he would make every effort to resolve the Kashmir issue bilaterally. From all accounts, Bhutto had promised to convert the CFL into a permanent border, which did not happen. It is noteworthy that India was also ready to accept a virtual partition of the state of J&K. No sooner than he reached home, Bhutto changed his tune and spoke of a 1,000-year war with India, and soon also began Pakistan's clandestine nuclear programme. India's reputation had risen substantively but it had gained little in concrete terms. Worse, India did not use the moment to put further pressure on Pakistan.[58]

In May 1974, India carried out a nuclear test and dubbed it a Peaceful Nuclear Explosion (PNE). While the major powers were quick to slap sanctions, India did not make any vigorous attempts to actually develop a missile delivery system or weaponise the nuclear device, but went on a decade-long futile campaign for global nuclear disarmament. It was only in 1983, nine years after the PNE, that India launched its Integrated Guided Missile Development Programme (IGMDP) and it took another six years to test the Agni missile in May 1989; showing lack of clarity on a critically vital issue of national security, perhaps due to the absence of a long-term strategy. A carefully formulated national security strategy and a determined effort to quickly weaponise the nuclear deterrent, would have saved India many anxious moments in the future. As happened, India had to finally choose the nuclear option in 1998, but by then it had already been subjected to nuclear blackmail in 1987 and 1990.

That the 1974 PNE was more to shore up Mrs. Gandhi's political position, than to give India a robust nuclear deterrent, is common knowledge. As in most other cases related to India's security, there was no follow up, but the test invited the wrath of the nuclear powers and sanctions followed. The most telling of these were related to technology denials, and as a result many of the Indian Space Research Organisation (ISRO), Defence Research and Development Organisation (DRDO) and other scientific programmes suffered.

This was also followed by a long period of political uncertainty and economic difficulties. When faced with a disqualification following irregularities in the Parliamentary election, Mrs. Gandhi declared a state of internal emergency in June 1975 that lasted for over 15 months. In the following elections, the ruling Congress (I) lost and a hastily cobbled combination of different opposition parties formed the Janata Party Government, which took over the reins, with Morarji Desai, a strong anti-nuclear leader, becoming the Prime Minister. India's nuclear weapons programme went into hibernation. The then Foreign Minister A.B. Vajpayee attempted to normalise relations with China by visiting that country in February 1979, but during the visit China invaded India's friend Vietnam (on February 17, 1979), and to add insult to injury, Deng Xiaoping declared that China invaded Vietnam to teach them a lesson as it had done to India in 1962.

China had been providing military aid to Pakistan from 1968, and after India's PNE in 1974, this assistance was expanded to the nuclear field.

The year 1979 was perhaps the most difficult for India. The Soviets invaded Afghanistan and brought the superpower rivalry to South Asia, the Shah of Iran was overthrown in an Islamic revolution, the Indian economy faltered under the weight of the second oil shock and Sikh militancy began to acquire serious proportions in Punjab. Pakistan was once again gifted another opportunity to bleed India. With the US deciding to fight the Soviet Army with Afghan mujahideen, Pakistan was given the role to train and arm these fighters, making it a frontline state with US financial and other assistance, mainly military/arms. Pakistan received some three dozen F-16 fighters in the early 1980s, as an effective counter to the IAF Jaguar, the Deep Penetration Strike Aircraft (DPSA). As usual, India had little room for manoeuvre.

Operation Blue Star, 1984

Following the spiralling of violence in Punjab and the occupation of the Akal Takht of the Golden Temple at Amritsar by Sikh extremists led by Sant Jarnail Singh Bhindranwale, the central government decided to send the army to flush them out. The assault was led by Major General K.S. Brar, himself a Sikh, with Lieutenant General K. Sundarji as the GOC-in-C of the Army's Western Command. On June 3, 1984 the army first laid siege to the Golden Temple and asked the terrorists to surrender, or at least, allow the innocent pilgrims to leave the temple premises. The terrorists did not show any inclination to surrender, and in fact, planned to use the presence of the pilgrims to foil any attack by the army. The army moved in on the night of June 4-5, but grossly underestimated the firepower of the militants. In the circumstances, the army was forced to use tanks and artillery, which resulted in extensive damage to the Akal Takht, the sanctum sanctorum. This further inflamed Sikh passions and some troops in the Sikh units mutinied. This was quickly brought under control, but to avenge the desecration of the Golden Temple, Sikh bodyguards of the Prime Minister Mrs. Indira Gandhi assassinated her on October 31, 1984. In retaliation, some 3,000 innocent Sikhs were killed in Delhi and some other places. This further worsened the security of the country as a whole and Sikh militancy showed no signs of abating. Sikh militancy was finally brought under control only in the early 1990s.

Exercise Brasstacks, 1986-87

Probably to show its military might, India staged a massive army-air exercise in the deserts of Rajasthan and mobilised a very large number of troops and armoured regiments, that raised Pakistan's fear of an imminent and massive Indian thrust to cut the country into two. Pakistan in turn, mobilised its troops, armour and aircraft and foiled India's plans for an offensive, if indeed there were any.

Pakistani scientist Dr. A.Q. Khan told a respected Indian journalist Kuldip Nayar, that Pakistan was only a screw's turn away from a nuclear device. Tensions rose with this sabre rattling, but were gradually defused.[59] In the book *Brasstacks and Beyond*, the authors paint a very grim picture of India and Pakistan on the brink of a conventional war during the fourth and final phase of the exercise in which actual mobilisation of troops took place. Exercise Brasstacks however, did not generate half as much excitement in the IAF as this account suggests. While there was some movement of fighter squadrons, no one really feared actual hostilities. The Indo-Pak face-off did not seem as charged as the one following ceasefire violations in 2013. The author was then in active service and most saw the Sikh militancy as a far bigger problem compared to the Pakistani threat. The crisis certainly highlighted India's vulnerability in the nuclear arena and spurred it to move forward to quickly begin the process to acquire a deliverable weapon. Calculated and well-timed leaks about the possession of a nuclear weapon by Pakistan worked to heighten Indian anxieties and deterred its leaders as India probably did not have a reliable counter to Pakistan's veiled threats. In December 1988, India and Pakistan signed an agreement of Non Attack on Each Other's Nuclear Installations and in what is termed as an important nuclear confidence-building measure (CBM) both sides have been exchanging relevant data every January since 1989. In spite of this CBM, there was another nuclear scare in 1990 when the US alleged that following Pakistan's heightened interference in the Indian State of J&K, which saw increased violence, there was the danger of a nuclear clash in South Asia. Although there was some heightened activity, those including this author who were then on active duty did not think that there was any chance of war. Robert Gates, the then US Deputy National Security Adviser visited Delhi in May 1990 and claimed that he had successfully defused the situation. Although General K. Sundarji, the then Indian Army Chief is reported to have remarked that Brasstacks was the last chance India had to sort out Pakistan, it is a moot point if anything substantive was actually planned. To be sure, according to journalist Raj Chengappa, Rajiv Gandhi was annoyed with his friend and Minister of State for Defence, Arun Singh and roundly castigated him for launching a major exercise without his express permission. Arun Singh maintained that he had informed the Prime Minister and obtained the necessary permission. Soon thereafter Arun Singh resigned.[60]

Indian Peace Keeping Force (IPKF) in Sri Lanka, July 1987-March 1990

Earlier in 1987, in an already charged situation, India had also decided to send its troops to bring peace to Sri Lanka and help it conduct elections in the vain hope that the dreaded Liberation Tigers of Tamil Eelam (LTTE) would be amenable to a negotiated peace on the basis of autonomy to the Northern

Provinces of Sri Lanka, the home of most Sri Lankan Tamils. Instead of the promised 'four or five days to bring the situation under control' the operation, codenamed Operation Pawan, took nearly three years during which the Indian Army suffered heavy casualties. This was seen as yet another example of India's hubris, to ride roughshod over its smaller neighbours. It was a classic case of delayed over-reaction. P.C. Alexander, a former Principal Secretary to Rajiv Gandhi, blamed the then Army Chief General K. Sundarji for the army's failure in the June 1984 Operation Blue Star and the June 1987 Sri Lanka intervention. Alexander quotes the late Rajiv Gandhi as saying, "senior army officers in charge of the IPKF operations, in particular General K. Sundarji had assured him categorically that the Indian forces would be able to bring the conflict in Sri Lanka under full control in a matter of four to five days." India had once again launched its troops without adequate intelligence and preparation. In reality, there was little coordination between the Research and Analysis Wing (R&AW), the external intelligence agency which had a far better knowledge of the situation, and the politico-military leadership.[61]

The IAF pressed its transport aircraft and helicopters into service in Sri Lanka and played a major role in providing tactical mobility and logistic support. Many of the helicopters were fired at by the LTTE rebels and sustained damage, but such attacks were mercifully restricted to only small arms fire, although the LTTE was known to possess small numbers of shoulder-fired missiles or Man Portable Air Defence Systems (MANPADS).

Kargil Conflict, May-July 1999

In May 1999, India was again surprised to find that Pakistan Army regulars had occupied a number of posts on the Indian side of the Line of Control (LoC) in the Kargil sector of J&K that were vacated during the previous winter. As in the past, the enemy began shelling the vital Srinagar-Leh Road that threatened to cut off Ladakh. Pakistan initially denied that its regular troops had infiltrated into India but following a strong Indian reaction in which sizeable elements of both the Indian army and IAF were employed, Pakistan was forced to admit that its army regulars were in fact the main force involved in the fighting. Unbeknown to India, the Pakistan Army was in the process of occupying these posts in late 1998, early 1999. It came as a shock to India, especially because on February 19, 1999, the then Indian Prime Minister, A.B. Vajpayee was visiting Lahore in Pakistan on a 'Bus Yatra' to mend Indo-Pak relations. This stab in the back utterly vitiated the peace in South Asia and cost India over 517 lives. It became clear that India could never let its guard down while dealing with this implacable neighbour. In an attempt to contain the scope of its response, India restricted its air force operations to its side of the LoC but it took until the end of July to fully throw out the enemy that was entrenched in the high mountains and was relatively invulnerable and safe from air and ground attacks.

Fighting Insurgencies and Terrorism

From about the late 1980s, Pakistan realised that it could not effectively address India's conventional superiority. Smarting under the Bangladesh defeat, Pakistan embarked on a modified strategy of using mujahideen, terrorists recently freed from the Afghan War, against India; first in J&K where local unrest proved helpful and later in other parts of India. India was still reeling under the Sikh militancy, which also received all help from Pakistan. Indian aircraft were hijacked and flown to Pakistan and sometimes further to Dubai, which housed many anti-India elements and criminals. Such was the fury of cross-border terrorism and support to insurgency that in 1990 the Indian Army had to raise special battalions of infantry (dubbed as a paramilitary force under the home ministry to get around manpower ceiling laws), the Rashtriya Rifles (RR) to tackle the terrorist menace in J&K. Even so, India had to eventually deploy some half a million troops in J&K. Through the 1990s, cross-border infiltration increased and terrorism spread to other parts of the country.

In 1990, the Indian economy took a turn for the worse and India was forced to mortgage its gold reserves with the World Bank to avoid defaulting on payments. In May 1991, Rajiv Gandhi was assassinated by an LTTE suicide bomber. Following the elections, the P.V. Narasimha Rao Government embarked on bold economic reforms designed to put the economy on a path of rapid and sustained growth. The December 6, 1992 demolition of the Babri Masjid at Ayodhya once again fanned communal flames. Although India successfully if belatedly brought under control the Pakistan-abetted Khalistan militancy in Punjab by the early 1990s, the menace of jihadi terrorism acquired dangerous proportions, when terrorists targeted the cities of Mumbai and Delhi.

On December 24, 1999 a Pakistan based terror group successfully hijacked an Indian Airlines aircraft to Kandahar in Afghanistan (Flight IC-814 from Kathmandu to Delhi) and compelled the Indian Government to release five dreaded terrorists. Jihadi terror now became the biggest threat to national security. Numerous terror strikes were carried out, including the Mumbai carnage of November 26, 2008 in which 10 Pakistan-based and trained terrorists mercilessly killed 166 innocents and injured hundreds.

India's security forces are still engaged in fighting several insurgent groups in the North-east and Maoists/Naxal militants in Central India who aim to overthrow the Union Government. The army and Rashtriya Rifles are also continuously engaged in fighting Pakistan-aided militancy, often described as Low Intensity Conflict Operations (LICO) in J&K for over 23 years. Successive Union

Governments have managed to safeguard India's unity, despite numerous internal and external threats and challenges, but India has continued to rely on an archaic and inefficient mechanism of security decision-making and responded only when the enemy was at the door. If only India had adopted a somewhat different and proactive, yet well-calibrated security strategy, some of these situations could have been handled more competently and with less harm to the country.

The departure of the US-led North Atlantic Treaty Organisation (NATO) International Security Assistance Force (ISAF) from Afghanistan in December 2014 is once again likely to exacerbate the security situation in South Asia and place additional pressure on India. In such a scenario, it is imperative that India takes urgent steps to remedy, at least, the major deficiencies in its security management. In the absence of a public document on India's security policy/strategy, one can only make an informed inference about how it works.

As we have seen, until the appointment of a NSA in 1998 by the Vajpayee government, management of the country's security affairs was the responsibility of the Prime Minister's Office (PMO) assisted by the Defence, Foreign and Home Ministers. The committee system – Defence Committee of the Cabinet (DCC), Cabinet Committee on Political Affairs (CCPA), Cabinet Committee on Security (CCS), Chiefs of Staff Committee (CoSC), Joint Intelligence Committee (JIC) – worked, but only when the civilian political leadership took some interest and tried to maintain direct contact with the military. India has followed a unique system in which the three Service Chiefs and the Service Headquarters are not an integral part of the Ministry of Defence (MoD), but operate as its attached offices.[62] The Rules of Business of the Central Government, thus place the responsibility of India's defence, solely with the Minister of Defence or Defence Secretary, who is a senior Indian Administrative Service (IAS) officer with or even without any experience of working in the MoD, and hence a 'generalist'. The MoD is charged with meeting all the needs of the three Services, and also coordinates with other departments of the government.

Why a National Security Strategy?

While chances of a conventional war might be remote, it cannot be totally ruled out, especially given that India shares disputed borders with two of its neighbours. The country, thus has little option but to maintain a certain minimum level of military capability, which would obviously depend on current and future threats. There can, however, be a wide variation in our understanding of the worst case scenario and the most likely scenario. It is often said that there is no such thing as absolute security. This is what is commonly referred to as a 'security dilemma': beyond a point your security will begin to impinge on the security of your adversary or neighbour, hence, it is important that a judicious balance is maintained between own sense of security and the genuine fears of the potential adversary. This will, however, be tempered by past experience, own concept of defence, and the continuously changing dynamic of mutual competition and threat perception. This cannot be done without regularly analysing the security situation and hence a formal or informal security policy or strategy is inescapable. Annual Reports of the Indian MoD expressly state, "India remains fully committed to the twin policies of (a) no territorial ambition and (b) no export of ideology".[63] In other words, while India will defend its territorial integrity and sovereignty, it will not invade another country. The record of its history since independence adequately proves this. Its neighbours nevertheless continue to have a different opinion and cite Goa (1961), Bangladesh (1971), Sri Lanka (1987-90) and Maldives (1988) to raise the bogey of India's hegemonic behaviour.

In simple terms, strategy is the process of harmonising ends with means. Those charged with the defence and security of the country, must follow a certain well-defined process to arrive at an appropriate national security strategy, which should logically flow from the country's Grand Strategy. Again, this is usually a statement of the broad goals that the nation wishes to pursue and even when not written down in a formal document, becomes evident from the statements of national leaders, parliamentary debates, defence expenditure and the general behaviour of the nation-state. Besides safeguarding national interests, such as living in peace, being allowed to pursue the general development of its people, and the freedom to make choices, a country also has to ensure that future generations would be able to enjoy these freedoms. It is therefore essential to take a long view of the past and current trends and project them into the future, before a country can decide on its security goals.

Former President Dr. A.P.J. Abdul Kalam wanted India to become a developed country by 2020. Former Prime Minister Manmohan Singh wanted to maintain high levels of inclusive economic growth to liberate the vast multitudes of Indians from poverty. The former NSA Shivshankar Menon has often said that India aims for 'total transformation and a peaceful periphery' to achieve that.[64] All of these statements and a visible attempt to keep India's defence expenditure at a reasonable level of around 2.5 per cent of GDP, should give a good idea of the general direction of India's national security strategy. A tendency to demonstrate strategic restraint, an unshakeable faith in peaceful resolution of international disputes, and extreme reluctance to resort to use of force, may be seen as the most important features of India's security behaviour.

Having articulated these broad objectives, the strategy maker has to examine the current trends and devise ways to build economic, ideational and military capabilities to meet them. Before identifying deficiencies in the strength, numbers, sophistication and technology levels of our weapons and equipment, the country's leadership must first look at the state of its economy and the social/human development index or level to make a broad assessment of the country's financial capacity to sustain its defence effort.

The next step would be to make a short and long-term perspective plan and lay down *inter se* priorities, visualise the kind of technologies that the country must obtain from abroad, or develop them indigenously and then regularly monitor them, to ensure timely revisions and corrections to achieve the short and long-term goals.

Some might argue that public articulation of defence strategy will unnecessarily forewarn the potential adversary and give it an opportunity to devise strategies of its own, to neutralise India's. Any self-respecting modern nation-state usually possesses a plethora of instruments and technical means to constantly decipher the intent and capabilities of a competitor or adversary and hence, a declared national security strategy does not give away any state secrets, but on the other hand, lays down the manner in which security challenges and threats would be handled, and reduces the chances of any miscalculation. Even when a country's strategy is cloaked in secrecy, its actions and responses to various situations normally give a fairly accurate idea of its intentions.

It usually takes a long time to build military capabilities and hence, this process cannot be neglected or left to the vagaries of democratic politics, nor can it wait for 'complete transformation'. Governments change but the foundations of national security must always remain strong. All this is easier said than done, simply because a democracy faces a faces a veritable political revolution every five years. With new governments at the helm, the influence of interest groups changes and so do their priorities. In India, mercifully, there is a broad consensus on national security and barring a few exceptions, the country's defence has received adequate funding. As a result, the country's defence budget has hovered around a modest 2.5 per cent of the national GDP, but this has often meant an increase barely enough to cater to annual inflation. Given that high-tech weapons and equipment usually show an annual increase of 10 per cent in their prices, there is little left for military modernisation. The fact that India continues to depend on foreign countries for up to 70 per cent of its defence needs, further exacerbates the problem. Inflation or upward price variation and above all, the value of the Indian rupee against the US dollar – the benchmark currency in which most purchases are made – further complicate the problem. Foreign exchange is always scarce and purchasing weapons, platforms and spares from abroad puts considerable pressure on the country's economy and foreign exchange reserves and hence, it becomes difficult for the government to assign a certain fixed amount of money for defence.

The vital role of a National Security Strategy, and/or Defence Strategy, and Long Term Integrated Procurement Plan (LTIPP) should now become evident. India has some nine major Defence Public Sector Undertakings (DPSUs) and 42

Ordnance Factories (OFs), many of them operating since before independence, and also a large DRDO staffed with world-class scientists and engineers, but alas, India has still not been able to achieve the requisite degree of self-sufficiency, which often constrains its choices. India's defence industrial base is not adequately developed and that makes technology absorption relatively difficult. India's policy of maintaining equal distance from any bloc, its decision to carry out a nuclear test in 1974, lending support to countries fighting colonialism and imperialism, its disputes with Pakistan and attempts to chart an independent course in international relations, have together resulted in many Western powers imposing economic and other sanctions and denying it sensitive technologies. While Indian scientists and engineers have successfully carried out space research and exploration, developed ballistic missile technology, launched a variety of satellites and most importantly, given the country a credible nuclear deterrent, their record in areas of aircraft, avionics, aero-engines, and airborne radars leaves much to be desired. A national security or defence policy and strategy has never been articulated. In light of the above, a national security strategy document is essential, for, without such a clear enunciation, various organs of the government including the armed forces, cannot make any long-term plans and are unable to anticipate and prepare for new challenges and threats.

But this is not all. There also exists a major and profound 'disconnect' between the political establishment and military leadership. As seen before, it was this gap that was the primary cause of India's humiliation in the 1962 Sino-Indian border conflict. It is not as if the political bosses have not given necessary directions to the military leadership on how India might resort to use of force, but only just. Such interactions have been rare. There has seldom been a regular dialogue between the military and political leadership. Government directives to the MoD were not updated for years.[65] Considering that India has faced threats of aggression and other disruptions from across the border for most of the last 68 years, this indifference is unfathomable.

Even an obliquely critical comment on their peace-loving nature, their deep-rooted faith in non-violence and their lofty goal of becoming a 'righteous nation-state' can raise disproportionately strong reactions amongst Indians. India, it seems, does not mind if the world sees it as indecisive, lethargic, hypocritical, ambiguous, unsure, timid, excessively cautious or even incompetent on matters of national security, but any slight to its upright and honourable image of a 'non-aligned country committed to promoting world peace and the welfare of mankind' is not tolerated.

The fact that throughout recorded history, the Indian sub-continent has been at the receiving end of numerous invasions from the north-west and also from the sea, should normally make an average Indian sensitive about national security, but the exact opposite is the case. Even educated and well-informed Indians are blissfully indifferent, even apathetic, to security issues. Indians often cite examples of their southern kings like the Cheras, Cholas and Pandyas, making forays into South East Asia and holding sway there for centuries. But they often forget that when the Portuguese ships began bombarding Calicut in 1501, the friendly and hospitable Zamorin was utterly stunned, because neither he nor his nobles had ever experienced the use of gunpowder. This was in spite of the fact that the Portuguese had already been welcomed in his kingdom and had been given permission to trade in spices. The story in the North was not very different, when the then mighty Indian kings faced the wrath of Babur's artillery.[66]

Contrast this with China. When the People's Republic of China (PRC) emerged from a long period of internal strife, caused by a bloody civil war and a 'century of humiliation', Chairman Mao only said, "China has stood up".[67] The Chinese are equally proud and conscious of their 5,000-year-long civilisational history and never let the world forget how far advanced that civilisation was. But such sentiments have never been allowed to interfere with China's core objectives of national reunification and economic advancement, leading to development and progress. For example, by the mid-1980s, the PRC had its own submarine-launched ballistic missile. Although not as yet a member of the UNSC, this nuclear status significantly enhanced its national power and also opened diplomatic opportunities.

In February 1972, the then US President, Richard Nixon, made a historic visit to China. Although the honeymoon did not last very long, China made full use of the short-lived friendship with the US. Soon after the death of Mao Zedong and Zhou En-Lai, Deng Xiaoping revitalised the 'four modernisations' strategy and embarked on an ambitious programme of economic development. This China could do, because its rudimentary nuclear capability had ensured a near threat-free environment. The PRC did not hesitate to take all necessary steps to first ensure its survival. Mao's policies no doubt caused many social upheavals and resulted in millions of deaths, but Deng Xiaoping, who also belonged to the first generation leadership, led that same China to unprecedented and spectacular growth. China soon became the second most powerful economy in the world and slowly but steadfastly developed its military power in the face of sanctions. Whether we like it or not, today China's voice counts. Not a day passes without a mention of China's peaceful rise in the global media. So much so, China's double-digit economic growth and its rapidly-modernising military, have together compelled the US to review its global strategy and begin rebalancing the deployment of its military, especially the navy in the Western Pacific theatre.

India, on the other hand, has constantly been plagued by bickering and internecine factional fighting. This has severely affected its decision-making and unduly delayed the implementation of urgent measures necessary to consolidate its security. The excuse is that in a democracy it takes a long time to build consensus and a democratic government cannot ignore the demands, rights and sentiments of the people. This is undoubtedly true, but procrastination and inaction cannot be condoned in the vital arena of national security. The first goal of any self-respecting national leadership must be to inspire the people to give their best and manage the differing perceptions of competing interest groups within reasonable limits. According to some observers, Indian democracy has certainly witnessed free and fair elections and ensured peaceful transfer of power, but has failed to provide effective governance. In almost all fields of national endeavour, India has consistently delivered sub-optimal performance and worse, the governments and people are both quite sanguine about the pace of progress. India does not lack thinkers. Indians have earned a name for themselves when working on the frontiers of technology in the US and other countries. In India, however, the same people somehow find it difficult to work as a team.

A group of highly accomplished and respected intellectuals has in a recently published report titled *Non-Alignment 2.0* recommended a mixture of Nehruvian and neo-liberal approaches to India's foreign and security policy.[68] The group suggests that India should lead by example while simultaneously building its economy. Ashley Tellis and Satish Chandra, two influential writers on Indian security, have however, roundly criticised the report, albeit for different reasons. Tellis says:

> Therefore, Nonalignment 2.0's dramatic claim that India's 'power has often been the power of its example' may be irrelevant even if true, because there is no evidence that it has paid off concretely in the international arena by buttressing either India's economic development or its rise in power.[69]

Former diplomat, K.S. Bajpai, also criticises the report as he feels calling it 'Non-Alignment 2.0' unnecessarily cloaks it in controversial terms. Briefly stated, the first two approaches (Nehruvian and neo-liberal) suggest a strong collective effort to ensure rapid economic growth, development and employment of India's vast reservoirs of 'soft power', while maintaining a high degree of political autonomy, to lead the world by 'example'. The writers of the report sincerely believe that it is this 'example' (68 years of democratic freedom, secularism, pluralism and an inclusive approach) that will ultimately triumph in this globalised and uncertain world. The third school, the so-called Hyper-Realists, essentially agree with all of the above, but also want India to modernise its military, reduce dependence on foreign powers by quickly reforming and remodelling its defence industry, and be ready in the event a situation requires the use of force. The Hyper-Realists also want India to build partnerships with advanced countries of the world, including the US, to access high technology in order that India's military modernisation comes to fruition without further delay.

In a recent book *Arming without Aiming*,[70] two American authors have discussed India's laudable tradition of 'strategic restraint' and wondered where its recent high visibility arms purchases are leading the country. Many Indian analysts have criticised the main theme of the book, but it is difficult to ignore its central message that in the absence of 'institutional and organisational reforms', merely procuring modern aircraft and weapons will not suffice to deter the enemy. Stephen Cohen and Sunil Dasgupta say, "The weak response to the terrorist attack on Mumbai is now the poster child of organisational incoherence – all of the personnel and equipment existed, but the system did not allow for timely deployment and coordinated use of force. India's systemic failure to anticipate and act beforehand is notable, but it is a price that the political leadership seems willing to pay",[71] a damning indictment of India's indecisiveness and the habit of living in a make-believe world.

India urgently needs a well-thought out and validated policy and strategy for use of military force, as reacting to every emerging situation 'on its own merits' by calling a meeting of senior bureaucrats cannot work, in the current atmosphere of unprecedented uncertainty. Little wonder then that Timothy Roemer, the former US envoy to India, blamed India's 'slow and grinding process of military mobilisation' for the absence of a military response to the November 26, 2008 terrorist attacks in Mumbai.[72]

Following a loud and persistent clamour for a thorough and purposeful review of India's Higher Defence Control Organisation, the United Progressive Alliance (UPA) II Government constituted a Task Force of experts under the leadership of Naresh Chandra, a veteran diplomat, bureaucrat and former Cabinet Secretary. The resultant report says: "Many of the key recommendations of the Kargil Review Committee (KRC), set up immediately after the 1999 conflict, have not yet been implemented."[73] The report advises India to be prepared militarily to deal with an "assertive" China even as it seeks to build bridges of cooperation with Beijing. The report calls for better coordination between the foreign and defence ministries.[74] That it needed a Task Force to suggest such obvious measures, especially after the KRC had made similar recommendations, is indeed shocking. It is also surprising that 68 years after independence, India refuses to change its archaic system of politico-military decision-making, but at the same time, goes on spending huge sums of money on import of aircraft, weapons and other equipment. It surely cannot be for lack of understanding of the seriousness of the problem. At a minimum, the political leadership must remove this 'disconnect' with the top military commanders. In a democracy, every citizen has the right to know the security policy/strategy that the government intends to adopt to address the myriad threats to the country. Even so, given a general air of policy paralysis, it is difficult to see India adopting a 'declaratory defence policy' although that was one of the main recommendations of the KRC.[75]

All this should have normally caused India's decision-makers to sit up and take notice of these criticisms. Alas, India continues to grope for a viable and workable national security policy, far less, strategy. Despite some very useful and candid remarks by the former NSA Shivshankar Menon, in the many lectures he delivered, the pace of security reforms appears to be decidedly slow. India seems to believe that its security would be enhanced by merely raising additional infantry/ mountain divisions and by purchasing more advanced aircraft, ships and submarines. Without a coherent security policy and strategy and a robust and visible display of national resolve and political will, India is unwittingly getting trapped in an arms race with its more powerful, smart and rich neighbour. In the circumstances, India's military modernisation attempts appear unsustainable and perhaps even counterproductive.

NOTES

1. See for example, Stephen P. Cohen and Sunil Dasgupta, *Arming Without Aiming: India's Military Modernisation*, Viking, New Delhi, 2010.
2. Durga Das, *India from Curzon to Nehru & After*, Rupa & Co., Delhi, 1969 (Reprinted 1974), pp. 44-45.
3. Cited in K. Shankar Bajpai, *India Engages the World* at the 11th Prem Bhatia Memorial Lecture, 2006 at http://www.prembhatiatrust.com/lecture11.htm (Accessed November 27, 2011).
4. Ibid.
5. Kanti Bajpai, "India: Modified Structuralism", in Muthiah Alagappa (ed.) *Asian Security Practice: Material and Ideational Influences,* Stanford University Press, Stanford, 1998, p. 164.
6. The definitions by Walt, Morgan and Buzan and Booth are from Alagappa, Ibid. p. 27.
7. Pierre Jacquet, "From Survival to Interdependence", *Survival,* Spring 1992, pp. 89-90.
8. K. Subrahmanyam, "Decision Making in Defence", *IDSA Journal,* 2 (4), April-June 1970, reprinted in N.S. Sisodia and Sujit Dutta (eds.), *India and the World: Selected Articles from IDSA Journals, Volume 1– Strategic Thought: The Formative Years*, Promilla & Co., New Delhi, 2005, pp. 78-107.
9. K. Subrahmanyam, "Grand Strategy for the first half of the 21st Century," *Indian Express*, February 3, 2012.
10. Shivshankar Menon, "The Role of Militaries in International Relations", Address by NSA at the Cariappa Memorial Lecture, New Delhi, October 5, 2011.
11. Neo-realism is another theory of International Relations which appears to be currently popular.
12. Muthiah Alagappa, no. 5, p. 38.
13. See for example, Stephen Walt, *Theory Talks,* August 25, 2009, When asked, 'What is, according to you, the biggest challenge or principal debate in current IR? And what is your position or answer to this challenge / in this debate?" Walt said, "For me, the biggest challenge is making my work relevant to the general population. For many people, world politics has an alienating effect, appearing as a product of distant, uncontrolled, and alien forces" at http://www.theory-talks.org/2009/08/theory-talk-33.html (Accessed July 26, 2013).
14. Shivshankar Menon, no. 10.
15. K. Shankar Bajpai, "India Engages the World", 11th Prem Bhatia Memorial Lecture, 2006 at http://www.prembhatiatrust.com/lecture11.htm (Accessed November 27, 2011).
16. Ibid.
17. A. Appadorai, *Contemporary India: Essays in Domestic and Foreign Policy*, Asian Publishers, New Delhi, 1988, p. 166.

18. Ibid., p. 169.
19. K. Shankar Bajpai, no. 15.
20. A. Appadorai, no. 17, p. 177.
21. P. Chidambaram, India's finance minister, in an address at IDSA, delivered on February 6, 2013.
22. See http://archive.indianexpress.com/news/naxalism-gravest-internal-security-threat-to-nation-pm/609303/
23. The Indian military normally uses the term 'jointness' which means synergy between the three services; the former NSA, however, coined this new term. "The Role of Militaries in International Relations", Cariappa Memorial Lecture, October 5, 2011 at http://indiatoday.intoday.in/story/nsa-shivshankar-menon-lecture-on-the-role-of-militaries-in-international-relations/1/153967.htm(Accessed November 15, 2011).
24. Ibid.
25. *Indian Express,* July 21, 2009.
26. "Government Admits Chinese Intrusions", *Mail Today*, May 17, 2012.
27. K. Subrahmanyam in a posthumously published essay, *Indian Express,* February 2, 2012.
28. P. Chidambaram, no. 21.
29. Although Indians do not readily accept it, countries such as Brazil and South Africa have also done far better than India in per capita GDP terms.
30. K. Subrahmanyam said that India's non-alignment was not a dogma but a strategy and India reaped many dividends by remaining friendly with both superpowers.
31. Major General Dipankar Banerjee (Retd.), "Geo-Strategic Balance", *Defence & Security Alert*, September 2012, pp. 44-46.
32. Shashi Tharoor, cited in Srinath Raghavan, *War and Peace in Modern India: A Strategic History of the Nehru Years*, Permanent Black, Ranikhet, 2010, pp. 1-2.
33. S. Kalyanaraman, "*The Indian Military Response to Threats From Pakistan, 1949-2010*", Paper presented at IDSA Fellows Seminar, July 8, 2011 (Unpublished).
34. Srinath Raghavan, no. 32, p. 31.
35. B.G. Verghese, "50 Years after 1962: A Personal Memoir", Presentation at Subbu Forum Round Table, September 6, 2012. Verghese was the assistant editor and war correspondent for the *Times of India* during the 1962 Sino-Indian conflict and was stationed at Tezpur.
36. C. Dasgupta, *War and Diplomacy on Kashmir, 1947-48*, Sage, New Delhi, 2002, pp. 36-37.
37. Ibid., pp. 12-13. This paragraph is based largely on Dasgupta's findings.
38. Ibid, pp. 14-18.
39. C. Dasgupta, no. 36.
40. K.P. Saksena, *The United Nations and Collective Security*, DK Publishing House, New Delhi, 1974.
41. UN SCOR-1948, 3rd year Supplement for November 1948, p. 143, as quoted in K.P. Saksena, Ibid., p. 71.
42. Ibid., p. 72.
43. Ibid.
44. Ibid., p. 73.
45. Ibid., p. 71, emphasis added.
46. Ibid., p. 73.
47. Ibid. Emphasis added. This discussion is based on the findings of K.P. Saksena in "United Nations and Collective Security" referred to in no. 40. Very few other books have ever made any mention of this grave blunder. The former NSA Shivshankar Menon in one of his lectures referred to the above lapse in passing but without any clarification. In his book, Srinath Raghavan, has devoted two full chapters to Nehru's handling of the Kashmir issue but for reasons best known to him has chosen to omit these details.
48. Rajmohan Gandhi, *Patel: A Life,* Navjivan Press, Ahmedabad, 2008, pp. 480-83.

49. P.V.R. Rao, "Governmental Machinery for the Evolution of National Defence Policy and the Higher Direction of War", *IDSA Journal*, (1), July 1968, reprinted in N.S. Sisodia and Sujit Dutta (eds.), *India and the World: Selected Articles from IDSA Journals*, Vol. 1, Promilla & Co., New Delhi, 2005, p. 64.
50. Jasjit Singh in a private conversation with the author at CAPS New Delhi, January 20, 2011.
51. J.K. Galbraith, *Ambassador's Journal*, Hamish Hamilton, London, 1969, pp. 428-530. Galbraith focuses on the Sino-Indian Conflict on which the summary in the text is based. He gives a good idea of the state of affairs during this crisis in New Delhi.
52. Ibid.
53. The previous two paragraphs are based on Galbraith cited above at no. 50.
54. Srinath Raghavan, no. 32, pp. 303-04. When V.K. Krishna Menon, Gen. Thapar, IB Chief Mallik and Lt. Gen. Sen, the Eastern Army Commander flew to Tezpur on October 16, 1962, Kaul in fact "strongly argued that the Namkachu positions were unstable."
55. R.D. Pradhan, *Debacle to Revival: YB Chavan as Defence Minister, 1962-65*, Orient Longman, Hyderabad, 1998, pp. 171, 173, 177, 300-309. Emphasis added.
56. Jasjit Singh (ed.), *Pakistan Occupied Kashmir: Under the Jackboot*, Siddhi Books, New Delhi, 1995, p. 4.
57. P.V.S. Jagan Mohan and Samir Chopra, *The India Pakistan War of 1965*, New Delhi, Manohar, 2005 (Reprinted 2006), pp. 62-63.
58. Inder Malhotra, "Revisiting Shimla", *Indian Express*, July 2, 2012.
59. See Kanti Bajpai, P.R. Chari, Pervaiz Iqbal Cheema, Stephen P. Cohen, and Sumit Ganguly, *Brasstacks and Beyond: Perception and Management of Crisis in South Asia*, Manohar, New Delhi, 1995 (reprinted 1997), pp. 96-113.
60. Raj Chengappa, *Weapons of Peace: The Secret Story of India's Quest to be a Nuclear Power*, HarperCollins India, New Delhi, 2000, pp. 321-26.
61. P.C. Alexander, *Through the Corridors of Power: An Insider's Story*, HarperCollins, New Delhi, (Second Impression 2004) pp. 296, pp. 304-06, 363-66.
62. Admiral (Retd.) Arun Prakash, "National Security Reforms: Ten Years After the Kargil Committee Report", *USI Journal*, Oct-Dec 2012, pp. 504-23.
63. India's Ministry of Defence Annual Report for the year 2005-06, p. 12.
64. P.C. Lal Memorial Lecture, delivered by Shivshankar Menon at the Air Force Association, New Delhi on April 2, 2012.
65. During the early 1990s, the government had not found it necessary to update its 1979 directive to the armed forces and despite many reminders from the Service HQs there was no response from the MoD. The directive was finally revised a few years later.
66. In 1526 at Panipat, Babur actually fought and defeated Ibrahim Lodhi of Afghan descent, then ruling from Delhi, but his grandson Akbar decimated his Rajput opponents at the Battle of Haldi Ghati with his famous long-range gun Mallika-a-Maidan. Total disinterest in developing war-winning technologies was the root cause of innumerable Indian defeats at the hands of foreign armies and navies supported with long-range artillery against which mere swords, lances, horse cavalry or bows and arrows were totally ineffective.
67. Wu Xinbo, "China: Security Practice of a Modernizing and Ascending Power," in Muthiah Algappa (ed), no. 5, p. 115.
68. *Non-Alignment 2.0*, 2012 at http://www.cprindia.org/sites/default/files/NonAlignment%202.0_1. pdf (AccessedJuly 15, 2012); see also Ambassador Satish Chandra, "Why Non-alignment 2.0 does us a Disservice?" at http://www.rediff.com/news/column/why-non-alignment-does-us-a-disservice/20120612.htm (Accessed July 15, 2012); Ashley Tellis, *Nonalignment Redux* at http//www.ceip [nonalignment_redux-ashleytellisjul 2012 pdf] (Accessed August 1, 2012).
69. Ibid. p. 37.
70. Stephen P. Cohen and Sunil Dasgupta, no. 1.

71. Ibid., p. 150.
72. Wikileaks: "US spied on India's military contingency plans", *Indian Express*, December 1, 2010, at http://www.indianexpress.com/news/wikileaks-us-spied-on-indias-military-contingency-plans/718517/ (Accessed June 4, 2012).
73. Josy Joseph, *Times of India*, July 26, 2012.
74. Ibid.
75. Report of the Kargil Review Committee at http://www.scribd.com/doc/152396717/Kargil-Review-Committee-Report-1999 (Accessed June 30, 2014).

4

Airpower Employment: Lessons from the Past

This chapter looks at major post-World War II conflicts in India and elsewhere in the world to derive important lessons pertaining to the employment of air power. This analysis first covers five significant conflicts: the four wars with Pakistan, the Sino-Indian conflict, and the one against LTTE in Sri Lanka. It then goes on to cover all other major wars since the end of World War II. The analysis focuses on air power lessons with only a very brief treatment of other relevant military lessons.

India-Pakistan War in Jammu and Kashmir, 1947-48

Pakistan's invasion of Kashmir came as a complete surprise. It is not as if there were no indications of things to come. As early as August 1947, Major O.S. Kalkat, an Indian officer serving at the General Headquarters (GHQ) Rawalpindi in Pakistan, came upon a top secret letter that gave the entire plan of Operation Gulmarg to be launched on October 20, 1947. The plan was to send up to 10,000 tribal fighters into the Kashmir Valley to start a rebellion which would pave the way for direct action by Pakistan. He managed to make his way back to Delhi on October 19 and disclosed the details of the plan to Sardar Baldev Singh, the then Defence Minister, Brigadier (later Lieutenant General) Kalwant Singh and Colonel Thapar, the acting Director of Military Operations. Unfortunately, no credence was given to this vital piece of information. Operation Gulmarg started on October 22, 1947 as planned, and Kalkat was brought from his home and presented to the Prime Minister. But by then the information was dated and not of much use.[1]

India decided to send a battalion of troops to Kashmir, but only after its ruler signed the Instrument of Accession, as Lord Mountbatten, the new Governor General of independent India, felt that India could not send its troops into a sovereign princely state that was technically not part of the dominion. By that time information was received that the raiders had reached Baramulla and were poised to threaten Srinagar. What happened then is now history, but for a variety of reasons the Indian response was delayed. Had it not been for the alacrity and professionalism of the few air force and army officers then present at Delhi, the crucial airlift could have been further delayed and the history of Kashmir and indeed India would have been very different. It is said that some officers had anticipated the airlift requirement and cautioned many private aircraft operators to be ready in case of emergency.

Need for Infrastructure

The runway at Srinagar was until then used mainly for the private aeroplane of the Maharaja and was unfit to undertake round-the-clock operations by heavily laden DC-3 aircraft that brought in men and material in an unending stream for weeks. The unpaved surface soon broke up and a cloud of dust was raised every time an aircraft took off or landed. The airfield also lacked Air Traffic Control (ATC), meteorological forecasting facilities and navigation aids so vital for safe air operations. Although the runway was somehow maintained, its condition continued to pose serious problems. Another major problem was lack of fuel, oil and lubricants (FOL) at Srinagar. In desperation, the Spitfires and Tempests of the Indian Air Force (IAF) routinely siphoned off excess fuel from returning Dakotas, in return for a hastily scribbled receipt for the amount of fuel received. According to Lieutenant General L.P. Sen, the audit objection for not raising a voucher in triplicate for such informal transfer of fuel was pending till 1965.[2] IAF fighter crews were also totally short of maps. For many days, a small portion of the situation map from the briefing room was cut out and used for offensive missions during the day and replaced in the evening. Such was the thoroughness with which the Pakistani leadership had planned the take-over of Kashmir by force, that at the time of partition, the departing Pakistani civilian and military intelligence officers had emptied out the central stores of all stocks of Kashmir maps, and details of the disposition of the Kashmir State Forces before they left India.[3] Yet, this was neither noticed nor reported to the higher military and political authorities in India. According to Durga Das, "(Muslim) League leaders had in any event made plans to occupy Kashmir by force."[4] Considering that the newly independent country was inundated with the many problems arising from partition and an unprecedented movement of refugees from both sides, this intelligence failure is perhaps not unusual, but it was not the last.

India was lucky to have a variety of civilian and commercial operators flying the venerable DC-3 Dakota aircraft in different parts of the country and these operators were alerted in the third week of October 1947 of an impending operation to ferry troops to Jammu and Kashmir (J&K). Even so the motley collection of these aircraft of mixed vintage was barely adequate to meet the task. Such was the success of the hastily mounted operation that Pakistan and indeed the world believed for a long time, that the airlift of Indian troops was a *pre-planned* operation.

Only three fighter and one transport squadron took part during this 14-month-long war with only 8-10 aircraft on their strength. The squadrons were running low on spares as most of the stores and equipment depots were located in Pakistan and the division of assets took considerable time. IAF men provided commendable maintenance support in trying circumstances and kept the fleet airworthy. Both the Tempest and Harvard aircraft were extensively used in the armed reconnaissance and ground attack role. The armament used consisted of front guns or cannons, rocket projectiles (R/Ps) and bombs. Given the mountainous terrain, it was difficult to accurately bomb targets such as bridges or gun emplacements tucked away in narrow valleys; bombing is difficult even in the most ideal conditions as these heavy 500 or 1,000-pound bombs are free-fall gravity weapons.

High altitude also adversely affected the performance of these piston engine aircraft and restricted operations due to the reduced flight envelope. When asked, a veteran of this war said, "We flew by the seat of our pants and did not bother too much about these (aerodynamic) problems." The attack on enemy positions at the Zoji La Pass in August 1948 was noteworthy as the Pass is well over 10,500 feet high and the Tempest was not designed for operations at this altitude.[5] Attacks on Skardu, Bunji and Gilgit also presented immense difficulties due to the terrain, bad weather and large distance from their operating bases. This meant that on many occasions the aircraft were forced to fly with internally mounted guns, as neither rockets nor bombs could be carried. Due to limitations on the number and range of aircraft and lack of political direction, attacks on these targets in Gilgit-Baltistan were not decisive.

The lone Dakota Squadron was woefully short of air crew, especially qualified experienced captains and flying instructors. This meant that the Commanding Officer (CO) and Flight Commander had to often undertake training sorties after completing rigorous day-long operations in the mountains. First based at Agra, some aircraft of this squadron were later moved to Palam near Delhi. The DC-3 Dakota was also often used to the limit of its designed capacity. Carriage of heavy guns, dropping of supplies and day and night landing on the hastily prepared short runway at Poonch under enemy fire by the only transport squadron of the IAF, was a major achievement of this war. The most noteworthy feat of the squadron was when Air Commodore 'Baba' Meher Singh landed the Dakota at Leh, an unpaved runway at 11,000 feet altitude after flying over mountains reaching 20,000-25,000 feet en route. The experience of the 1947-48 Indo-Pak War thus clearly brought home the following important lessons. The IAF urgently needed:

- A sizeable number of medium and heavy transport aircraft with adequate range and load carrying capacity, suitable for operations from high altitude airfields; a fleet of fighter and light bomber aircraft with adequate range and armament carriage for operations in the mountains; a number of all-weather airfields with runways of adequate length; ATC; Met forecasting facilities; fuel, oil and armament storage; parking and manoeuvring areas and ground handling equipment and vehicles;
- Expanded training facilities and rapid induction of pilots, navigators, flight engineers and signallers.

In fact, the IAF had to quickly expand to at least 15 squadrons. As brought out in the chapter on Development of IAF Force Structures, the IAF managed to get these requirements only by the late 1950s. These shortages also seem to have influenced the thinking and options of the national leadership when Pakistan again held out threats of war in the 1950s.

The Sino-Indian Conflict, 1962

For nearly 14 years after the end of the first India-Pakistan war over Kashmir, India did not face war but unfortunately this long period was not used to strengthen its defences, especially along the Sino-Indian frontier. Sometime in 1957, to its utter horror, India discovered that the Chinese had already built a road in the Aksai Chin sector of Ladakh, an area claimed by the Chinese. A recently published account by Sidney Wignall – an Englishman – claims that he had in fact travelled to Tibet and gathered vital information about the Xinjiang-Tibet Highway and passed it on to the Indian Army, at least two years before the Chinese announced the building of the said road, but the Indian leadership did not take him seriously.[6] It was, however, too late to do anything about it. India nw decided to beef up its army presence in the border areas and this required an even larger air maintenance effort on a daily basis. Many generations of aircrews of the IAF transport fleet cut their teeth in these operations, wich became the virtual lifeline for the troops deployed in the forward areas. Maintaining the army and civilian population of the forward areas by air supply alone also gave rise to the need for helicopters, as many of the posts and villages were inaccessible to fixed wing aircraft; the dropping zones were too small and often located on muntain tops, such that even a slight error due to strong winds resulted in the precious loads rolling off the hill slopes. Narrow valleys that often abruptly ended in a cul-de-sac presented serious challenges for the supply-dropping aircraft flying at the limits of their performance. Although the Border Roads Organisation (BRO) came up in the late 1950s, surface roads and infrastructure took a very long time to develop, with the result that the task of air maintenance increased with every passing year. Moreover, fixed wing aircraft could not be used for casualty evacuation from remote posts. (Please see Appendix V).

The newly founded (October 1, 1949) People's Republic of China (PRC) showed its hand when it invaded Tibet in 1950, with the ostensible aim of reunification of territories that it had allegedly lost to imperialist forces during its period of weakness. In one stroke, India's northern borders that had until then seen no threat from the peaceable Tibetans, became alive to possible Chinese expansionism. As if to add insult to injury, the PRC maps showed vast areas of India, in fact the whole of he North East Frontier Agency (NEFA, now Arunachal Pradesh) and large parts of Ladakh as Chinese territory. When India pointed out this erroneous depiction of India-China borders Zhou En-Lai, the PRC premier in a dubious reply said that the maps were old and needed to be revised, giving the impression that the maps would be corrected. Soon, however, the PRC howed its true colours and repudiated the McMahon Line that formed the border between the two countries. India signed a trade agreement in April 1954, giving up all its privileges in Tibet under which India had carried out trade, maintained Post and Telegraph Department facilities and enjoyed freedom for its citizens to cross into Tibet without any visa requirements. India surprisingly demanded nothing in return. Such professions of good faith and good neighbourliness fell on deaf yearsand the PRC soon began engineering border incidents with Indian border police and guards who were invariably unarmed. The first such incident occurred "when shortly after the 1954 agreement, the two sides began to contest the ownership of a grazing ground called Bara Hoti in the middle sector"[7] on the Uttar Pradesh (UP)-Tibet border but was amicably resolved and perhaps lulled India nto a false sense of security.

Four years earlier, Sardar Patel, the then Home Minister and Jawaharlal Nehru's deputy had, in a much-talked-about letter in October 1950, raised the issue of a possible threat from the PRC, but it was ignored, as India was vigorously and assiduously cultivating Chinese friendship. In another lesser-known letter to Nehru, Patel had actually evinced his apprehensions of a Communist Chinese military threat as early as in March 1949, seven months before the founding of the PRC. Patel had also engaged in a discussion with the then Secretary General in India's External Affairs Ministry, Sir Girija Shankar Bajpai, an experienced former Indian Civil Service (ICS) officer, who also had similar apprehensions about China' expansionist behaviour. By the end of the 1950s, relations between the two countries had deteriorated to such an extent that there was open talk in the Indian media of a possible military conflict, and yet the decision-makers allowed themselves to be lulled into believing that whatever India said or did, *the Chinese would never attack*. India, by publishing the entire correspondence with China as white papers in 1960-61 to meet public demand and to garner its support, perhaps unwittingly made it even more difficult to find a mutually acceptable solution to the border problem. The Chinese had apparently wanted the negotiations to remain confidential.

In the absence of a clear directive from the government, the IAF was not quick to address the problem of poor access to the remote border areas and somehow managed to acquire in the mid-1950s, an assortment of helicopters. The American Sikorsky S-55C in 1954, Bell 47G, S-62B and Russian Mi-4 were inducted from 1954 to 1960. These played an important role in taking vital supplies to our beleaguered troops when the crisis erupted. The Bell light helicopters evacuated casualties in dangerous situations and often faced Chinese small arms fire. For various reasons that are still not fully explained, the IAF contribution during the Sino-Indian border war of 1962 remained confined to the use of helicopter and transport aircraft for casualty evacuation and air supply.

The IAF had moved some Toofani squadrons to reinforce the combat assets in the East but their serviceability was poor.[8] By 1962, the IAF in fact possessed some 23 combat squadrons comprising Hunter, Mystere, Toofani and Vampire, and Canberra light bomber aircraft suitable for air interdiction and photo reconnaissance. (For details please see Appendix I) Air Marshal Randhir Singh who commanded No. 106 PR Squadron and flew a Canberra PR aircraft on a photo reconnaissance mission over Aksai Chin in Ladakh and the border areas of NEFA, found that the Chinese were well entrenched along the McMahon Line and could be seen living under proper but temporary huts and tin sheds.[9]

There are many plausible reasons for the IAF not being used in an offensive role. The official history of the 1962 Sino-Indian Border Conflict claims that Air Commodore H.C. Dewan, then Director of Operations at Air HQ, had said that due to the mountainous terrain air power would not prove useful and yet some fighter squadrons were moved to Bagdogra, Tezpur, Jorhat and possibly Chhabua. Late Air Marshal Y.V. Malse, however, strongly refuted this claim and categorically said that the IAF combat aircraft were ready to enter the fray. Malse, in fact, himself flew a sortie in a Hunter trainer aircraft to recce the areas along the McMahon Line.[10]

Air Marshal Subroto Mukherjee, the first Indian Air Chief, had enjoyed a good relationship with Nehru but he had passed away in November 1959. Air Marshal A.M. Engineer, who succeeded Mukherjee, apparently did not enjoy the same equation with the Prime Minister. According to Randhir Singh, although Air Marshal A.M. Engineer was present in person at Jorhat to brief him (Randhir Singh) for his photo reconnaissance mission and was obviously in the know of developments on the ground, his advice was apparently not sought or, worse, disregarded. He, as a member of the Chiefs of Staff Committee, would have attended all meetings and frequently interacted with V.K. Krishna Menon who, till the end, did not believe that the Chinese would actually attack. Menon was known for his brusque and condescending ways and often dismissed the advice of the military top brass. It seems that Engineer, who did not enjoy a good equation with the Defence or Prime Minister, was simply sidelined. It is also well known that when tensions rose, Menon ordered that minutes would not be recorded at any meetings that he had with the Chiefs. As a result, there are no official records of what exactly transpired at these meetings.

B.C. Roy, the then Chief Minister of West Bengal, is also reported to have advised Nehru to refrain from bombing Chinese positions for fear of retaliation against Calcutta (now Kolkata). This concern about the risk of cities being bombed, was to heavily influence the thinking that led to the decision not to use combat air power during the war with China in 1962. As discussed in Chapter 3 another influential person to advise Nehru against the use of combat air power was the then US envoy at Delhi, John Kenneth Galbraith, but this advice came only three days before the ceasefire. Galbraith's advice was based on many other considerations, the most important of which was to avoid inadvertent escalation.[11]

Apparently, the Indian Army also did not brief or formulate joint plans with the IAF but Lieutenant General S.P.P. Thorat, who relinquished his post as the General Officer Commanding-in-Chief of the Eastern Command (then based at Lucknow), only in May 1961 and had been in charge of the defence of NEFA from around 1960, claims that the Army Chief General K.S. Thimayya directed 'Exercise: Lal Qila'. All the Principal Staff Officers at the Army Headquarters and some very senior Air Force officers were present at Lucknow for this exercise in March 1960, to assess, understand and devise ways to thwart a possible Chinese attack across the northern borders. Thorat had a serious difference of opinion with Menon on the implementation of the so-called 'forward policy'. He stated: "Advised by Lieutenant General B.M. Kaul, he (V.K. Krishna Menon) wanted me to organise the defences for NEFA in very close proximity of the McMahon Line, with which I entirely disagreed."[12] It would have been obvious to anyone that deploying our troops in penny packets without mutual fire support and assured logistical backup strung all along the border would be suicidal; but since both the Prime Minister and Menon strongly believed that there would be no war, it was impossible to convince them of the folly. Some writers have unfairly said that senior military officers did not give adequate options or alternatives to the political leadership even after having seen evidence to the contrary.[13] Another author candidly writes about how Y.B. Chavan, the next Defence Minister, succeeded in saving the reputation of the Prime Minister by ensuring that all the flak was directed at Menon and Kaul who undoubtedly deserved it. Nehru was, however, not very happy when Chavan accepted Kaul's resignation and tried to reinstate him in some other appointment and sacked Menon only when the Executive Committee of the Congress demanded Menon's head and implicitly threatened an open rebellion against Nehru if he did not agree.[14] It is also clear that neither Menon nor Nehru paid much attention to the needs of the military since they were hoping to avoid a clash through diplomacy; Menon said this in so many words. There is also no evidence of the Minister of Defence or Prime Minister ever sitting together with the top military brass to discuss the Chinese threat.

Earlier in 1948, Nehru was quite happy to discuss details of the various operations in J&K during the 1947-48 war, with Mountbatten and all the British senior officers of the army and air force, along with the then Defence Minister Baldev Singh, Deputy Prime Minister Sardar Patel and Rajaji (C. Rajagopalachari) in the Emergency Committee of the Cabinet, later Defence Committee of the Cabinet. Why then did he not speak with his own Generals or Air Marshals? Was it out of distrust? Did he think the Indian military brass was not competent to advise the government? Was Menon the main reason for keeping vitally important information from the Prime Minister? A year and a half after his retirement, Thorat was called to personally brief Nehru. During this meeting, Nehru carefully read Thorat's recommendations for the defence of NEFA and asked why these plans were not shown to him before the Chinese attack. To which Thorat said that the question should be addressed to Defence Minister V.K. Krishna Menon.[15]

Two inferences can be drawn from this narrative. The political leadership was over-confident and misread the Chinese signals by rigidly refusing negotiations, even when India's claims in Aksai Chin were not unassailable. Nehru strongly and sincerely, if innocently, believed that a Chinese attack on India would lead to immediate intervention by the Great Powers to avoid a world war.[16] Secondly, there was simply no one among the senior officials to forcefully argue against the strongly held views of Menon, Mullick and Nehru and as a result of 'group think'[17] no one else could offer any way out. It is little wonder then, that in this air of doom and utter confusion, no one ever thought of employing air power to thwart or at least check the Chinese advance. Given Nehru's towering personality and larger than life persona no Air Marshal, however courageous, could have confronted him and invited humiliation.

Absence of communications, infrastructure, roads, readily actionable intelligence about the actual capabilities of the People's Liberation Army Air Force (PLAAF), inter-service consultations and joint planning, greatly diminished the chance of India even giving a fair and equal fight in NEFA. Shortage of helicopters, transport aircraft and most importantly, a complete absence of resolve on the part of the national leadership are some of the major lessons of this war. A dysfunctional civil-military interface, a print media baying for the blood of the Defence Minister, and India's inability to read Chinese signalling, made it impossible to put up a coherent response and the poor ill-clad and ill-equipped jawan (Hindi for soldier) paid the price for these blunders.

In spite of these glaring deficiencies, three years later, India was once again caught on the back foot. Pradhan reports that Y.B. Chavan made a concerted effort to raise the morale of the armed forces by first embarking on a long-term programme for the re-equipment and modernisation of the army and the air force. He began daily morning meetings with the three Service Chiefs and the Defence Secretary where a number of issues were discussed, solutions found and actions initiated. Above all, Chavan ensured that minutes of these meetings were ready by three in the afternoon every day, which should have facilitated action on a war footing. He was also worried that the Chinese might launch another attack once the mountain passes opened the following summer.[18] In July 1963, India quickly reinforced its posts in Sikkim to prevent the Chinese from advancing into North Bengal from the Chumbi Valley and cutting off Assam and the North-eastern states. Both the army and air force were to be expanded; the army with three mountain divisions and the air force with 20 additional squadrons. Recruitment of officers for the two services and their training facilities were expanded. Pakistan, it seems, kept a close watch on these developments and struck, taking full advantage of the Indian preoccupation, before any major expansion plans came anywhere near fruition.

Indo-Pak War, 1965

The 1965 Indo-Pak War should actually have begun in November 1964, when both sides fought a ferocious encounter at Tithwal; or in April 1965, when Pakistan intruded into the Kutch sector and claimed territory; or at least when forward posts in Kargil and Haji Pir pass changed hands in August; and lastly, when Pakistan sent in intruders under its plan codenamed Operation Gibraltar on August 5,1965 into the Kashmir Valley, but did not because India tried its utmost to avoid an all-out war for which it was not ready.

India's policy to avoid war till the very last moment is indeed laudable, but that should not have stopped its political and military leaders from preparing contingency plans for a possible conflict if diplomacy failed, as it finally did. In the early hours of September 1, 1965 Pakistan struck at India's jugular, the Chhamb salient in close proximity of the main road linking Kashmir with the rest of India; an obvious target. The Chhamb-Jaurian salient extends north-westwards from the bridge at Akhnoor on the road to Kashmir and this was the major objective of the Pakistani assault. Here again, geography favoured Pakistan as it could maintain a sizeable force in the near vicinity, whereas India under the United Nations (UN) proposals was not allowed to keep any major army units close to the Ceasefire Line (CFL) in J&K. Strangely enough, India again failed to anticipate this threat.

On the afternoon of September 1, 1965, Y.B. Chavan, the Defence Minister, was discussing air force modernisation plans with Air Chief Arjan Singh, when General J.N. Chaudhuri barged into his office and demanded immediate air support to stabilise the situation in Chhamb, where the army was under immense enemy pressure. Air Marshal Arjan Singh was expecting such a request and had readied a sizeable force of fighters at Pathankot, a forward airbase close to the scene of action. Chavan gave the go-ahead and in less than 45 minutes, some 12 Vampires and 14 Mystere IVA fighter bombers were heading to the area as the sun was setting, and this adversely affected their visibility. The IAF succeeded in halting the Pakistani armour, but lost three pilots and four Vampires in air encounters with the Pakistani Sabres. While the IAF claimed some 10 enemy tanks and a number of guns and other vehicles, it also caused damage to its own forces. Such fratricide was inevitable, for there was little briefing and/or prior planning. The loss of four Vampires in the very first air action was naturally a shock, but considering that the Vampires were no match for the Pakistani Sabres, they should not have gone without fighter escort; but that is hindsight. Pakistan Air Force (PAF) radars had far better coverage and the Sabres used that to full advantage. It is said that the plan was to send only the relatively faster Mystere, but the Vampire Squadron Commander argued and won the privilege of leading the first strike of the war. The first two Vampire formations did in fact return unscathed.[19]

It is surprising that although the IAF had known of the Pakistani attack early that morning, it still chose to await a formal request by the Army Chief, General J.N. Chaudhuri. The two new Chiefs were both experienced professionals, yet there were no prior consultations. As has happened again and again with disturbing regularity, the Indian Army continues to keep its plans close to the chest, and demands that the air force jump into the fray at the last minute, simply because it has tended to treat air power only as a bonus. Probably because it does not fall under its direct purview, the IAF too, is not proactive in keeping tabs on the day-to-day developments in forward areas and offering its support, even at the risk of being brushed off. IAF says that-safeguarding the land borders is not its mandate. Even the official history, which remains classified, but is freely available on the internet, is silent about why there was such total absence of army-air force consultations, especially when the three Chiefs of Staff, according to Pradhan, were supposedly meeting the Defence Minister *every morning*, unless that practice had fallen into disuse as happens with most Indian schemes. India was once again absolutely and completely surprised. Air action remained restricted to the Chhamb area for the next four days during which the IAF drew its first blood, when the tiny Gnats flown by Squadron Leader Trevor Keeler and Flight Lieutenant V.S. Pathania, shot down a Sabre each on September 3 and 4.

To relieve Pakistani pressure, India, as per its oft-repeated threat, now decided to open a second front across the International Border in Punjab. This, however, did not happen for five full days. The IAF also did not mount an offensive until the 7th morning, but only after the PAF had launched devastating strikes on IAF airfields on the evening of the 6th. Apparently, due to heavy losses, daylight counter air operations against each other's airfields by both sides were discontinued after the first day, with this task being taken over by IAF Canberra and PAF B-57 light bombers by night. These night attacks did not prove very effective, but caused much nuisance and in the case of the IAF, further aircraft losses on ground.

The IAF flew a total of 3,937 combat sorties of which Combat Air Patrol (CAP) over own airfield consumed nearly a third – 1,352 sorties. Inadequate radar cover and close proximity to the border of IAF airfields, and perhaps a defensive mindset were the main reasons for this.

In 1965, India lost 75 aircraft with 37 of these being lost on the ground, compared to PAF's 19. PAF losses were perhaps far higher. Air Chief Marshal Arjan Singh on a post-war visit to Peshawar noticed signs of severe damage, but Pakistan was able to effectively camouflage it. The PAF destroyed 10 IAF aircraft at Pathankot in a single attack, and 10 at Kalaikunda in two strikes, on the same morning (September 7). The IAF committed a blunder by first striking Chittagong in East Pakistan without any cohesive overall plan and then, not retaliating to PAF strikes on Kalaikunda, Barrackpore, Bagdogra and Agartala, because by mid-day September 7, Delhi had forbidden all offensive action against East Pakistan. Not only was there little joint planning or coordination between the army and the air force, IAF's Offensive Air Support (OAS) to the army was also not appreciated, as it did not seem to change the course of events or cause serious damage to the enemy except in Khemkaran. As a veteran of this war succinctly put it:

> My impression about all air operations, whether in the East or West, was that nobody seemed to know what to do. According to me, the level of professionalism at all levels was extremely low and I do not exclude my own performance. The lessons learnt in 1965 were all negative ones – in other words, what not to do should there be another conflict. These lessons were so numerous and cogent that they were more valuable than any positive lessons.[20]

A damning indictment, if there ever was one.

The major lessons of this 22-day-long war can be summarised as follows: Inadequate radar cover forced the IAF to devote a disproportionately large effort to CAP sorties over its forward airfields located close to the border; Pathankot being a mere two minutes flying time away.

Absence of covered bomb-proof shelters commonly known as Blast Pens resulted in excessive loss of aircraft on ground. After the first few days of the war, the IAF began the practice of pulling back most of its fighters to depth airfields like Ambala after their last sortie of the day, for night halt. Ambala had some 50 Gnats and many more Hunter and Mystere aircraft lined up on the tarmac. According to Air Marshal Randhir Singh, the Gnats at Ambala were feeding the three 'active' squadrons, Nos. 2, 9 and 23, then fighting from Pathankot and Halwara. At one time, there were nearly 100 aircraft at this base, when the PAF B-57 dropped bombs which fortunately skipped in the wrong direction and hit the cathedral nearby. If the bombs had skipped in the other direction, we would have lost a huge number of aircraft on ground in a single attack.[21]

The PAF B-57 night raids were a serious nuisance as the crews could not get enough rest, but these strikes, often inaccurate, also destroyed a number of aircraft on ground. For example, on September 12-13 night, in four raids over Jamnagar, India lost a Hunter trainer, and a Dakota at the Repair and Servicing Unit (R&SU) hangar. Some 23 bombs fell in residential military quarters. On 13-14 night, two Vampires, one Dakota and a Hunter were destroyed.

At Jodhpur, which was raided frequently, the damage was little, as there were no operational aircraft based here and the damage to runways and installations was slight. Soon after the war, it was decided to move the Air Force Flying College away from Jodhpur, but it took nearly five years before the Air Force Academy at Dundigal near Hyderabad was ready for use. When the author's course which was terminated for a month recommenced at Jodhpur, there was no evidence of any damage by the enemy.

At Adampur, the bombs hit a fuel dump and the fire could have been a beacon for further strikes but none came. A Mystere, along with a refuelling browser was destroyed at Pathankot. Thirteen of the 37 aircraft lost on ground were bagged by B-57 night raids. At Khem Karan, the PAF Sabres took a heavy toll on the Indian Army. Eleven Sherman tanks were destroyed and some 200 men of Mahar and Gorkha regiments were killed, captured or wounded.

IAF Mystere fighters flew so low that these aircraft sometimes came back with overhead High Tension (HT) cables in their under-wing pylons. Such was the apprehension of enemy fighters that all pilots were flying at ultra-low levels, 40-50 feet off the ground. Lack of radar cover added to this fear, as there was no warning. The enemy Air Defence (AD) also took a big toll of our aircraft on Close Air Support (CAS) missions, because the pilots also carried out multiple passes, for example five passes by the then Flight Lieutenant Vinod Patney who admitted to being 'reckless' but lucky all the same. Flight Lieutenants Micky Jatar, P.C. Chopra, Vinod Patney and Jimmy (V.K.) Bhatia (later Air Marshal) were members of the charmed formation that came back unscathed after every mission.

There were some shining examples of selfless sacrifice by civilians. Chaman

Lal, a civilian fireman at Gurdaspur railway station, won the Ashok Chakra for disconnecting the two tankers on fire from the rest of the train, but in doing so lost his life.[22]

A Combat Air Patrol (CAP) is often needed for daylight activity such as own convoy movement or advance/retreat of own ground forces, rail and road movement of stores. Forward Air Controllers (FACs), operating with own ground forces can then direct friendly fire and warn own troops and aircraft of the presence of enemy fighters. This becomes critical if we have not been able to neutralise offensive capabilities of the enemy air force or in other words, not achieved a Favourable Air Situation (FAS). Although many offensive sweep missions were flown by the Gnat and MiG-21 squadrons, these did not prove effective as the enemy simply waited until these had vacated the area and then pounced on our troops. The war also proved that to be successful, the air force must resort to sustained offensive action.

The F-104, F-86 Sabre-Sidewinder combination initially inhibited IAF options. Although the F-104 did not prove effective in intercepting IAF Canberra night attacks, these remained risky because unlike the United States (US)-built B-57 version of the English Electric Canberra, the Indian Canberra did not have an ejection seat for the navigator, who was obliged to bail out manually; a near impossibility in an emergency.

CAS to the army was also not effective, due mainly, to the archaic communications and demand procedures. Each IAF forward airfield had a Ground Liaison Officer (GLO) but his information and briefings were invariably poor, as he was not getting updated information from his army Corps/Formation Headquarters. Although the IAF interdicted enemy trains carrying ammunition, vehicle convoys, armour and even troop concentrations and launched many 'search & destroy' missions, the army said it was bombing the wrong targets and hence, these strikes did not support ground action.

Soon after the war, the IAF began building blast pens at all its forward airfields and completed this task by early 1968. More forward airfields were built at locations, even closer to the border, and these were invariably provided a parallel taxi track of about the same length as the runway, for landing and take-off, if and when, the main runway became unusable due to enemy bombing or other reasons such as landing accidents.

Another possible reason for a less than optimum relationship between the army and the air force was that until 1965 the Chief of Army Staff (COAS) was a full four-star General whereas the Air Force and Naval Chiefs were of the rank of Air Marshal and Vice Admiral respectively; a rank lower than the COAS. Soon after the war, Defence Minister Y.B. Chavan removed this glaring anomaly. In the 1950s and 1960s, the age-old tradition of demanding and offering respect and deference to age, seniority and experience was in evidence across all organisations. Born in 1908, General J.N. Chaudhuri was 11 years older than Air Marshal Arjan Singh. Air Chief Marshal P.C. Lal draws a vivid pen picture of the army chief.

> Whether or not the use of the air force would have turned the Chinese tide is difficult to say. The point to note is that the 1962 war saw our military competence at its lowest ebb. This was largely because an over confident Defence Minister (Menon) set out to direct the war on his own, putting hastily assembled troops without the benefit of consultation or advice and assistance from the Chiefs of the three Services. Air Marshal A.M. Engineer, the Chief of the Air Staff at the time, was an extremely frustrated man in consequence.
>
> Except for minor variations, this story was repeated in 1965, though by then Krishna Menon had been gone for nearly three years from the Ministry of Defence. The Defence Minister was Mr. Y.B. Chavan, a strong and silent man who restored *constitutional rule* in the Armed Forces, with the Chiefs of Staff being given the consideration that their positions deserved and the assistance that their Services required.
>
> This time there was another dominant personality to reckon with: General J.N. Chaudhuri, Chief of the Army Staff (COAS). A tall, handsome cavalry man, educated in England, trained for the Army at Sandhurst, with battle experience gained in World War II, well-read, much travelled, with a highly sophisticated taste in clothes, food, music and fine living, a witty raconteur and conversationalist, ebullient and full of confidence in his own abilities, he had led the military operations that secured the State of Hyderabad for India in 1948 and Goa in December 1961. By 1962 it seemed that he had been passed over by Mr. Krishna Menon for the top job in the Army. The Chinese came to his rescue as they did to mine! Along with Krishna Menon went General P.N. Thapar, who had the misfortune of being the Chief of the Army Staff when the Chinese came into India. General Chaudhuri, with his record of successes and impressive personality, was just the man for the job of reviving the Army's morale and the country's fortunes. Soon after becoming the COAS he also succeeded to the Chairmanship of the Chiefs of Staff Committee. This came about when Air Marshal Arjan Singh succeeded Air Marshal A.M. Engineer as the Chief of the Air Staff and Vice Admiral S. Soman succeeded Vice Admiral R.D. Katari as the Naval Chief about the same time.[23]

General J.N. Chaudhuri also did not come out of this war unscathed. Lieutenant General Harbaksh Singh, the Western Army Commander, openly defied him when he was ordered to pull back his forces to the East of the Beas

River. Chaudhuri also invited criticism when he allegedly feared low ammunition stocks whereas in reality there was no such dearth.[24]

Offensive spirit and audacious action together, often pave the way to success. To illustrate the point: During the 1965 war, East Pakistan had only one Sabre squadron, but it played havoc by destroying a total of 12 precious aircraft of the IAF in just four strikes; proving what a single squadron can do if the enemy is clueless, careless, confused and disorganised. In retrospect, the IAF should not have attacked targets in East Pakistan; but once begun, should not have stopped but gone on relentlessly to destroy the PAF assets based there. The IAF had adequate assets to achieve that in the Eastern theatre. By the time the ceasefire came into effect at 3.30 am on September 23, 1965. India's total losses were 3,621 killed and 8,444 wounded. The dead included 359 missing.[25]

Pakistan claimed the destruction of 104 Indian aircraft and admitted a loss of only 19. Of these, 35 were claimed in air-to-air combat and 34 were destroyed on ground; all, except four, to Sabres and the remainder to F-104s. Only two, Lowe's Canberra and Devayya's Mystere were confirmed F-104 kills. Pakistan's claims were highly exaggerated. It claimed five over Halwara when in fact only two, Pingle and Gandhi, were shot down; but not before they had shot down one each of the attacking Sabres. Only 18 aircraft were actually lost in air-to-air combat.

There was also little army-air force coordination in assessing claims of the anti-aircraft artillery units of the army. Army gunners often claimed a kill when they saw Sabres dropping their external fuel tanks. Most Indians believe that 1965 was a stalemate, but the armed forces certainly succeeded in thwarting Pakistan's plans to wrest control of Kashmir by force, albeit at heavy cost in men and material. The IAF and the Indian Army had also managed to blunt the offensive capability of the enemy by destroying 250 US-made Patton tanks. Even so, the IAF could have done much more. According to Sam Manekshaw, the army failed to cash the blank cheque that the Indian Government had issued, by declaring that any attack on J&K would be met by a similar attack across the International Border (IB) in Punjab. Another army officer called it a clear case of missed opportunities.[26]

In the 1965 war, the IAF fielded the only MiG-21 squadron (No. 28), five Mystere IVAs (Nos. 1, 3, 8 31 and 32), three Hunters (No. 7, 20 and 27), two Gnats (No. 23 & 9) and two squadrons of Vampires (45 and 220) and three Canberras (5, 16, and 106) on the Western front. The successful Canberra strikes on Peshawar and Badin became part of the Canberra legend. No 5 Squadron alone flew 150 sorties. One Hunter squadron (No. 37), and one Canberra squadron (No. 16), were moved from the Eastern theatre to the West, but were hardly used since the war ended soon after their arrival.

This shows that the IAF used only 16 combat squadrons for actual operations whereas it possessed a total of 25 squadrons. At an average serviceability rate of approximately 70-75 per cent, this translates into a little under one-third of the strength of the air force. The IAF could well have caused far more damage to the enemy if all its assets had been fully employed. The corollary is that a small, but determined and audacious air force, (such as the single PAF Sabre Squadron at Dacca, now Dhaka) can change the complexion of any conflict and this is true even today.

In their book on the war, P.V.S. Jagan Mohan and Samir Chopra write:

> As part of the agreement reached at Tashkent under the auspices of the Soviet Union, Pakistan and India agreed to the establishment of diplomatic relations, halting of hostile propaganda, and restoration of economic and social ties. India gained little from the Tashkent Declaration, except six years of uneasy peace; India was forced to hand over all the captured territory (including the strategically important Haji Pir Pass in J&K. India's main objective of having Pakistan labelled as the aggressor was also not achieved. The Tashkent Declaration only ensured a return to an unsatisfactory status quo.[27]

As brought out above, this 22-day war ended inconclusively but India achieved its limited objective of stopping Pakistan from wresting Kashmir by force and its army captured a sizeable chunk of Pakistan's territory which had to be returned under the Tashkent Agreement. India's Prime Minister Lal Bahadur Shastri showed firmness and resolve in dealing with Pakistan and his government withstood the combined pressure of the Western bloc for an early ceasefire and repeated Chinese threats on the northern border. The outcome of the war would have been different had the Indian Government and the three Service Chiefs made detailed joint plans to meet Pakistani aggression especially after the Kutch episode.

Bangladesh Liberation War, 1971

It is now over four decades since the 1971 India-Pakistan War that resulted in the birth of Bangladesh. Whichever way one looks at this event, it added a glorious chapter to India's independence history. Every air force veteran that this author has spoken to now, and in these over 40 years, readily agrees that it was indeed a high watermark in the history of the IAF. Much has been written about this surprisingly short 14-day war but the current generation of young members of the air force and sister services, need to be told that no one really expected Pakistan to capitulate in such a short time.

The official history records a short conversation which went something like this:

> When asked by a senior air force officer as to why he had surrendered when his army was intact, General Niazi, the Pakistani Army Commander

> in Dacca pointed at the wings on the chest of this officer and said, "because of this, you, the Indian Air Force". At first glance this might appear a gross over-simplification of the events and an exaggeration of the role played by the IAF but on deeper reflection it is an accurate description of the short war.[28]

The IAF attained total air superiority or control of the skies over the country in just 48 hours by effectively neutralising the PAF assets at Dacca, which consisted of only a single F-86 Sabre squadron, some 20 aircraft and a few T-37 trainers. The IAF, on the other hand, had 11 fighter-bomber squadrons in the Eastern theatre. It was no doubt an uneven contest, but total control of the air over East Pakistan again proved the old air power adage: 'With air superiority anything is possible; without it everything is at risk.' The IAF, soon after putting the runways at Dacca's Tezgaon and Kurmitola airfields out of action, began to provide the Indian Army with all kinds of support. It carried our relentless strikes on enemy positions, destroyed bridges, river barges and boats, ammunition dumps and generally made it extremely dangerous for the enemy to think of any concerted counter attacks. The IAF transport fleet not only carried out a battalion-size para-drop over Tangail, north of Dhaka, without a hitch, but its Mi-4 helicopters flew an astonishingly large contingent of the army, some 3,000 troops across the mighty Meghna River, to hasten the capitulation of the Pakistan Army.

So proactive, intense and whole-hearted was the IAF's role in these operations – codenamed Cactus Lily – that it left little room for complaints or bickering. Such was the speed of the Indian Army's advance that the participants themselves, and the leaders and decision-makers in Delhi, and indeed, the world were totally stunned. While it is difficult to single out an operation for special credit, the hastily mounted strike by four rocket-firing MiG-21 fighters on the Government House at Dhaka at about noon on December 14 that turned the tide of the war, would surely be one such. Here it is in the words of Wing Commander (later AVM) B.K. Bishnoi:

> On 14th December I had just returned from a close-support mission in the morning from Mainamati Cantonment when Group Captain Wollen came rushing to our operations room and said, "Bhoop, a very critical and urgent task has come from Air HQ. There is a very important meeting going on at Circuit House, Dacca and this building needs to be attacked at 1120 hrs."
>
> I told him that, first it was already 1055 and it required 21 minutes to be at Dacca and then "Where in God's name is the Circuit House located in Dacca?"
>
> He said, "If you hurry up you can just about make it. Here, I have tourist map of Dacca and here, next to this road crossing is the Circuit House."

I looked back at him, the Circuit House was part of a densely populated area of Dacca and from the air one could see hundreds of road crossings, how was one to pick that one? I simply said, "Yes Sir, it shall be done." I borrowed that map from him to be taken along and with this, search for that Circuit House after getting overhead Dacca.

For this mission I was taking four MiG-21s loaded with 32 high explosive rockets each. I was strapped in the cockpit of the aircraft and started the engine, just when I saw one of our Flight Commanders waving a paper and run towards me. "Sir, this is for you." It read, "Target is Government House, repeat Government House and not Circuit House". Confirm understood. Best of luck and good shooting. Mally."

"I raised my thumb to confirm that I had noted the change. I quickly scanned the tourist map in my lap and located the Government House and taxied out. At this stage I did not inform of the change to the other three members of my team which consisted of Flight Lieutenant Vinod Bhatia, Flight Lieutenant Raghavachari and Flight Lieutenant Malhi as I did not want to announce this on R/T for the whole world to know."

"(We got) Airborne and as we were approaching Dacca and had barely a minute to go, I gave the new target to my numbers 2, 3 and 4. I described the rough location of the target and asked them to look for it. Flight Lieutenant Bhatia spotted it first, calling that the target was at 11 o'clock, 500 yards away. It was a magnificent old styled palatial building with a high dome, situated in the middle of a lush green compound. There were quite a few vehicles inside the entrance gate".

"I did a "chakkar"[29] around it to reconfirm its identity and then ordered the attack taking the building from broad side. I aimed at the room below the dome, others took on other portions. We did two passes each and fired 128 rockets into the Government House."

"By the second attack smoke and dust could be seen rising from many locations from the abode of the mightiest in East Pakistan. It obviously broke the backbone of the civilian government. Two days later General Niazi, the Supreme Commander of the Pakistan Military in East Pakistan was to surrender to the Indian Defence Forces along with 93,000 troops."[30]

This successful strike was followed by two MiG-21s and two Hunters, to ensure that this vitally important target was indeed fully destroyed. "This sudden and spectacular attack carried out with pinpoint accuracy destroyed a third of the Government House and caused severe damage to the rest of the buildings. It so completely unnerved and demoralised the persons present at the meeting that the Head of the East Pakistan Government Dr. A.M. Malik along with his entire

Cabinet resigned then and there."[31] This attack also proved that 'decapitation' of national leadership might work in certain circumstances. Although it took three more days for the formal surrender, the war in the East was effectively over.

India had decided to maintain a defensive posture with the sole aim of 'holding the front,' simply to prevent Pakistan from gaining large chunks of Indian territory, but that was easier said than done. Maintaining a purely defensive posture all along the long International Border (IB) and the ceasefire line in J&K was nearly impossible, because it meant spreading out troops along the entire length of the IB, not knowing when and where the enemy might strike. Some contingency actions would no doubt have been planned, but at the national level the aim was to maintain the status quo. Pakistan started the war with a pre-emptive air strike at 1740-45 hours on December 3, 1971 on some of the forward airfields of the IAF. The attacks appeared to be half-hearted and failed to cause any significant damage, to any runway or installations. The IAF had learnt its lessons from the 1965 conflict. At most bases, its aircraft were under bomb-proof shelters and/or were widely dispersed. Improved radar cover, regular exercises, drills and close liaison with the railways and other civilian agencies had ensured a far more efficient and conducive air defence environment. The IAF retaliated on the same night with Canberra strikes on some PAF air bases. Air Chief Marshal P.C. Lal, the then Chief of the Air Staff had given very clear instructions that the army would be given full support.

The main objectives of the IAF were:

(a) To defend the home base against enemy air attacks;
(b) To support the army in the field, and to take all actions to achieve a Favourable Air Situation over the tactical area, besides carrying out Counter Air Strikes, carry out interdiction and armed recce having a direct bearing on the outcome of the land battle;
(c) Carry out necessary reconnaissance missions;
(d) Provide air transport support;
(e) Provide maritime air support to the navy.[32]

In reality, the IAF finally expended very little effort on counter air missions and strikes on special/strategic targets such as the Karachi harbour, the Sui gas plant, the hydro-electric power station at Mangla Dam and oil refineries at Attock, although these attacks did not have any immediate effects in the short war. These strikes, also did not in any way, reduce the IAF's effort in support of the army, a persistent complaint of the previous war. The two most noteworthy exploits on the Western Front were the total decimation of a Pakistani armoured regiment in Longewala, and the spectacular strikes on the Karachi complex. The experienced and specially selected aircrews of the newly formed Tactics and Air Combat

Development Establishment (TACDE), located at Ambala, carried out single aircraft night attacks on PAF air bases with MiG-21 and S-22 aircraft. Although they dropped only two 500-kg bombs in each attack, they caused much nuisance and even frustration to the enemy; and except in one case, all of them returned unscathed.

Major Lessons of the War

Although the IAF emerged with flying colours, there were some important lessons:

The Radius of Action (RoA) and armament carrying capacity of the IAF fighter bomber fleet was extremely limited, and this constrained its freedom to attack depth targets. Even so, Hunters and S-22s bombed rear airfields such as Peshawar, Sargodha, Shorkot Road (Rafiqy) and others.[33] This, counter air campaign, was given up due to high attrition and negligible damage to the runways.

The Canberra could carry up to 4,000 kg (or 8×1000 lb.) bombs whereas all the other aircraft could barely carry two 500-kg bombs. Their range restricted their choices for evasive action and freedom of manoeuvre to engage the enemy if needed; the limited bomb load meant insignificant damage to concrete runways and hardened installations, except when attacks were repeated in quick succession. Limited range also precluded 'tactical routing', enabling the enemy air defences to easily pick up IAF fighters and lie in wait for them. The PAF also mounted offset CAPs away from the airfields, giving full freedom to the anti-aircraft guns to engage IAF attackers, and allowed the PAF interceptors to convert their height or potential energy into speed, by diving while chasing the intruders. This once again showed PAF's emphasis on training with the United States Air Force (USAF). After the war, the IAF concentrated on developing new and innovative tactics at the TACDE and regularly conducted courses for training fighter leaders. The PAF air defence network, especially radar and visual observers, proved quite effective. Another shortcoming due to limited range was the inability of the IAF to provide dedicated fighter escort to strike formations.

The newly acquired Soviet Sukhoi S-22 also called Su-7, was used both for OAS and counter air missions. Most pilots tended to carry out multiple passes over the targets, thus exposing their aircraft to lethal small arms and anti-aircraft fire. As a result, the IAF lost many S-22 aircraft in these operations, especially on the Western Front. Electronic Warfare (EW) capability was then non-existent. The MiG-21 had a rudimentary Radar Warning Receiver (RWR) while the non-Soviet fighters did not have even that. The K-13, the only air-to-air missile (AAM) in the Indian inventory, was carried by the MiG-21 (Type-77) but proved totally ineffective at low altitudes.

Tactics and Air Combat Development Establishment (TACDE), then a newly raised unit, was equipped with the MiG-21 and S-22. The highly experienced and hand-picked pilots of this new unit, carried out low-level single aircraft missions against Pakistani airfields by night. On reaching the enemy airfield, the anti-aircraft batteries invariably put up a barrage and gave away the exact location, thus facilitating the strike but since these fighters carried only two 500-kg bombs each, the damage they caused was not very significant. These strikes, however, had a huge nuisance value, as they kept the enemy awake and on alert every night. Considering these single-aircraft missions were totally unprotected, their losses were minimal. This was a bold and innovative employment of a short-range fighter/interceptor.

In the six years since 1965, the procedures and signal communications for army-air coordination/cooperation had improved. Radar cover was still patchy. The Srinagar Valley and parts of Rajasthan were still without radar cover.

The Surface-to-Air-Missile (SAM-II) (NATO Code Name Guideline) was designed to engage only high-altitude threats, and while these might have forced the enemy to fly at low levels, these missiles were not really effective; some seven of these were fired without success. These were sited mainly for the defence of large and important cities, such as Delhi, Agra and Chandigarh but a determined enemy could have got through.

Use of forward airfields at Sirsa, Jaisalmer, Nal, Utarlai and Amritsar helped mitigate, to some extent, the problems of range and time over target, but staging through these Forward Base Support Units (FBSUs) as they came to be called, added to maintenance and logistical difficulties. Except in a few cases, aircraft were not regularly pulled back to rear bases.

The IAF was also forced to carry out a large number of reconnaissance sorties as very little information was available about PAF airfields, since the IAF could not obviously enter Pakistani air space prior to war. Recce sorties were also flown for Bomb Damage Assessment (BDA) by single unescorted fighters, mostly the Su-7, with no self-protection except the integral guns. Although the recce requirements of the army were invariably met, there was no feedback from the army on its efficacy. The IAF had since the 1965 war managed to phase out some old types such as Vampire, Toofani and Mystere. Their replacements, mainly the MiG-21 and the S-22, although more modern and capable of very high speeds, lacked range.

Although strategic and special operations constituted only 1.4 per cent of the total effort, their results were often spectacular. The attacks on oil refineries and storage tanks at Karachi and Attock, the hydro-electric power station at Mangla Dam, and the Sui gas plant in the west and the very short notice strikes on the Government House and the Radio Station at Dhaka were notable for their success. The Tangail para-drop and the helicopter-lift of a brigade – 3,803 troops and 100 tons of other loads in 400 sorties – across a river in record time, are the other examples of the IAF's notable achievements.

This 'feint' of a major heli-lift by night was successfully attempted when the noise of many Mi-4 helicopters and the heli-lift of 4/5 Gorkha Rifles troops from Kailashahar to a point north of Surma river effectively locked up two Pakistani brigades at Sylhet and Maulavi Bazar. War is after all a game of defeating the enemy by all means available. This was possible due mainly to smart thinking at the local level. The IAF once again used an excessively large effort for CAP missions. The airfield at Bareilly in western UP, was also provided CAPs to protect aircraft movement; a totally avoidable waste of effort. Although Western Air Command (WAC) deployed a few Gnats for the air defence of the Srinagar Valley, their success was limited on account of poor visibility and non-availability of a radar set.

In 1971 too, the single Sabre squadron based at Dhaka took more than two days to be neutralised, and that too, only when the runways at Tezgaon and Kurmitola airfields were damaged beyond repair. The IAF no doubt attained total air superiority but against just one enemy squadron. Similarly, on December 14, 1971, a single attack on the Government House in Dhaka did not kill the East Pakistan leadership, yet it forced the enemy to surrender in less than two days. Although the Indian Army had only some 3,000 troops in the vicinity while Pakistan had over 30,000, their morale was completely shattered and hence they surrendered.

Nineteen seventy-one was indeed IAF's finest hour. The victory showed that in the post-1965 period, much work was done to hone our skills and streamline inter-service relations and procedures. Most important, the nearly eight-month-long warning period was also fruitfully used for military preparations and for garnering political support of many friendly countries.

In the victory celebrations that followed, many deficiencies were glossed over or simply forgotten. When this author asked the then Station Commander at Srinagar immediately after the end of hostilities why our squadron was not given the necessary administrative and logistical support, his laconic reply was, "There are no courses of instructions for Station Commanders". (All of us felt that the planners at Headquarters WAC and Air Headquarters were unaware of the actual conditions in the Srinagar Valley: poor visibility, poor communications; non-availability of the Awantipura runway as a diversion, which resulted in the Gnats having to keep extra fuel to divert to Udhampur; restriction on the total number of Gnats that could be based at Srinagar; the total absence of radar cover in the Valley and did not realise our frustration at our inability to successfully intercept the PAF intruders. (Please see Appendix VI). At the strategic level, it seems no one really knew or cared about what role the IAF elements were expected to play in the larger scheme of things. It is often said that the national aim was to fight a 'holding battle' in the Western Sector. India was more or less successful in blocking Pakistani attempts in Baramulla, Chhamb, Sialkot and Rajasthan sectors, but it is equally true that it did not use the opportunities that presented themselves to strengthen or consolidate the CFL, in the critical state of J&K. Inadequate joint planning and consultations between the army and the air force and the general lack of interest of the political masters, were perhaps the cause for this sub-optimal outcome on the Western front.

Sri Lanka, 1987-90

Begun with a promise of quickly ending the Tamil-Sinhala conflict in Sri Lanka, India's intervention proved ineffective, and extremely costly. The IAF flew a total of 70,000 sorties mostly to provide helicopter support to the army; fixed wing transport for airlift of stores and victuals; and only a few Mirage-2000 fighter sorties at the very beginning of the war. This time too, the services did not find it necessary to formulate a joint plan. The IAF was asked to provide transport and helicopter support which it did admirably, but as in the past, the IAF learned its lessons and continuously innovated and modified its tactics as the conflict progressed. Besides massive fixed wing transport support for the army, the IAF helicopter fleet played a vital role in providing tactical mobility to the army. It also performed commendably in the casualty evacuation role. On many occasions, the IAF helicopters came under small arms fire of the Liberation Tigers of Tamil Eelam (LTTE) insurgents that caused damage to the Mi-8 rotor blades. The LTTE was rumoured to possess the deadly shoulder-fired heat-seeking anti-aircraft missiles, but luckily this proved to be untrue. Given the thickly forested terrain, the low-flying helicopters would have been extremely vulnerable to such weapons. It is also possible that the LTTE did not use these missiles for fear of further escalation.[34] The major shortcoming of this military intervention, however, was a total absence of joint planning, poor intelligence and the gung-ho attitude of the top army and political bosses.

Maldives, 1988

India reacted with alacrity to a Save Our Souls (SOS) from the President of this tiny island neighbour and in a matter of 15 hours, airlifted a para battalion to Hulule, the only airfield close enough to Male – the other airfield at Gan with a longer runway being 400 km away. While the operation was concluded quickly without any loss as in many earlier cases, neither the IAF nor the army had any intelligence, or even estimates of the strength of the rebels, their actual location, or knew whether the airfield at Male was indeed in rebel hands. According to a knowledgeable source, the operation could easily have ended in disaster, if the rebels had simply blocked the Hulule runway with a few heavy vehicles. The operation, in which the lumbering Il-76 planes carrying the crack troops of the Indian Para Brigade landed in the dead of night, without any runway lights and only limited radio contact with the ATC, could well have ended in disaster. The operation would have been much more challenging if the troops had faced major opposition on landing. Absence of intelligence seems to be the leitmotif of all Indian military operations but the information provided by the Indian Ambassador to Male who happened to be in Delhi, when the emergency arose, proved to be very useful to the aircrews of the Il-76, and the CO of the para battalion (6 Para Commando).

Kargil, 1999

Since the end of the 1971 Bangladesh war, the IAF did not employ its combat elements for 28 years, until the 1999 Kargil border war with Pakistan. This localised conflict, however, went on for over two months, and threw up a number of important lessons. The IAF lost a total of three fixed wing aircraft and one helicopter in the first three days, and was forced to change/modify its weapon delivery tactics. These changes were necessitated for two main reasons: the availability of US-supplied shoulder-fired Stinger anti-aircraft missiles with the enemy, and the unusually high altitude and the very small size of enemy targets. The enemy having entrenched its troops in well protected and camouflaged 'Sangars' or makeshift battlements of rock, found it easy to rain fire from dominating defensive positions, onto the Indian troops who were forced to mount frontal attacks after first climbing near-vertical rock faces. The IAF used laser-guided bombs and rockets and continuously modified its attack patterns to improve accuracy. Low density, strong winds and very low temperatures together substantively altered the trajectory of these air-delivered weapons, which in turn affected the predictability and sighting/aiming methods for successful engagement. Even so, in almost total white-out conditions, and often by night, the IAF fighters delivered devastating fire on the enemy and completely destroyed the main enemy logistics base at Munto Dhalo, which was otherwise inaccessible to Indian ground troops. From May 26 to July 12, the IAF fighter-bombers flew a total of 1,200 missions; comprising 580 strike, 460 air defence and 160 reconnaissance missions. In addition to a large number of fixed-wing transport sorties, flown to provide tactical and strategic mobility, the IAF helicopters flew some 2,500 sorties, transported 800 troops, rescued 600 casualties and airlifted 300 tons of material for the ground forces. Army aviation helicopters also flew a large number of sorties for communication, casualty evacuation and tactical recce. According to one senior army officer, Kargil was mainly an artillery war, where the 155mm Bofors howitzers played a vital role.[35] The main aim of the enemy, of interdicting the Leh-Kargil highway was effectively thwarted. India suffered a total of 517 killed and over 1,200 wounded.

The major lessons of the two-month-long border war can be summarised as follows:

- India was once again surprised by the Pakistan Army's audacious and, as proved later, foolhardy attempt to infiltrate some five battalions of its regular troops alongwith a few jihadi fighters across the Line of Control (LoC) in the Kargil sector of J&K. All five battalions reportedly came from the Northern Light Infantry consisting of troops recruited from Gilgit-Baltistan (earlier called the Northern Areas) of Pakistan-occupied Kashmir.
- The Indian Army did not detect these intruders until they were reported by civilian nomadic 'Gaddi' shepherds, since all of these posts were vacated during the winter months.
- It is claimed that Indian intelligence had reported unusually high activity around Skardu in the winter months of 1999, but these reports were not seriously acted upon.
- The army demanded that the IAF employ armed helicopters to engage the well-entrenched enemy. The IAF was initially reluctant to use helicopters as these were not suited for high-altitude offensive operations and were vulnerable to enemy small arms fire and Man Portable Air Defence Systems (MANPADS). In the event, 16 rocket-equipped Mi-17 sorties were launched but these did not prove very effective and one helicopter, not equipped with IR flares was lost to enemy MANPADS.
- The IAF also believed that use of offensive air power added a new dimension to the conflict and that this was likely to lead to escalation and hence needed prior approval of the government, which came only on May 26, 1999.
- The Indian Government also restricted the air operations to our own side of the LoC, which cramped the freedom of manoeuvre of the high speed fighters.
- Almost all the strike missions were provided an air defence escort to keep the PAF out of the fray. While a few PAF F-16 fighters were sighted, there was no aerial engagement as the enemy aircraft stayed well away from the combat zone.
- The IAF like the army, alerted almost all its units and stations located in the Western Sector and was ready for a wider conflict if it had escalated. Pakistan characteristically and unsurprisingly called this over-reaction on the part of India.
- As in the past, Pakistan not only surprised India but also forced the Indian military to fight at a place and time of its choice, thus severely constraining India's options.
- The IAF had not given adequate attention to air operations in the high mountains.

- Absence of prior consultations between the army and air force resulted in avoidable bickering and heartburn.
- The IAF lost a MiG-27 to technical problems, and enemy Stingers shot down a MiG-21 and a Mi-17 and severely damaged one engine of a Canberra on a photo recce mission.
- While remaining on own side of the LoC certainly earned India some diplomatic advantages, it also severely affected the efficacy of air power.
- In the future too, the IAF might be called upon to employ its offensive air power according to such restrictive Rules of Engagement and as one recent book has claimed, IAF performance may once again be termed as *marginal*.[36]

Air Power Lessons from Other Wars

Arab-Israeli Wars

Since its birth in 1948, Israel has fought four major wars and numerous skirmishes with its Arab neighbours. The Israeli Air Force has invariably been in the vanguard of these conflicts. Israel is often criticised for overreaction and use of disproportionate force, but its leadership insists that eternal vigilance and military readiness are the only guarantors of its survival in the midst of hostile Arab countries. It used the fledgling air arm in the 1948 and the 1956 Suez Crises, but it came of age in the '1967 Six-Day War,' when in just three hours on the morning of June 5, 1967, it decimated the Egyptian Air Force in pre-emptive strikes before it could even get airborne. Simultaneous strikes were carried out at 8.30 am when it was breakfast time for the Egyptian Air Force men and most of its senior leadership was on its way to work. There was much tension and Egypt, Syria, Iraq and Jordan were probably planning to attack Israel. By striking first, the Israeli Air Force caught them napping and attained total air superiority in a matter of hours, which finally helped bring the war to an end in a mere six days. In the end, Israel claimed 452 Arab aircraft destroyed, of which 49 were in aerial combat. The IAF lost only 20 of its aircraft. Only after it had achieved total air supremacy in the first two days did it focus its attention on the enemy's ground forces when it effectively broke the Egyptian Army, at the Mitla and Giddi passes, destroying seven Egyptian divisions with 1,000 vehicles (including 800 tanks). The Arabs had apparently learned no lessons from the Indian experience of 1965 and had failed to protect their airfields against surprise air attacks. "The inability of the Arab air forces to survive air attacks on their bases resulted in their effective destruction within two days."[37]

Yom Kippur War, 1973

Six years later, however, Egypt and Syria chose to strike when most Israelis were celebrating Yom Kippur, a national holiday. The Israeli Air Force played a key role in containing the Syrian Army's surprise attack on the Golan Heights when Israeli ground forces were still in the process of deploying for the war.[38] Even so, it soon turned the tables on its enemy. The Egyptians had, with Soviet assistance, built a formidable air defence umbrella employing older SA-II & III, mobile SA-VI Surface-to-Air Missiles (SAMs) and shoulder fired SA-7 Strella MANPADS. Initially, the Israeli losses were heavy but the Israeli Air Force overcame these defences with ingenuity and clever use of Electronic Counter Measures (ECM) and evasive tactics. It lost five aircraft in aerial combat and 104 aircraft to anti-aircraft fire and SAMs. It claimed a staggering 334 enemy aircraft in aerial combat, and a further 180 due to other causes. The Arabs relied too heavily on their missile-based air defence system and lost many of their aircraft to fratricide. The Israeli Air Force suffered heavy attrition in the opening phases of the war, and had to stop offensive action for some time but eventually gained air superiority.

In another surprise attack on June 7, 1981, the Israeli Air Force destroyed an under-construction Iraqi nuclear reactor located a mere 20 km from Baghdad. The strike involved flying a round trip of over 1,800 km over Saudi Arabia and Jordan. It used eight F-16s with two Mk-84 bombs each, escorted by four F-15 fighters. Israel claimed it had carried out the attack in self-defence, as in its view the Iraqi reactor was on the verge of becoming operational.

Lebanon War (Bekaa Valley), 1982

This time Syria had with Soviet help built up a formidable and overlapping network of SAMs of various types in Lebanon's Bekaa Valley. In a coordinated artillery and air attack, the Israelis destroyed many Syrian SAM batteries in a matter of minutes. In the air battles that followed, the Israeli Air Force shot down 86 Syrian aircraft for the loss of just one of its own. This unprecedented kill ratio of 86:1 has not been achieved before or since. The secret of Israeli success, however, was the effective use of ECM that blinded the Syrian radars and rendered its Command and Control System, deaf and dumb. In addition, AH-1 Cobra helicopter gunships destroyed a large number of Syrian T-72 tanks and other armoured fighting vehicles. Again on October 1, 1985, in response to a Palestine Liberation Organisation (PLO) terrorist attack that killed three Israeli civilians in Cyprus, the Israeli Air Force bombed the PLO Headquarters in Tunis, a distance of 2,300 km using air-to-air refuelling.

Lebanon War, 2006

The Israeli Air Force again played a critical role in this conflict that lasted 34 days and was waged mostly against Hezbollah, with the aim of stopping its rocket attacks on Israeli civilian targets. On the second day, the Israeli Air Force destroyed a large number of Hezbollah rocket sites. The air force lost two helicopters to mid-air collision on the last day of the war.

In September 2007, in yet another surprise attack, the Israeli Air Force destroyed a Syrian nuclear reactor. A specially programmed Unmanned Aerial Vehicle (UAV), similar to the US Suter airborne network attack system, had apparently sent an embedded bug as part of the reflected radar echo, to one of the Syrian air defence radars. This false echo had in turn disabled the entire Air Defence (AD) network for a considerable period of time to allow the Israeli Air Force strike aircraft to enter Syrian air space without detection. The Israeli Air Force also carried out a number of surgical strikes against Hamas in the Gaza Strip.

The one major lesson of all Arab-Israeli conflicts, is the decisively offensive nature of Israeli employment of air power. The Israeli Air Force has been heavily criticised for causing extensive collateral damage and civilian casualties, but to be fair, Israel has also lost many civilians to terrorist and indiscriminate rocket attacks. Even if one does not subscribe to its aggressive philosophy, Israel has shown the grit and determination, to not just survive, but prosper in a neighbourhood that does not acknowledge its right to exist. The Israeli Air Force with consistent American support is probably the most experienced and potent air arm in the world.

US Air Power in Vietnam, 1964-75

Conventional wisdom says, that the US lost this long and costly war despite the use of sophisticated aircraft and hi-tech weaponry. There is much truth in this statement. The war, however, has many lessons for air power operators, as it saw the use of massive air power in every conceivable role. From aerial reconnaissance to air cavalry, from strategic bombing to combat search and rescue, and from strategic lift to special operations, the war saw extensive employment of air power. Air power proved ineffective against a determined enemy bent on waging a guerrilla war, with little concern for own well-being. The Communist regime of North Vietnam under Ho Chi Minh and its military, led by the legendary General Vo Nguyen Giap was so well indoctrinated and motivated, that it finally forced the US military out of Vietnam with heavy losses of men and material. US casualties numbered a staggering 58,000 dead and wounded. The North Vietnamese air defence based mainly on Soviet AM II Guideline first generation missiles and MiG-21 fighter interceptors, also took a major toll of American aircraft. Very often, US air power was micro-managed from distant Washington, where decision-makers such as Robert McNamara, an eminent economist, often dictated the selection of targets, go-no-go areas, and used air power in fits and starts, giving ample opportunity to the enemy to recoup its losses and devise new tactics. Operation Rolling Thunder, Linebacker I and II and later vertical envelopment tactics, by using a variety of helicopters, contributed to the larger aim even if these succeeded only at the tactical level.

In a memorable post-war conversation, Colonel Harry G. Summers told his North Vietnamese counterpart, "In this long war, you did not win a single battle." The laconic reply was, "True, but it does not really matter, we won the war."[39]

China-Vietnam War, 1979

The PRC began this war in March 1979, ostensibly to teach the Vietnamese a lesson for invading Cambodia, which was then under PRC-supported Khmer rule. The Central Military Commission (CMC) mobilised a very large number of army formations and also a sizeable section of People's Liberation Army Air Force (PLAAF). In the event, the PLAAF was in such poor shape, that in the absence of adequate number of trained and experienced aircrews (pilots) many Squadron Commanders from different regions were forced to take command of the fighting units. The PLA army's performance was below par and although the Chinese managed to make incursions into the border areas of Northern Vietnam (which had a large population of Chinese origin) they found it difficult to hold ground and finally withdrew after an agreement was signed between the two sides. It is generally agreed that instead of teaching the Vietnamese a lesson, the Chinese themselves were taught a lesson. The major lesson of this otherwise short localised war was how not to commit air power. In 1979, the Chinese military was in poor shape – its equipment was old, training was unremarkable, conscripts had little combat experience and the PLAAF was averaging very little flying training, as it simply did not have enough aircraft. Almost all squadrons were equipped with Soviet-era machines, which were plagued with spares shortages and major maintenance difficulties. China was then producing a large number of aircraft of old design with very limited range and armament, obsolete electronics and above all, poor reliability. It also seems that the PRC leadership underestimated the enemy resolve. China did not follow a very sound strategy but soon realised its folly, and quickly withdrew while the going was good. That the Chinese who had all along mentored the Vietnamese could not correctly assess the strong points of the adversary is indeed surprising.[40]

The Falklands War, 1982

On April 2-3, 1982 Argentina invaded and occupied the South Atlantic British Territory of Falklands (Malvinas) and South Georgia. The conflict lasted 74 days and ended with the surrender of Argentinian forces. Casualties were heavy on both sides. The then British Prime Minister Margaret Thatcher, the 'Iron Lady', warned the Argentine leadership of war, if they did not immediately vacate the occupation of the Falklands; but the Argentine military leadership, especially Admiral Jorge Anaya, a member of the ruling junta, made the mistake of convincing themselves that Britain will never attack. That Britain could pull off an operation of this magnitude, 7,500 km away at the other end of the Atlantic, was indeed laudable and speaks volumes for the resolve of the British Government, whatever the verdict at this distance in history. The British, under the leadership of Margaret Thatcher, did not dither for a moment, even when it became clear that the operation would prove extremely costly in men, material and money. Whether or not the gains of victory outweighed the costs is – with the benefit of hindsight – a moot point. The sheer scale and the scope of the effort, transporting two brigades and marines across the world, and sustaining them with the necessary logistic support, is without parallel in post-World War II military history.

The major lessons of this war are as follows:

- In a series of five single-aircraft missions, the Royal Air Force (RAF) Vulcan strategic bombers bombed the airfield at Port Stanley and rendered it unusable for Argentine jet fighters, thereby assisting the RAF and Royal Navy to gain some control of the air. On the way to the Falkland Islands on a 15,000-km round trip, the bombers conducted multiple air-to-air refuelling operations; the Victor tankers themselves taking fuel from other Victor tankers in a 'buddy' role.
- As many as 24 of 26 enemy ships were sunk or disabled, in air action. The average distance of the Argentine airfields on the country's mainland was 700-1,050 km and this restricted their armament load and time over target. Due to intense anti-aircraft fire, the Argentine pilots released their bombs at very low levels, not giving the fuses time to function properly. As a result, many of these bombs did not explode but a live unexploded bomb stuck in the innards of a ship, was still a serious hazard and caused casualties. An Argentine Super Etendard of French make fired an AM-39 Exocet missile at the *HMS Sheffield* and sank it. Three ship-based British helicopters also sunk the Argentine submarine *Santa Fe,* that was caught on the surface. With the sinking of the light cruiser *General Belgrano* by the Royal Navy's nuclear-powered submarine, the *HMS Conqueror,* 323 sailors died but 700 more were rescued in cold and stormy weather. Thus the threat posed by the Argentine Navy was effectively eliminated.
- The British Task Force sailed out within three days of the Argentine invasion.
- This war clearly brought out the difficulties of launching a major operation at far-off places but also proved what aircraft carrier-based air power could achieve against heavy odds. The British had a total of 42 Harriers as against 122 Argentine fighters of various types including Mirage IIIs, IAI Dragons, A-4A Sky Hawks and the turbo-prop-powered Pukara COIN aircraft.
- The British lost 24 helicopters and 10 Harriers, in addition to two destroyers, two frigates, two amphibious crafts and one container ship. Two hundred and fifty eight personnel were killed and 775 injured. The Argentine forces lost a light cruiser, a submarine, four cargo vessels, two patrol boats, 35 fighters, 25 helicopters, two bombers, four transport planes

and 34 COIN and lightly armed trainer aircraft. Argentina also sustained 649 casualties, 1,068 were injured and over 11,300 were captured.

Gulf War, 1991

Being the first major war after the disastrous experience of the decade-long Vietnam War, the Americans wanted to validate the new found doctrine of air power employment, which postulated that a relentless stream of offensive strikes against the major 'centres of gravity' of the enemy would be needed to break the will of the enemy. The US-led Allied air forces were to first mount a 'Suppression of Enemy Air Defences' or SEAD campaign to reduce to the minimum, any possibility of enemy air forces interfering with own strategic strikes/operations. It was only after the enemy's offensive capability both in the air and on ground had been comprehensively degraded, that the US ground forces would be released with full air support. Fighters and attack helicopters would be on call at a minute's notice or when required would provide airborne stand-by.

There was widespread condemnation when Saddam Hussein's forces marched into Kuwait on August 2, 1990. There soon began a massive airlift that saw a slow but steady build-up of troops, aircraft, armament and equipment in Saudi Arabia. By August 15, the US had sent 48 F-16 and 36 F-15 fighters to Saudi Arabia, which immediately began patrolling the Iraq-Saudi border to prevent Iraqi incursions into Saudi Arabia. Strangely, Saddam failed to employ Iraqi air power to disrupt the Coalition build-up that went on for months. The United Nations (UN) Security Council authorised a US-led Coalition of 34 countries to oust the invading Iraqi forces from Kuwait.[41] This was the first major war that was broadcast live on TV screens across the world and the role of the electronic media came to be known as the 'CNN Effect'.

Coalition air strikes began on January 17, 1991 with a variety of aircraft taking part from airbases in Saudi Arabia and neighbouring Arab countries, ship-borne aircraft from the Persian Gulf (two US Navy carrier battle groups) and some from bases in Europe and continental US or CONUS. Two more US Navy ships were dispatched to the region and another 48 F-16 fighters of the US Air National Guard also moved to Saudi Arabia. By the end of the year (1990) some 540,000 US troops had been stationed in Saudi Arabia. The Coalition Air Forces flew more than 107,000 sorties dropping 88,000 tons of bombs and other weapons. Precision Guided Munitions (PGMs) constituted only 8 per cent of all ammunition dropped in the war. During the first 38 days of the Gulf War nearly 100,000 sorties were flown, 226,000 munitions dropped and 1,200 targets engaged. This gives a clear idea of the size of each package,[42] the number of times the same targets were engaged and the limited efficacy of the destructive power of free-fall bombs and unguided munitions.

Although the Coalition airpower destroyed some 340 hardened bomb shelters and rendered almost all the Iraqi airfields unusable, 200 bomb shelters and a substantial portion of Iraqi aircraft remained undamaged. Many of the Iraqi fighter aircraft escaped by flying out to Iranian airfields, and remained there, as the Iranians naturally refused to return them at the end of the war. It is difficult to understand why the Iraqi leadership permitted the country's assets to go to Iran, with whom Iraq had fought an inconclusive war for eight years. This once again proves that mere acquisition of fancy aeroplanes and weapons, cannot be a substitute for national resolve and determination.

Iraq's tactic of employing Scud missiles in random attacks against Israel aimed at breaking the Coalition, failed to provoke that country to action but diverted considerable air effort to Scud hunting operations. USAF pilots in a post-war analysis found that Air Tasking Orders (ATO) were invariably delayed, and this entailed the aircrews working late into the night throughout the war. Another important lesson was that all knowledge of the enemy's strengths and weaknesses must be gathered well before the beginning of the war, as once the shooting starts there is little time to learn new tactics.

Kosovo, 1999

Kosovo was acclaimed as the most successful air campaign ever. "A turning point in the history of warfare," wrote the noted military historian John Keegan, positive proof that "a war can be won by airpower alone."[43] In fact, the 78-day (March 24 to June 9, 1999) US-led North Atlantic Treaty Organisation (NATO) air campaign against the Serb forces in Kosovo was largely ineffective. NATO claimed that its fighter aircraft flew a total of 37,465 sorties of which nearly half were strike and SEAD operations, with another 10,808, for strike and attack. NATO fighters engaged Serb military targets and claimed the destruction of 120 tanks, 220 armoured personnel carriers and up to 450 artillery guns and mortars. Kosovo ostensibly began to throw the Serbian military out before UN peace-keepers could be sent. Air power it seems, offered the option of a clean and relatively bloodless war. The air strikes were expected to achieve this aim in a short period of time, without the need for the army to undertake any ground operations. But by publicly announcing this strategy in the opening phases of the air campaign, the US President Bill Clinton gave away NATO's plans, and relieved the Serb leadership of much anxiety and preparations for dealing with a full-fledged ground invasion. In reality, only a fraction of Serbian armour was actually destroyed. The Kosovo Force (KFOR) counted 250 tanks, 350 Armoured Personnel Carriers (APCs), and 650 artillery pieces returning to Yugoslavia, or leaving Kosovo, at the end of the war. NATO aircraft also bombed high value targets such as bridges and power stations and power lines in Belgrade and other civilian areas. It was when his people went without water and electricity that the Serbian leader,

Slobodan Milosevic decided to withdraw his Serb troops from Kosovo. But this might have been counter-productive for two reasons. First, the "Serbian population which was desperately dependent on the well-being of its infrastructure was made to pay the price for Milosevic's deeds". Second, it was the European members of the NATO that would pay to rebuild the shaken country.[44]

The Serbs made extensive use of camouflage, concealment and decoys (using logs and aluminium coated card board cut-outs) which fooled the striking pilots who, in order to remain outside the enemy SAM envelope, were carrying out their attacks from medium levels of around 15,000 feet. A large number of PGMs and cruise missiles were used; the latter often going haywire due to some ingenious methods adopted by the Serb defenders. A cruise missile is pre-programmed to fly at a height of some 20-30 metres above ground, at subsonic speeds. These missiles depend on their temperature and altitude sensors to maintain correct course and height and are equipped with a terrain-following radar to avoid obstacles. By lighting small fires along their expected track, the Serbs successfully misled many of these hi-tech missiles. NATO did not lose even a single pilot as the crews of the F-117 stealth fighter, F-16 and two AH-64 attack helicopters, lost to enemy action/other causes, were quickly rescued by the readily available Combat Search and Rescue teams. Some 700 SAMs and MANPADS were fired but proved largely ineffective against the high-flying NATO aircraft. Equally, only a few of these SAM sites were actually destroyed. Some seven MiG-29s and a few Galebs of the Serbian Air Force were shot down in aerial combat, with no loss to NATO aircraft. These Russian fighters were hampered by poor serviceability and unreliable avionics.

As was shown earlier during the Bosnian campaign, it is impossible for modern high-speed jet fighters to target small armed groups of people, indulging in violent activity, for example, ethnic cleansing. NATO planners should have concentrated on targets of strategic importance rather than Serb army tanks, artillery, APCs and mortars, which in the absence of a ground invasion could be hidden without fear of being seen. Even so, in a TV interview, Milosevic showed no intentions of backing down in the face of sustained bombing, until the Russians announced the withdrawal of their support, giving rise to further criticism of air power ineffectiveness. Unfortunately, some air power protagonists claimed that 'modern air power could alone win a war'. There was also much bickering among NATO members on target selection, mainly due to fears of unduly high collateral damage and loss of civilian life and property. In short, this air campaign proved very costly in terms of air effort. Although the Serbs were finally forced to leave Kosovo, it was not due entirely to the air strikes. In the words of Supreme Allied Commander Europe (SACEUR), General Wesley Clark, the "most decisive moment came when the Russians stopped supporting Serbia"[45] indicating that air operations were indeed ineffective.

To be fair, part of the blame must lie with the wrong strategy of placing excessively high reliance on air power alone, and publicly declaring that NATO did not envisage a ground invasion. In the words of Elliot Cohen, "Air power is an unusually seductive form of military strength, in part because, like modern courtship, it appears to offer gratification without commitment."[46] This view poses a major challenge to air power operators because policymakers often see air strikes as a low risk, low commitment option. When weighing the balance of ground and air forces, policy makers must consider not only what they seek to accomplish through coercion, but also what they seek to prevent. Successful coercion requires not only effective threats but also the neutralisation of adversary responses.[47] Air power contributed to pushing the Serbs out of Kosovo, but it was a hollow victory as it did not prevent the Serb armies from forcing out and murdering the hapless Kosovars. The activities of the Kosovo Liberation Army (KLA), a militia-type outfit and Russia's diplomatic pressure forced Milosevic to finally pull out his forces from Kosovo. This was one clear example of how air power should not be used.

Gulf War, 2003

Unlike the first Gulf War which was somewhat open-ended, and stopped with the surrender of the Iraqi Army, this war was waged with the specific aim of ousting Saddam Hussein. The US and United Kingdom (UK) leadership falsely claimed that Iraq possessed Weapons of Mass Destruction (WMD) which needed to be destroyed, urgently. In the event, no such weapons were found. The absence of post-war stabilisation plans turned a very successful military campaign led by formidable air power elements, into a political quagmire of enormous proportions. It also spawned Sunni insurgency and Al Qaeda-assisted terrorism that destroyed Iraqi society, especially since the then US Secretary of Defense, Donald Rumsfeld, had refused to commit the minimum necessary ground troops to control the situation, once the Iraqi military and the Saddam regime were defeated. It also brought worldwide condemnation of the American policy of unilateralism and preventive war that the neo-conservatives of the George Bush regime had propounded. Another major air power lesson of this much-hyped campaign was the questionable value of the 'campaign of shock and awe'. Even the civilian population quickly adapts to these strikes, takes measures to minimise its effects, raises issues of collateral damage and human rights of non-combatants, and finally flees the urban areas for sheer survival. Air power can and often does put immense pressure on enemy governments, but unless follow-up action such as possible negotiating strategies, alternative regime rehabilitation and above all, power sharing options are fully thought out, a successful air power campaign can prove to be a pyrrhic victory. In the event, the US-led NATO forces got bogged down in a country, relentlessly devastated by internecine warfare between different ethnic and religious groups, jockeying for power.

The American and British air forces used a highly sophisticated array of PGMs supported by satellite-based communications and navigation (GPS) systems, that made it a truly network enabled war and dramatically reduced casualties. Weapons such as the then newly introduced Joint Direct Attack Munitions (JDAM) and later special measures to detect and destroy Improvised Explosive Devices (IEDs), received much acclaim. The NATO air forces also made extensive use of attack helicopters to hunt insurgents and terrorists planting IEDs. Surveillance and drone attacks by UAVs/Unmanned Combat Aerial Vehicles (UCAVs) respectively, proved both effective and economical. Last, but not least, like the first Gulf War of 1991 and the Kosovo war of 1999, US air power once again operated in a relatively benign environment, as there was virtually no air opposition.

Another major lesson of the two Gulf Wars, fought a decade apart (1991 and 2003), was that while force multipliers such as AWACS, Air-to-Air Refuelling (AAR) Tankers and satellite-based communication and navigation support systems, are absolutely essential for waging a high-tech war, they do not allow for any significant reductions to fighter inventories and to that extent, these systems multiply the 'effects' and not numbers. Force multipliers have not reduced the absolute numbers of aircraft, Su-30 vs. Hunter or even Canberra, although costs and weapons carriage and range are vastly different. All the recent wars that the Western allies have fought have been against very weak powers, at least in air power capabilities.

Afghanistan, 2001

The Afghan war began in October 2001 with the United States Air Force (USAF) bombing Taliban and Al Qaeda targets and has continued for 13 years with mixed results. In the aftermath of 9/11, when the US began bombing Afghanistan, it faced a whole host of questions. Sadly, many of them remain even today. First, the Americans did not know how to obtain access to this landlocked country, and once there, what targets to bomb. Fortunately for the US, the Northern Alliance, that was then fighting the Taliban regime proved amenable to US assistance, and the Central Intelligence Agency (CIA) renewed their old contacts and sent in a small number of agents who performed exceptionally well as Forward Air Controllers (FACs) when the US decided to open the bombing campaign. Not only was the bombing completely successful, despite some early setbacks, the Northern Alliance rallied round and soon pushed the Taliban out of Kabul, and eventually to the mountain hideouts of the Pak-Afghan border. But this did not change the ground situation, and then began a clamour for 'boots' on the ground. The US-led NATO forces have been in Afghanistan since 2006-07 with a major 'surge' in their numbers, beginning 2010 but success, if any, has been fleeting. Mainly due to Pakistani support to Taliban elements and Pakistan's persistent refusal to engage the Haqqani and other elements operating from Pakistani soil, the NATO air forces have been rendered largely ineffective. Intermingling of armed Taliban groups with the civilian Afghan population, makes it nearly impossible to effectively neutralise them from the air. This, however, should not be seen as a failure of air power, as the conflict is now apparently not amenable to any military solution.

For the last few years, NATO air forces have increasingly been relying on UCAVs or what are commonly called drone attacks, and have succeeded in eliminating a substantial number of Al Qaeda and Taliban militants, sometimes inside Pakistan's borders. Pakistan usually registers nominal protests of breach of sovereignty but tacitly allows the US to continue these strikes. Employment of UCAVs in a conventional war scenario may, however, require far more careful planning and execution, due to the presence of enemy and own air forces in congested airspace.

Libya, 2011

Being the most recent and major air campaign, employment of air power in Libya deserves detailed study. The 2011 NATO intervention in Libya was a success in several important respects: it helped topple Muammar Gaddafi's 42-year-old regime without the deployment of ground forces, with very low levels of collateral damage, and no NATO casualties.[48] France opened the air campaign on March 19, 2011 on its own and the UK joined soon thereafter. After the passing of United Nations Security Council Resolution (UNSCR) 1973 others joined the campaign but Germany stayed out. According to Adam J. Hebert, "If US and NATO air forces had not intervened in the Libyan civil war this year, Muammar Gaddafi would still be alive and Libya's ruling dictator." He says, "[T]housands of the civilians who had protested or taken up arms against his regime, however, would all be dead." That is airpower's contribution to the now-complete operation. In March 2011 before NATO air power intervened, "Gaddafi's forces were in the process of routing the rebels. Resistance forces had been pushed into an enclave at Benghazi, where many anticipated a last stand. Gaddafi himself promised no mercy to those who had opposed him." "NATO aircraft flew more than 26,000 sorties. There were nearly 10,000 strike missions, 90 per cent of them flown by nations other than the United States." As stated earlier, some of these were flown from RAF bases in the UK, and involved nearly 3,000 km return flights. As a joint operation conducted by some 18 participating nations, it was a major success for air power. Strike and other aircraft were launched from bases in several European nations and also from ships in the Mediterranean. The US only provided its naval forces in the Mediterranean, Intelligence, Surveillance and Reconnaissance (ISR) and Air-to-Air (AAR) support. "The operation lasted seven months, and was a relative bargain, costing the United States $1.2 billion."[49]

According to the Royal Aeronautical Society Paper on 'Operation Unified Protector', on the NATO air campaign:

- Lack of boots on the ground limited NATO's situational awareness which had to rely totally on ISR to gain and maintain the ground picture.
- Advocating non-invasive intervention through air is more acceptable than the presence of foreign troops on the ground. Committing ground troops is a truly momentous decision with major implications. Such campaigns are generally very lengthy and costly. The Iraq and Afghanistan examples are striking.
- Policing the no-fly zone (from 1991 to 2003) in South and North Iraq was relatively less expensive.
- Air forces should be ready to emphasise this advantage to the politicians, the public and other services.
- In seven months (March to October 2011) some 26,000 sorties were flown. Of these 25,000 were by fixed wing, 400 by rotary wing and 500 by Remotely Piloted Aircraft (RPAs) or UAVs/UCAVs. A total of 7,600 PGMs, 3,600 laser-guided bombs and 3,500 GPS-guided munitions/bombs were dropped.
- Superior training, especially on sophisticated aircraft, support infrastructure and correct targeting is the key that achieved desired effects. Weapon accuracy is futile without intelligence accuracy. Simply attacking and ticking off target lists does not work as happened in the NATO's Serbian (Kosovo) campaign of 1999. NATO did not understand the cultural importance of Kosovo to Serbia and it took 78 days of air power application and political pressure and (also the threat of a ground invasion) to get Milosevic to bow down.
- The Libyan air campaign took 227 days and hence quick results should not be expected. Communication with ground troops is very important or else ISR is useless.
- No plan works without amendments, tweaking, common sense and experience.
- Air-to-air refuelling played a key role in long-range strikes.
- No single NATO member could afford the full range of capabilities.
- Situational awareness is fundamental to operational success. ISR is vital. A clear understanding of 'Forward Line of Own Troops' (FLOT) or a 'no man's land' is vital to avoid fratricide. Close coordination with ground forces, use of Ground Moving Target Indicators (GMTIs) for tracking of regime vehicles, their movement, origin and direction and use of Litening Targeting Pods increased air power effectiveness.
- There was only one cautionary engine change in 3,000 hours of flying and even that engine was found undamaged. This speaks volumes for technology,

tactics and maintenance especially with austere base facilities.

- The French Air Force maintains flying training currency of its aircrews posted on staff so that they are immediately available for operations in an emergency. Although expensive, this confers surge capability when needed.
- British Tornados flew a total of 8,000 hours and 3,000 km-long sorties from bases in the UK.
- None of the crews had trained specifically for Libya but they were ready for it. Being prepared for any contingency and eventuality was dependent on good training and also on the agility of the approach and flexibility of the mind.
- Carrier aviation has much to offer including mobility, full range of spares support and maintenance support plus proximity but for all that air superiority is essential. Air and naval systems are complementary and together can offer great flexibility and capability in many cases.
- First strikes came just in time. Even a little delay and Gaddafi would have pulverised the rebels or would have caused far more bloodshed.
- The RAF Tornado squadron had just returned from an exercise in the US on March 14. The UNSCR was issued on March 17. The squadron prepared for Libya on 17-18 and launched its first Storm-shadow cruise missile strike from a UK base on March 19 that flew a 3,000-km round trip. This speaks volumes for RAF training, flexibility and operational readiness.
- As a result of the kinetic effects achieved, the Gaddafi regime stopped using armour and switched to civilian SUVs. Use of inert weapons worked to stop hostile action and kept collateral damage at low to nil level. Air weapons were often used to persuade rather than to kill, in what came to be called 'knocking on the door' strikes, in which inert weapons warned the enemy. Just four Brimstones destroyed eight regime vehicles in a single attack.[50]

The campaign lasted for nearly a year. This long and protracted intervention raised logistics, and economic costs and at times, stretched the willing contributions by NATO and other Arab countries. The air effort of over 26,000 sorties including 10,000 strike sorties was colossal and would be difficult for a single country. Without the signal contribution of the US, in providing surveillance, Airborne Warning And Control System (AWACS) tanker and intelligence support missions, the UK and French air forces would have found it nearly impossible to sustain a year-long commitment. Air power did not in any way preclude the use of ground forces – in this case anti-Gaddafi rebels – and even they had to be guided and trained by NATO Special Operations Forces (SOF) experts. The geographical proximity of Libya to NATO countries and the presence of coalition naval ships in the Mediterranean Sea, close to the Libyan coast also helped. Above all, Libyan Government Air Forces were neutralised in the first few days and NATO enjoyed complete freedom over the Libyan skies.

Conclusion

For all its ubiquity, flexibility and reach, air power should never be seen as a panacea for every situation. Air power assets will always be in great demand and therefore the tendency to employ them simply because these are seen to be idling on ground must be checked. As we have seen, gaining control of the air is undoubtedly a vital task, but it is only an enabling condition. Once achieved, the condition must be quickly used to prosecute other military tasks and missions or else the effort would be wasted. Simply carrying out medium or high-level offensive sweeps to entice the enemy to provoke it to fight might prove – though temporarily – that the enemy is reluctant to fight, but it may, in fact, be waiting for a more opportune moment to strike at more important and vulnerable targets.

Given the availability of AWACS and longer-range air superiority fighters with the IAF, the next conventional war might see a different and more efficient employment of air power resources and may, in fact, stop the enemy well before it reaches the border. The AWACS-AAR combination is also bound to dramatically extend the range and safety and success of IAF's strike missions deep into enemy territory. But such bold and sustained actions are unlikely for two reasons. First, it is still not clear if India's political leadership has really understood the impact of modern technologies like stealth, PGMs and/or Network Centric/Enabled Warfare. Unless India comes to terms with the essentially offensive nature of modern air power, there is every possibility that all the advanced combat aircraft, and combat support elements such as AAR, AWACS, PGMs and EW would once again be under-employed or not at all. Second, the chances of a conventional war appear to be slim and India might once again find itself inhibited by Pakistan's 'low' nuclear threshold. Even so, the IAF must train for operations other than a classic copy book conventional war.

NOTES

1. Air Marshal Bharat Kumar, *An Incredible War: Indian Air Force in Kashmir War 1947-48*, Knowledge World, New Delhi, 2007, pp. 203-04.
2. Lt. Gen. L.P. Sen, *Slender was the Thread*, Orient Longman, New Delhi, 1969, p. 61.
3. Ibid., p. 19.
4. Durga Das, *From Curzon to Nehru and After*, Rupa & Co, New Delhi, 1969 (Reprinted 1974), p. 251.
5. Interview with Air Marshal Randhir Singh (Retd.) at Chandigarh on January 15, 2012.
6. Claude Arpi, "The Englishman who Spied for India", June 1, 2012 at http://www.rediff.com/news/report/the-englishman-who-spied-for-india/20120601.htm, (Accessed September 9, 2012).

7. Srinath Raghavan, *War and Peace in Modern India: A Strategic History of the Nehru Years*, Permanent Black, Ranikhet, 2010, p. 243.
8. Interview with Air Marshal P. Rajkumar (Retd.) at Bangalore on February 12, 2011.
9. Interview with Air Marshal Randhir Singh, See no. 5.
10. Interview with Air Marshal Y.V. Malse on July 12, 2000. See also Air Cmde. Jasjit Singh, "The Role of Airpower" in Brahma Chellaney (ed.) *Securing India's Future in the New Millennium*, Orient Longman, New Delhi, 1999, pp. 99-123.
11. J.K. Galbraith, *Ambassador's Journal*, Hamish Hamilton, London, 1969, pp. 428-530.
12. Lt. Gen. S.P.P. Thorat, *From Reveille to Retreat*, Allied Publishers, New Delhi, 1986, pp. 213-15.
13. Srinath Raghavan, See no. 7, pp. ix-x.
14. R.D. Pradhan, *Debacle to Revival: Y.B. Chavan as Defence Minister, 1962-65*, Orient Longman, Hyderabad, 1998, pp.161-81.
15. Lt. Gen. S.P.P. Thorat, no. 12, p. 191. I have relied more on Thorat's views simply because Nehru called him after the debacle, patiently heard his side of the story and asked why Thorat's plans were not shown to him. Nehru also appointed Thorat on the National Defence Council which was chaired by the PM himself.
16. Srinath Raghavan, no. 7, p. 279.
17. Yaaov Vertzberger, 'Bureaucratic-Organisational Politics and Information Processing in a Developing State', *International Studies Quarterly*, 28, 1984, pp. 69-95.
18. R.D. Pradhan, no. 14, p. 25.
19. P.V.S. Jagan Mohan and Samir Chopra, *The India-Pakistan Air War of 1965*, Manohar, New Delhi, 2005 (Reprinted 2006), pp. 69-72.
20. Air Cmde. P.M. Wilson quoted in the *Official History of the 1965 India-Pakistan War*, p. 273 at http://www.bharat-rakshak.com/LAND-FORCES/Army/History/1965War/PDF/1965Chapter09.pdf, (Accessed July 14, 2012).
21. Interview with Air Marshal Randhir Singh. See no. 5.
22. P.V.S. Jagan Mohan and Samir Chopra, no. 19, pp. 234-36.
23. Air Chief Marshal P.C. Lal (Retd.), *My Years with the IAF*, Lancer International, New Delhi, 1986, p. 159. R.D. Pradhan also endorses these views, see no. 14, p. 23. Also see Lt. Gen. Harbaksh Singh, "War Dispatches –A Soldier Remembers", *Indian Defence Review*, January 30, 2014.
24. R.D. Pradhan, no. 14, p. 286-88.
25. P.V.S. Jagan Mohan and Samir Chopra, no. 19, p. 290.
26. Maj. Gen. Joginder Singh, *Behind the Scene: An Analysis of India's Military Operations, 1947-1971*, Lancer International, New Delhi, 1993, p. xi and 8.
27. P.V.S. Jagan Mohan and Samir Chopra, no. 19, p. 245.
28. *Official History of the 1971 Indo-Pakistan War*, at Bharat Rakshak.com.
29. 'Chakkar' is a Hindi word for orbit.
30. AVM (Retd.) B.K. Bishnoi, "Thunder Over Dacca 1971", excerpted from *Air Space*, January 1997 at http://www.bharat-rakshak.com/IAF/History/1971War/Dacca.html (Accessed July 17, 2012).
31. *Official History of the 1971 War* available at, http://www.bharat-rakshak.com/IAF/History/1971War/Dacca.html, p. 611 (Accessed July 17, 2012).
32. Ibid.
33. In an interview on June 4, 2012, Air Cmde. (Retd.) A.V. Sathaye, Vir Chakra, a veteran of these operations questioned the usefulness of these strikes since the IAF did not persist with these strikes nor did these fulfil any higher strategic objectives.
34. From October 1989 to July 1991, the author commanded the IAF 43 Wing at Sulur near Coimbatore that provided the helicopter support for Operation Pawan, codename for the Sri Lanka air operations.

35. In an email by Lt. Gen. J.F.R. Jacob (Retd.) dated December 4, 2013.
36. Stephen P. Cohen and Sunil Dasgupta, *Arming Without Aiming: India's Military Modernisation*, Viking, New Delhi, 2010, p. 79.
37. Andrew G.B. Vallance, *The Air Weapon: Doctrines of Air Power Strategy and Operational Art*, St. Martin's Press, London, 1996, pp. 18, 49, 76 and 153.
38. Ibid. p. 18.
39. Col. Summers was a military aide to Henry Kissinger when the latter negotiated peace with Lee Duck Tho, the North Vietnamese interlocutor.
40. Air Commodore Ramesh Phadke, *China's Power Projection*, Manas Publications, New Delhi, 2005, pp. 70-73.
41. The UNSC passed Resolution No. 678 giving Iraq upto January 15, 1991 to withdraw all Iraqi forces from Kuwait and authorised a US-led coalition of 34 countries to use 'all necessary means' to force Iraq out of Kuwait after the passing of the deadline.
42. A strike mission comprising several fighter-bombers, air defence and ECM escorts is termed as a package.
43. John Barry and Evan Thomas, "The Kosovo Cover Up" at http://www.newsweek.com/kosovo-cover-160273 (Accessed June 2. 2014); and *The Daily Beast*, May 14, 2000.
44. Martin Aguera, "Air Power Paradox: NATO's 'Misuse' of Military Force in Kosovo and its Consequences", *Small Wars and Insurgencies*, 12 (3), Autumn 2001, pp. 115-28. The quotes are from p. 123.
45. John Barry, no. 43.
46. Elliot A. Cohen, "The Mystique of US Air Power", *Foreign Affairs*, January/February 1994 at http://www.foreignaffairs.com/articles/49442/eliot-a-cohen/the-mystique-of-us-air-power (Accessed February 03, 2014).
47. Ibid.
48. Erica Borghard and Constantino Pischedda, *Parameters*, Strategic Studies Institute, Spring 2012, pp. 63-74 at http://strategicstudiesinstitute.army.mil/pubs/parameters/Articles/2012spring/Borghard_Pischedda.pdf(Accessed June 25, 2013).
49. Adam J. Hebert, "Libya: Victory Through Airpower", *Air Force Magazine*, Air University Press, Maxwell Air Force Base, Alabama, December 2011 at http://www.airforcemag.com/MagazineArchive/Pages/2011/December../ (Accessed June 25, 2013).
50. "Lessons Offered from the Libya Air Campaign", Paper by the Royal Aeronautical Society at www.aerosociety.com, pp. 07-14. (Accessed June 25, 2013). Also see Dr. Christian F. Anrig, "Allied Air Power over Libya: A Preliminary Assessment" at www.airpower.au.af.mil/digital/pdf/articles/winter/2011/II-VA-Anrig.pdf (Accessed June 26, 2013).

5

Development of IAF Force Structures

The IAF came into being in 1932, more to meet the demands for 'Indianisation' of the defence forces and to assuage the feelings of a few strong Indian nationalists, rather than to play any specific role in the defence of British India. The only threat to India at the time came from the restive, violent and unpredictable tribesmen of the North West Frontier Province (NWFP, now Khyber Pakhtunkhwa). The strategic threat from the Soviet Union was distant, and handled by British diplomacy and the balance-of-power games. The Indian Army was used mainly to fight colonial wars in China, Iraq, and Africa. Although World War I did not come to India, India's contribution to the war effort in military manpower and economic terms was considerable. Upwards of a million Indians fought under the British flag in the War. It was in the aftermath of World War I that Indian political leaders began demanding a bigger role in the armed forces. In 1925, the Government of India formed the Indian Sandhurst Committee, also known as Skeen Committee, under General Sir Andrew Skeen, the then Chief of General Staff of the British Indian Army. The Committee recommended the induction of suitable Indians in the officer cadres of the Indian Army and also recommended the formation of the Indian Air Force (IAF).

Early Developments

The Indian Air Force Act became effective on October 8, 1932 but the first unit, No. 1 Squadron was formed only on April 1, 1933 and that too with just one flight of four Westland Wapitis. At the outbreak of World War II in September 1939, the IAF had technically been in existence for seven years, but it had barely expanded from a single flight of four Wapiti biplanes in 1932, to two flights by

1938. It was initially manned by five Indian officers trained at Cranwell in Britain. The 'A' Flight, in fact, the only flight, was commanded by a British officer, Flight Lieutenant Boucher. To begin with, the flight concentrated on the intensive training of the recently commissioned Indian pilots, Sarkar, Mukherjee, Bhopinder Singh, Awan, Amarjit Singh and Tandon. At independence, Awan opted for Pakistan. During flying training at Cranwell, Tandon was found to be shorter than the prescribed height, as his feet did not reach the rudder pedals of the aircraft and hence his training was discontinued. Later, he was commissioned in the Equipment (now Logistics) Branch.

"In the autumn of 1936, a serious rebellion broke out in North Waziristan. The Wazirs of Tochikhel revolted against the Government." The flight was moved to Miranshah in support of the army where the IAF cut its teeth, and in a mere three-month period flew 1,400 operational hours while maintaining its aircraft serviceability of 100 per cent. In time, the second or 'B' Flight of the squadron was formed and was based at Karachi. In 1938, the two flights of No. 1 Squadron moved to Ambala, which was then a major Royal Air Force (RAF) flying base, and remained there until the outbreak of World War II. In order to face the immediate threat posed by an aggressive Germany, the British Government pulled out all RAF squadrons deployed in India back to Britain. Until the entry of Japan in the war in December 1941, the IAF did not see any further growth or action. The NWFP was once again in turmoil with increasing violent activities of the rebel tribes. It was found that a single squadron was not adequate to support the troops in the area. To augment the existing forces, No. 2 Squadron was formed on April 1, 1941.[1]

With the coming of hostilities to India, five Coastal Defence Flights were formed with a wide assortment of the remnants of RAF and civil aircraft then operating in India and were manned by personnel of the IAF Volunteer Reserve (IAFVR) formed at the outbreak of the war. These flights were located at Bombay (now Mumbai), Calcutta (now Kolkata), Madras (now Chennai), Cochin (now Kochi) and Karachi, and were tasked with surveillance of the vast coastline of India. Later, No. 6 Coastal Defence Flight was formed at Vishakhapatnam.

Soon after their attack on Pearl Harbour in Hawaii on December 7, 1941, the Japanese advanced at lightning speed and in quick time occupied the British territories of Hong Kong, Singapore, Malaya and were soon knocking at the doors of Burma. With this threat developing to the Indian mainland, No. 4 Coastal Defence Flight was moved from Karachi to Burma in December 1942, making it the first Indian unit to operate outside India. According to Air Marshal M.S. Chaturvedi, these Coastal Defence Flights rendered invaluable service by keeping an alert eye on Japanese activities, especially on their submarines, in the Indian Ocean and the Bay of Bengal. Given their vintage and limited range, this socallèd maritime surveillance was of little strategic or deterrent value but it prepared the young Indian pilots of the IAFVR for operations in Burma. With the relentless advance of the Japanese into Burma, the IAF underwent rapid expansion and saw operational service in the first and second Burma Campaigns. By February 1944, Nos. 3, 4, 6, 7, 8, 9, and 10 squadrons were raised. No. 12 transport squadron was formed on December 1, 1945 and No. 5 Squadron in November 1948.[2]

At the end of World War II, the IAF had grown from a single flight to some 10 squadrons, each with considerable operational experience, first with the assorted aircraft of Coastal Defence Flights, such as Wapiti, Audax and Hudson and later Lysander, and Vultee Vengeance dive bombers. None of these aircraft were capable of facing the Japanese fighters and were of little use to the RAF squadrons operating in Burma, but were allotted communication and reconnaissance tasks which they performed with great enthusiasm.

Although unsuitable for bombing operations, Squadron Leader Jumbo Majumdar, an illustrious pilot of the IAF, had bomb racks fitted on the lightly armed Lysander and led No. 1 Squadron at tree top height on February 3, 1942 to a Japanese air base at Mae Hon Son. He achieved complete surprise and inflicted heavy damage on the enemy. It was during the second Burma campaign that all the recently raised IAF squadrons were re-equipped with Hurricane and Spitfire fighters and quickly gathered operational experience in tactical reconnaissance, strafing, dive bombing, photographic reconnaissance, top cover, interdiction of enemy roads and bridges, and earned the respect of the various army formations in support of which they were employed.

The IAF did not possess any transport aircraft squadrons at that time, but its men were witness to the large-scale troop-lift and air supply effort which very often proved invaluable for the beleaguered army in the long and arduous Burma campaign. Although the IAF was essentially employed in support of the army, the chance to work alongside RAF bomber and transport units gave the young Indians a good understanding of airpower roles, effectiveness and limitations. They also learned vital lessons in moving and operating their squadrons from makeshift airfields in different parts of India and Burma. Thick jungles, mountainous terrain, incessant rains and bad weather during the long and often severe monsoon season tested their initiative and innovative skills. It was a truly Indian affair with almost all of the squadrons under command of Indian officers and with maintenance and administrative support from Indian technical officers and men. The contribution of the fledgling service was much appreciated and its personnel won a number of gallantry awards and more importantly the respect of the whole nation.[3]

The British, who were at first reluctant to 'Indianise' the military in the 1930s, realised that when it came to valour and fighting skills, the 'native' was second to none. Even so, many doubted their leadership abilities. General Sir Arthur Smith, the departing Commander-in-Chief of the Indian Army, in 1947 expressed serious doubts about the future of the Indian military. At a farewell dinner on the eve of independence when asked about the future of the Indian Army he bluntly said: "I do not give your army six months. It will crack up before that. You see, the Jawans are like bricks and the 'officer' provides the mortar that holds them together. The Indian officer will not provide the mortar because his leadership has not been tested and the Jawan has no respect for him." When told that patriotism was a great force that will provide the mortar, Smith snapped back, "No, not with the Jawans. They have loved their British officers because they took care of them. Your boys are too selfish and snobs."[4]

During the six-year long World War II, a very large number of Indians were trained as pilots, navigators and in other support roles, such as the Technical, Equipment and Administration branches and were employed in units and squadrons, at the many RAF Stations that had sprung up throughout India. The period also saw a number of ground training establishments, coming up in different parts of the country where technical trade training was imparted. Although its growth was driven by emerging war-time requirements and was not well planned, by the end of the war a sizeable nucleus of trained and experienced personnel was available to support the 10 IAF squadrons. Today, it is difficult to visualise the colossal mobilisation that took place during World War II. It resulted in tens of thousands of young Indians joining the defence services as civilians and uniformed men. This offered new vistas for employment, with these young Indians learning new skills, in hitherto unknown professions. Most of these adventurous men became experienced engineers, administrators and pilots and formed the backbone of the IAF, and independent India's government and the private sector. In a sense, World War II was a blessing in disguise, for without it, newly independent India would have found it very difficult to train such a large body of professionals.

Post-war demobilisation, however, resulted in many war veterans leaving for greener pastures in civil and commercial fields. All RAF squadrons were also soon withdrawn from the Indian theatre. At the time of independence, the IAF had a total of 10 squadrons, but the division of assets after Partition resulted in two fighter squadrons and one transport squadron going to Pakistan. There was much wrangling at the Armed Forces Reconstitution Committee (AFRC) whose terms of reference were to divide the assets on communal ratio which was 80 per cent non-Muslim to 20 per cent Muslim; and hence Pakistan's share came to only two squadrons. But some British officers opined that Pakistan's operational requirements in the NWFP should also be considered while dividing the assets. This was not accepted by the Indian members who (rather disingenuously) said that the Indian Government was opposed to the use of air force against its own people.[5] But Pakistan eventually got two fighter and one transport squadrons. The process of the actual division continued well into 1948, as most of the Equipment Depots and Air Stores Parks were located in Pakistan, while many important air force bases and training establishments were located in India. There were allegations on both sides of, unfair division, delay and wilful damage to equipment. This had an adverse effect on aircraft availability during the Kashmir War.[6] The two transport squadrons, one each for India and Pakistan, were equipped with C-47 Dakota twin-engine aircraft. In addition, there were two RAF transport squadrons, one based at Karachi and another at Palam (New Delhi) that were made 'available' for non-operational and training tasks and remained in India until the end of 1948.

According to Chaturvedi, 1946 was a year of confusion. Wholesale demobilisation had rendered hundreds of thousands of skilled and experienced Indians, jobless. The RAF squadrons were leaving India; a number of air force bases and hastily prepared airfields had become redundant. It was a strange situation. The IAF by then, had a total of 10 squadrons and possessed many other assets, bases and considerable reserves, but no air headquarters or controlling organisation. There was no 'Command and Control' set-up and hence it lacked direction.[7]

Before independence, the Commander-in-Chief (C-in-C) India controlled all military activity and was next only to the Viceroy/Governor General. The C-in-C India, an army officer, was in command of all the three Services. The recently raised IAF squadrons and units thus came under Air Officer Commanding (AOC) RAF India, who was part of the vast defence department in Delhi, with all decisions about the defence of India being taken at Whitehall in London. India thus did not have a Ministry of Defence but only a Defence Department. The first task at independence, therefore, was to create a suitable organisation for the fledgling units and squadrons of the IAF.

IAF in Independent India

At independence, India naturally did not have many senior and experienced Indian military officers. (Indian members of the civilian bureaucracy, the Indian Civil Service (ICS), were also relatively young, but had considerable administrative experience in the government except in matters of defence.)[8] As a consequence, Nehru reluctantly agreed to the suggestion of the Governor General, Lord Louis Mountbatten, to retain some senior British officers as heads of the three Services. Field Marshal Sir Claude Auchinleck, until then the C-in-C India, was retained as the Supreme Commander of the militaries of the two newly formed dominions and was charged with overseeing the division of assets. He was also to exercise control over the movement of units allotted to the two dominions and the British military units still in India. He, however, had no operational control over any Indian or Pakistani units.

Once Lord Mountbatten was invited to become the First Governor General of free India, it was only natural that he would wield considerable influence over India's defence decision-making.[9] He presided over the Partition Council to which the AFRC that was responsible for the division of assets, reported. Strangely, later, he also chaired the newly formed Defence Committee of the Cabinet (DCC) and selected the British officers to head each of the three services, although as the Governor General, he was merely the constitutional head and had no executive powers.

Air Marshal Sir Thomas Walker Elmhirst, then serving as the Chief of Inter-Services Administration at General Headquarters (GHQ) Delhi, was recommended for the post of the Chief of the Royal Indian Air Force (RIAF). Elmhirst agreed to take on this responsibility only if the Indian Prime Minister met two conditions; first, that the IAF would be an independent fighting service with him as its C-in-C being subordinate only to the Minister of Defence and second, he would be allowed to choose six officers of the RAF to assist him during the first two years. These conditions proved to be a blessing in disguise, as without them, the very small and young IAF would in all probability have come under the Indian Army. Air Marshal Elmhirst, with the help of the six British officers, quickly set about the task of putting the IAF organisation on a firm footing.[10]

As brought out earlier, the officers and other personnel of the RIAF had gained considerable operational experience during the war, but were not exposed to higher defence responsibilities, nor did they have any experience of working at higher formations as these were invariably manned by British officers. None of them held a rank higher than Squadron Leader with a very few Wing Commanders and Group Captains doing ground jobs. On taking over as the C-in-C and the Chief of the Air Staff, Elmhirst held consultations with the Defence Ministry and appointed Air Commodore S. Mukherjee, the then seniormost Indian, as his Deputy Chief of the Air Staff, in the rank of Air Vice Marshal; Group Captain A.M. Engineer as Air Officer in-charge Personnel & Organisation, in the rank of Air Commodore; and Group Captain R.H.D. Singh as Air Officer in-charge Technical & Equipment Services, in the rank of Air Commodore.

In addition, two groups were formed: No. 1 Operational Group under command of Air Commodore Meher Singh at Palam near Delhi; and the Training Group under command of Air Commodore Narendra at Bangalore. These appointments became effective on August 15, 1947. Some of the important Sections at Air Headquarters, later re-designated 'Directorates' were assigned to Group Captain P.C. Lal, Training & Plans; Group Captain K.L. Sondhi, Personnel; but the Directorate of Operations was, however, kept under an RAF officer. The major IAF stations and bases at the time were: Palam at Delhi; Ambala; Jodhpur;

Bangalore and Tambaram near Madras (now Chennai). Group Captain Ranjan Dutt, the first among emergency commissioned officers trained in India, was appointed as Senior Air Staff Officer (SASO) of No. 1 Operational Group. (Opl. Gp).[11]

War Intervenes

The next item on Elmhirst's agenda was to organise the operational and training plans of the new service but the Kashmir war intervened. While operational details and lessons learnt from this 14-month-long war are dealt with in Chapter 2, it should suffice to say here, that the young IAF that had gained the honorific, 'Royal' for its performance during World War II, rose to the occasion and organised, in record time, the air lift of a battalion of troops from Delhi to Srinagar. Srinagar then, only had a small infrequently used airfield with a dusty unpaved runway unfit for sustained transport or fighter operations, a makeshift air traffic control set-up, no meteorological centre or weather forecasting facility and no radio telephony (R/T) or other signal communications for air traffic control. Elmhirst and his staff successfully organised the airlift of troops, ammunition and other warlike stores by commandeering a sizeable number of civilian/commercial and privately run Dakota DC-3 aircraft at Palam, and by mid-morning on October 27, 1947 the first company of No. 1 Sikh Battalion had been airlifted to Srinagar. In fact, in the following week, one full Infantry Brigade (No. 161) was airlifted to Srinagar. Such was the speed and efficiency of this first ever IAF airlift, that most observers did not and even today do not believe that the operation was not pre-planned. Three fighter squadrons Nos. 7, 8 and 10 and the only transport squadron No. 12 and an Army Air Observation Post (AOP) Squadron took part in this war. The airfields at Srinagar, Jammu, and later at Leh and Poonch, were developed and upgraded on a war footing for military transport and fighter aircraft operations.

At the time, RIAF fighter squadrons were established for 16 Tempests[12] and two Harvard aircraft, and the only transport squadron (No. 12) for 10 DC-3 Dakota aircraft. But the latter was woefully short of aircrews, as very few qualified twin-engine captains, co-pilots, navigators and signallers were available. To make matters worse, the same squadron was also assigned the task of training fresh aircrews. This experience spurred the efforts of the planners and catalysed the quest for a balanced air force. In April 1949, the Air Headquarters presented a plan to the government that envisaged an expansion of the air force to 20 squadrons.[13] The government, while approving only a 10-squadron force, directed that the training and other supporting establishments should, however, be built up for a 20-squadron force. The logic of building the 'training and support' facilities for a much larger force was to provide for rapid expansion in an emergency. But these facilities in fact, got used up by the then existing squadrons and units and support units, which after partition were woefully short of trained manpower.

Threat Assessment

At the beginning of World War II, the IAF strength was 16 officers and 244 other ranks, which by January 1945 had swelled to 1,200 officers, including 500 pilots, 200 officer cadets, 20,000 airmen, 6,000 airmen under training and 12,000 enrolled followers; in today's parlance, Group D employees of different trades such as washermen, sweepers, lascars, labour, cooks and the like. The 12,000 enrolled followers recruited during the war were disbanded and sent home at the end of the war.[14] The remaining manpower became the nucleus around which the new air force gradually expanded.

By invading the Indian state of Jammu and Kashmir (J&K), Pakistan had demonstrated its enmity towards India and it was quite obvious that it would continue to pose an existential threat to India, as it remained in illegal occupation of a large portion of Indian territory known as Pakistan-occupied Kashmir (PoK). China had only recently emerged from a civil war and although it showed some interest in controlling Tibet, it was not as yet seen as an immediate threat.

Although only one-third the size of China, India is a vast country with the high Himalayas in the north and the sea on three other sides. While the high Himalayas afforded a reasonable defence, a determined enemy could always come across the numerous passes in the high mountains. At the time, there was little or no threat from across the seas. Although India had faced many invasions from the north-west in the past, the country is too big to be easily conquered, defeated, subdued or occupied unless internal cohesion breaks down. There was thus, no justification for being paranoid about imaginary threats.

In its long civilisational history, India has never invaded any country nor has it shown irredentist or expansionist tendencies. It was thus natural, if naïve, for its leadership to believe that independent India did not face a major external threat, and that the world would leave it alone to pursue peaceful economic development and emancipation of its masses. The political leadership was only too conscious of the abject poverty, food shortages, lack of basic health, education and civic facilities, and above all a very weak economic and industrial base, from which to plan development. Any expenditure on a large standing army, air force or navy was, therefore, seen as wasteful and even counter-productive. By the early 1950s, it was also becoming clear that a newly independent People's Republic of China (PRC), now under Communist control, would pose a variety of security challenges to India, especially after its invasion of Tibet.

Although somewhat less experienced, the senior officers of the IAF were fully aware of present and future threats to India's sovereignty and territorial integrity.

The proposal for expanding the air force to 20 squadrons was thus based on a thorough understanding and analysis of the events in India's neighbourhood. They visualised and planned for a 'balanced air force'; an air force capable of carrying out all its roles and missions. There being many outstanding problems with Pakistan, Indian planners saw a 'short-term' threat of limited war with Pakistan and it was to meet this threat that they now devoted their energies.

Since India wished to follow a defensive policy, it was clear that the initiative would always remain with the enemy. An aggressor can focus on a relatively small area, but a defender has to necessarily remain alert along the entire length of the border, until the attack actually materialises. This not only requires a constant vigil but also the ability to stop the aggressor without losing too much ground. In the case of the air force, a defensive posture does not allow a pre-emptive strike nor any other action until the enemy has already struck. Air Defence (AD) thus became a vital component of the IAF's capability. It was thus imperative for the air force planners to develop an all-round capability, so that the enemy was deterred in the first place or appropriately dealt with if and when deterrence failed.

All of the air force senior officers had just recently participated in the long-drawn-out World War II and learnt important lessons. They did not want India to make the mistake of emphasising one capability at the expense of another. The first ever plan of air force expansion, therefore, envisaged a 20-squadron force. Its composition was as under:

- 8 fighter/bomber squadrons
- 1 night fighter squadron
- 1 photo reconnaissance squadron
- 2 light bomber squadrons
- 1 maritime reconnaissance squadron
- 2 transport squadrons
- Other ancillary and supporting formations and training units[15]

Even a cursory glance at the above composition will show the general trend in the thinking of the time. The number of fighter/bomber squadrons appears to have been decided, both by the length of the borders with Pakistan and the requirements of air defence, as no separate air defence squadron was planned. The two light bomber squadrons signify a limited offensive capability. The choice of a night fighter squadron may, at first glance, seem a little strange, as at that time there were very few radar stations. The aircraft of the period also did not have airborne interceptor radar. In the absence of these two vital capabilities, the night fighter would have been quite useless. The IAF in fact actually raised a night fighter squadron and equipped it with two-seat Vampire fighters, which had very rudimentary air interception radars operated by a radar operator occupying the second seat, but their exact role was never quite understood as these fighters were never really used in this role. Neither Pakistan nor any other adversary then possessed a bomber or fighter capable of night operations, and hence this particular capability somehow did not make sense. Here, a brief digression is necessary to understand the thinking behind this ambitious if unusual air force expansion plan.

Dependence on Outside Advice

The reason for this decision on the strength and composition of the air force is to be found in the recommendations made by Professor P.M.S. Blackett, a famous British physicist and a Nobel laureate, who was invited by Nehru to assist India in planning its defence forces. He was requested to make a report outlining the measures necessary for India to become near self-sufficient in defence production over a period of seven years but at the same time retain adequate defence and security.[16] This, according to Chris Smith, was due mainly to the inexperience of the Indian leadership.

> Neither he (Nehru) nor his civilian advisers understood sufficiently the intricacies of military technology and strategy, and the advice of the service chiefs alone would have been inappropriate and insufficient. In addition, there existed gaping holes in the decision-making process. It was only during World War II that the Indian Civil Service (ICS) officers were deputed into South Block (of the Ministry of Defence)...Moreover, it took a long time to change the Department of Defence into anything more than a post office.[17]

Blackett submitted his report in the latter half of 1948 which followed an earlier report by another British adviser, Wansborough Jones, which was commissioned by the Interim Government prior to independence and formed the basis for the defence science organisation in India. His (Jones's) terms of reference were to outline four central roles for the armed forces: (a) to secure the land frontier against raids from border tribes or from attack by a second-class army, (b) to support civil power; (this role was later dropped and ignored by Blackett), (c) to provide a small expeditionary force capable of protecting India's regional interests; and (d) within available financial resources to develop a force capable of taking the field in a first-class war. With the exception of the second element Blackett followed these guide-lines.[18]

There was, however, a significant difference. The Jones' report was prepared at a time when India was not partitioned and hence only the threat from border tribes, with which the British were only too familiar, was taken into account. But now as a British dominion, *India was also expected to look to the Commonwealth for its external security needs and hence the omission of the second clause relating to support to civil power*. The Blackett report, on the other hand, was commissioned by the Prime Minister of an independent country that was only a member of the Commonwealth. It was thus made keeping in mind Nehru's basic requirements of self-sufficiency in defence, and more importantly its affordability. The obvious focus was on what India could afford given the high priority for the process of planned development of the country. Keeping in mind 'India's extreme economic weakness', Blackett, therefore, suggested a modest capability that centred on defensive or what he called *non-competitive weapons,* rather than on *competitive* weapons such as modern fighter aircraft, heavy tanks and aircraft carrier task forces. In this scheme, the *army was to play a major role* as it could well provide a reasonable assurance of defence without too much expenditure on modernisation. The navy's role was: (a) to provide protection of coastal shipping; (b) to escort a small number of ocean convoys between Aden (now Yemen) and Singapore[19]; (c) co-operation with the army and the air force in repelling enemy landing operations; advance along coastlines and to be able to undertake similar operations against the enemy. Blackett found cruisers both expensive and vulnerable but while opting for small cost-effective and non-prestigious systems, he nevertheless recommended the acquisition of *a small escort carrier for convoy protection.* In all fairness, he also pointed out that India's assumed enemy, Pakistan, was unlikely to acquire the capability to threaten Indian convoys for the foreseeable future.[20]

His recommendations for the air force were similarly modest. While ruling out strategic bombing on humanitarian grounds, he also vetoed a 'long-range bombing' role on the basis of cost and efficacy. He thought that India could not hope to acquire a precision bombing capability and hence, it would have to go for counter-value targets, i.e. civilian population centres which for obvious reasons, was not advisable. He therefore, recommended smaller single-engine fighters with adequate strike capability. He did not think India needed jet fighters as these were *too fast* to be able to identify and attack the enemy's army. He also believed that jet operations in the dusty and high ambient temperatures of the arid and semi-arid north of India would require careful evaluation. Blackett, however, accepted the procurement of light bombers, night fighters, photo reconnaissance aircraft and trainers and recommended a major boost to the Hindustan Aircraft Factory (later Hindustan Aeronautics Limited or HAL).[21] These recommendations seem to be the basis for the composition of the proposed 15-squadron force given above. This brief analysis still does not give a convincing answer, for the need for a single night fighter squadron, which appears to be an aberration. But according Robert Anderson[22] – who cites Blackett's interviews of 1967 – Blackett held a number of discussions and briefings, with the senior serving officers of the Indian army, navy and the air force, and hence they would have been fully aware of the reasoning behind his recommendations. Blackett, in fact, was the official defence consultant and visited India on a dozen occasions from 1947 to 1972, had access to Nehru and was friends with noted scientists like Sir Shanti Swarup Bhatnagar, Dr. D.S. Kothari, the first Scientific Advisor to the Defence Minister, Homi J. Bhabha and P.C. Mahalanobis – all in the inner circle of the Prime Minister and influential decision-makers in the field of defence science policy. He also vigorously supported the decision to manufacture the Gnat in India. In hindsight, it is possible and perhaps even likely that Blackett had a good idea of the real threats India faced in the early 1950s, the state of the Indian economy, and hence advocated a modest defence capability.

New Acquisitions

Notwithstanding economic constraints, India soon acquired a sizeable number of Vampire jet fighters and trainers from Great Britain. This was possible because:

> ...[w]hen India gained independence in 1947, its foreign exchange reserves were substantial. These were held chiefly in the form of sterling securities, . an IOU from Great Britain to the Government of India, its colony for the unrequited exports which India had supplied to England during the war, which in 1948 amounted to British £1,200 million.[23]

Britain would have gone bankrupt if it had attempted to pay back this debt in one lump sum. An agreement was therefore reached, whereby India could draw a maximum of £40 million every year for 30 years, until the total debt amount was liquidated. India, however, purchased considerable defence equipment including several aircraft, tanks, ships and many other items for civilian use from Britain, and exhausted these sterling assets in the first few years after independence. According to the Anderson Report cited above, India's sterling reserves were still healthy at £542 million in 1955.[24]

Although the Kashmir issue had been referred to the United Nations (UN) in 1948, Pakistan's hostility showed no signs of abating but in fact increased, and hence it now posed a long-term threat. By the early 1950s, on the recommendation of the three Chiefs of Staff, the government formed a high-powered Armed Forces Re-organisation Committee. In 1952, it accepted in principle the Committee's recommendations, one of which was that the air force should be expanded to a 15-squadron force. In fact, during the 1950s there were three force structure reviews. The first, an internal review at Air Headquarters, proposed a '20-squadron-force' but the government accepted only 10 squadrons. The second committee recommended a 15-squadron force, while the third review conducted by another committee suggested 20 squadrons. Finally in 1963, the third, the Tata Committee, under the chairmanship of the noted industrialist J.R.D. Tata that went into the question of the size of the Indian military, recommended a 45-squadron air force to be gradually built up over a *period of time*. No time frame was, however, specified and as will be seen, this ambitious level was never really achieved.[25]

Initial Consolidation and Reorganisation

The experience of the 1947-48 Kashmir operations had raised many questions about the operational readiness of the IAF, which had fought the war with available equipment of World War II vintage. Many deficiencies such as shortage of suitable aircraft, equipment, logistics and maintenance support and Command and Control were addressed. The year 1949, thus proved to be one of consolidation and reorganisation in almost all the major departments based on the primary roles of the IAF, Air Defence, Strategic Offensive Operations and support to the army and navy. In April 1949, the Directorate of Policy and Plans at Air Headquarters submitted a paper to the DCC through the Chiefs of Staff Committee (CoSC) for a minimum of 20 squadrons with necessary support units. Due to financial constraints, the DCC accepted for immediate implementation the expansion to only 10 squadrons but allowed the IAF to raise support and administrative establishments to cater for an eventual expansion to 20 squadrons.

Some of the important decisions were:

- The flying schools at Jodhpur and Ambala were renamed Nos. 1 and 2 Air Force Academies with the former doing initial flying training; and the latter advanced training. The training establishment at Coimbatore was renamed No. 3 Air Force Academy to carry out ground training of officers.
- The No. 1 Operational Group at Palam was upgraded to Operational Command and the Training Group at Bangalore to Training Command.
- Air Force Technical College (AFTC) was established at Jalahalli, Bangalore for training officers of the Technical Engine, Electrical, Signals and Armament branches. Until then, technical officers promoted from ranks were trained at the No. 2 Ground Training School (GTS) Tambaram Madras, (now Chennai) and direct entry candidates were sent to the United Kingdom (UK) for training. Indian instructors began to gradually replace British instructors at AFTC with the last British Commandant of the college leaving India only in 1956.
- Nos. 1, 2 and 3 Ground Training Schools for airmen were established for non-technical, airframe and aero-engine, electrical, signals and radar trades at Jalahalli and Tambaram.
- An Air Mission was established at London to assist in procurement of spares which were mainly of British origin and also to keep IAF informed of developments in the field of aviation in the UK.
- An RAF Transport Command Team was invited in May 1951, to properly standardise and categorise IAF transport aircrews.
- Another team from the Examination Wing of the RAF Central Flying School also assessed the standard of flying training imparted at IAF schools.

- In September 1950, steps were taken to establish the Armament Training Wing (ATW) at Jamnagar for live air armament training.[26]

As we have seen above, IAF expansion and modernisation was aimed at meeting the challenge posed by Pakistan, and hence it will be instructive to briefly study Pakistan's military strategy. It was evident from the early 1950s that Pakistan had learnt some vital air power lessons from the 14-month-long Kashmir War in 1947-48. While it had succeeded in diplomatically and militarily pressurising India, to avoid being called the 'aggressor' and in fact, a legitimate 'party' to the dispute, it did not have the air power capability to take on the IAF and face the Indian military threat. India certainly enjoyed superiority in conventional arms. Faced with a far bigger country and a stronger economy, Pakistan had to co-opt friends and allies to meet the Indian threat. Pakistan began making efforts to address this perceived inferiority in right earnest. As early as 1950, Pakistan's Prime Minister Liaquat Ali Khan had begun asking the United States (US) Administration for military assistance, including modern fighter aircraft ostensibly to fight the Communist threat.[27]

In 1950, during one of the many crises between India and Pakistan, when India moved an armoured division to the west of Beas River in the Amritsar area as a precautionary step, Liaquat Ali Khan visited Washington and asked the Americans for arms aid. "He met the Secretary of Defense and the Chairman Joint Chiefs of Staff and stressed his desire to obtain arms and equipment. He also privately met the US Navy Chief Admiral Chester Nimitz and re-emphasised Pakistan's need for arms. Pakistan, he assured Nimitz, would act as a bulwark against pro-Communist India...both American and British diplomats felt that he made it clear where Pakistan stood in the Cold War." When asked how big an army Pakistan wanted to maintain, he replied, "If your country will guarantee our territorial integrity, I will not keep any army at all.[28] It then became clear that the arms sought by Pakistan would eventually be used against India. India expressed its concern to the US and the US decided not to supply arms to Pakistan 'at this stage'. A worried India began a renewed search for modern arms and equipment from other sources.

In March 1955, Nehru made a very successful high profile visit to the Soviet Union during which he invited the Soviet leadership to visit India. While remaining non-aligned, India wanted Soviet arms. In November 1955, Nikita Khrushchev and his deputy Marshal Nikolai Bulganin visited India to cement the friendship, and promised all assistance to India's planned development; the steel plant at Bhilai was one such example.

By 1955, Pakistan had joined the Central Treaty Organisation (CENTO) and soon thereafter the South East Asia Treaty Organisation (SEATO); it began receiving considerable arms aid from the US including some 120 F-86 Sabre fighter jets and 28 Canberra B-57 medium bombers and a little later (in 1961) a dozen F-104 supersonic Starfighter aircraft. The entry of a supersonic fighter into South Asia changed the overall military balance between India and Pakistan and there arose a clamour in India for a supersonic fighter to match the F-104.

Pakistan had in one stroke changed the qualitative air power balance in its favour. Both the F-104 and Sabre F-86 were equipped with the heat-seeking Sidewinder missile that had by then acquired a reputation for high lethality. Pakistan also managed to obtain two high-powered static radar stations, one of which was located at Badin in Sindh, and the other at Sakesar in Punjab. In addition, it also received some early warning radar sets which together strengthened Pakistan's AD network and provided its aircraft considerable warning when these were on an offensive mission.[29]

This advantage was only partly neutralised when India received the first batch of MiG-21 fighter interceptors from the Soviet Union in the early 1960s. By the time the 1965 Indo-Pak War began, India had only a handful of MiG fighters, but managed to exert some psychological pressure on the Pakistan Air Force (PAF); but only just. Although Pakistan's strategy was essentially defensive, it adopted an 'offensive' rhetoric and kept needling India whenever an opportunity arose; American and Chinese help was always at hand to restrain India.

More Aircraft Join the IAF

The next major purchase in 1953 was the 71 MD-450 Ouragan (Toofani) fighter from Dassault of France, followed by a batch of another 33 of these fighters in 1957. The aim was to diversify the sources of arms and to reduce dependence on one foreign power. The Toofani was neither tested in battle, nor extensively used for operational training and had by the 1960s become obsolete. By the end of 1959, the IAF had also acquired 110 Mystere IVA fighters from Dassault France, 182 Hunter F-56 fighters and T-66 trainers, 74 Canberra light bombers and strategic reconnaissance aircraft from the UK. The proposal to manufacture the Gnat fighter under licence at Hindustan Aircraft (later Aeronautics) Limited (HAL) was vigorously pursued and the first of these fighters had begun to fly in 1958.[30] (Please see Appendix II – The Gnat Story). The transport fleet was augmented with a sizeable number of twin-engine C-119 Packet medium lift aircraft from Fairchild Company of the US, and more DC-3 Dakotas. In addition, about 20 IL-14 light transports, and in 1961 a squadron of An-12 heavy lift transports were acquired from the Soviet Union. The IAF strength had rapidly expanded to 23 squadrons by 1960 (Please see Appendix I).

It is often claimed that India's decision to purchase these fighters and light bombers was in response to Pakistan joining the Western Alliance (CENTO and SEATO) in 1954-55 but according to Chris Smith many of these purchase decisions were made well before that happened. This author, however, feels that these decisions were necessitated by Pakistan's renewed hostility and the efforts of its leadership in the early 1950s, to convince the US to supply arms for defence against the Soviet Union.

The most amazing part of this acquisition is that such formidable capability was not employed during the Chinese aggression of 1962. The PAF had almost no offensive capability until it began to receive military assistance from the US in the mid-1950s. The PAF acquisition was quite well thought out and was designed to thwart a perceived Indian threat. Some 120 Sabre F-86 fighter/ bombers, 24 B-57 US-manufactured Canberra light bombers were followed by 14 F-104 Starfighters in 1961-62. The F-86 was known for its manoeuvrability since its turning radius in air combat was quite small, but was inferior to the Gnat in its climbing performance. It carried six nose-mounted guns of 0.5 inch calibre with a good rate of fire, so that an enemy in the range of about 400-600 metres was a sure kill. PAF Sabre kills in 1965 and 1971 were, however, from much closer ranges. The PAF soon obtained from the US the Sidewinder AIM-7 air-to-air heat-seeking missile, which when mounted on the Sabre, made it even more lethal. The F-104 being a supersonic fighter interceptor raised much anxiety among Indians. Like the early models of the MiG-21, it was also specifically designed to intercept enemy (Warsaw Pact) strategic bombers at high altitude, well before the bombers reached their weapon release line. Both the MiG-21 and F-104 fighters were equipped with an 'after burner' which helped the engine to produce extra thrust by burning more fuel, thereby giving the fighter a very high rate of climb, acceleration and supersonic speeds. But both these aircraft had limited endurance, a 25-30 minute duration flight being the norm. With a reliable Ground Controlled Interception (GCI), high-powered, long-range radar, well-trained radar controllers, a dependable air-to-air missile and finally an alert pilot, the F-104 posed a major threat. For trans-sonic fighters flying at low altitude, the F-104 or the MiG-21 were not much of a threat as these possessed better turning performance and the Sidewinder and the Soviet K-13 missiles usually missed the target, when fired on an enemy flying at very low altitudes; proximity to the ground would simply cause the heat-seeking missile to hit the ground. The F-104 had one advantage; the 20mm Gatling rotary gun with a very high rate of fire fitted to the side of the front part of its fuselage, while the early models of the MiG-21 had none. In hindsight, the clamour in India for a supersonic aircraft to match the PAF F-104 was, therefore, justified, if a little, overestimated. The performance of the F-104 in the 1965 and 1971 Indo-Pak wars was below expectation, but it nevertheless posed a threat due to its generally better performance (higher speed, acceleration), airborne radar, and a rotary cannon, to Indian fighters and especially to Canberra night bombing operations. The night-fighting capability of the F-104 also caused some psychological inhibition, although most Indian Canberra crew learnt to make a quick bombing pass and exit the target area at low levels and high speed.

In the early 1950s, a committee had calculated the IAF strength on the basis of one fighter squadron per division. India then had about nine active divisions, so besides these nine squadrons, the air force was to have six to eight squadrons for air defence, two/three light bomber squadrons and a photoreconnaissance unit.[31] This probably explains the magic figure of 15 combat squadrons in the 1950s and also the traditional view, that the IAF was essentially a tactical air force, a supporting organisation in the service of the army. Once the planners had focused on Pakistan as the major threat, it was only natural that the range, or more correctly, Radius of Action (RoA) of the proposed fighter-bombers did not receive much attention. As a result, most IAF fighters, until recently, had very limited range or 'short legs' and barely managed to reach Pakistani airfields, like Sargodha. To be fair, India was not able to buy long range fighter-bombers, as none was really available. At the time, fighter interceptor and Fighter Ground Attack (FGA) aircraft the world over had a short range, as these were essentially designed to intercept incoming enemy bombers near, or over a country's own borders, and for tactical operations in support of surface forces. The only aircraft with relatively longer ranges were the bombers. The Canberra had adequate range and was relatively slow, but nevertheless made up for its speed by flying at night and thus avoiding enemy reaction, except the PAF F-104 Starfighter, that was really the only fighter capable of night interception.

For several reasons, the acquisition of the MiG-21 turned out to be a blessing in disguise. First, the Soviets allowed India to manufacture the aircraft under licence. Second, in due course they also provided three different versions, the MiG-21 M, MF and 'bis,' with marginally higher thrust, better avionics, especially the Airborne Interception (AI) radar, and additional under-wing stations to carry a modest variety of armament stores. It still lacked range, but with two/three external drop tanks it could reach some enemy targets, albeit with limited weapon loads. (Please see Appendix III – The MiG-21 Story). The first MiG-21 squadron was just about entering service when the 1965 Indo-Pak war broke out in September 1965. Most of these fighters were used only as 'top cover,' or as escorts, to Mystere IVA fighter-bombers, attacking enemy positions in support of the army, in areas close to the Pakistani border. In one such encounter, a MiG-21 fired its missiles but these missed the enemy fighter due to the aircraft flying in very close proximity of the ground.[32]

By early 1965, the Gnat fleet was also gradually overcoming its teething problems and the IAF was able to raise a total of three squadrons (Nos. 2, 9 and 23) of this tiny fighter, which not only had the advantage of very good manoeuvrability, but also of size, as it could not easily be 'spotted' by the enemy. It also presented a very small radar signature, and hence to some extent possessed 'stealth' attributes. One of the most serious drawbacks of this indigenously produced fighter, however, was that its 30 mm Aden Guns were prone to frequent jamming or stoppages. As a result, many an opportunity was lost, with the enemy fighter in cross-hairs and within firing range.[33] Similar disappointments were also faced during the 1971 war.

Fleet serviceability and availability were also a matter of concern with most of the Mystere IVA, Gnat, and even Hunter aircraft although these were relatively new. Even so, during the 1965 Indo-Pak war, the IAF employed a total of just about 16 fighter squadrons in the Western theatre. This seriously curtailed sortie rates during the war, and severely reduced their availability despite the hard work of the maintenance crews. In the post-1965 period, non-availability of aircraft also delayed peacetime training schedules. Many young pilots found themselves languishing in ground jobs, when in fact, they should have been flying to get their Fully Operational (F/Ops) status. In times of such shortage, some of the forward bases had to be given fighters on loan, so that they could at least maintain a Live Air Defence alert on the Operational Readiness Platform (ORP).

HF-24 Marut

Even though this Indian fighter aircraft lacked a suitable engine and had to make do with two Orpheus engines, already being licence-produced for the Gnat, it was inducted into the IAF only in 1967, when its first squadron was formed. Nos. 10 and 220 were the only two units that were equipped with this aircraft. The HF-24 was to be fitted with a Rolls Royce engine, made for the Egyptian Air Force, but Cold War sanctions came in the way and the aircraft remained underpowered. Being markedly underpowered, the HF-24, like the Mystere IVA, used to get airborne nearly at the end of the 3,000-yard runway, with both the onlooker and the pilot missing a heartbeat. HAL also manufactured a trainer version of the HF-24 Marut but could not really overcome all the teething problems. Two of its illustrious test pilots, the legendary Group Captain Suranjan Das (killed January 10, 1970) and Squadron Leader Arun Keshav Sapre (killed November 21, 1971), were lost in HF-24 accidents. The HF-24 performed well during the 1971 war and even bagged a Sabre in an air-to-air encounter, but limited armament and RoA, came in the way of further development. HF-24 serviceability was also generally poor, and in any case the IAF decision-makers were already looking at Soviet fighters, such as the MiG-21 and S-22 aka Sukhoi-7. India was then subject to a stringent technology denial regime imposed by the West, because of the 1971 Friendship Treaty with the Soviets, which gave the impression that India was 'firmly in the Communist Camp' and had to finally phase out this promising fighter by 1985. In hindsight, the IAF and HAL should not have abandoned this indigenous programme, but put it on hold and then revived it when the Western markets opened up, soon after the disintegration of the Soviet Union in 1991. Some believe the HF-24 could have at least filled the Advanced Jet Trainer (AJT) need of the IAF, at a fraction of the cost and could well have avoided the delays that eventually saw the British Aerospace (BAe) Hawk AJT enter IAF service only in 2004, some 18 years after the search for the AJT began.

Soon after the 1965 war, Pakistan also came under US sanctions, but succeeded in diversifying its arms suppliers by obtaining a sizeable number of F-6s (MiG-19s) from the PRC, and Mirage III and V fighters from France, once again attempting to balance IAF's quantitative superiority. Experience of the 1965 conflict clearly showed that IAF airfields were highly vulnerable to PAF strikes, due to their close proximity to the International Border (IB). PAF airfields on the other hand, were located relatively deep inside Pakistan and were invulnerable to IAF fighter/bombers which were woefully short of range. This was to become abundantly clear in the 1971 war, when India decided to maintain only a defensive posture in the west. The IAF used Hunters for attacks on Peshawar and other depth airfields, while the Canberra light bombers were used for night attacks, as these were too vulnerable by day.

The IAF had inducted only one new type of aircraft during the inter-war years. The S-22 also known as Sukhoi-7 was capable of carrying more armament, but its range was limited. The MiG-21 fleet was also growing fast, and together the availability of these fighters, boosted the confidence of the IAF pilots. In just two years from 1968, the IAF raised or re-equipped some six-and-a-half squadrons with the S-22 and eight-and-a-half squadrons with the MiG-21.[34] The IAF thus had 15 squadrons of supersonic fighters. During the 1971 war, both S-22 and MiG-21 aircraft were also used for single aircraft night attacks on PAF airfields. While innovative and daring, the value of these night raids could not be fully assessed. Some daylight attacks on PAF airfields were fairly successful, but IAF losses to Pakistan's AD fighters and anti-aircraft guns were heavy. The newly acquired S-22 fleet was used extensively in the Offensive Air Support (OAS) and Interdiction roles, and proved very effective, but the losses to anti-aircraft and enemy small arms fire were once again very high. This attrition was mainly due to IAF pilots carrying out multiple or repeat dive attacks in the S-22 aircraft, giving ample time to the enemy to anticipate and properly aim anti-aircraft fire. Its large size made it easier to visually spot the S-22 and this added to its vulnerability.

The IAF once again, found itself incapable of inflicting serious damage to the Pakistani assets in the west, even though some important strategic targets such as the Mangla Dam, the Sui gas plant and railway communication systems were effectively struck and damaged. Limited range or RoA of the IAF fighter-bombers was seen as the main cause of its reduced effectiveness. Thus began the search for a Deep Penetration Strike Aircraft (DPSA) capable of reaching the farthest PAF airfield in Pakistan. Many fighters such as the SAAB Viggen and French Dassault Mirage F-1 were also in contention, but in 1978, India finally selected the Jaguar aircraft that was manufactured by an Anglo-French consortium, some 10 years after it was first offered to India.[35] Deliveries of the Jaguar began in 1979, with the first batch of 18 aircraft given on loan from the RAF, followed by 40 more built in the UK and another 45 being manufactured at HAL Bangalore, with the kits provided by the manufacturer. HAL went on to produce over 100 of these aircraft and also participated in an extensive electronic upgrade. The IAF equipped a total of five squadrons with this fighter-bomber: Nos. 5, 14, 16, 20 and 27. Sometime later, No. 6 Squadron was equipped with the shipping-strike version of the Jaguar. One other role for the DPSA was nuclear weapon delivery, if and when, India decided to weaponise its nascent nuclear capability. To be sure, the 1974 nuclear test was officially termed a 'peaceful nuclear explosion' (PNE), and India did not follow it up with any major weapons programme, but the long overdue induction of the Anglo-French Jaguar ensured a delivery system when needed. India began its Integrated Guided Missile Development Programme (IGMDP) only in 1983, nearly a decade after the 1974 PNE Test and finally tested its nuclear deliverable devices or weapons only in May 1998. According to Stephen Cohen and Sunil Dasgupta, "After three decades of focusing on air defence interception, the IAF acquired a modern two-engine strike aircraft; the Anglo-French Jaguar, supplanting the slower and more vulnerable Canberra. British Aerospace, the Jaguar manufacturer, had offered the plane to India as early as 1968, but New Delhi had rejected it for fear of accepting another orphan aircraft such as the Gnat."[36]

The IAF and indeed the Indian Government have shown marked reluctance to choose an aircraft under development, perhaps because Indian aviation industry was not confident of maintaining an unproven aircraft. Costs and distrust of Western vendors in the Cold War climate might also have been two other major factors. Except for the few Gnat and Jaguar squadrons, the IAF during this period was largely equipped with Soviet fighters.

Just when India felt confident of deterring Pakistan by acquiring a deep penetration strike capability, the latter once again managed to upset the qualitative balance by inducting the formidable F-16 'Fighting Falcon' from the US in the early 1980s. Today, even after 30 long years, the F-16 remains a formidable opponent for the third and fourth generation fighters of the IAF, a tribute to American technology and Pakistan's farsighted approach to aircraft procurement. Pakistan became the so-called 'frontline' state when the Soviets invaded Afghanistan in late December 1979, and extracted a high price for its cooperation. The US did not want the Soviet Union to come close to the oil-rich region of the Arabian Sea and decided to raise a force of Islamic mujahideen fighters to evict the Russians. In this scheme, Pakistan's Inter-Services Intelligence (ISI) worked closely with the Central Intelligence Agency (CIA), providing training and logistical support while Saudi Arabia provided the finances. Such total dependence on Pakistan meant that for almost a decade, the US had little option but to go along with Pakistan's demands. Pakistan received massive economic aid and 40 F-16 fighters. Pakistan also got round the US to ignore its clandestine nuclear weapons programme, that finally fructified in the late 1980s, but was kept under wraps until 1998, when it overtly tested its nuclear weapons. Pakistan also received generous technological and other help from the PRC. The Chinese not only provided Pakistan with the design of a fission bomb but also gave it the use of their nuclear firing range, to test it on 26 June 1990.[37] In the F-16, the PAF had found an antidote to the IAF's Jaguar. Although only a relatively small number of F-16s – 36 fighters plus four trainers – were procured, the purchase gave the PAF the confidence to face the IAF. Pakistan also, thus got a fighter that was capable of nuclear delivery.

India almost immediately reacted to this new Pakistani threat and ordered, in a great hurry, 49 Mirage-2000 air superiority fighters from France, followed by some 60 MiG-29 fighters from the Soviet Union. These two types were finally inducted into the IAF, only in 1985 and 1987 respectively. But such was the urgency to find an answer to the PAF's F-16, that India once again turned to its old and reliable supplier, and purchased a limited number of MiG-23 BN and MF, fighter-interceptor and fighter-bomber versions, as an interim measure. Both these types also had only limited range, but carried a bigger armament load than the MiG-21.[38] The MiG-23 had the advantage of being quite cheap in the early 1980s. For example, the MiG-23 MS was priced between $3.6 million and $6.6 million, depending on the customer; on the other hand in 1980, the F-16 Fighting Falcon was priced at $14 million, and the Flogger's closest Western competitor was the Israeli Kfir C2 at $4.5 million.

From about the early 1980s, the IAF saw slow but gradual expansion, and improvements in all major departments. By the second half the 1970s, it had also inducted some 30 squadrons of Soviet SAM III Pechora AD missiles. These were deployed mostly at forward airfields and other important Vulnerable Areas (VAs) and Vulnerable Points (VPs). The army also soon purchased the mobile self-propelled Quadrat SAM System to give protection to its armour, and in addition both the army and the air force also received a modest number of Igla shoulder-fired quick reaction Surface-to-Air Missiles (SAMs), also known as Man Portable Air Defence Systems (MANPADS). The Il-76 heavy transport and An-32 Medium Tactical transport or METAC, Mi-17 helicopters, Mi-25 and later Mi-35 attack helicopters, were also inducted in 1984-85. In fact, the 1979-89 decade saw major expansion and modernisation of the IAF. Except for the Jaguar and Mirage-2000, all the armament and equipment came from the Soviet Union. One noticeable fact about India's efforts at modernisation was – and to some extent still is – that both Russian and Western sources invariably offered aircraft and equipment on temptingly attractive terms, just when Indian defence industry appeared close to a breakthrough. Given the ever-present threat from Pakistan, India had little option and showed little enthusiasm for its indigenous defence programmes.

The PAF had by then acquired the French Crotale SAM, RBS-70 Quick Reaction Missiles (QRMs) and the Mirage III and the Mirage V fighters and FGA aircraft respectively, and as we have seen in the early 1980s, some 40 American F-16 fighters, that fundamentally changed the air power balance in the sub-continent, to the extent that Pakistan could not be treated casually. The Pechora SAMs were inducted to free a larger number of fighters from AD duties. The IAF also tried to develop and integrate this missile system and the accompanying mobile radars to strengthen India's AD. The PAF had also modernised its AD by deploying a very large number, some say up to 40, German Mobile Pulse Doppler Radars (MPDRs) along the IB and automated its Control and Reporting System (C&R) to frustrate the low-level fighter threat from India.

By the 1990s, the remaining few Hunter, HF-24 and Gnat fighters were phased out. The S-22 had also been phased out rather early, as its flight safety record was not exactly noteworthy, and the fleet also faced an acute shortage of spares, coupled with maintenance problems. The IAF was thus again faced with fast-dwindling numbers of its fighters, but this time there was no easy solution, as unit costs of aircraft had skyrocketed and the indigenous Light Combat Aircraft (LCA) programme was languishing for want of an engine, multi-mode radar and suitable and reliable digital fly-by-wire (FBW) flight control system and was unlikely to reach fruition before the turn of the century. In fact, the LCA made its first flight only in February 2001. The Indian economy was in dire straits and it seemed the 1990s would prove to be a very difficult decade, which it was. The Narasimha Rao government decided to liberalise the economy and succeeded in showing some early gains. The buzz in the Defence and External Affairs Ministries was to avoid war at almost any cost.[39]

Expansion of Capabilities

By the late 1980s, the IAF possessed some six squadrons of the DPSA Jaguar, two each of Mirage-2000 and MiG-29 and some 30 squadrons of MiG-21, when another Russian fighter-bomber, the MiG-27 began entering service. This aircraft had greater armament payload and range but once again posed serious and recurring maintenance problems. The R-29 engine often suffered from fourth-stage compressor blade failure and the decision to use a de-rated engine caused engine surge at the most critical times, such as on the take-off run. This aircraft is currently undergoing mid-life upgrade, but it is not clear if its maintenance problems have been resolved.

The Mirage-2000 is seen as being one of the most versatile and reliable multi-role fighters, with adequate range and armament, but according to some knowledgeable sources its maintenance and lifecycle costs have been prohibitively high. In 1993, when foreign exchange was in short supply, routine maintenance of the Mirage fleet alone used up more than half of the Rs. 90 crore worth foreign exchange allocated to the Directorate of Air Staff Requirements (DASR) for minor expenses.[40] At the time of its induction in the early 1980s, the Mirage-2000 was also an expensive and unproven fighter with few export customers, but proved to be a good buy despite its high cost. It also reinforced the widely held notion that Western equipment was decidedly better than its Soviet/Russian counterparts. The current plans to upgrade, mainly the avionics and radar, of the 52 strong Mirage-2000 aircraft fleet are estimated to cost a whopping $2.3 billion. Dependence on foreign suppliers for aircraft, armament and avionics puts an unduly heavy burden on the exchequer, and raises serious doubts about the operational preparedness of the air force. To be fair, the initial cost of the Russian equipment was invariably much lower than its Western counterparts, and the terms of payment were also generally favourable, but their lifecycle costs were invariably high and difficult to calculate.

The Soviet Union offered the MiG-23 in the 1970s, when India was in search of a DPSA as a replacement for the ageing Canberra. The IAF rejected it because of inadequate range and performance. India then purchased the Jaguar from the UK, which was also quite costly. The Russians again made a better offer and said, "Take the aircraft now, start payment only after two years, complete the payment in 17 years at two per cent rate of interest." The Indian government told the IAF to accept the aircraft even if it did not fully meet its requirements. The Air Staff Requirements (ASRs) for the MiG-23 were allegedly written after the deal was already finalised.[41]

Despite all out efforts, the strength of the IAF fighter fleets was fast dwindling on account of ageing, technological obsolescence and maintainability issues. During the 1980s and early 1990s, while pilots of the Jaguar and some of the new types of Russian aircraft were flying 120-150 hours a year, those of Sukhoi S-22, HF-24, Hunter and Gnat were barely managing to get 80 hours a year. Many of the units were thus struggling to maintain the operational status of their pilots. The IAF is normally expected to maintain a daily serviceability and availability of around 50-60 per cent of the authorised strength of 16 fighters and two trainers in a squadron; but this was often not possible. Some believe that the IAF over-maintains its aircraft. The Americans say, "If it ain't broke, don't fix it." In other words, a machine is likely to start giving trouble if one unnecessarily tinkers with it, when it is working perfectly well. Every aircraft has to follow a servicing schedule laid down by the manufacturer – check, change and replace parts such as filters, seals at regular intervals. But when a fleet faces shortage of spares, users are prone to 'cannibalise', that is, take out a part from an already unserviceable aircraft that is on ground for scheduled servicing or snag rectification and use it to fix a problem on another aircraft. Very soon the subject aircraft becomes a 'Christmas tree' because repeated demands reduce it to a mere skeleton. At the root of this problem is the low MTBF or (Mean Time Between Failure), poor forecast of spares requirements, procurement delays in the pipeline, especially when it stretches to an Original Equipment Manufacturer (OEM) in another country and lastly the inability of the local industry Hindustan Aeronautics Limited (HAL) or IAF Base Repair Depots (BRDs) to repair/service it in time. Earlier the Russian aero-engines, for example, were designed for a service life of just 200-300 hours as against some 600-800 hours for their Western counterparts. Tropical conditions, where dust, high humidity and temperatures and corrosion are routinely experienced, add to the difficulty of aircraft maintenance. This subject will be discussed in a later section, but suffice it to say that for decades poor serviceability and reliability have plagued the IAF.

Search for the Advanced Jet Trainer

A committee under Air Marshal D.A. Lafontaine was set up in the early 1980s to enquire into causes of fighter accidents in the IAF. The committee held 'pilot error' as one of the main causes and attributed it to poor training due to the non-availability of the AJT. The Kiran was considered too slow for a direct transition to MiG-21 aircraft, the mainstay of the IAF. The BAe Hawk and the French Alpha Jet were shortlisted and extensively tested. The IAF wanted a minimum of 99-106 aircraft but the Ministry of Defence (MoD) was prepared to sanction only 66. The differences arose because until then a trainer was expected to fly 30 hours per month, but given its experience, the IAF wanted that calculations be made on the basis of only 20 hours per month and to this, the Finance Ministry officials naturally did not agree. The Alpha Jet had two engines, a better thrust-to-weight ratio and an equally good avionics suite, with the French offering to transfer the entire manufacturing line with all the jigs and fixtures to India. The IAF however, wanted only the Hawk, because the spinning characteristics of the Alpha Jet were seen as 'disconcertingly oscillatory'. The deadlock was resolved only after a lapse of 18 years (because in the early 1990s the Indian economy experienced a downturn that effectively delayed all defence procurement decisions) when the BAe Hawk finally arrived in India in 2004. Only 66 trainers were allowed, with the first 18 being shipped directly from the UK, while the remaining 48 were assembled at HAL. The HAL has reportedly handed over the last of the Hawks only in 2012, effectively stretching the AJT acquisition process to a mind-boggling 26 years. It is difficult to say if the timely availability of the AJT would have automatically reduced accidents, but this long-drawn selection process does not augur well for defence decision-making. As we shall see later, this appears to be a direct result of poor teamwork and general absence of accountability. The PAF, on the other hand, has used the American T-33 and T-37 trainers for over four decades and successfully trained its pilots to fly a variety of fighters, such as F-7P and F-7MG, the Chinese versions of the MiG-21, Chinese J-6 and J-5, Mirage III and V, and the F-16 and more recently the JF-17 without much apparent difficulty.[42]

New Challenges

Although India had spent considerable sums of money on the modernisation of the IAF during the 1980s, by the early 1990s, the writing was on the wall. Almost all aircraft, helicopters, missiles and other equipment like radar, airfield infrastructure and even armament were reaching the end of their useful life. The An-32s and IL-76s, the mainstay of the transport fleets, had no respite, as air maintenance of forward troops, tactical and strategic lift and humanitarian assistance missions together, constituted a colossal task even during peace-time. The Mi-8 and Chetak helicopters were showing signs of ageing. The Pechora squadrons and their radars were short of spares. The five different types of MiGs, 21, 23, 25, 27 and 29 were in a similar state, mainly due to supply chain disruptions in the wake of the collapse of the Soviet Union, with different sovereign states manufacturing different spare parts. Although neither the Indian nor the Russian governments admitted these problems, serviceability plummeted across the IAF. It took considerable diplomatic effort and worldwide searches to obtain the urgently needed spares. It took some time before the supply chains were re-established. The MiG-21 upgrade to Bison was delayed and so were many other projects. The Narasimha Rao government had only recently embarked on an ambitious economic liberalisation drive and the Indian economy was only just taking off.

The 1991 Gulf War in which the US-led Allied air power played a decisive role, came as a wake-up call for China, India and many other countries whose air forces needed modern technology. The IAF and more importantly the Government of India (GoI) also realised that air power capabilities could not be ignored. In 1992, the PRC signed a major deal with the then cash-strapped Russia for the purchase of some 36 Sukhoi-27 air superiority fighters and licence production of another 200 units of this modern multi-role fighter. In addition, the Chinese also, soon employed a very large number of jobless Russian aviation experts, designers and engineers following the disruption of the Russian economy.

The IAF too saw merit in bidding for a similar type, since Russia appeared to be loosening its control on the sale of such high technology aircraft. The IAF wanted the Su-30, an improved and more capable multi-role version of the Su-27, which was roughly in the same class as the US F-15 Strike Eagle. Sometime in the mid-1990s, India approached Russia for the purchase of the Su-30 and the request was quickly accepted. The IAF was to first receive some 20 aircraft of a slightly older version of the fighter in a flyaway condition. The deal was that these aircraft would be returned to Russia once the India-specific models became ready. After the Bison experience, which saw a very successful mating of Western avionics with Russian platforms, the Indians wanted the Su-30 to be extensively modified with a host of Western avionics suites. The IAF also demanded that the Al-31F engine be fitted with a thrust vectoring nozzle, to further enhance the manoeuvrability of the already impressive fighter. The Su-30 has an RoA, much in excess of any other aircraft in the IAF inventory and can carry up to 8,000 kg of weapon load, including advanced Air-to-Air-Missiles (AAMs) and other stand-off weapons. India, it seemed, had finally obtained a capable fighter to effectively meet the needs of a truly multi-role fighter. The induction of the Su-30 was a windfall of sorts, as its licence manufacture with Western avionics would give India an option to quickly replace the rapidly ageing MiG fleets.[43] But as with other aircraft, this also took its own time and could not arrest the rapid decline of the IAF fighter inventory.

Conclusion

By the end of World War II, the IAF had barely expanded to a 10-squadron force, when the division of assets following the partition of the country, again brought down its strength to six-and-a-half squadrons. In October 1947, when Pakistan launched its aggression in Jammu and Kashmir (J&K) the IAF had only one transport squadron and six-and-a-half under-strength fighter squadrons equipped with obsolete aircraft such as the Spitfire, Tempest and others.

In the next 15 years or so, the IAF revived/raised 10 more fighter squadrons, 11 transport squadrons and four helicopter units, with the result that by the time of the Sino-Indian border war, the IAF had some 25 fighter squadrons, 12 transport squadrons and four helicopter units. India's air defence was weak, as it had only a few World War II vintage Marconi radars.

Between 1962 and 1971, the IAF raised some 10 fighter, three transport squadrons and three more helicopter units. As a consequence, in December 1971, the IAF had a total of 37 fighter squadrons composed of six Hunters, eight Gnats, five Canberras (including 106 Strategic Recce Squadron and Jet Bomber Conversion Unit (JBCU), six S-22s, eight MiG-21s and two HF-24s and two Mystere IVA squadrons. In addition, it had raised the Tactics and Air Combat Development Establishment (TACDE) equipped with an equal number of S-22 and MiG-21 fighters. The IAF had also operationalised all six high-powered radar units of American origin and received some four Soviet P-30 radar units, considerably strengthening its air defence capabilities.

Its transport fleet comprised two An-12s, four C-119 Packets, three Dakota DC-3s, one Caribou, one Il-14, two Otters making a total of 14 squadrons and an assortment of other light communication aircraft such as Devon, AVRO HS-748 and a mixed squadron of L-1049 Super Constellation airliners discarded by Air India, and a few surviving Liberator B-17 bombers, used mainly for maritime surveillance duties. The IAF also had 10 helicopter units equipped with Mi-4, Alouette and Bell. The 1980s saw major re-equipment and modernisation, with five new squadrons being raised with MiG-21, 23, 25 and 29 aircraft.

In 1947, India began with the hope of diversifying foreign sources of aircraft and equipment, but until the entry of the former Soviet Union, Britain and France remained the only exclusive foreign vendors. Although India purchased many C-119 Packet and a few Sikorsky S-62 helicopters from the US, Cold War politics did not permit this relationship to flourish further.

India began its experiment in self-reliance by developing the Gnat and HF-24 fighters, but both these programmes were constantly plagued with major uncertainties and maintenance problems and hence, were not pursued with vigour or necessary perseverance. In the case of the HF-24, it was the non-availability of a suitable engine that killed the programme. When the Cold War ended, the IAF could have revived this promising twin-engine fighter, had it carefully preserved it, but as in many other cases, retired fighter aircraft were sent off for decoration and 'motivation' displays to schools, city squares and small towns, with little or no benefits.

The choice of the MiG-21 and the subsequent modification of this aircraft to a ground attack role made the IAF somewhat complacent. Easy availability of a reasonably modern fighter in the 1960s, at low prices, in Indian currency (against rupee payment), influenced all procurement decisions. The choice of the MiG-23 BN and MF was based on political considerations. India's aviation industry faithfully licence-produced the MiG-21 with little or no modification or improvements. The Chinese, as we shall see in a later chapter, followed a totally different philosophy for their military modernisation and made many improvements to this Soviet fighter.

The delayed entry of the DPSA Jaguar affected the overall operational preparedness of the IAF but once the six squadrons became operational, flying training picked up. The IAF and HAL successfully collaborated to develop an indigenous solution to improve the Nav-Attack system of the Jaguar, and the DARIN Jaguar was the result. Further work has now delivered the more advanced DARIN III version of the DPSA. Plans to replace the Jaguar Rolls Royce Adour engine with a more powerful Honeywell engine are in the pipeline, but as with other projects, this is also delayed. Considering that the Jaguar is over 33 years old, the decision to replace the Adour with a more powerful engine should have come much earlier.

By the early 1980s, except for the Mirage-2000, all other purchases, Il-76, An-32, Mi-17, Mi-26 heavy-lift, Mi-25/35 attack helicopters, MiG-29, 25, and 27, a variety of AAMs and Surface-to-Air Missiles (SAMs) were of Soviet origin. Changing over to Western arms suppliers is therefore, not as easy as some observers appear to suggest. The Russians have also readily given India considerable assistance in the nuclear field, submarines, and surface ships and missiles. The Russian contribution to India's military preparedness is thus varied and pervasive, and for those who favour Western equipment, this umbilical cord cannot be severed easily.

Foreign vendors have always kept a close watch on India's defence modernisation and offered it aircraft and equipment at throwaway prices, when it appeared that India was on the threshold of developing its own indigenous option. This has sometimes influenced India's commitment to indigenisation.

It is a truism that an aviation industry has to first satisfy its major customer – in this case the IAF – and only then can it rely on the customer placing further orders. Despite the consistent support from the Ministry of Defence (MoD), HAL has not always kept this requirement in mind. As a result, the IAF is often criticised for always demanding 'top-of-the-line' foreign (read Western) aircraft and equipment, while HAL is praised for producing aircraft under licence.

Last but not least, Indian decision-makers have always linked the development of indigenous aircraft with IAF force structures. The MoD and Defence Research and Development Organisation (DRDO) somehow fail to understand that the IAF cannot but ask for immediate replacements, if and when, its strength and operational preparedness are lower than acceptable levels vis-à-vis the threat. Unless a programme becomes mature, viable and truly reliable, the government must not order the service to await the outcome of any indigenous effort. The IAF, for example, has been asked to place orders for some 40 LCA Tejas fighters when in fact the grossly underpowered LCA, now weighing over eight tons, will not meet IAF needs and worse, might not be available before the end of 2017, a full 30 years after its development commenced.

Since Russian aircraft and equipment constitute a major share, their serviceability and availability also need closer attention. The author believes that if India were to give to the Russians, even a small fraction of the money that it lavishes on Western OEMs for spares and maintenance, the IL-76 and Su-30MKI serviceability will show dramatic improvement. There are, however, others who disagree, because they believe that the cause of poor serviceability lies in Russian technology and not better coordination with Russian manufacturers. The IAF and HAL will, however, also have to put in sustained hard work, especially now that the IAF has decided to purchase an additional 42 Su-30MKI from Russia. It is time India asked Russia to accelerate the plans for establishing a joint venture company for aircraft maintenance and logistics support in India.

Finally, there has also been excessive emphasis on the numbers of fighter squadrons and insistence on hi-tech equipment, rather than on new and innovative tactics and strategies, and suitable organisation for their employment. The army's insistence on Close Air Support (CAS)/Offensive Air Support (OAS) demands and the IAF's supporting role in conventional war scenarios, and the IAF's stress on air superiority, instead of a truly innovative joint strategy, is unlikely to help enhance India's ability to deter its adversaries.

Despite these never-ending arguments, it is also equally true, that a nation-state such as India needs a modern air force and its own military aviation industry.

NOTES

1. The quotes and details are taken from Air Marshal M.S. Chaturvedi's, *History of the Indian Air Force,* Vikas, New Delhi, 1978, pp. 1-15. While Chaturvedi gives March 1941 as the date, the official history of the squadron gives April 1, 1941 as its date of birth.
2. Details of the dates and types of aircraft of these squadrons are given in Appendix I.
3. Air Marshal M.S. Chaturvedi, no. 1, pp. 49-51.
4. Durga Das, *India: From Curzon to Nehru & After*, Rupa & Co., New Delhi, 1969 (Reprinted 1974), pp. 250-251. This is an extract of a conversation that Durga Das had with General Smith at a farewell party hosted by General Sir Claude Auchinleck on August 14, 1947. Durga Das, then editor of *Hindustan Times*, thought that there was an element of truth in the General's statement and that the Pakistani invasion of Kashmir came as a godsend, as it provided the mortar to build a cohesive army and gave the opportunity to the officers belonging to the so-called non-martial races to provide inspiring leadership.
5. Air Marshal Bharat Kumar (Retd.), *An Incredible War: Indian Air Force in Kashmir War 1947-48,* Knowledge World, New Delhi, 2007, pp. 10-20. India, however, used fighters to bomb the Mizo rebels in 1966.
6. Ibid., p. 21.
7. Air Marshal M.S. Chaturvedi, no. 1, p. 53.
8. Today we look at 'age and experience' of our leaders in a totally different light. At the time it was quite normal and indeed common to have relatively young people filling important positions. Lord Mountbatten, the Viceroy, was only 47 years old, Nehru 58, and most of the senior military officers were in their late thirties and some in the early forties. It was in fact the towering personality of Pandit Nehru and the aura of greatness attached to his persona that made others look inexperienced, even when many of them had over 15 years of military service, command experience in fighting a five-year-long war, and managing sizeable numbers of troops and military assets.
9. Air Marshal Bharat Kumar, no. 5, p. 13.
10. Ibid. p. 13.
11. Air Marshal M.S. Chaturvedi, no. 1, pp. 59-60.
12. Chris Smith, *India's Ad Hoc Arsenal: Direction or Drift in Defence Policy?* SIPRI, Oxford University Press, 1994, p. 68 gives 1948 as the year in which the RIAF received 100 Spitfire and Tempest fighters. But this seems incorrect as these aircraft took part in the Kashmir Operations from October 1947 onwards.
13. Air Marshal M.S. Chaturvedi, no. 1, p. 99.
14. Ibid., p. 54., The figures given by Chaturvedi at page 187 are somewhat different.
15. Ibid., p. 107.
16. Chris Smith, no. 12, p. 48.
17. Ibid.; Also see Air Marshal Bharat Kumar, no. 5.

18. Ibid., p. 49. There was, however, no clarity on which the second-class army might be and which first-class war India might be faced with. Blackett probably meant Pakistan.
19. Also see Lorne J. Kavic, *India's Quest for Security: Defence Policies 1947-1965*, EBD Publishing & Distributing Co., University of California Press, Berkeley & Los Angeles, 1967, pp. 51-57.
20. Ibid., p. 51.
21. Ibid., p. 52.
22. Robert S. Anderson, *Patrick Blackett in India: Military Consultant and Scientific Intervenor, 1947-72. Part One*, The Royal Society at http://www.jstor,org/stable/532210, pp. 263-69. (Accessed June 19, 2013). Also see Ramdas P. Shenoy, *Defence Research and Development Organisation 1956-1982*, DRDO Monograph Series, DESIDOC, Ministry of Defence, New Delhi, 2006, pp. 16-22 at http://drdo.gov.in/drdo/pub/monographs/Introduction/defence_hod.pdf, (Accessed June 20, 2013.)
23. Cheryl Payer, *The Debt Trap: The IMF and the Third World*, Penguin Books, London, 1974, p. 167.
24. Robert S. Anderson, no. 22, p. 269.
25. Air Marshal M.S. Chaturvedi, no. 1, pp. 99, 107-109; Chris Smith, no. 12, pp. 53-54.
26. Ibid., pp. 100-109.
27. Srinath Raghavan, *War and Peace in Modern India: A Strategic History of the Nehru Years*, Permanent Black, Ranikhet, 2010, p. 186.
28. Ibid., p. 187.
29. With active American assistance, Pakistan once again achieved the same effect when in response to India acquiring the Jaguar, it managed to get some 40 F-16 air superiority fighters in the early 1980s. The entry of the F-16 radically changed the very complexion of the air power balance in South Asia.
30. Chris Smith, no. 12, pp. 68-69.
31. In an interview Air Marshal Y.V. Malse also confirmed this as the basis of rough calculations.
32. Wg. Cdr. M.S.D. Wollen, an experienced pilot, was at the controls of the MiG-21 aircraft. See P.V.S. Jagan Mohan and Samir Chopra, *The India-Pakistan Air War of 1965*, Manohar, New Delhi, 2005 (Reprint 2006), pp. 85-86.
33. Ibid., Wg. Cdr. M.R. Murdheshwar had an enemy Sabre in his gunsights at very close range, but his Gnat guns failed him on September 4, 1965 over Chhamb. p. 84.
34. Nos. 1, 4, 8, 28, 29, 39 45, 47 and one flight of TACDE were equipped with the MiG-21 (Type 77) and Nos. 26, 32, 101, 108, 221, 222 and one flight of TACDE were equipped with the S-22 aka Sukhoi-7 fighters.
35. The British had asked India to join them in the Jaguar development programme, but lack of foresight or inherent aversion to risks, resulted in loss of an excellent opportunity to get a modern aircraft as well as invaluable experience in its development.
36. Stephen P. Cohen and Sunil Dasgupta, *Arming Without Aiming: India's Military Modernisation*, Viking, New Delhi, 2010, pp. 77-78. Their comment that the IAF is wary of purchasing aircraft that are not in the inventory of the country that manufactures them does not give the full picture. The IAF declined the American offer of Northrop F-20 in 1986 simply because the US had already supplied 40 F-16, a far superior fighter, to Pakistan. India naturally did not want to be weighed down by this obligation and get stuck with an inferior aircraft.
37. K. Subrahmanyam, "India's Grand Strategy", *Indian Express*, February 3, 2012.
38. According to Air Marshal Philip Rajkumar (Retd.), the purchase of the MiG-23 was not based on any serious evaluation but simply because the Soviets had offered it at a low price to the Indian Government. According to Chris Smith, around the same time, India's Defence Minister R. Venkataraman also approved the purchase of a sizeable number of MiG-27 aircraft from the USSR, without ascertaining if the IAF really wanted or needed these.
39. The author was then posted on the Joint Planning Staff of the Cabinet Secretariat that was

in the process of being transferred to the MoD, and saw at close quarters the goings-on in the higher echelons of the military, and indeed the MoD.

40. Interview with Air Marshal Philip Rajkumar (Retd.) at Bangalore in February 2012.
41. Interview with Air Cmde. S.P. Tyagi on September 29, 1999 at New Delhi. He later rose to become the CAS.
42. According to media reports, the PAF accident rate has also been a cause of concern, but it is not as alarming as that in the IAF.
43. A story then doing the rounds of the Delhi circuit went something like this: In order to prop up the Yeltsin government, the US allegedly told P.V. Narasimha Rao that it (the US) would look the other way if India pledged \$300-400 million to Russia. Rao then called A.B. Vajpayee and said, "Let us help our old friend with whom we have a long defence relationship. In case the Congress does not win the next election, the money can always be adjusted against any other defence purchase." So came the Su-30 in 1996 for Rs. 6,000 crore or \$1.8 billion as per *Jane's World Aircraft*. This was confirmed later in Shekhar Gupta's column, "The Mulayam Touch", National Interest, *Indian Express*, September 22, 2012.

6

The Indian Air Force Today

The Never Ending Process of Modernisation

Before assessing the current status of the Indian Air Force (IAF), it is essential to examine what mission it is likely to be used for. Will it be: (a) conventional war; (b) limited border skirmish; (c) nuclear delivery or; (d) limited punishment/compellence strikes? The last appears the most likely but the Indian military seems to always prepare for a set-piece, copy-book conventional war. With China assisting Pakistan in the military and nuclear fields for decades, a strong possibility of collusion and hence a combined threat has always existed. But by raising the two-front threat, the military, especially the army, appears to ensure that its numbers are not slashed. This also seems to serve the government's purpose as it generates employment and keeps the armed forces, especially the army, happy. After all, it is the army on which the government depends for tackling numerous internal security challenges and threats. The insistence of the IAF to prepare for 'Full Spectrum Dominance', however distant its possibility, also follows the same line of thinking, i.e. preparing for a worst case scenario of an all-out conventional war. In light of the above one wonders if the Indian military is trying to bite off more than it can chew. Given the slow speed of decision making it may be increasingly difficult to sustain this kind of military modernisation and incremental expansion.

Ever since independence Indian security thinking has been rooted in 'loss of territory'. The Pakistan-sponsored tribal invasion of Kashmir in 1947, and the 1962 border war with China have only reinforced this deep-rooted apprehension. Separatist elements in Jammu and Kashmir (J&K) and the North-east and the

Maoist or Left-Wing Extremist challenge continue to add to these fears. The result is a huge infantry-heavy army, suited to holding every square inch of ground and a stunted navy and air force.[1] Suggesting that national security has to look 'beyond' frontiers, Rear Admiral Raja Menon says that merely making political statements that our armed forces are employed in some kind of 'chowkidari' (watchman's role) or 'border defence' tasks to keep out trespassers cannot obviously substitute for national security planning.[2] Such a defensive and outmoded approach not only encourages the tendency to look inward but also fails to derive the most out of the inherent strength of air power. Once again, the result is its sub-optimal utilisation.[3] That air power is essentially offensive but flexible, and hence can be employed in multiple ways is routinely forgotten. With the result, India's response to multiple cross-border threats fluctuates from total inaction at one extreme, to full-scale conventional war at the other. This shows a markedly narrow, unimaginative and inadequate understanding of air power and also a general lack of innovative thinking. Simply stating that India does not covet territory and wishes to live in peace with others does not automatically guarantee that others will not covet Indian territory. An oft-repeated vow to defend every square inch of Indian territory is also impractical and very often works against the basic tenets of military strategy, as India realised in the 1962 border war. To ensure optimal utilisation, the IAF must, as far as possible, be used to prevent or pre-empt aggression/intrusion at the first available opportunity.

The first and most important task of the air force, is the defence of the nation's skies. It is also equally important to ensure air dominance; i.e. dominance of the air and dominance from the air of the events on the surface below. Not only does air power influence events on ground and sea but if employed in time, very often prevents their occurrence without firing a shot in anger. The 'flour bombing' or dropping of food to the Tamil population of Jaffna in Sri Lanka by IAF An-32 transport planes on June 5, 1987, is perhaps the best example of such benign but effective use of air power. To achieve this the IAF has to maintain a constant alert to ensure immediate response; and it goes without saying, that it must be suitably equipped for a variety of tasks during peace and war. It is in this department that the IAF has been facing major challenges for some time. Although it embarked on a massive and comprehensive modernisation programme over a decade ago, it has not as yet completed this process, due to India's total dependence on foreign countries for modern arms and aircraft. While modernisation is a time consuming and continuous process and some delays are often inevitable, but today this is beginning to weaken India's military preparedness.

While it is true that the chances of a conventional war in the sub-continent are somewhat low, but military preparedness continues to be crucial for effective deterrence. The IAF aims for full spectrum dominance, which in other words means that it must be ready to meet all kinds of threats – from a sub-conventional conflict to nuclear war. This appears to be somewhat ambitious or even unrealistic, because preparing for a 'worst case scenario' might diminish its ability to respond to the 'most likely scenario,' which in India's case might well be another 26/11 type of terrorist attack or Kargil-type intrusion. The two-front threat therefore, needs to be seen in the correct perspective. China has an able and willing partner in Pakistan to play the role of its 'cat's paw,' and hence all threats are essentially combined. It is thus clear that to be an effective deterrent the acquisition of high tech equipment or modernisation must be a time-bound process.

The Pakistan Threat

How does India implement its policy to 'deter' Pakistan and 'dissuade' China from launching a conventional war? In reality, it seems Pakistan has effectively neutralised India's perceived conventional superiority. By adopting a policy of cross-border terrorism or proxy war under a thinly veiled nuclear threat, Pakistan does not need to launch a conventional war. Simply deterring Pakistan from launching a conventional war is, therefore, not the right strategy because Pakistan does not have to resort to open conventional war, if India is effectively prevented from taking even limited retaliatory military action. Such deterrence is useless, since Pakistan neither has the capability to challenge India in a conventional war nor does it need to. India must devise ways to effectively neutralise Pakistan's 'nuclear strategy', for a calibrated military response in which the IAF can play a major role.

The China Threat

China, on the other hand, appears to be satisfied so long as it can keep India on the back foot, for which it adopts a smart strategy. First, it maintains that the resolution of the vexed border issue will take a long time. Second, it provides a variety of assistance – military, economic, nuclear and above all political – to encourage Pakistan to keep India unbalanced, fully occupied and yet diplomatically engaged. Third, it administers its own kind of pinpricks: water-use threats, occasional intrusions across th Line of Actual Control (LAC), denial of visas and other such actions across the whole spectrum of relations. Fourth, it encourages India's smaller neighbours to up the ante, when possible, and finally provides economic and other assistance to India's neighbours. China's People's Liberation Army (PLA) troops have maintained an active presence in infrastructure development activities in Pakistan-occupied Kashmir (PoK), so that India gets a clear message, but cannot really resort to any retaliatory measures.

China also cleverly shows readiness to take limited palliative measures to prevent a major rupture in bilateral relations; or in other words, uses 'smart' power to constrain India's options.

A very sophisticated politico-military strategy is therefore needed to address these challenges. Without such a strategy expressly tailored to meet Pakistani adventurism and frequent Chinese pin pricks, mere military modernisation or selective additions, such as the reported raising of a mountain strike corps[4] for the Eastern Front may not ensure effective deterrence against the calibrated yet unfriendly, behaviour of the two neighbours. IAF's current capabilities and its future modernisation programmes, need to be assessed in light of these realities. Merely acquiring new aircraft and weapon systems without developing specific strategies to meet the above challenges may prove costly, and even unsustainable. India must guard against an unintended arms race with China. It is thus axiomatic that the IAF maintain its readiness, by maximising and further sharpening the power of its existing assets, so as to enlarge the available options. The political leadership must be assured of this capability, so that it can exercise the option of instantly resorting to use of force in a future contingency.

Prospects of Modernisation

Irrespective of what India does, however, it cannot quickly arrest the dwindling numbers of IAF fighter squadrons. It is not as if this situation was not anticipated. Sometime in the early 1990s, the IAF had begun to take a hard look at its true combat strength. With the prospect of the majority of its fleets coming up for gradual but certain retirement, the IAF began searching for alternatives. The induction of the Su-30MKI in the late 1990s was aimed at enhancing the quality and reach of the IAF and not a mere quantitative replacement of its second-generation fighters. The indigenous Light Combat Aircraft (LCA) Tejas, it was hoped, would gradually fill the void created by the phasing out of the numerous MiG variants. Although the LCA made its first flight in February 2001, it achieved Initial Operational Clearance (IOC) only in December 2013, a full 12 years down the line. The LCA Tejas Limited Series Production (LSP-8) carried out its maiden flight sometime in early April 2013.[5] Full Operational Clearance (FOC) is, however, due only by the end of 2015 or early 2016. Hindustan Aeronautics Limited (HAL) is in the process of manufacturing the 40 LCA Tejas fighters ordered by the IAF.

It was in these circumstances that the search for the Medium Multi-Role Combat Aircraft (MMRCA) began in early 2004. Given the slow and grinding processes of defence procurement the selection of the Dassault Rafale was announced on February 1, 2012 with the hope that price negotiations would be completed and the contract signed in fiscal year 2012-13. But that has not happened and current indications are that it will not be signed before March 31, 2015. A marked economic slowdown in 2011-13 forced the Indian Government to make significant cuts in the 2012-13 defence budget. This was followed by only a marginal increase in the budget for 2013-14. It is therefore likely that the MMRCA induction schedule would have to be revised with the Rafale entering service only by 2017-18 or even later. Some pessimists believe that the deal might unravel if economic difficulties continue.[6]

Just as the IAF was forced to extend the operational life of its oldest MiG-21 (Type-77) fleet due to procurement delays, it would once again have to find similar options. Presently the MiG-29, Mirage-2000 and Jaguar fleets are all slated for extensive upgrades which leaves only the Su-30MKI, as the IAF's mainstay. The already upgraded but ageing MiG-27, MiG-21 Bison and its M and MF variants will have to continue being used, in relatively low-threat areas or in combination with the Su-30MKI. The IAF is thus faced with a stark choice of serious depletion in its offensive capabilities, at least in terms of numbers. While the government and IAF must already be conscious of these difficulties, it is not clear how they would address this problem.

The induction of six Hercules C-130J has been completed and a contract for six more signed.[7] Three C-17 heavy lift aircraft have also been inducted in the service. The fourth C-17 was inducted in September 2013. *The Military Balance 2015* brought out by the Institute for Strategic Studies, London reports that C-17A are now on the IAF inventory.[8] The IAF has ordered six more of these and they are expected to enter service by the end of 2015. The IAF C-17 fleet will thus comprise 16 aircraft, giving the country a major strategic airlift capability. The Il-76 fleet is showing signs of ageing; and the An-32 fleet is also equally old.

While the new Mi-17-V5 medium helicopters are in the process of induction, a majority of the Mi-8, Cheetah and Chetak light helicopter fleets are fast reaching the end of their useful life. The IAF has only a small number of air-to-air refuelling tankers and just three Airborne Warning And Control System (AWACS). It is reasonable to assume that it would take some time before these new systems and technologies are fully absorbed. The contract for 75 Swiss Pilatus PC-22s was signed but these only began to join service in mid-2013, with the 'basic' and 'advanced' training continuing on the Kiran Mk.1, 1A and Mk.2 trainers of 1970s vintage. A total of 49 Pilatus PC-22s are now in IAF service for basic training.[9] All of the 66 BAe Hawks have been inducted, but it is not known if their supply chain and maintenance schedules are working smoothly, and if HAL is able to provide the necessary spares and maintenance backup. Any shortfalls in this area may have an adverse impact on both basic and operational training.

The 25-odd Pechora Surface-to-Air Missile (SAM)-III squadrons have already become obsolete, and two squadrons of the indigenous Akash SAM system have joined service only in 2014. There is also no guarantee of the Short and Medium Range SAM (SR/MR SAM) systems being developed with Israel, becoming available in the near future.

The Challenge

Let us now briefly examine the state of the Pakistan Air Force (PAF) and People's Liberation Army Air Force (PLAAF), the two main challengers of the IAF. China and Pakistan are continuing to build their strategic partnership, with the PAF fast reaping its benefits. Three JF-17 squadrons have been already formed, with Pakistan Aeronautical Complex (PAC) at Kamra reportedly producing at least one JF-17 fighter per month. According to the Chief of Air Staff PAF, "With the capability of carrying a variety of weapons, it is a true multi-role aircraft and in time would become the PAF's mainstay."[10] The Russians have not only reconciled to China selling the Russian origin RD-93 aero-engine to Pakistan but Russia, in fact, is showing clear signs of mending diplomatic and economic relations with Pakistan, in the run-up to the departure of North Atlantic Treaty Organisation (NATO) forces from Afghanistan.

China has already demonstrated two new prototypes of its indigenous fifth generation fighter aircraft (FGFA), the CAC J-20 and SAC J-31. Production of the J-10 and J-10B is also proceeding apace. Thus, the number of fully ready and operational fourth generation fighters in the PLAAF inventory is steadily increasing. Both these countries are also collaborating in other areas. Pakistan is already fielding the Swedish SAAB-2000 Erieye and the Chinese Y-8 ZDK03 Airborne Early Warning and Control (AEW&C) aircraft. China is also providing the PAF with a variety of modern missiles. The United States (US) has also supplied the PAF with BVR missiles such as the AMRAAM AIM-120 Sparrow, and has also completed the upgrade of all PAF F-16 Fighting Falcons, of which it now possesses 76 units. The PLAAF is regularly exercising/training/deploying its modern fighters from airfields in Tibet and Xinjiang, further sharpening the combined challenge from across the borders. The challenge to the IAF is thus rapidly acquiring a serious dimension.[11]

Despite frequent changes and modifications in India's defence procurement policy and efforts to galvanise its defence aviation industry, the military, especially the IAF, continues to depend on foreign vendors for close to 70 per cent of its needs. The government has also introduced many changes and further liberalised its defence offset policy, but this has not as yet attracted much foreign direct investment. In the circumstances, India has little choice but to reinvigorate its own defence industry, however slow the process may be. The United Progressive Alliance (UPA) Defence Minister A.K. Antony had repeatedly said that continued dependence on outside/foreign sources for India's defence needs is, 'dangerous and shameful' but to no avail. What with rapidly increasing costs of high tech weapons, a falling rupee and the current economic/budgetary constraints, the habit of simply purchasing ever more costly weapons and aircraft is neither affordable nor sustainable.

To further illustrate this point, in the first 20 years after independence, from 1947 to 1967, India purchased a large number of Vampires, Toofanis, Mysteres, Hunters, Canberras, C-119 Packets, DC-3 Dakotas, Canadian Caribous, An-12s, Il-14s, Mi-4s, Sikorsky, Bell helicopters, SAM-II Guideline missiles and MiG-21 and S-22 fighter bombers from various sources. During the next 10 years, 1968-78 it obtained as aid, an array of static high powered radar sets, and some transport aircraft from the US and Canada. India also purchased a large number of Pechora SAM-III missiles and Mi-8 helicopters from erstwhile USSR. In 1979, India purchased the Jaguar Deep Penetration Strike Aircraft (DPSA) or long-range strike aircraft from the UK. Although it had licence-produced a large number of Vampire, Gnat Mk.1, HT-2 basic trainers and HS-748 AVRO medium transport aircraft, and most notably numerous MiG-21 variants during the period, by the end of the 1970s it had to once again look to foreign suppliers for its modernisation programme.

Beginning in 1980, India purchased: the MiG-23 MF/BN; MiG-25; Mirage-2000; MiG-29; Il-76; An-32; Mi-17; Mi-25; 35 attack and Mi-26 heavy lift helicopters; Igla MANPADS; OSA-AK SAM and a host of radar sets, air delivered weapons and Air-to-Air Missiles (AAMs) and other equipment. The process of licence production of some of these aircraft and systems, and their maintenance was not yet fully over, when India had to once again start searching for a suitable replacement for its large fleet of MiG-21 variants. As a result, aircraft serviceability and availability, adversely affected sortie rates, training schedules, maintenance load and practices, servicing schedules and spares procurements. The collapse of the Soviet Union in 1991, further adversely affected the availability of spares and thus, aircraft serviceability. In 2015, the IAF is once again, at nearly the same decision point, with little hope of an early solution. Fortunately, with a sizeable number of Su-30MKIs, Il-76s, Il-78s, C-17s, C-130Js and Mi-17s, the IAF is in a much better state compared to the early 1980s.

According to *The Military Balance 2015*,[12] the IAF has the following assets:

Name	Strength	Remarks
Su-30MKI	215	A total of 272 fighters planned
MiG-29	74	Being upgraded
Mirage-2000	50	To be upgraded
MiG-27	126	Some 40 upgraded
Jaguar (includes 10 aircraft of maritime strike version)	105	Under DARIN III and Re-engining upgrade
Bison (Upgraded MiG-21bis variant)	116	Strength reducing
MiG-21 bis	31	Due for phase-out by 2017
MiG-21 M	54	Due for phase-out by 2017
MiG-21 MF	16	Due for phase-out by 2017
MiG-21 UB	40	Two seat trainers fast ageing
BAe Hawk	66	Mk. 132, AJT
Kiran Mk I	120	Trainers
Kiran Mk. II	55	Trainers
Total	1,068	Including Kiran trainers

Transports

Name	Strength	Remarks
Il-76	24	Heavy Transport
Il-78	06	Tankers
Il-76	03	AWACS
EMB-145	02	AEW&C, two more on order
C-130J	05	Six more may be added later
An-32	103	Medium Tact Transport
HS-748	56	Due for early replacement
DO-228	35	Light Transport
Gulfstream	03	ISR Duties
Boeings, 707, 737, & EMB-135	08	For VVIP duties
Total	245	All types

Helicopters

Name	Strength	Remarks
Mi-25/35	20	Attack
Mi-17	179	Including Mi-17 V5
Mi-8	94	Including 4 Mi-26
Chetak	60	Lama SA-315B
Alouette	40	SA-316
Dhruv	40	150 on order
Total	433	All types

Note: In addition, the army has 232 Dhruv and Chetak/Cheetah helicopters while the navy operates 94 fixed wing aircraft including 11 MiG-29K; 11 Sea Harriers; 05 Il-38; 04 Tu-142; 14 Do-228; 37 BN-2 Islanders light communication aircraft; 12 Kiran HJT-16 trainers; and a variety of Anti-Submarine Warfare (ASW), Airborne Early Warning (AEW) and Maritime Reconnaissance (MR) helicopters, totalling 127 units.

Let us now take stock of how the IAF can meet its primary responsibilities, in the near future.

Air Defence

The air defence (AD) capability of the IAF has received a big boost with the arrival of three AWACS in the recent past. In close coordination with the six Il-78 Air Refuelling Tankers, and the already long range of Su-30MKI, it is now possible to actualise the concept of 'forward defence' in which own AD fighter-interceptors, can theoretically intercept the enemy aircraft well before they reach their targets. Although the 250 odd MiG-21 variants have a relatively short range, these can now be more effectively utilised for airfield defence, and defence of important Vulnerable Areas (VAs) and Vulnerable Points (VPs) in depth. These can also be utilised for providing AD cover or 'top cover' in areas not covered by the AWACS. AWACS and the Air Force Net (AFNET), the recently inaugurated digital communication network of the IAF, will also facilitate air space management and help reduce 'friendly-fire' incidents. The absence of a dedicated secure link for air-to-air and air-to-ground communications, however, is a major deficiency and will be filled up only when indigenous efforts to build a link on the lines of NATO Link 16, fructify. This is vital, as without secure communications, air operations can face major disruptions and jamming problems. It is not known, but assumed, that the IAF would have ordered or already possesses the required numbers of AAMs since it is the Beyond Visual Range (BVR) missiles, that are needed to really exploit the advantage conferred by the long range surveillance capability of the AWACS. Peacetime AD is thus adequate and wartime requirements are gradually, but steadily improving.

Counter Air and Deep Strike Operations

As previously discussed in Chapter 1, depending on the type of conflict, the IAF may have to allocate considerable effort for these two vital tasks. In a border skirmish restricted in time and space, and hence mission objectives, it might not be necessary to launch deep strikes. In a larger conflict, however, the IAF will have to undertake Suppression of Enemy Air Defences (SEAD) operations on a scale commensurate with the military objectives. As is well known, the establishment of air superiority over a defined geographical area, is always necessary. During Kargil operations, the MiG-29 provided air defence cover and ensured non-interference of the PAF F-16 fighters based at Skardu, even when the Rules of Engagement (RoE) dictated that the IAF not cross the Line of Control (LoC). With the gradual build-up of the Su-30MKI fleet to its proposed strength of 272 aircraft, this long range offensive capability of the IAF is well taken care of.

Counter Surface Force Operations

Availability of the Jaguar and MiG-27, capable of delivering a much larger armament load than the MiG-21 or Hunter class of Fighter Ground Attack (FGA) aircraft will make the task of Counter Surface Force Operations (CSFO) much easier, more effective, and hopefully less contentious..The IAF has already assured the army and navy that it will not be found wanting in this department, provided that such operations form an integral part of overall plans and detailed prior consultations, to avoid delays and misunderstandings at the eleventh hour. Some army analysts have often argued for a dedicated ground attack fighter like the American Fairchild A-10 or Russian Sukhoi Su-25/39 for Close Air Support (CAS)/Offensive Air Support (OAS) Operations in a conventional war. This they believe is necessary because the MMRCA are often too fast and costly which makes it difficult for them to be utilised in larger numbers and high speeds also make target identification difficult.[13] This comparison is not valid for various reasons. First, MMRCA are capable of switching roles without any difficulty and that is precisely why these replaced the dedicated Air Defence or Ground Attack fighters. Second, a relatively slow moving ground attack fighter would be vulnerable to enemy fighters (as happened on September 01, 1965 in the Chhamb sector in the Tactical Battle Area (TBA) and would have to be provided air superiority fighters as escorts. Third, use of dedicated aircraft goes against the grain of air power employment as it restricts the inherent flexibility of air power. The IAF already has a sizeable number of BAe Hawk and MiG-27 aircraft that can be utilised for CAS/OAS missions. Finally, the A-10 and Su-25/39 would not be more effective than other multi role fighters in the high mountains and may in fact suffer a more marked drop in their performance at high altitudes.

Force Multipliers

A force multiplier as the term suggests, is the capability that when added to and employed by a combat force, significantly increases the combat potential of that force and thus enhances the probability of successful mission accomplishment. AWACS, Air-to-Air Refuelling (AAR) Systems, Precision Guided Munitions (PGMs), Electronic Counter Measures (ECM), Unmanned Aerial Vehicles (UAVs), Surveillance, Communication and Reconnaissance Satellites, Operational Data Link (ODL), and AFNET, are traditionally known as force multipliers. Together these give invaluable support for the success of combat operations.

AWACS

In March 2004, India placed an order with Israel for three Phalcon radar systems for $1.1 billion and another for three, Beriev A-50 (Il-76) heavy transport aircraft at the cost of $500 million. The IAF received the first of its three A-50 AWACS equipped with the Israeli Phalcon radars on May 25, 2009.[14] The radar uses the fuselage mounted 'rotodome' but the Active Electronically Scanned Array (AESA) radar, does not actually require a rotating antenna that was used by older systems. A typical AWACS carries a mixed crew of some 16, that includes two/three aircrews to fly the aircraft and a dozen or so fighter controllers, who man the multiple radar screens in separate cubicles in the large fuselage. With an assured coverage of some 300 km, the AWACS can provide early warning, as it can, depending on its position, detect enemy aircraft on the ground at their bases, or soon after they get airborne, well before they pose a threat to own VAs and VPs. The AWACS is thus capable of performing the task of many ground radars. Although vulnerable to enemy action, it can be protected by dedicated fighters under its close control. A typical AWACS has a range of 6,000 km and can remain on station for considerably longer periods of time, its efficiency limited only by the endurance of the crew and total fuel carried.

Air-to-Air Refuelling

In-flight refuelling system is not a new concept but has only recently entered the Indian skies. AAR can significantly extend the range of fighters and strike aircraft. The last time the IAF sent a Su-30 squadron to an American air base, the only support aircraft that accompanied them, was one Il-78 tanker and another Il-76 heavy transport that carried the maintenance crews and ground equipment. Typically, when on a long ferry, the tanker follows a 'trail' procedure, which means that it gets airborne earlier to meet with the main fighter elements on the way, refuels these and then lands at a predetermined airfield enroute, and the process is repeated until both reach the final destination. Another method is to set up a tow line, usually a race course pattern with several fighters receiving fuel from the tanker, when needed. Weather, visibility, light conditions, turbulence and enemy activity during hostilities are some of the important factors that affect these operations. Given the fact that in the past IAF fighters typically had extremely limitedRadii of Action (RoA), the addition of six tankers is a boon to the service.

Precision Guided Munitions

Precision Guided Munitions (PGMs) are not a recent addition to air power arsenals, but are nevertheless a major force multiplier. A Laser Guided Bomb (LGB); Air Launched Cruise Missile (ALCM); Joint Direct Attack Munitions (JDAM); and a whole host of anti-ship, anti-radiation, AAMs both close combat and Beyond Visual Range (BVR), have vastly improved and enhanced the safety, lethality and cost effectiveness of modern combat aircraft. The small diameter bomb; Bunker Buster; Brimstone; Javelin; Hellfire; and other such multi-purpose missiles, have in the recent past reuced the chances of collateral damage through better accuracy and a reduced spread.[15] The IAF, however, reportedly possesses a limited number of PGMs.

Unmanned Aerial Vehicles

At present, the IAF has only the Heron and Searcher Unmanned Aerial Vehicles (UAVs) and a few Harpy ant-radar UAVs. All three are of Israeli origin, and are used maily for surveillance, with the Harpy providing limited anti-radar strike capability. Following its huge success in the Af-Pak region, the Hellfire equipped Predator or Reaper UAVs, are now popularly known as 'drones'. The IAF must also acquire these, as they have more than proved their worth in the operations against the Taliban and Al Qaeda insurgents, in the mountainous areas of Afghanistan. Both armed and surveillance UAVs can be of immense help against Maoists and other insurgents. These can also be useful in weather forecasting, disaster relief, counter terror, anti-narcotics, anti-smuggling and coastal defence duties. The UAV/UCAV must, however, not be seen as a substitute for manned aircraft. High Altitude Long Endurance (HALE) type of UAVs may become the preferred option for strategic reconnaissance missions. UAVs have yet to prove their reliability in operations in congested and contested airspaces. Producing an indigenous UAV/UCAV should not pose a major problem and this option must be pursued with far greater vigour. India's Nishant and Rustam UAVs, the vehicle and rail-launched and parachute-recovered types, are still at the trial stage and a few more have reportedly been under development, for some years. The Government of India must give these projects the necessary impetus on a war footing.

Helicopters

India has not really used the 20-odd Mi-25/35 attack helicopters that it obtained from the ormer Soviet Union in the 1980s. An excellent platform for counter insurgency operations, attack helicopters have yet to prove their immense potential in India. There is some reluctance to use them, perhaps due to their inherent offensive character. Inter-service issues also need to be addressed before these assets can be optimally utilised. The purchase of the AH-64 Apache and the CH-47 Chinook heavy lift helicopters is on the anvil, but the doctrine for their employment is not yet clear. Inter-service consultations are urgently required to formulate the necessary Standard Operating Procedures (SOPs) for their effective employment, in peace and war, especially in the mountains.

Other Force Multipliers

The Defence Research and Development Organisation (DRDO) has been making Radar Warning Receivers (RWRs), Electronic Counter Measures/Electronic Counter-Counter Measures (ECM/ECCM) and Electronic Support Measure (ESM) suites for some years, but these are now reaching obsolescence. The IAF has also bid for a dedicated satellite for its exclusive use. A dedicated satellite for the navy was launched in September 2013. Three joint or inter-Service commands, viz. Space, Cyber and Special Forces have also been announced. The recent induction of six C-130J Hercules aircraft with grealy improved performance and the projected purchase of 10 C-17 strategic-lift heavy transports, add to India's force projection capability. 'Persistent' surveillance from 'near space' (20-100 km) is yet another possibility. A European aviation major has also recently announced that its 'passive radar' is undergoing trials. Although this concept is not new, advances in computing have made it possible to use it. The radar reportedly analyses television and radio transmissions and fixes the position of a flying object, as it crosses these waves; hence it can detect even stealthy aircraft. It is bound to pose a major challenge as and when it becomes operational.[16]

IAF Modernisation: Work in Progress

IAF's modernisation is characterised by production and procurement deadlines that are frequently missed. While some of the big-ticket purchases have fructified in the recent past, many more are stuck at various levels. The MMRCA contract continues with little clarity on its approval and delivery time lines. This time the reasons are a budgetary crunch and the apparent disagreement on whether the HAL should be the lead integrator or the recently floated Dassault-Reliance JV. Dassault is reportedly insisting that the latter be given the responsibility to ensure smooth and timely induction, and local production of the remaining 108 Rafale fighters, but the Ministry of Defence (MoD) favours the HAL for this task. In any event, the delivery of the first 18 Rafale fighters is expected to begin, only after a minimum of three years, from the date of signing of the final contract which as per the revised schedule, was due by the end of 2014. But this has not happened and may in fact be delayed further to the middle or late 2015. This means that the first batch of Rafale will begin arriving only in 2018-19 and local production will start thereafter. There is a big question mark on whether the offset, and other negotiations, will be successfully completed in the following three years. Given the present economic difficulties, some doubts have been expressed about the government approving this major purchase. Some believe that India might be forced to abandon the MMRCA deal and simply choose to buy additional Su-30MKI aircraft. The new Defence Minister Manohar Parrikar has reportedly said that IAF may have to make do with the Su-30MKI.[17] If all goes well, the Rafale induction will be over only by 2030.[18]

In an interview to a defence journal, the former Chief of Air Staff, Air Chief Marshal N.A.K. Browne said, "The induction of Rafale in the IAF along with associated weaponry will indeed prove to be a game changer in the IAF's combat capability." He also noted that, "At present the IAF has 34 fighter squadrons against the sanctioned strength of 42 squadrons and will have to live with this situation until the XIIth Plan."[19]

The LCA story is not very encouraging either. Although a preliminary (also called notional) IOC was awarded on January 10, 2011, in reality the IOC was awarded only in December 2013. The FOC was due in end 2014 but that has not happened, instead two LCA Tejas fighters of Limited Series Production were handed over to the IAF on January 17, 2015.[20] In December 2012, the LCA was sent to Leh for 'very low-temperature conditions' trials but these could not be completed as the engines failed to start. Earlier, the testing process was delayed due to insufficient space between the top of the pilot's helmet and the canopy and the canopy had to be modified to ensure minimum safe clearance. The LCA took part in the IAF's Iron-Fist Fire Power Display in February 2013 and also delivered some weapons, but that has not helped to remove the doubts about its timely induction. The first 40 LCA Tejas' will be fitted with GE-F404 engines, as the more powerful GE-F414 is not due for some time. The LCA currently does not have the latest Electronic Warfare suite, mid-air refuelling and long range missile capabilities, due only when FOC is awarded by the end of 2015. What with the LCA weighing more than its designed weight of 5.5 tons, these fighters will be underpowered, and may not actually meet IAF requirements. The trainer version of the LCA will also have to be readied in time to ensure smooth induction and conversion of new pilots. The IAF plans to raise a total of six LCA squadrons by 2021-22 but at the present pace, this goal appears to be ambitious.

The DARIN III (avionics upgrade) version of the Jaguar flew in November 2012. "This will result in major operational improvements with regard to all-weather, air-to-ground, air-to-sea and air-to-air capabilities through the incorporation of the multi-mode radar."[21] According to a HAL report, however, much work including some structural modification to the airframe would be required to accommodate the new equipment.[22] The Request for Proposals (RfP) for a new and more powerful engine for the Jaguar has also been issued, but this upgrade, though planned for some time, will also take at least three to four years to fructify.

During the visit of the Russian President Vladimir Putin to India in December 2012, a contract for additional 42 Su-30MKIs was signed. According to one report, the total cost of these 42 fighters is estimated to be around $4.3 billion, as these are expected to have better specifications. Rumour has it that these additional aircraft were specially configured for nuclear delivery and were to cost less than those produced by HAL. Whatever the truth, it is clear that the IAF is placing a higher degree of reliance on the SU-30 to maintain the minimum desired levels of operational readiness. The IAF presently has eight squadrons equipped with the Su-30MKI and plans to increase the strength to 15 squadrons, or according to some reports 272 aircraft. It is thus evident that the Su-30MKI will in all probability remain the mainstay of the IAF for the foreseeable future and these fighters will in fact fill the gaps that the gradual if delayed, phasing out of the remaining MiG-21s will create from 2017 onwards.[23]

The IAF's transport fleet of 24 Il-76s and 105 An-32s is also now nearly 30 years old and would require careful nurturing, with generous spares and maintenance support, as these two aircraft along with the Mi-8 and Mi-17 helicopters form the backbone of its air maintenance capability, on which depends the very survival of the troops and civilians in forward areas. The IAF has already received six special purpose C-130J Hercules transports from the US, and six more are likely to be added in the future. Although these aircraft are meant primarily for special forces operations, these may eventually be used for air maintenance and routine airlift tasks.

Infrastructure

MAFI or Modernisation of Airfield Infrastructure and GAGAN, Global Positioning System (GPS)-Aided GEO-Augmented Navigation programmes are two important projects that the IAF is now pursuing. MAFI is slated to upgrade 30 IAF airfields while GAGAN will provide satellite based navigation and digital communications.[24] There are also reports of the IAF fast acquiring a variety of light weight mobile radars for use in the mountainous regions of the North and North-east.

As previously noted, the large 25-squadron-strong, Pechora SAM force of the IAF is overdue for replacement, but only two squadrons of the indigenously produced Akash missile squadrons, have so far been inducted. Reports indicate that the IAF has placed orders for Medium Range Surface-to-Air Missiles (MR SAMs) with DRDO, which is planning to make these in collaboration with Israel, but there is no clarity on when these would be inducted.[25]

The Sukhoi-HAL FGFA or T-50 PAK-FA[26]

Another ambitious project on the horizon is the joint development of the T-50 PAK-FA fifth generation Russian fighter, the first prototype of which was expected to come to India sometime in 2013 but is currently delayed by at least three years. This project envisages the joint development and manufacture of up to 250 of these highly advanced fifth generation fighters in India.

On December 21, 2010 India and Russia signed a landmark deal to co-develop the T-50 PAK-FA (Perspektivny Aviatsionny Kompleks-Frontovoy Aviatsii), or Perspective Airborne Complex-Frontline Aviation aka the Fifth Generation Fighter Aircraft (FGFA), in India. Signed during the visit of the Russian Prime Minister Dmitry Medvedev, the MoD described it as the 'biggest defence programme ever in the history of India'. Depending on who looks at it and how, it can be called 'unnecessary splurging' or 'calculated risk-taking' in this exceedingly complex game of defence acquisitions.

India is slated to get a work share of some 25 per cent in the development of the FGFA and finally purchase 50 single-seat and 250 two-seat versions for the IAF. The deal is reportedly worth $30 billion and the unit cost of the fighter is likely to be around $100 million. The fighter flew for the first time on January 29, 2010 and had completed over 40 flights by the end of 2010. The second prototype began flight-testing in early 2011, but the design has actually been under development for over 10 years. The fourth prototype of the T-50 flew on December 12, 2012 from Komsomolask-on-Amur. Flight testing on three earlier prototypes has already crossed 200 flights. Its Western counterparts, the American F-22 and F-35 Joint Strike Fighter or JSF are already flying and the Chinese J-XX or J-20 flew for the first time on January 11, 2011. On October 31, 2012 China also flight-tested another fighter, the SAC J-31, to build internal competition and improve its prospects of exports.

The FGFA is stealthy (uses 'very low observable' technology) that makes it nearly invisible to a radar. It has: an Active Electronically Scanned Array (AESA) airborne radar with 'artificial intelligence'; super-cruise or the ability to fly at supersonic speeds without after-burners, i.e., without consuming too much fuel; a long operational range of over 2,100-2,500 km and a ferry range of some 5,500 km; the ability to carry next generation air-to-air, anti-ship and air-to-surface missiles; and thrust vector control (TVC) that gives it incredible agility. All these features make it a truly advanced FGFA, capable of performing a variety of offensive and defensive tasks in the future.

The relentless march of technology sometimes makes it extremely difficult to choose the right option, because of the prohibitively high costs of modern weapon systems and aircraft and the attendant uncertainty, due to time delays and cost escalations. A quick reminder from history should, however, be of help. Had the British not quickly developed and operationalised the radar and the AD communication network, that helped detect the direction, distance, speed, height and numbers of German bombers early on in World War II (the Battle of Britain for example), the Germans would certainly have retained the upper hand for a long time. At the time, the Germans were also well ahead in the development of their own radar system, but were late in operationalising it. Soon thereafter, began the effort to further improve the radar by making it less bulky, smart, jamming-resistant and mobile.

Along with these efforts the scientists also started looking for ways to make the aircraft less visible to the radar, by reducing the radar cross section (RCS) or reflectivity of the fighter aircraft and soon, the stealth fighter was born. The discovery of the radar had put major constraints on strike fighters by forcing them to fly low to avoid radar detection, which in turn reduced the range and weapons-carrying capacity of these aircraft, due to the very high fuel consumption at low levels. The so-called Revolution in Military Affairs (RMA), at least in combat aviation, is in fact nothing but a combination of stealth, long range, highly accurate fire power (PGM) with airborne radar, that is capable of detecting threats and directing BVR missiles, to the targets. In the meantime, AWACS, Airborne Early Warning (AEW) and Aerostat also have dramatically improved radar detection capabilities, further increasing the need for a truly stealthy aircraft. India's decision to buy the FGFA must, therefore, be seen as an important step towards obtaining the most advanced technology available, even if the costs appear to be very high and its delivery schedules uncertain.

Not surprisingly, the American, Russian and the Chinese versions of the FGFA look strikingly similar, although the Chinese J-20 is somewhat larger. The most noteworthy feature of the T-50 is the absence of a traditional rudder with the vertical twin-tail providing control surfaces. With a pair of Saturn 117S engines producing 142kN (~15,000 kg, 32,000 lb.) of thrust, the thrust-to-weight ratio is 1:1.19, which makes the fighter truly agile. Both the engines would be capable of individually vectoring their exhaust/thrust nozzles, to provide superior manoeuvrability to the aircraft. The T-50 also sports an extended leading edge, blended into the jet engine air intake, to meet the needs of super-cruise and relaxed stability.

The FGFA will carry all armament internally, so that airframe drag and radar reflectivity will be kept to a minimum. In theory, the FGFA will be capable of climbing to 60,000 feet in under two minutes, and reconnoitring the entire length of the border detecting any enemy air activity, neutralising threats if any, landing at distant airfields without air refuelling, and remaining invisible to enemy radar, and above all without any external assistance or AWACS guidance.

Some believe that India's contribution to its development would be quite low since the fighter is already flying. It is said that the Russians had offered the deal in early 2002, and again in 2004, but India was reluctant as it did not know enough about the programme, and had wanted to post its own scientists and engineers at the Sukhoi laboratories, which the Russians naturally did not approve. Another reason for India dragging its feet over the deal could have been the uncertainty of such high-tech and high-cost programmes, which makes it difficult to commit funds, especially when resources are limited. A 25 per cent work share is something HAL may be able to deliver on time. It is reported that HAL would be tasked to produce advanced avionics, including mission computer, critical software, cockpit displays, Counter Measure Dispensing Systems (CMDS) and perhaps composite materials, as its part of the share. It must be noted that the LCA and even the Su-30 MKI are already flying with HAL avionics and composites. Besides, HAL would get valuable experience of working on the development of a truly modern platform.

As part of the deal, the Russians are also allowing India access to the Global Navigational Satellite System (GLONASS) global positioning system, a navigation system that is reportedly more accurate than the non-military grade American GPS. The US allows access to military grade GPS to its allies only and perhaps friends that sign CISMOA and other-end user agreements.

Given that the Chinese military aviation industry will likely produce its own FGFA, the J-20 by 2020, it is prudent for the IAF to also become familiar with such advanced fighter designs. While there is an urgent need to reduce dependence on foreign suppliers for India's defence needs, especially modern combat aircraft, it would be unwise to unduly delay acquisition of technology simply because India's efforts at self-reliance have not fructified. Ten years from now, the aircraft might be even more expensive or worse, might not be available and hence, India has little option but to grab this opportunity. Analysts would remember the criticism that was levelled at the Su-30 purchase in 1996, but no other country would then have given India a fighter in the same class as the US F-15. Needless to add, the Su-30 MKI is now the backbone of the IAF along with the MiG-29 and Mirage-2000.

The IAF is sometimes criticised for buying every new toy in the latest glossy defence magazine, or chasing high-tech weapons, simply for the sake of technology, without linking its employment and utility to the national defence policy. Given the capital-intensive nature of airpower, such criticism is sometimes justified but it is equally true that India cannot afford to lag too far behind its likely adversaries in technology. Since India's own defence industry has not progressed as yet to a level where it can build such advanced aircraft on its own, India has little choice but to depend on its old friends. If all goes well, by 2020 the IAF may possess a reasonable number and suitable mix of high-end and medium-performance fighters.

While the 2013-14 economic indicators are not encouraging, and budgetary allocation for defence might come under stress, as the 2013-14 figures have shown, the government would have to find funds for these modern machines. Interestingly, both the F-22 Raptor and the F-35 Lightning II programmes have also faced major funding cuts. Although the unit cost of the Sukhoi-HAL FGFA is expected to be around $100 million, it would not be surprising if the programme also faces reduced orders in the future. India has probably ordered 48 single-seat and 166 twin-seat units to derive the benefits of economies of scale, but whether or not, such large numbers finally materialise, would depend largely on the state of the Indian economy and the capacity to spend large sums on defence procurement. According to a recent report, the IAF has already cut down the number of FGFA to 144 single-seat fighters, down from the original 214 aircraft.[27] According to another media report, the IAF is unhappy with the FGFA because (a) the Russians are reluctant to share critical design information with India (b) the fighter's current

AL-41F engines are inadequate, being mere upgrades of Su-30MKI's AL-31 engines; and (c) it is too expensive – with India paying $ 6 billion for co-development of the FGFA, a large percentage of IAF's capital budget will be locked up.[28] In order to preclude the spares/re-supply problems that the IAF faced after the collapse of the Soviet Union, there is a need to include in the contract agreement, maintenance and upgrade support *ab initio*. The IAF must also have considered lifecycle costs. Russian aircraft, airframe and aero-engine servicing cycles and total technical life are usually much lower than their Western counterparts and this adds to overall lifecycle costs. India must now ensure that it quickly establishes a local servicing facility and where possible, encourages Indian Small and Medium Industries (SMEs) to manufacture spares for the new aircraft.

The IAF would also have to seriously and quickly re-assess its manpower requirements. Both the Su-30 MKI and the FGFA are two-seat fighters, the rear cockpit being occupied by either a pilot or a Weapon Systems Operator (WSO). As is well known, basic and operational training takes time and requires resources in qualified flying instructors and suitable trainer aircraft. Currently, the IAF faces a shortage of basic trainers, and delays in the HAL Intermediate Jet Trainer (IJT) Sitara programme would further add to training woes. The IAF has already ordered an additional 57 BAe Hawk trainers and may also get more PC-7 basic trainers.

The foregoing clearly shows that the present scenario is fraught with uncertainties; but there is also hope that some of the on-going programmes will bear fruit by the end of the current decade.

NOTES

1. Raja Menon, "Components of National Security and Synergising them for Envisaged Security Threats in 2025", National Security Paper 2011, *USI Journal*, January-March 2012, pp. 104-43.
2. Ibid., p. 105.
3. *Basic Doctrine of the IAF*, Directorate of Operations (Space), Air Headquarters, September 2012, p. 4.
4. Rahul Bedi, "India approves mountain strike corps", *IHS Jane's Defence Weekly*, 50 (23), June 5, 2013, p. 14.
5. Rahul Bedi, "Antony sets December deadline for Tejas IOC", *IHS Jane's Defence Weekly*, 50(27), July 3, 2013, p. 14; also see *SP's Military Aerospace and Internal Security (MAI)*, 3 (8), April 16-30, 2013, p. 15.
6. M.K. Bhadrakumar, "India's MMRCA Deal Unravels" at http://blogs.rediff.com/ymkbhadrakumar/2012/03/13/indias-mmrca-deal-unravels/ (Accessed June 4, 2013).
7. One C-130J was lost in an unfortunate accident on 28 March 2014. See http://indianexpress.com/article/india/india-others/pilot-error-led-to-c-130j-hercules-crash-iaf-sources/
8. *The Military Balance 2015,* International Institute of Strategic Studies, Routledge, London, 2015, p. 251.
9. Ibid.

10. Interview with Air Chief Marshal Tahir Rafique Butt, *IHS Jane's Defence Weekly*, 50 (31), July 31, 2013, p. 34.
11. Mohan Guruswamy, "Will India and China fight a war again?" *SME Times*, September 26, 2012 at http://www.smetimes.in/smetimes/in-depth/2012/Sep/26/will-india-and-china-fight-a-war-again74911.html (Accessed on July 2, 2014).
12. *The Military Balance 2015*, no. 8.
13. Gurmeet Kanwal, 'Air Power and Future Battlefields: India's Needs', at http://www.ipcs.org/article/india/air-power-and-future-battlefields-indias-needs-4833.html (Accessed on February 28, 2015).
14. The IAF may eventually field ten AWACS aircraft. See Gulshan Luthra, "IAF to go in for 10 more AWACS: Rafale Deal hopefully by July", athttp://www.indiastrategic.in/topstories1910_IAF_to_go_in_for_10_more_AWACS_Rafale_deal.htm. (Accessed March 5, 2015).
15. Caitlin Harrington, *Jane's Defence Weekly*, 47, March 31, 2010, pp. 24-31.
16. "'Passive Radar' from Cassidian remains invisible", *Airbus Defence and Space*, July 19, 2012, at http://www.cassidian.com/en_US/web/guest/Passive%20radar%20from%20CASSIDIAN%20remains%20invisible (Accessed on July 20, 2012).
17. "Rafale in Storm Clouds, Parrikar says IAF can make do with Sukhoi-30", at http://www.business-standard.com/article/current-affairs/rafale-in-storm-clouds-parrikar-says-iaf-can-make-do-with-sukhoi-30s-114123100706_1.html (Accessed March 5, 2015).
18. Air Chief Marshal N.A.K. Browne in an interview to a Delhi-based defence journal *India Strategic* in October 2013, opined that the signing of the Rafale contract was likely to be delayed. The first 18 Rafale would join the IAF three years after that, and the delivery of the remaining 118 would be completed only in the 4th to the 11th year. See http://indiastrategic.in/topstories3054_IAF_transformation_happening_but_delay_on_MMRCA_is_worrying.htm (Accessed March 5, 2015).
19. *SP's Aviation*, October 2012, p. 20.
20. *IHS Jane's Defence Weekly*, 49 (21), August 31, 2012; Also see http://www.financialexpress.com/article/economy/32-years-after-tejas-light-combat-aircraft-to-be-handed-over-to-indian-air-force/31144/ (Accessed March 05, 2015).
21. *SP's Aviation*, 12, December 2012, p. 32.
22. See http://www.hal-india.com/futureproducts/products.asp (Accessed March 20, 2013).
23. Interview with Air Chief Marshal N.A.K. Browne, no. 18.
24. See http://www.indianexpress.com/news/indian-air-force-projects-mafi-gagan-to-benefit-pune-airport/778566, (Accessed March 21, 2013).
25. See http://www.globalsecurity.org/military/world/india/mr-sam.htm (Accessed March 21, 2013).
26. The next few paragraphs related to T-50 FGFA are based on the author's article in *Force* magazine, December 2011. In an interview on October 8, 2013 the Chief of the Air Staff admitted to delays in the procurement of the FGFA, at http://www.janes.com/article/28125/iaf-chief-plans-more-c-17s-admits-fgfa-delays (Accessed February 3, 2014); also see Gulshan Luthra, "IAF decides on 144 Fifth Generation Fighters", *India Strategic*, October 2012, at http://www.indiastrategic.in/topstories1766_IAF_decides_144_fifth_generation_fighters.htm; "Pak-FA/FGFA/T50: India, Russia Cooperate on 5th-Gen Fighters", *Defence Industry Daily*, June 11, 2014 at http://www.defenseindustrydaily.com/india-russia-in-negotiations-re-nextgeneration-fighter-03133/#more-3133 (Accessed on July 2, 2014).
27. See http://aviationweek.com/defense/india-cuts-orders-fifth-generation-fighter-aircraft (Accessed March 5, 2015).
28. See http://www.business-standard.com/article/opinion/ajai-shukla-how-rafale-is-killing-the-air-force-s-future-115021601822_1.html (Accessed on March 5, 2015).

7

The Future of Air Power in India

Introduction

Late 2014 witnessed a noticeable spurt in ceasefire violations by Pakistan along the Line of Control (LoC) and the International Border (IB) in Jammu & Kashmir (J&K) adjoining areas of Punjab.[1] India's response to these was seen as prompt and measured, yet robust. The comprehensive dialogue between the two neighbours had remained stalled since the cancellation of Foreign Secretary level talks in August 2014. In early March 2015, India's Foreign Secretary visited Pakistan as part of his interactions with all members of South Asian Association for Regional Cooperation (SAARC) and media reports indicated that talks with Pakistan may resume in the near future.[2]

Chinese army intrusions in Ladakh during the visit of the Chinese President Xi Jinping to India in September 2014 also became a cause of concern, especially since the Chinese army personnel returned to their side of the disputed border only after the departure of the Chinese President from India.[3]

As is its wont, China again objected to Indian Prime Minister Narendra Modi's visit to Arunachal Pradesh on February 20, 2015 but this time its tone and language was harsher. While China has regularly protested against visits of Indian Prime Ministers to Arunachal Pradesh on the grounds that it is a disputed area, it did not bother about India's sensitivity when its troops intruded into India, during its President's visit to India. Such behaviour does not help build mutual trust and makes it difficult to understand Chinese intentions.[4]

The United States (US)-led North Atlantic Treaty Organisation (NATO) forces in Afghanistan known as the International Security Assistance Force officially ended their mission on December 31, 2014 and were replaced by another NATO force named the Resolute Support Mission (RSM) comprising 13,195 military personnel from 42 NATO member countries, with effect from January 1, 2015. The RSM will provide advice, assistance and training to the Afghanistan National Army. At least as of March 2015, there are no indications that the RSM or any other part of NATO will participate in actual combat operations. The possibility of the US increasing the number of its soldiers cannot be ruled out. Pakistan has all along sought to play a major role in Afghan affairs to achieve what it calls 'strategic depth' and may once again become more active in its support to elements of the Afghan Taliban. With the withdrawal of NATO's combat forces from Afghanistan, sub-conventional threats across the border may become more widespread and sophisticated if the situation in Afghanistan worsens.[5]

In early March 2015, a People's Democratic Party – Bharatiya Janata Party coalition government came to power in J&K. Its Chief Minister Mufti Mohammed Sayeed thanked Pakistan, the Hurriyat leadership and the Kashmiri militants for allowing smooth conduct of elections in the state and also announced an amnesty for political prisoners in the state of J&K. While these may be viewed as normal populist measures that many political leaders resort to, such statements may nevertheless embolden forces inimical to India to create trouble with renewed vigour.[6]

On November 20, 2014 the Russian Defence Minister Sergey Shoigu visited Pakistan and the two countries signed a landmark defence deal. Although its details were not available, Russia had reportedly made an offer to consider the sale of Mi-35 attack helicopters to Pakistan. Pakistan and Russia also signed a US$ 1.7 billion worth energy deal. During his visit to Russia in November 2014, the Pakistani Finance Minister also evinced his country's interest in grabbing a maximum share in Russian markets. Pakistan may also be able to purchase the RD-93 aero-engine that powers the JF-17 fighter, currently being produced at Pakistan Aeronautical Complex (PAC) Kamra, with Chinese collaboration. Pakistan presently obtains these engines via the China route. Although Indo-Russian relations remain vibrant, it is clear that with the changing strategic situation in Afghanistan, Russia is keen on mending its relations with Pakistan, a country that was responsible for training the Afghan mujahideen and finally ending its occupation of Afghanistan in 1988. Although it is too early to assess its impact, Russia's eagerness to build a defence relationship with India's implacable neighbour will only further embolden Pakistan to harden its stand against India.[7]

In light of the above it can be safely assumed that India's borders with Pakistan and China will remain live and their relations problematic for the foreseeable future. India's armed forces cannot therefore lower their guard. The modernisation of the Indian Air Force (IAF) and its operational preparedness thus acquire added urgency and salience.

The Current Air Power Balance

The Military Balance 2015 shows the IAF fighter squadron strength as 37, whereas the Chief of Air Staff, IAF had put this number at 34. To avoid confusion, therefore, we will rely on the number of aircraft rather than on number of squadrons. As shown in the previous chapter, the current strength of the IAF is 1068 fighters, including 66 BAe Hawk AJT and 175 Kiran trainers, which are essentially advanced jet trainers but are also capable of limited strike operations. The Pakistan Air Force (PAF) has some 450 fighters, including 76 F-16s and 49 JF-17s, while the People's Liberation Army Air Force (PLAAF) possesses some 2239 combat capable aircraft. In the last decade alone, its J-10 fleet has shwn an impressive growth to 270 and the JH-7 to over 240, including 120 with the PLA Navy.[8] Numbers alone do not necessarily signify the real combat strength of any air force, which depends on many factors such as training, combat experience, doctrine, synergy with surface forces and comprehensive national power. But numbers nevertheless, give a good indication of current and future trends. These numbers or the numerical strength of the PAF and PLAAF clealy highlight the combined challenge posed by these two adversaries.

Force Structures

Force sructures are invariably constructed on the basis of affordability, access to technology, current and future threats and above all, service doctrine. In the case of the IAF, however, doctrine seems to have played onlya marginal role. This is so because India continues to depend on other countries for its military hardware. With the economy showing a marked upward trend in the last decade, India's options widened and the result was the introduction of a number of aircraft and systems that were unaffordable until then. India's quest for modern weapons is unlikely to end in the near future. With demand slackening in the West, India became a major customer for arms imports. India, it is widely believed, is planning to spend a minimum of $100 billion in the next 10 years. The 30 per cent mandatory offset clause in all major purchases, it is hoped, would also make India an attractive investment destination. Some major Indian companies such as Reliance, Larsen & Toubro (L&T), Mahindra and Tata have already formed joint ventures with Western defence industry majors and it is hoped that these will play an increasingly important role in India's defence industry.

The likely development of aerospace power in the next two decades would depend on many of these factors. Given the high cost of research, progress of the Indian defence industry is likely to be incremental rather than dramatic.

While it is too early to write off the future of manned fighters, there is a possibility that unmanned aerial systems and missiles will probably play an increasingly bigger role. While the US and its Western allies will continue to dominate the air power arena, there is a possibility of some of the developing countries of Asia, especially China, becoming more self-reliant in this field. India's indigenous military aviation industry may also grow at a faster pace, if the government gives it the right support and encouragement. Its past record does not, however, raise high hopes. The IAF is also likely to continue giving greater importance to advanced manned fighters rather than to missiles and UAVs/UCAVs.

Of the 1,042 combat capable aircraft of the IAF, as many as 259 are the old and ageing MiG-21 and 241 trainers. This leaves only 194 Su-30MKIs, 63 MiG-29s and 52 Mirage-2000s, clearly highlighting its 'air defence orientation'. The 100-odd recently upgraded MiG-27s and the 106 Jaguar Deep Penetration Strike Aircraft (DPSA) would be on their way out by 2030, unless the Jaguar re-engining programme fructifies in time. The Request for Proposal (RfP) for the same was withdrawn in March 2011, because of a 'single vendor situation', anathema to India's Ministry of Defence (MoD). It is believed that a new RfP has now been issued again with Honeywell's F-125 engine being the only contender.[9] The contract to upgrade the 52 Mirage-2000H to Mirage-2000-5 level has also been signed, but that will take another two to three years up to 2016-17. There is already some criticism about the very high cost of these projects.[10] The Tejas Light Combat Aircraft (LCA) and the Rafale Medium Multi-Role Combat Aircraft (MMRCA) will be available only by the end of the current decade, or perhaps even later.

Given India's expanding strategic horizons, the emphasis would be on long-range multi-role capability. In 2030, the IAF can hope to possess some 272 Su-30MKIs, 100 Tejas LCA, 60 MiG-29s and about 50 Mirage-2000s and if all goes as per plan, at least 126 Rafale fighters that are currently on order. A sizeable number of Fifth-Generation Fighter Aircraft (FGFA) Indo-Russian fighters may also form part of the IAF inventory by 2030.

Given that the PLAAF has already inducted 249 J-10 fighters, it can safely be assumed that China will produce 40-50 fighters every year. This trend is likely to continue for the next two decades. With the Chinese fighters becoming more and more sophisticated and reliable these may also gain a sizeable export market. There are already reports of Egypt's interest in locally manufacturing the JF-17, jointly produced by China and Pakistan. Given the current levels of defence cooperation between China and Pakistan, it is likely that a majority of PAF aircraft will be of Chinese origin and this will place added stress on the IAF.[11]

The high cost and restricted availability of the F-22 Raptor and F-35 Joint Strike Fighter (JSF) make it difficult for these to enter the region by 2030, except possibly for a few US allies such as Japan, South Korea, Taiwan and Singapore. It must, however, be remembered that in 1980 Pakistan was the first country in the region to get F-16 fighters, and may possibly get advanced American aircraft in the future.

But in the meantime, "under its Next Generation Air Dominance (NGAD) programme, Boeing has unveiled its design concepts for a sixth-generation fighter to replace the US Navy's F/A-18E/F Super Hornet after 2025, and to succeed the US Air Force's F-22 Raptor two or three years later. These are said to be stealthy, tailless, and super-cruise capable and would include optionally manned cockpits." One of the defining characteristics of the programme is likely to be its affordability.[12] In sum, the prohibitively high costs of the modern fighter platforms may compel India to look for other options such as mid-life upgrades, and life extension/refurbishing of the available fleets.

Airborne Weapon Systems

The quest for accurate delivery of bombs and munitions gained added urgency in the Vietnam War and the Laser Guided Bomb (LGB) soon became the most sought after weapon. The LGB can, however, go awry due to smoke, clouds and other atmospheric obscurities. The LGB's popularity was due to the simplicity with which a 'dumb' bomb was converted into a 'smart' weapon. This was done simply by adding a kit that included the laser seeker and fins to guide the bomb to the target illuminated by the laser designator, which was carried either by the fighter bomber in 'autonomous' mode or by a 'buddy' fighter. Where possible, a Forward Air Controller (FAC) was also used for laser designation. In Operation Desert Storm (1990-91), only 229 US aircraft were capable of delivering laser-guided munitions. By 1996, the expanded installation of Low-Altitude Navigation and Targeting Infrared by Night (LANTIRN) pods on F-15Es and block 40 F-16s had increased this capability, within the air force, to approximately 500 platforms. These weapons known as Precision Guided Munitions (PGMs) became increasingly popular, as they promised reduced collateral damage. It is noteworthy that the IAF used its MiG-27 and Mirage-2000 fighters in 'buddy' mode, to target camouflaged enemy positions with LGBs, in the high mountainous terrain during the 1999 Kargil operations. Most if not all IAF Jaguars, MiG-27s, MiG-29s, Mirage-2000s and Su-30MKIs either already possess the capability to deliver PGMs, or will soon acquire it.

In the West, the limitations of the LGB resulted in the development of Joint Direct Attack Munitions (JDAM) and later the Joint Standoff Weapon (JSOW) family of air launched ordnance, that rely on the Inertial Navigation System/ Global Positioning System (INS)/(GPS) for guidance, and make it possible for these weapons to be delivered even in bad weather, so long as the correct geographical position of the target is available. Although countries other than the US have also produced such weapons, they remain expensive and are not easily available to developing countries of the region. It is likely India will try to indigenously produce more advanced weapons. A new family of the Sensor Fused Weapons capable of firing small 'bomblets' at specific targets, such as the hot engine of tanks and vehicles is also being used, but their efficacy in operations other than conventional wars is questionable, since these 'smart' weapons still cannot differentiate between the engine exhaust heat of an armoured vehicle, and that of a school bus.[13] A family of anti-tank weapons such as the Milan, TOW, Eryx, FGN-148 Javelin, and AGM-114R Hellfire are once again in demand and are increasingly being used in counter-insurgency operations both from ground and airborne platforms. "Raytheon has delivered more than 30,000 Javelins and about 3,300 have been fired in combat, with production running at between 1,300 and 2,000 per year.[14]

The air-to-air missile has also seen major improvements with the All-Aspect-Missile and Beyond Visual Range (BVR) Missile entering service, with most air forces of the region. India is also reportedly testing its first air-to-air missile, the Astra. It is said to be a BVR with a range of 44 km that may be increased to 80 km in the future. This is another area where self-reliance will become even more important for cost and access considerations. These missiles will become even more effective with the introduction of Airborne Warning and Control System (AWACS) in the region.

Air Defence

The region has seen the induction of more sophisticated surface-to-air missiles (SAMs) in the recent past, with China receiving a large number of Russian S-300 PMU SAMs, with ranges exceeding 150-200 km. These are also effective against enemy missiles. India too has obtained a few of these missiles and has inducted two batteries of locally produced Akash SAM systems. With the gradually increasing reach of modern fighters and the induction of the air-to-air refuelling tankers and AWACS in Pakistan, China and India, the air defence envelope has expanded with the fighter/interceptor set to engage the enemy at far off ranges. This trend is likely to continue. Ranges may further increase with new BVR missiles entering service with some of these air arms. Operations with these force multipliers are, however, very complicated with the tanker and the AWACS platforms themselves needing protection.

Support Platforms

Fixed wing transport aircraft and helicopters have proved their usefulness in peace and war and have been regularly employed for strategic mobility, troop lift, disaster relief, evacuation of own citizens from troubled areas, providing support to the civilian authority and in Counter Insurgency Operations (COIN). In India, the task of air-maintenance of troops and also civilians in the high altitude frontier areas, will remain a major responsibility, even after the ongoing development of surface infrastructure in forward areas is accomplished. In the absence of infrastructure in the mountains, these aircraft of the IAF have proved to be the lifeline of the inhabitants of these remote regions of the country. The IAF has been using the Il-76 and An-32 as the main platforms for over two decades. The Hercules C-130J that entered service with the IAF in 2012, would likely continue well beyond 2030, but the Il-76, An-32 and HS-748 will need replacements or midlife upgrades much earlier. India is currently planning to produce its own Medium Tactical Aircraft (MTA) with Russian collaboration, which may enter service by the end of the next decade.

India received all three of its AWACS aircraft in 2012. Pakistan has ordered six SAAB Erieye AEW&C aircraft from Sweden, the first of which rolled out on March 26, 2008.[15] India and Pakistan may add to their existing assets of tankers and AWACS. India has plans to purchase ten AWACS aircraft. China has already inducted its locally developed AWACS, the KJ-2000. This aircraft led the flypast at the 60th Anniversary Parade of the PLAAF in 2009.

Helicopters have proved their versatility both in war and peace and hence, are likely to remain in great demand in the foreseeable future. India's Advanced Light Helicopter (ALH) 'Dhruv' is already flying with the army, navy and the air force, and is also available on the export market. China has produced the Z-8 support and Z-9 attack helicopter and both of these are also likely to be exported in the future. India's order for 197 Light Observation Helicopters (LOH) for its army is delayed once again, but the IAF may get its Mi-17V5s on schedule. India has reportedly finalised the contract for 22 AH-64 Apache attack helicopters and Chinook heavy helicopters. The Indian Army is also expected to receive some 22 Apache helicopters. Given the mountainous nature of India's northern borders, the helicopter would continue to remain important in all its roles: armed/attack, scout/reconnaissance, support, tactical troop lift, medical casualty evacuation, combat search and rescue, even if its effectiveness in the attack/combat role is restricted to about 10,000 feet Above Mean Sea Level (AMSL).

UAVs/UCAVs

The Unmanned Combat Aerial Vehicle (UCAV) as also High/Medium Altitude Long Endurance (HALE, MALE), Unmanned Aerial Vehicle (UAV) are now fast becoming more popular with all armed forces. The success of the US in the October 2001 Afghanistan Air War, in the early and effective targeting of the Taliban and Al Qaeda fighters with the Predator MQ-1 launching Hellfire anti-tank missiles, made this modified UAV a legend. This kindled renewed interest in the UAVs with many countries developing their own. Small UAVs that can be launched by an infantryman are also becoming more and more commonplace. A variety of UAVs, UCAVs and Man-portable and Micro-UAVs will see a resurgence in the near future because of their low cost, relative ease of import and local manufacturing. Presently, the market is expanding, but fully autonomous types are not being fielded, for reasons of safety to other users of airspace, and the need to first confirm that the target is indeed hostile, before its engagement. Unmanned Autonomous System or UAS operations are not as yet commonplace, though much work is being done in this area.

Some low-cost UCAVs, such as the Harpy, designed to home in on the radiations of a radar set and destroy the radar by diving into it, are already in use in the region. According to the *Aviation Week & Space Technology* (*AWST*), the US remains the dominant producer and operator of the UAV and from a mere 1,000 flight hours in 1987, the figure went up to 600,000 in 2008.[16] Northrop Grumman, the manufacturer of the famed Global Hawk HALE UAV, has recently offered for trials the X-45 that will display stealth characteristics, and carry Precision Guided Munitions (PGMs) such as the JDAM and the small diameter bomb. The X-47B technology demonstrator capable of carrier operations is currently undergoing trials. With the rapidly increasing costs of manned fighters, there is a strong possibility of the UAV/UCAV combination becoming more popular with the armed forces in India, but whether these would replace the manned fighter is still uncertain. There is greater uncertainty about their being available in the Western arms markets, as also about their affordability.

Missiles

For some years now, more and more countries in the region have been producing conventionally armed surface-to-surface missiles of the Prithvi, M-9, and M-11 variety. India has recently unveiled its solid fuel version of the Prithvi with a conventional warhead. In the recent past, rudimentary short-range missiles and rockets have caused two major conflagrations in West Asia: the 2006 Lebanon War and the 2008 Gaza conflict. A variety of ship and air launched missiles for use against ships and ground targets already fill the inventories of many countries, with the People's Republic of China laying considerable stress on this 'easy-to-produce' simple weapon system. Both Iran and Pakistan are also busy producing different types of missiles, including the cruise missile. The reason for such interest is perhaps their relatively low cost and ease of manufacture, high accuracy and their usefulness in the initial stages of a conventional war, when air superiority is not attained.

According to a recent report:

> In 1970 there were only two countries developing cruise missiles with ranges of more than 150 km, but by 2009 this figure had increased to

17. Cruise missiles cost between 10 per cent and 25 per cent of the price of a ballistic missile; they use general aircraft technologies and tend to be more accurate.[17]

Defence Research and Development Organisation's (DRDO's) Nirbhay cruise missile was tested in March 2013, but the test was not fully successful as the missile had to be destroyed, when it veered off course in flight. It was once again tested on October 17, 2014 and this time the test was termed successful. It is reported to be stealthy and has a nominal range of 1000 km. Pakistan, on the other hand has already developed a nuclear capable cruise missile Babur with a range of 700 km and is testing an Air Launched Cruise Missile (ALCM), the Ra'ad (Hatf VIII) with a range of 350 km.[18]

It is quite possible that the next two decades will see more and more of these missiles in the region. As seen during the 1995-96 Taiwan Straits Crisis, the missile may also become the weapon of choice to signal the intentions of a country. Selectively targeting the enemy's military assets such as fuel dumps, ammunition storage depots, forward airfields, command posts, regional headquarters and communication nodes can prove a very 'safe', cost effective and decisive option in the opening days of the war, with low risk of attrition to own aircraft and collateral damage to enemy civilians. This may thus become the preferred tool for the developing countries of the region. As Iran has shown, the poor man's weapon will be the missile. The American Stinger man-portable SAM or Man Portable Air Defence System (MANPADS) has over time acquired a high reputation for accuracy and lethality. During the 1999 Kargil conflict, the IAF lost a helicopter and a fighter aircraft, and sustained damage to a Canberra, due to Stingers. It must, therefore, be remembered that a low cost MANPAD SAM can be a major deterrent to offensive air operations and a major force multiplier for the defender.

The Brahmos supersonic missile, jointly developed by India and Russia, is another example of effective long-range engagement of the enemy with relative safety. The Brahmos was successfully tested from an underwater platform in the Bay of Bengal on March 20, 2013. An air-delivered version is also under development for carriage on the Su-30MKI. The next two decades may see a proliferation of missiles of all types, as manned fighters/bombers become costlier and out of reach of the developing countries. The aircraft and the helicopter lose their overall effectiveness, due to reduced aerodynamic lift and engine thrust at high altitudes. The ballistics of the shell and bomb also become more unpredictable at higher altitudes. Interdiction of enemy supply lines is, therefore, a preferred strategy, relative to attacks on enemy targets, in close proximity of own troops. Future air operations in the mountains would have to allow for these limitations of the aircraft and helicopters. Man-portable Anti-Tank (MANPAT) and anti-aircraft missiles and Multiple Launch Rocket Systems (MLRS) may be more effective in the mountains. In fact, the intelligent use of the UCAV-missile combination might prove a winning future strategy and enhance their attractiveness in the future, as has already been proved by the success of 'drone' attacks in the Afghanistan-Pakistan region.

Aerostats

The IAF began experimenting with tethered balloons in the early 1990s, but the two barrage balloon units were designed as a passive air defence measure on forward airbases. These were designed for deployment at different heights, over or in close proximity to the airbase or a Vulnerable Area (VA), to deter low-level attacks by the enemy. Later, the IAF purchased two Aerostat systems from Israel, for deployment in areas close to the border. The aerostats are balloon-mounted, low-looking radars, for the detection of ultra-low level enemy attacks. By raising the aerostats to a few hundred feet, the radar is able to pick up targets at considerable distances. One of these was unfortunately lost while it was being lowered in strong wind conditions. The Aerial Delivery Research and Development Establishment (ADRDE) a DRDO laboratory at Agra, is reported to have successfully tested and indigenously designed and built Akashdeep, a medium-sized aerostat system in late 2012. If successful, the IAF could vastly improve its low-level radar cover and make its air defence more effective. The IAF needs 20 of these high endurance surveillance systems, developed by the DRDO. The high-performance PU-coated nylon fabric, aerostat balloon, electro-optical tether, electro-hydraulic control system and helium gas management system developed by DRDO were successfully tested.[19]

Use of Near Space

Officially designated as extending from 75,000 feet to 62 miles, 'near space' has been attracting the attention of aerospace research scientists for a variety of reasons. Deployment of airships and tethered balloons or 'aerostats' at very high altitudes, on the fringes of the earth's atmosphere, is likely to prove very useful for reconnaissance, long duration continuous surveillance and Electronic Intelligence (ELINT) gathering, and has been evolving for some time. Absence of severe weather, strong winds, and above all, the low cost of manufacturing and operation of these air ships/balloons are the main points in favour of such efforts. The major advantage is that such platforms could remain on station for weeks, if not months, and would be much cheaper than satellites and provide a continuous picture of activities in the 'footprint' of the platform and may prove very useful in the future.[20]

LEMVs

The old airships are likely to come back in vogue not for carriage of passengers, but for long endurance surveillance. The US Army Space and Missile Defence Command conducted a test of a Long Endurance Multi-intelligence Vehicle (LEMV) on August 7, 2012. An airship not unlike the old 'blimp', the LEMV is designed for long-term Intelligence Surveillance and Reconnaissance (ISR) and 'persistent stare' type missions. The LEMV can operate at altitudes greater than 22,000 feet and has a radius of action of over 3,600 km; it carries an ISR payload of 1,300 kg, can stay aloft for more than 21 days, and is reputed to have very low fuel consumption.[21]

Solar and Renewable Energy Platforms

Much work is under way to develop solar and hydrogen cell powered aeroplanes and UAVs. Initial difficulties in obtaining/generating more usable power and hence limitations of all-up weight, might restrict these technologies to UAVs and light reconnaissance platforms, but the potential is as yet not fully realised. For example, the solar-powered Zephyr flew for 82 hours in a test flight in 2008.[22]

End of Fossil Fuel/Alternative Fuels or Energy Sources

Availability and desirability of using fossil fuel for aviation may soon become a hotly debated issue, if fears of climate change come true. Military aircraft would be most vulnerable to these pressures by environment and climate change advocates. According to one estimate, the US Air Force (USAF) alone uses 2.5 billion gallons (approximately 10 billion litres) of fossil fuel each year. In 2008, it cost the US Government nearly US$7 billion, slightly more than half the total fuel bill of the entire US Government, to fuel its air force. It is also said that aircraft release about 600 million tons of carbon dioxide each year, but have a greater impact on the environment than other sources of combustion products, because the aircraft deliver it directly into the atmosphere. Thus, even though aviation accounts for just eight per cent of the total use of refined oil, and only three per cent of greenhouse emissions, the overall climate effect is about 13 per cent. Military aviation would have to search for alternative sources and types of fuel.[23] Many alternative fuels and even solar energy is being considered but which of these, if any, would suit the requirements of military aviation is difficult to say at this time. In the near future, fuel may thus become a major constraint for military aviation and may even adversely affect the production of some of the fighters and other platforms. The USAF has already demonstrated successful use of bio-fuels in military aircraft. India is yet to begin looking at these alternatives.

Conclusion

From the present indications, the IAF is unlikely to reach its target of 42 combat squadrons in the foreseeable future, for that would translate into about 900 fighters and is unlikely to be achieved, even if all ongoing procurement programmes reach their fruition on schedule. With a maximum of 272 Su-30MKIs, 126 and possibly 200 Rafales, 150 LCA Tejas', and all other combat aircraft that are available in 2015, the IAF cannot hope to get 900 modern fighters, as more than 30 per cent or approximately 300 (MiG-21s and MiG-27s) of these would be phased out well before 2030. The IAF Air Chief also said the MiG-21 bis could be used until 2025, instead of the projected phase-out in 2017.[24] The Light Combat Aircraft (LCA) programme is also behind schedule, with the Initial Operational Clearance (IOC) awarded in December 2013 and the Full Operational Clearance (FOC) likely in end 2015 or early 2016. Although the IAF has ordered 40 LCA Tejas' (fitted with the GE F-404 engine) these are also unlikely to be available before 2020. The Tejas Mk. II with the more powerful GE F-414 would also be delayed further to at least 2025 or beyond. The IAF will thus have to be content with about 33-35 squadrons for the next 10 years and modify its strategy to meet future threats with the available numbers.

Pakistan's reliance on nuclear weapons and its dependable friends China and the US, will ensure that a rough strategic balance is maintained with India, so that the latter is unable to take any major retaliatory military action. Unless India fine-tunes its retaliatory options, declares its red lines and also issues clear warnings, it would be impossible to check Pakistan's adventurism. The modernisation of the IAF must be aimed at achieving and maintaining this capability to deter Pakistan and defeat its 'nuclear threat' strategy since air power is the best – probably the only—instrument for instantaneous, yet calibrated response, with a high degree of escalation control.

As referred to in this and previous chapters, the present 'hardware' or in other words aircraft, equipment, and weapons shortages, would most probably be made up through outright purchases and indigenous solutions, but other 'software' issues—such as civil-military relations, jointness, common strategies for joint missions, greater synergies with the sister Services and with the civilian government, the DRDO/scientific community and industry—will require much more diligent, sincere and careful handling.

NOTES

1. "2014 Records 562 Ceasefire Violations in J&K, Highest in 11 Years", *Times of India*, December 28, 2014 at http://www.timesnow.tv/2014-records-562-ceasefire-violations-in-JK-highest-in-11-yrs/articlesho (Accessed March 5, 2015).
2. "Foreign Secretary S. Jaishankar Breaks Pak Ice to Clear Way for Talks", *Indian Express*, March 4, 2015 at http://indianexpress.com/article/india/india-others/saarc-yatra-jaishankar-meets-

paks-foreign-secretary-aizaz-chaudhary (Accessed March 5, 2015).

3. "China Tests India in Ladakh", *The New Indian Express*, September 25, 2014 at http://www.newindianexpress.com/columns/China-Tests-India-in-Ladakh/2014/09/26/article2449159.ece (Accessed March 5, 2015).
4. Inder Malhotra, 'Border in the Middle', *Indian Express,* March 6, 2015 at http://indianexpress.com/article/opinion/columns/border-in-the-middle/ (Accessed March 6, 2015).
5. "Resolute Support Mission in Afghanistan", February 27, 2015 at http://www.nato.int/cps/in/natohq/topics_113694.htm (Accessed March 5, 2015).
6. "Historic PDP-BJP Government in Kashmir Gets Off to a Controversial Start", *Times of India,* March 2, 2015 at http://timesofindia.indiatimes.com/india/Historic-PDP-BJP-govt-in-Kashmir-gets-off-to-a-controversial-start/articleshow/46424404.cms (Accessed March 5, 2015).
7. See http://www.claws.in/1340/russia-pakistan-engagement-concerns-for-india-ramya-panuganty.html, February 23, 2015 (Accessed March 6, 2015). Also see "Russia Pakistan Defence Accord signals shifting Regional Alignments", *World Politics Review,* November 23, 2014 at http://www.worldpoliticsreview.com/articles/14526/russia-pakistan-defense-accord-signals-shifting-regional-alignments (Accessed March 6, 2015).
8. *The Military Balance 2015*, International Institute for Strategic Studies, Routledge, London, p. 251.
9. "Re-engining Jaguar", *SP's Aviation*, (10), October 2011, p. 56.
10. *IHS Jane's Defence Weekly*, 50 (11), March 13, 2013. A.K. Antony, India's Defence Minister, justified the cost of US$ 30 million per aircraft as being reasonable, on the basis of 3.4 per cent annual escalation, since the Mirage-2000 was first purchased in 1985.
11. Interview with PAF Chief, *IHS Jane's Defence Weekly*, 50 (31), July 31, 2013, p. 34.
12. *Jane's Defence Weekly*, 47 (20), p. 5.
13. David R. Mets, *Airpower and Technology: Smart and Unmanned Weapons*, Praeger Security International, Westport, 2009, pp. 128-29.
14. Caitlin Harrington, *IHS Jane's Defence Weekly*, 47(13), March 31, 2010, pp. 24-31.
15. *IHS Jane's Defence Weekly*, March 26, 2009, p. 19.
16. Larry Dickerson, "New Respect for UAVs", *Aviation Week and Space Technology*, January 26, 2009, pp. 94-97.
17. Duncan Lennox, *IHS Jane's Defence Weekly*, 47 (13), March 31, 2010, p. 22.
18. "India Successfully Test-Fires Cruise Missile 'Nirbhay'", *The Hindu,* October 17, 2014 at http://www.thehindu.com/news/national/indigenously-developed-cruise-missile-nirbhay-testfired/article6509942.ece (Accessed March 6, 2015); Also see "Pakistan Conducts Flight Test of Ra'ad", *The Dawn,* February 2, 2015 at http://www.dawn.com/news/1161034 (Accessed on March 6, 2015).
19. *SP's Aviation,* (12), December 2012, p. 32.
20. See http://www.gaerospace.com/press-releases/pdfs/Near_Space_SpaceToys.pdf.
21. "LEMV takes to the skies", *IHS Jane's Defence Weekly*, 49 (33), August 15, 2012, p. 4, and *SP's Aviation*, (9), September 2012.
22. Hue Williams, *Jane's International Defence Review*, 43, June 2010, pp. 82-87.
23. Mark J. Lewis, "Military Aviation", *Aerospace America*, September 2009, pp. 24-31.
24. Air Chief Marshal N.A.K. Browne in an interview to a defence journal on October 7, 2013 at http://indiastrategic.in/topstories3054_IAF_transformation_happening_but_delay_on_MMRCA_is_worrying.htm (Accessed November 2, 2013).

8

Perspectives on Some Important Issues Influencing Air Power Employment

Introduction

As we have seen in previous chapters air power employment depends wholly on its ground-based infrastructure and organisational strength. To be effective, every modern hi-tech machine is required, after all, to be operated by a well-trained and motivated human being fully supported with a responsive logistics and maintenance organisation. This in turn is built on a firm foundation of air strategy and doctrine that is derived from past experience and is aimed at fulfilling future national political objectives. Further, air power employment, like any use of force, must also consider the overall threat environment. The 1998 nuclear tests by India and Pakistan have added a new dimension to warfare in the subcontinent and raised the risks and complexities of conflict. This makes it necessary to briefly touch upon the nuclear dimension. This chapter attempts to deal with some of these important issues.

Human Resource Development or Personnel Planning

Although Human Resource Development (HRD) is the more widely used term in the business world, the Indian Air Force (IAF) continues to call its HR department the Directorate of Personnel. This is headed by the Air Officer-in-Charge Personnel or AOP, who holds the rank of Air Marshal and is also one of the Principal Staff Officers (PSO) at Air Headquarters, and looks after the recruitment, retention, retirement and promotion, of all air force personnel. The IAF's current strength is over 127,000 and includes some 5,000 officers, 110,000 airmen and 15,000 enrolled non-combatants and civilians. Like its sister Services, the IAF has also seen considerable growth in the last four decades.

Until the late 1960s, besides the General Duties Pilot GD (P) and Navigator or GD (N) Branches to which pilots and navigators belonged, other branches of the IAF comprised Administration and Special Duties (A&SD), Technical Engine (Tech. Eng.), Technical Armament (Tech. Armt.), Signals, Equipment and Medical. During a service-wide reorganisation in the early 1970s, these branches were renamed and rationalised. The two main and 'executive' branches the GD (P) and (N) were renamed the Flying Pilot and Navigator or F (P) and F (N) for short. The A&SD Branch was renamed Admin. or Administration, with technical branches being merged into Aeronautical Engineering – Mechanical and Electronics or AE (M) and (L). The Equipment Branch was now called Logistics Branch. Air Marshal Y.V. Malse, and some other PSOs at Air Headquarters, were opposed to Air Chief Marshal I.H. Latif's plan to change the branch nomenclature from GD (P) to Flying Branch. They felt that in a service whose *raison d'etre* was flying, it was essential for the executive branch to gain experience in jobs, other than pure flying appointments. It was therefore incorrect to keep the pilots and navigators out of the vacancies in other branches, especially Administration which also included the special element of Air Traffic and Fighter Controllers, and who also held important portfolios in administrative fields such as, works, discipline and morale, human resource development or personnel and related fields.[1]

Earlier, the A&SD Branch comprised directly recruited officers of the Administration Branch as well as the pilots and navigators who were found unfit to continue flying, for one reason or another, as until then most of the Administration Branch vacancies could be filled by either an A&SD or GD Branch Officer. Many of the personnel serving in Administration and Logistics branches who were known as A&SD and Equipment Officers respectively until the early 1970s also came with some flying experience, as they were recalled to join ground duties after being suspended from flying training. This arrangement ensured that a very large proportion of the IAF officers had personal experience of the flying environment and this facilitated their understanding of air power issues. Fighter Controller (FC) and Air Traffic Controller (ATC) duties were, and are today carried out by Administration Branch Officers, both of which require a sound understanding of flying, airmanship, fighter tactics and employment. According to a very senior Air Marshal, even during World War II, the rejection rate for trainees in the GD (P) Branch was invariably as high as 75-80 per cent and this ensured that a large pool of cadets with some flying experience was invariably available for induction into other branches.[2] In the recent past the IAF has relaxed the stringent standards somewhat, and hence the number of suspensions are now relatively small.

Until the 1980s, a Pilot Officer of the General Duties (GD) Branch became eligible to be promoted to the rank of Flying Officer after one year of service; and to the rank of Flight Lieutenant after five years. For all other branches except the medical, the period was two and six years respectively. The rank of Squadron Leader was conferred after nine and 11 years for flying and ground duties branches, respectively. The objective was to keep the fighting force as young as possible and to give incentive to officers to remain fit for flying. This difference in eligibility to promotion, was done away with in the late 1980s with corresponding adjustments to the retirement age, in the rank of Wing Commander and above. As a result, the Flying Branch, considered as being the only executive branch, lost some of its sheen. One privilege or advantage to the aircrews, pilots and navigators, as also flight engineers and signallers was the payment of a flying allowance, earlier known as 'flying bounty' (FB). This was later renamed 'flying pay' although it was never considered a part of the basic pay, and hence officers of the Flying Branch never became eligible for perks associated with, or based purely on pay scales. Flying pay was reduced on attainment of the rank of Air Commodore, and as a result the total emoluments of a newly promoted Air Commodore of the Flying Branch, strangely, were less than when he was a Group Captain.

In the 1950s, the FB was Rs. 150 or some 30 per cent of the basic pay of a Pilot Officer and this went up to Rs. 250 in the 1960s. FB was an allowance and had to be claimed separately after completing a minimum of six hours of flying in a month. In the late 1960s, fighter aircraft serviceability was so dismal that many young fighter pilots had to fly as 'Second Pilot' in transport aircraft to claim FB. Perhaps as a reward for our victory in the 1971 war, FB became part of the pay in January 1972 and was also raised to Rs. 350, and in January 1975 to Rs. 375. In September 1981, it was further raised to Rs. 750. When the pay scales were revised upwards as a result of the recommendations of the Fourth Pay Commission, it was raised to Rs. 1,250 and remained at that level until it was raised to Rs. 7,500 in 2006, by which time the overall pay scales had been raised quite considerably. Flying Pay as percentage of basic pay thus remained insignificant.

Doctors or Officers of the Medical Branch were the only other branch entitled to additional allowance, called the Non-Practising Allowance or (NPA). The Sixth Pay Commission granted a substantial increase in pay and allowances to all branches and removed this difference, but as a result, the incentive to join the Flying Branch also disappeared. It is well known that the numbers opting to join the three wings of the armed forces, especially the combatant branches are continuously dwindling, with a majority of promising young students invariably preferring civilian or corporate/business sectors to the armed forces. Today, few young men in their teens are ready to commit 20 years of their life to service with the armed forces. Although the government has opened short service commissions in some branches, the response is reportedly less than expected. Lack of service accommodation and schooling facilities for children in far-flung airbases and frequent transfers are said to be the other major obstacles to joining the armed forces.

As previously noted, following the Sino-Indian border conflict of 1962, the IAF embarked on a massive expansion programme to induct over 1,000 additional pilots. In the early 1960s, the IAF was in the throes of a major upheaval due to the induction of a large number of pilots and other branch trainees. Training establishments were overflowing with new trainees and there was much chaos, as the sole purpose was to quickly train as many pilots as possible, in the shortest possible time. Some 10 pilots' courses or batches had already commenced training or passed out in the two years after the 1962 Chinese aggression. Five flying clubs, one each at Tambaram in Madras (now Chennai), Nagpur, Kanpur, New Delhi and Patiala were chosen to give 25-30 hours of flying experience to *ab initio* or new cadets. Thereafter, the cadets went through three more stages of training namely: Basic Stage on HT-2 at Allahabad; Intermediate Stage at Air Force Flying College (AFFC) Jodhpur on Harvard/Texan T6G trainers; and Advanced Stage on Vampire Mk. 55 and 52 fighters at Hakimpet, near Secunderabad, where the cadets were commissioned. The arrangement and sequence of flying training had undergone many changes in the previous two years. Those of the fighter stream were then sent to the two Vampire squadrons Nos. 220 and 221 at Pune, for what was then known as the Applied Phase of flying training, during which pilots learnt tactical flying that included live firing of cannons or front guns and rockets, at the firing range nearby.

The aim of the first stage was to weed out at the least expense, those trainees unlikely to make the grade for military flying, safely and economically. The Basic Stage, where this was normally done, was used for consolidation; the Intermediate Stage was for learning military flying; and the Advanced Stage was the one in which the cadets were trifurcated to fighter, transport and helicopter streams. The Applied Phase, as the name suggests, was meant to introduce the newly commissioned pilot to the basics of fighter, twin-engine transport and helicopter flying. The Hunter fighter on which most cadets of the 1960s-70s courses were thereafter trained, was then used both as Lead-in-Fighter-Trainer (LIFT), or Advanced Jet Trainer (AJT) as well as an operational aircraft. An Operational Training Unit (OTU) equipped with Hunter fighters and trainers was formed at Armament Training Wing (ATW), Jamnagar in late 1966 because it was felt that operational squadrons could not train such a large number of new pilots, and also simultaneously prepare for their operational tasks. The OTU was, however, disbanded in 1969 due to shortage of Hunter trainers. The intake into pilots' courses was reduced in 1968. The Hunter OTU was reformed a few years later.

The post-1962 emergency inductions came to a halt by the end of 1968-69, when the IAF went back to a peacetime training routine. The induction of approximately 1,000 additional pilots in a short span of five to six years, generally called the 'bulge', later posed great difficulty in career management as they could not be given the necessary operational flying training in the squadrons in time, because the IAF simply did not have enough aircraft. Both the Toofani and Mystere IVA were due for retirement and the MiG-21 fighters were not as yet available in large numbers, i.e., until the early 1970s. Some of the Hunter squadrons in the Eastern sector had as many as 40-45 newly commissioned Pilot Officers waiting to commence their operational training.

The situation in transport squadrons flying the Russian Il-14, the Canadian Caribou and the American Packet and Dakota aircraft, was equally bad, with a huge number of newly commissioned pilots cooling their heels. Many of them were sent on ground duties, such as Air Traffic Control Officers (ATCOs) and Base Operations Officers or were transferred to helicopters; but all this took time and many of them were unnecessarily wasted out or prematurely left the IAF. The civil/commercial aviation scenario was then equally bad, with only two commercial airlines, Air India and Indian Airlines operating in the country. Many flying clubs were also languishing, due to poor demand and lack of funds. As the 'bulge' began to progress towards the rank of Flight Lieutenant and then Squadron Leader, it faced increasingly tight bottlenecks. There was little increase in the number of squadrons but aircraft availability and serviceability had started to slowly improve, at least in the MiG-21 and S 22 squadrons.

The main reason for the bottlenecks, however, was that too many cadets had passed out between 1963 and 1966 with just 10-15 months of training. Later courses, e.g. the author's course, 97th GD(P), took much longer (30 months), to complete its training due to the delays caused by the 1965 Indo-Pak war and poor resource availability. The Pilots' Training Establishment (PTE), that had begun training IAF pilots in 1964, at the Civil Aviation Training Centre (CATC) at Bamrauli, Allahabad, presented a picture of total chaos, with even the instructors often unaware of who and where their cadets/wards were. It was a miracle that the cadets passed out or graduated from PTE in just over six months without any major accident. The IAF had called up some 15-20 flying instructors from the Auxiliary Air Force who were often found to be unfamiliar with air force life, but nevertheless imparted flying training with reasonable success. Some instructors for example, did not have much experience on the HT-2, and hence found it difficult to teach aerobatics to their pupils. This fact was, however, known to the Chief Flying Instructors (CFI) who gave necessary guidance when they flew a check sortie with the cadets.

By the time the 'bulge' members began reaching operational squadrons in 1968, both Hunter and Gnat serviceability hit rock bottom, which meant a very long wait to get the coveted Fully Operational (F/Ops) Status, which required at least 80-100 hours of flying. It was with difficulty that they became F/Ops before the 1971 Bangladesh War. There was no urgency to train more pilots because there was no real shortage, and as a result many younger pilots sat out the 14-day war, performing the duties of Forward Air Controllers (FAC), Combat Air Patrol or CAP Controllers, Base Operations Officers or sundry other jobs such as Mess Secretary and Security Officer.

With the induction of more MiG-21 aircraft in the early 1970s, the situation began easing but pilots posted to Hunter, Mystere and Gnat squadrons continued to struggle to maintain their operational status. They also found themselves out of the selection process for professional courses such as Qualified Flying Instructor (QFI), Pilot Attack Instructor (PAI) and the newly started Fighter Combat Leader (FCL) Course. Not surprisingly, the pilots commissioned before or after the 1962-68 period found themselves well placed for career progression. Pilots in transport squadrons also faced a bleak future till the arrival of An-32 and Il-76 aircraft in the mid-eighties. Such was the imbalance between rank, expertise and experience that it was a common sight in 1986-88, to see two Flying Officers flying the An-32 as Captain and Co-pilot while a senior Wing Commander Navigator kept a watchful eye on them!

By the late 1970s, the Personnel Staff or P Staff (as it is popularly known) in Air Headquarters managed to get government sanctions for a Cadre Review, under which some additional vacancies of Group Captain and above were sanctioned, but these were invariably used up in the very first year, with the result that the bottleneck did not clear. Once when the author congratulated a newly promoted Group Captain, the Chief Operations Officer (COO) of a fighter base in 1980, the latter laughed out loud and said it was not a great achievement as ten out of the eleven officers considered for promotion were in fact promoted. With the entry of Pechora SAM III missiles in the second half of the 1970s, many of the overlooked Squadron Leaders and Wing Commanders found some respectable jobs, but little upward movement. The post-'bulge' officers posted to S-22 and MiG-21 squadrons were, however, far better placed. It must be said to the credit of the much-maligned 'bulge' officers, that they held important and often thankless posts, in the air and ground jobs, across the Indian Air Force (IAF), and acquitted themselves well even when there was little chance of promotion.

Another major reason for poor career management in the officer cadres of the IAF was that sometime in the late 1970s and early 1980s, the policy makers at Air Headquarters managed to abolish the 'tenure system' under which a Group Captain, Air Commodore or Air Vice Marshal (AVM) was allowed to remain in that rank for a maximum period three or four years and was expected to retire in case not promoted, even if he had not reached the age of superannuation. As a result of the abolition of the tenure system some senior air force officers enjoyed two or three star ranks for as many as 8-10 years. The army and the navy also faced these problems, but with less severity, because their officers were permitted to leave the service prematurely, usually at Commander level and found job opportunities in the civilian sector. The air force or the government argument was that pilots could not be released because of the large sums of money spent on their training, a specious argument, but powerful nonetheless.

The 1975 Emergency bred sycophancy across all government departments; the armed forces did not remain unscathed. The result was that it encouraged 'yes' men and the so-called zero error syndrome and work culture. This soon stifled initiative and those close to their 'Godfathers' prospered. Until then frugal and spartan living, or at least living within one's means, was the norm, if not the hallmark of a young service officer, but the gradual increase in pay and allowances gave birth to what came to be known as 'five-star culture' and adversely affected professionalism in the service. Soon MiG, Jaguar, and Sukhoi lobbies became all-pervasive and powerful with the result that 'blue-eyed' boys prospered. In a well-known case, an officer was on the personal staff of two Air Chiefs, commanded two stations, wangled a diplomatic post abroad and became an Air Marshal without ever leaving the vicinity of Delhi.

In his 1995 essay on the IAF, George Tanham commented that the IAF is dominated by fighter pilots.[3] This is to some extent true, and the reasons for this perception are not far to seek. Unlike the other two Services, in the air force it is the fighter pilots who actually do the fighting and have to be trained to be ready for war at all times. This requirement, from the very beginning of their career, results in the young fighter pilots being groomed as 'gladiators' and in order to nurture this gladiatorial spirit, they seem to enjoy greater importance at work, but not any additional power in the military fraternity. In the Indian environment, transport and helicopter pilots also perform the equally risky and challenging task of flying, to and from high altitude runways, and Advanced Landing Ground (ALG) in the mountains. Attack helicopter and transport pilots flying specialised aircraft, such as the C-130J are undoubtedly engaged in equally important and risky tasks and this distinction or special place, that the fighter pilot enjoyed until recently, is changing as time goes by. What is, however, vital is that the IAF spend adequate time and resources to build true leaders and not merely 'stick & throttle' pilots or managers.

Until April 2007, all Air Chiefs had flown fighter aircraft – some of the World War II era – and began as fighter pilots, but later switched to transport flying. In April 2007, a helicopter pilot was chosen for the top job of the Air Chief, which speaks volumes for the way the IAF is changing. Another marked feature of IAF personnel or HR policies was that almost every Air Chief invariably changed the existing promotion policy. It is not as if those promoted were incompetent, but when competition is tight, even a small change such as increased emphasis on one or the other trait or qualification, can change the entire equation. The Air Force Staff Course at Defence Services Staff College (DSSC), Wellington, for example, has been given more or less importance depending on the views of the Air Chief. For some time, it was said that only those Flying Branch Officers with a 'Directing Staff' or instructor grading, were eligible for the command of a squadron, but that policy was soon abandoned. For many decades, only pilots and navigators or Flying Branch Officers were eligible for a posting on 'staff' of the DSSC, but this practice has thankfully been changed with almost all branches being given an opportunity to serve as Directing Staff, at this prestigious inter-service institution. This is of great significance for ground duty officers, as this and other instructional assignments at the Air Force Administrative College (AFAC) at Coimbatore and the Air Force Technical College (AFTC) at Jalhalli, Bangalore and a few other training units and establishments, are the only opportunities provided to them, where their service accomplishments can be recognised and rewarded.

With changes at the helm, that is, at the level of the Chief of the Air Staff (CAS), the QFI and PAI/FCL courses have likewise been given more or less importance, as a prerequisite for promotion. Given the ever-dwindling assets, the prime appointment of the 'Commanding Officer' of a frontline flying squadron, has also become even more valuable and extremely competitive, unleashing all kinds of undesirable characteristics of one-upmanship. Further, due to pressure of competition, some commanders are only interested in somehow completing fault-free command tenures, at a squadron or flying station. This tendency further reinforces the zero error syndrome and robs young leaders of initiative and opportunities to gain confidence from their own experience.[4]

Frequent postings to meet the requirements of a 'desirable' career profile also adversely affect the work output, quality and overall efficiency of the Service. Recognising the vital role that HR plays, the IAF under the leadership of Air Chief Marshal N.A.K. Browne coined a new motto: 'People First, Mission Always' clearly emphasising the vital role that humans play in the country's defence. With the entry of more complex and high-tech aircraft and equipment, HR will become increasingly critical to the success of the IAF. Many of the current and future fighter aircraft have two cockpits, and hence will need two aircrews. This requirement will place additional training burden on the IAF. Inspirational leadership and command challenges will be essential to keep the men and women of the IAF fully motivated and committed to organisational goals.

Recruitment and Retention

In today's globalised world, competition is becoming increasingly intense, with more and more young people aspiring to higher levels of job satisfaction, as also financial security. While India might boast of the so-called demographic dividend, finding the right candidates for the IAF might prove increasingly more difficult, as with the country's economic progress more avenues and options open. Recruitment and retention of experienced and skilled technicians, pilots, engineers and administrators is already posing a big challenge. Lateral movement at the right age into other government departments, paramilitary forces, Defence Public Sector Undertakings (DPSUs) and the burgeoning private sector would have to be considered with imagination and sensitivity. Given our large population, we often tend to show scant regard for the desires and genuine aspirations of our people. The best way to ensure high morale is to shift one's loyalties to our subordinates rather than to superiors.

As seen above, for some time now, armed forces and particularly the air force have not been an attractive career option for young Indians. The IAF, to be sure, gets a large number of applicants but they are apparently, not the best available. IAF maintains that it has not experienced much difficulty on this count, yet it is a widespread belief that a young 18-year-old is not ready to spend three years at the National Defence Academy (NDA) and another year at the Air Force Academy (AFA) and then make a commitment for a minimum of 20 years – and this is the main reason for the disinclination of the young generation to join the armed forces. Risk to life in aircraft accidents also dampens the spirit of the wards and their parents alike.

The IAF has for some time now opened short service commissions for some of the branches, yet these have not proved very attractive. Like in the United Kingdom (UK), the IAF could offer three options for release at 10, 15 and 20 years of service, with suitable incentives. Another option is to grant release after 20 years of service, and/or offer lateral separation to paramilitary organisations and other departments of the government. The government could also consider creating a separate cadre of ex-Service officers for employment in the Ministry of Defence (MoD), Ministry of Home Affairs (MHA) and Ministry of External Affairs (MEA) to encourage better understanding of security and closer cooperation with the defence services.[5]

The Indian National Defence University (INDU) proposal has been on the anvil for over a decade but has for some reason not progressed, although the government has reportedly allocated suitable land for it in Haryana. The foundation stone for the university building was laid by Dr. Manmohan Singh, the then Prime Minister, on May 23, 2013[6] Like the national defence universities in many advanced countries, INDU will help train leaders in national security. Military officers will benefit by pursuing post-graduate and doctoral studies between 10-15 years of service or once the officer has completed his/her command assignment. INDU graduates can then fill a larger proportion of vacancies in the MoD, MHA and MEA, and/or join the private sector, especially the defence industry. INDU will meet the prime requirement of Professional Military

Education (PME), and fill the existing gap in the field of security and defence studies. There are unconfirmed reports, however, that INDU may in fact play only a limited role of managing the award of degrees to the graduates of NDA, DSSC, Institute of Defence Management (IDM), National Defence College (NDC) and other training establishments of the three Services.

Maintenance

In 1978, the IAF adopted the so-called 'C' Flight concept by which the third or 'C' flight of a flying squadron that had until then provided second-line servicing support, was placed under and pooled as part of the airbase or wing engineering organisation. The Chief Technical Officer (CTO) was renamed Chief Engineering Officer or C Eng. O and upgraded to the rank of Group Captain. The aim of this exercise was to pool the human resources of two or more flying units based at a Wing. The Station Logistics Officer who had been independent until then, now reported to the C Eng. O. In one stroke, a third of each squadron's personnel began working directly under the C Eng. O while remaining on the posted strength and establishment of the squadron.

This arrangement, according to many veterans, diluted the authority and responsibility of the Squadron Commander, and increased the dependence of the squadron on the parent wing. With the raising of a large number of radar, Tropospheric Communication or 'Tropo' communication units and other supporting units in the 1980s and 1990s from within existing manpower resources, there was also considerable strain due to widespread manpower shortages, which on occasion caused avoidable difficulties and misunderstandings in the flying wings. Diffusion of responsibility also added to already existing problems of spares shortages, and aircraft and equipment serviceability dwindled. In one case, in the 1970s the Air Officer Commanding-in-Chief (AOC-in-C) of a Command was known to routinely visit equipment depots in search of spares for the squadrons under his command. While this unusual practice invariably improved the serviceability and availability of aircraft in his Command, it short-circuited the normal logistics procedures and adversely affected the serviceability in other Commands.

It is often said that the IAF over-maintains its aircraft. In many cases, the Jaguar being one example, the IAF engineers added their own additional checks and revised servicing schedules laid down by the manufacturers. The result was poor availability, without any attendant increase in safety. When on deputation to the Iraqi Air Force in the early 1980s, the author found that the Iraqis did not unnecessarily tinker with the MiG-21s, L-29s and L-39s that were based at the Iraqi Flying College in Tikrit. Consequently, the reliability and serviceability of these aircraft was quite high, even though the flying environment was dry, hot and subject to regular sandstorms. As mentioned earlier, the Chinese origin MiG-21 aircraft of the Iraqi Air Force had already undergone the modifications that the IAF was still struggling to incorporate, and according to Indian instructors deputed to Iraq, were a delight to fly. Aircraft serviceability and availability has thus been a subject of much contentious discussion in the IAF. Delays in procurement decisions may further exacerbate this problem in the future.

Trade Restructuring

In the 1990s, the IAF suddenly decided to change and merge the six groups in which airmen trades were organised. At around the same time, it was rumoured that a proposal to raise the flying pay was submitted to the Fifth Pay Commission. These two proposed changes caused a near mutiny in the IAF. Between December 1997 and January 1998, there were many instances of airmen and their families openly protesting at a number of air force stations and disrupting their daily routine. In one case, the airmen picketed the gates of an air force base and successfully blocked the entry of an AOC-in-C. In another, young airmens' wives blocked a railway track just outside a major air force base, which resulted in the stoppage of a long-distance express train. This serious 'law and order' situation was brought under control with persuasion and by tactful handling by the local commander. Many engineering officers also wanted to proceed on leave *en masse* and some even submitted resignations. While the situation was slowly brought under control, the incident dealt a big blow to inter-branch relationships in the IAF, which have not fully recovered even after 19 years. Many promising careers were unnecessarily ruined and the reputation of the IAF came under a cloud at a time when the security situation in the country was already delicate. Needless to add, the originators of these hare-brained ideas got away unscathed. According to some senior members of the service, this was undoubtedly a low point in the otherwise glorious and blemish-free record of the IAF.

Militaries work on faith and comradeship. A pilot has implicit faith in the integrity of the technical personnel that repair, service and maintain the flying machine, for in the ultimate analysis, his or her life, and above all national security, depend on their honesty and dedication. He cheerfully accepts to fly the machine, with only a minimal visual inspection, before flight and is ever ready to face any challenge or threat. Such relationships take a long time to build and nurture and hence Commanders need to remain particularly vigilant with regard to any fissures among the various branches and trades that make up this great service. Human resource management thus acquires critical importance in the armed forces. Recent reports of fragging and violence between officers and men, in some army units, only highlight the delicate nature of these relationships and the paramount need to maintain morale, especially when faced with an ever-present external and internal threat.

Flight Safety

The IAF has often been severely criticised on account of its flight safety record but at least outwardly, neither the MoD nor the air force seems particularly exercised about it. Accident rates are normally calculated per 10,000 or 100,000 hours of flying, with the IAF choosing the former method. As per the *MoD Annual Report* of 2011-12, the accident rate dropped from 1.48 per cent in 1972 to 0.40 per cent in 2007-08 – a significant decrease – but as always, there is scope for further reduction. The print and electronic media also takes an episodic interest in the subject, but rarely informs the general public about the true nature and causes of aircraft accidents. This results in avoidable misgivings about an already risky career in military aviation.

The IAF does not release all the data on accidents but in June 2012, A.K. Antony, the then Defence Minister, while answering a question in the Rajya Sabha (Upper House of the Indian Parliament) declared that the IAF had lost 482 of the 872 MiGs that it had procured in the previous 40 years. Such statistics unfortunately do not give enough information for a comprehensive analysis and are very often confusing and even misleading. In another instance reported in the media, the CAS, Air Chief Marshal N.A.K. Browne was apparently of the view that inexperience was the root cause of IAF accidents, but the then Minister of State for Defence, Pallam Raju publicly contradicted him, and said that it was pilot error that was in fact one of the major causes of accidents and not inexperience.

According to a media report quoting a statement of March 21, 2013 by the then Defence Minister, in the Rajya Sabha, "In the last five financial years, i.e. from 2008-09 to 2012-13 the IAF has lost a total of 37 fighters and 13 helicopters in which 17 pilots, 18 other service personnel and 06 civilians were killed." Breaking this down year-wise, the MoD says eight fighters and two helicopters crashed in 2008-09; 10 fighters and two helicopters crashed in 2009-10; six fighters and six helicopters crashed in 2010-11; nine fighters and one helicopter crashed in 2011-12; and four fighters and two helicopters crashed in 2012-13. "In the above accidents, a total of 17 pilots and 18 Service personnel were killed. Also, six civilians were killed and 25 injured."[7] The same report goes on to say that the IAF has been losing the equivalent of one fighter squadron every two years.

The flight safety record of the MiG-21 seems to be particularly worrisome since many of the mishaps were on this type. In the 1960s, Luftwaffe (German Air Force) flew only two major types of fighters, the Fiat G-91 and the F-104 Starfighter, with the latter being more accident prone. The Luftwaffe, however, said that because most of the flying was done on the F-104, the accidents were also on that type. Similarly, the MiG-21 has been the maistay of the IAF since the late 1960s and has had its share of accidents. Opinions on the safety and reliability of the MiG-21 have, however, been divided with some pilots swearing by its robust and reliable construction, with others taking a somewhat contrary view. The fact is that both are only partly correct. As we have seen before, the MiG-21 was designed essentially as a high-level interceptor but the IAF requested and received modified versions that could carry a modest armament load for ground attack missions. By the 1970s, more than half the IAF squadrons were equipped with various marks of this fighter. (See Appendix III for details).

From about the late 1960s, the Hunter fleet had begun receiving a large number of young pilots, fresh from training institutes, as the Toofani and Mystere fleets became due for retirement. A Hunter Operational Training/Conversion Unit (OCU) was formed in 1966 to give pilots coming from Vampire squadrons, a minimum of 40 hours of experience on the Hunter. The IAF then had a two-seat trainer version of the Hunter in fairly large numbers. Hunter serviceability, however, did not prove very encouraging, and hence by the late 1970s many of the Hunter squadrons were re-equipped with the Deep Penetration Strike Aircraft (DPSA) Jaguar. Hunter was a relatively benign aircraft to fly, and hence its accident rate was not very high. In the early 1970s, the Gnat squadrons also began facing spares shortages, and were plagued with poor serviceability and as a result the IAF did not possess a reliable LFT or the AJT for many years. As a consequence, from the early 1970s, many young and relatively inexperienced pilots were sent direct to MiG-21 units. Most of them coped well and soon became competent, and ably led by their experienced seniors, effectively carried the main burden of IAF's air defence and strike effort.

The MiG-21, however, is not an easy aircraft to fly and in the 1970s and 1980s when young pilots began going directly to MiG Operational Flying Training Unit (MOFTU), it took them time to master the aircraft. Type-77, the earliest mark of the MiG-21, used at the MOFTU suffered from poor forward visibility, high landing speeds and high rates of descent on final approach. It also had a marked tendency to enter 'super stall', a condition in which unlike other conventional fighters, the aircraft nose continues to remain high at low speeds, when in fact, the aircraft is rapidly losing height, thus confusing the inexperienced pilot. Despite many specific changes and added emphasis on recovery from such stalled flight conditions, the IAF lost many MiG-21s, effectively increasing the share of Pilot Error (PE) accidents.

Strangely, in the 1980s, young pilots were first trained on a difficult aircraft like the MiG-21 and then moved to relatively easier, more modern and reliable aircraft like the Mirage-2000 and Jaguar. The Gnat, which was used as a lead-in, or intermediate fighter trainer, also had its share of accidents, because of longitudinal control, the hydraulic system and engine problems. The Gnat did not have a two-seat trainer version. Pilots were given two-three dual sorties on the Hunter trainer before being sent 'solo' on the Gnat; not exactly a perfect solution but most pilots coped well. The Gnat was thus, not considered a suitable LIFT.

The Air Marshal D.A. Lafontaine Committee set up in the 1980s to investigate the causes of IAF accidents, squarely blamed the absence of a suitable trainer and recommended the Type-69 or MiG-21 trainer. The logic was sound, since the IAF then had a very large number of MiG-21 and other Soviet origin aircraft. The T-69 advantages included an identical cockpit, instrumentation, markings, cockpit layout, and handling characteristics similar to other MiG types. India was already licence-producing the MiGs in large numbers and there were good prospects of export as the type was no longer produced in the USSR.[8] The MiG-21 with its 'after burner' and very limited internal fuel was, however, a more difficult and less forgiving aircraft but was nevertheless used as an operational trainer.

The IAF already had many of these trainers, but accepted the Committee's recommendation only as a temporary solution, probably because the T-69 was essentially a MiG-21 trainer and was not exactly the ideal choice for a LIFT or AJT. This spurred the search for the AJT. The Air Staff Requirement (ASR) for the AJT was ready in 1986. Two aircraft, the French Alpha Jet and the BAe Hawk were extensively tested and their performance exceeded the ASR. The French offered to sell the used Alpha Jets of the West German Air Force with 'zero' life and all help in setting up the manufacturing line in India. First the Bofors scandal and later foreign exchange shortages, however, delayed decisions. The air force test pilots rejected the Alpha Jet for its 'disconcerting' oscillatory spin characteristics. With only the BAe Hawk remaining in the fray, it became a 'single vendor situation'. The IAF then raised the requirement of these trainers to 99 from the earlier 66, because it was felt that the utilisation rate of trainer aircraft should have been calculated at the rate of 20 instead of 30 hours per month. In the prevailing climate of economic difficulties, the government did not accept this change and the BAe Hawk deal was, once again postponed. Finally, the IAF grudgingly accepted the lower number but it was another 18 years before the Hawk deal was finally signed, and the BAe Hawk AJT actually reached India only in 2004. All these developments adversely affected IAF training schedules and flight safety record.

Bird hits have also taken a big toll of IAF fighters, as single-engine fighters are particularly vulnerable to bird ingestion. In India, rapid urbanisation and congestion have resulted in the unplanned expansion of cities, with the IAF airfields having to coexist in close proximity to heavily populated areas. Inefficient systems of garbage disposal and the absence of arrangements for speedy removal of animal carcasses, attract birds in large numbers. In spite of continuous efforts, including close liaison with civic authorities, the IAF has unfortunately not fully succeeded in reducing this menace.

The fact that the IAF has a plethora of aircraft types of Western and Russian origin, also adds to its maintenance difficulties, with trained and experienced technicians frequently moving to newly received aircraft, and thus depleting expertise at the units operating older aircraft.

For a variety of reasons, the IAF has always faced severe challenges in managing its logistics and aircraft maintenance activities. The end of the Cold War and the collapse of the Soviet Union in 1991, further aggravated these problems, although these were not publicly acknowledged. Russian technology was relatively less developed when compared to its Western counterpart, and hence a Russian engine had to be sent for major overhaul after 200-300 hours of flying; whereas its American, British or French counterparts could fly more than twice as many hours.

Foreign Object Damage (FOD) or ingestion of small pebbles or other such objects, when sucked into the powerful jet engine intakes of fighters also damage IAF aircraft, with poorly maintained runways, contributing their fair share of such cases. Indian climatic conditions often give rise to wide diurnal variation of temperatures, which affects the coal tar-based joint filling material used to fill the gaps between concrete slabs of the runway; loose pieces of which get sucked into jet engines on take-off.

Poor supervision, both flying and technical, has also been seen as contributing to IAF accidents. When the author asked a former Air Chief to give his view on the high rate of IAF accidents, he blamed poor supervision and advocated stringent punishment for those found responsible. He strongly believed that culpability had to be fixed and corrective action taken in time. Another retired Air Marshal firmly believed that due to poor aircraft serviceability, the IAF fighter squadrons have never really been able to fly the government-authorised monthly flying task and this has sometimes resulted in operators resorting to short cuts. In addition, the skewed and constantly changing personnel and promotion policies have further added to these woes.[9]

As seen before, the introduction of the C Flight concept of centralised servicing at IAF flying stations, also contributed to difficulties. According to some observers, this system of divided responsibility has resulted in neither the Commanding Officer nor Chief Engineering Officer being held to account. Although many senior officers do not accept this to be the cause of poor aircraft serviceability, this nevertheless continues to be a widely held view. Inter- and intra-branch understanding, or the lack of it, is perhaps the primary cause of this problem. The second generation fighter aircraft such as the MiG-21, 27 and 29 have limited endurance, with routine sortie profiles lasting just 30-45 minutes. This increases the number of landings and take-offs for every hour flown when compared to the Jaguar, Mirage-2000 and Su-30MKI. In addition, the Mirage fleet maintenance is even today, very largely dependent on direct support of the Original Equipment

Manufacturer (OEM), with Hindustan Aeronautics Limited (HAL) producing only a very small percentage of spares under licence. As a result, the Mirage fleet serviceability has always been very high.

Poor serviceability, susceptibility to repeated failures or malfunctioning of subsystems, or in other words a low Mean-Time-Between-Failure (MTBF) rate also increases the chances of in-flight emergencies, in turn reducing the margin for aircrew error. According to some, this contributes to a high percentage of pilot error accidents. While pilots are undoubtedly trained to handle emergency situations, they can sometimes make mistakes, if the aircraft experiences multiple system failure more frequently.

Despite its best efforts, the IAF accident rate continues to be a source of serious concern, especially since, between 2011-2014 it lost three Mirage-2000 and five Su-30MKI aircraft, both with excellent safety records. The IAF also lost a C-130J Hercules transport aircraft (March 27, 2014) and three Mi-17 helicopters (August 30, 2012 and June 25, 2013) during the same period. With the ever-increasing cost of modern aircraft, the country cannot afford to lose costly aircraft and precious lives. The IAF and the MoD must together find ways to improve its flight safety record.

At an Institute for Defence Studies and Analyses (IDSA) seminar in 2013, the Chair, discussants and other experienced active duty officers were of the view that the IAF must improve its aircraft serviceability and availability, simply because smaller numbers (34 squadrons) would demand a much higher sortie rate and operational tempo in any future conflict. It must be noted that the flight safety record of types other than the MiG-21, has also been quite poor. According to one privately maintained website, by the 1990s, the IAF had lost a total of 315 MiG-21s, 23 MiG-23s, four MiG-25s, 21 MiG-27s, seven MiG-29s, 23 Jaguars and three Mirage-2000 fighters.[10] These numbers, however, cannot be confirmed.

The case of the HPT-32, the basic trainer locally produced by HAL, is also a curious one. In the early 1970s, when the IAF was thinking of a replacement for the HT-2, the Italian SIAI Marchetti basic trainer was freely available, at a very reasonable price of just Rs. 12 lakh per unit. India did not choose this trainer since the HPT-32 was likely to be available for just Rs. 4 lakh each. Eventually, the HPT entered service only some 15 years later, in 1988, and cost more than Rs. 60 lakh, with Rs. 48 out of 60 lakh in foreign exchange.[11] The Lycoming 540-D-485 engine fitted in the HPT-32, experienced frequent failures, allegedly due to fuel starvation which made it unsafe to fly. Strangely, more than half the general aviation fleet of the world uses over 580 different models of the same Lycoming 540-D-485 piston engine, cleared for all aerobatic manoeuvres including spinning, without any apparent difficulties. Sadly, neither the IAF nor HAL have been able to rectify this apparently simple problem of fuel starvation/ vapour lock. The result: frequent crashes; 114 HPT-32 aircraft were prematurely withdrawn from service in August 2009. The IAF was forced to switch to all-jet training. Basic and even operational training has often been subjected to such shocks and disruptions. It is an irony that a country that boasts of building complicated and complex high-technology aircraft such as the Tejas LCA and Su-30MKI, has been unable to produce a reliable basic trainer. The IAF was then compelled to purchase the Pilatus PC-7 turboprop trainer from Switzerland. Some 75 PC-7s have been ordered at the cost of Rs. 3,000 crore.[12] The MoD has rejected the HAL proposal for a locally manufactured Basis Turbo Trainer (BTT) as its cost is said to be Rs. 40 crore, double that of the imported PC-7.

According to some observers, the IAF and the MoD do not seem to take a serious view of the high accident rate. Air Chief Marshals Moolgaonkar[13] and Dilbagh Singh were two Chiefs who flew regularly and took great interest in flight safety and ensured a low accident rate during their time and were widely seen as very strict about flying discipline.

The IAF has traditionally been somewhat indifferent to the use of flight simulators. The HAL-made Gnat/Ajeet simulator became available for use only a year or so before the Ajeet aircraft was phased out in the late 1980s. Although the Hunter and MiG-21 simulators were installed at Ambala and Chandigarh respectively, in the 1960s, few if any insisted on deriving real benefit from these useful aids to flying training. The very modern and advanced Jaguar and Jaguar-Darin simulators at Ambala and Gorakhpur respectively, have also not been regularly utilised to their capacity. Even today, when simulators of various types are widely available, this remains a low priority area in the IAF. In a recent interview to a defence journal, the then Director General Flight Safety and Inspection (DG FS&I) Air Marshal A.P. Garud said, "With regard to human error, *increased and mandatory use of simulators* by aircrew to practise procedures, develop skills and handling emergencies is being ensured".[14] While simulators alone cannot arrest accidents, if their use is made mandatory and accurately recorded, as is the practice with commercial airlines, it may prove very beneficial.

Understanding Defence Budgets

India's defence budget was only Rs. 2,868 crore in 1978-79 when it went on a shopping spree but ballooned to a staggering Rs. 1,14,223 crore, three decades later in 2008-09, an increase of over 40 times. The value of one dollar in 1978-79 was approximately Rs. 8 which increased to about Rs. 60 by 2014, an increase of over seven times. Even if we go by the devalued rupee, the increase in India's defence budget has been colossal. Worse, since India's defence industry has not made any significant advances, except routine licenced production of old models of aircraft and equipment at Defence Public Sector Undertakings (DPSUs) and ordnance factories, a big chunk of the capital budget is spent in foreign exchange and adds to the current account deficit. In the seven years since 2008-09, the budget again swelled to Rs. 2, 47,000 crore in 2015-16. The encouraging sign, however, is that despite such huge increases, it has remained at around 2.5 per cent of the Gross Domestic Product (GDP); the current budget is even less, at 1.79 per cent; no small achievement.[15]

In 2013, the government slashed the current capital budget by Rs. 10,000 crore, further adding to the 10 per cent cut in revenue budget that was imposed on all government expenditure, except salaries and allowances in June 2012. The GDP growth has slowed to about 5.8 per cent, the Indian rupee has lost more than 20 per cent of its value, and the budget deficit is unlikely to come down below five per cent of the GDP. Given these adverse economic conditions and the ever-increasing prices of foreign arms, the government was not able to maintain the nominal 10 per cent increase in the defence budget for 2015-16 and this will undoubtedly affect new acquisitions and modernisation.

In the nine years since 2001-02 to 2009-10, the IAF alone had spent a whopping Rs. 1,00, 681 crore or US$ 21.8 billion on aircraft and aero-engines, heavy and medium vehicles and other equipment, on modernisation, but this has not arrested the dwindling of its fighter assets. As was widely expected, the Medium Multi-Role Combat Aircraft (MMRCA) deal for 126 Rafale aircraft was not concluded before March 31, 2014, as this would have entailed a minimum payment of 10 per cent of the total contract amount, which is close to Rs. 10,000 crore.

This brief overview clearly shows that India's military modernisation efforts are at serious risk if the economy does not pick up in the next few years. The IAF has only inducted six C-130J Hercules, three Il-76 PHALCON AWACS and six Il-78 Air-to-Air Refuelling aircraft. It has signed contracts for the upgrade of the Mirage-2000, MiG-27 (since completed) and MiG-29 aircraft and for Akash and Medium Range (MR) SAM Air Defence missiles in the last 10 years. The first two of the modified Mirage-2000 aircraft were handed over to the IAF only on March 23, 2015 at the Dassault facility at Istress France. It is said that it would take at least seven years to complete the modification of all the 50 Mirage-2000 aircraft in the IAF's inventory. It is not known if the government has already paid for the recently concluded contract for the purchase of 42 additional Su-30MKIs, 77 Mi-17 V5s and for the co-development of the Fifth Generation Fighter Aircraft (FGFA) or PAK-FA. At first glance, this expenditure of Rs. 100,681 crore ($21.8 billion) under the capital/acquisition head appears to be disproportionately high, since it has not made any material difference to the IAF inventory and military preparedness of the country.

The budgetary process, which is the responsibility of the MoD and the Ministry of Finance, Government of India (GoI), usually begins in the month of September every year. Although critically important for the operational preparedness of the armed forces, it is essentially a routine bureaucratic activity that is subject to constant changes until it is finally presented in the end of February every year. The Indian Parliament can approve or reject the budget or any of the demands but cannot modify them.[16] The Defence Finance Wing of the Finance Ministry attached to the MoD plays a vital role in the budget preparation, which is invariably dictated by the nominal amount allocated by the Finance Commission, and except in a national emergency it has hovered around 2.5 per cent of the GDP for most of the past 68 years, since the founding of the Indian Republic.

The three Service Headquarters begin the annual exercise by first accounting the expenditure already incurred in the first two quarters of the current financial year. They then calculate the funding requirements for the remaining year and assess current expenditure trends. To avoid bunching of expenditure in the last quarter or excessively hasty purchases to exhaust sanctioned amounts, the Defence Finance Wing only sanctions a maximum of 80 per cent of the funds expended up to the end of the third quarter, for the last quarter, which means that if the Service Headquarter has not maintained an even outflow of funds, the Finance Ministry would invariably not allow it to spend the budgeted amount or Budget Estimate (BE). It is for this reason that a Revised Estimate or (RE) is presented to the Finance Ministry in the month of September and the budget is finalised by the end of December. Service budgets are made as per GoI guidelines which lay down instructions for economy, rationalisation of expenditure, savings, avoidance of duplication, unnecessary or excessive expenditure; and since 2006 also a Modified Cash Management System to ensure greater evenness in expenses, so that the last quarter expenditure does not exceed 33 per cent of the BE.

The defence budget comprises revenue and capital heads and relates to the requirements of the Army, Navy, Air Force, Defence Research and Development Organisation (DRDO), Department of Defence Production and the MoD. For some years now, expenditure on pensions is not included in the defence budget but indicated separately. The three Service Headquarters make their projections based on the expenditure patterns of the past years, current trends and inflation, committed liabilities, anticipated requirements of stores, annual acquisition plan, annual works programme and planned new raisings.

As would be evident, the revenue element of the budget is relatively simple as it comprises salaries and allowances, and routine expenditure incurred mainly on maintenance and running of the armed forces and includes fuel, oil and lubricants, rations, stores, clothing and the like. Expenditure under the capital head, which includes expenditure on land, construction of capital works, plants and machinery, equipment, tanks, ships, aircraft and aero-engines, and dockyards however, presents a different set of difficulties. This is because in most cases aircraft and equipment are purchased from foreign vendors, for which contracts have to be signed in time and funds released, based on delivery schedules and quality assurance. Very often, planned purchases are delayed for a variety of reasons, such as delayed trial reports or deficiencies in the performance of the equipment. Funds under the capital head are surrendered at the end of the year. For example, in the nine years from 2001-02 to 2009-10, in only three years, the average utilisation under the capital head was 97-100 per cent, while during the remaining six years, it fluctuated between 65 and 92 per cent; and yet the IAF alone spent Rs. 100,681 crore on the purchase of aircraft and aero-engines and other major equipment.

The GoI appears to follow a pattern: at first it declares a respectable figure for new acquisitions, and then delays the process, so that the air force and the two sister Services are forced to surrender substantial amounts every year. On rare occasions, the government has also spent much in excess of sanctioned budgets but only to meet contractual obligations and committed liabilities. This is only the 'mechanical' part of budget making. The truly vital part of allocation of funds to individual services is concerned with what the country really expects of the armed forces. In the absence of a declared strategy or national security policy document, or any serious joint consultations on national defence strategy, the three Service Headquarters are often left groping for direction, or perhaps they are now quite used to making their demands based on *'their'* perception of India's security needs and finally haggling for every rupee, during the numerous rounds of meetings for budget approvals. Being the specialists, it is the Services that carry out detailed studies of the trends in technology, the changing balance of military capabilities of potential adversaries, newly emerging threats and responsibilities. These assessments are based on available intelligence and are often gleaned from the addresses and statements of the Prime Minister, Defence Minister and directives and instructions received from the Cabinet Committee on Security (CCS), the highest decision-making body of the government.

As stated elsewhere, foreign policy imperatives also play a crucial role in the selection of weapons and equipment. India has all along been trying to diversify its sources of aircraft, weapons and equipment, but has not fully succeeded due to a weak defence industrial base. Inter-Service rivalry also plays a negative role as each Service wants a bigger portion of the budgetary cake. The air force, being inherently capital intensive, requires a much larger slice of capital/acquisition funding, but the army which is nearly 10 times the size of the air force, also cannot reduce its revenue expenditure on account of salaries and allowances and rations, Fuel, Oil and Lubricants (FOL) and other stores. With rising prices of imported oil and the urgent need to protect the environment, the IAF as also the army and the navy would have to find ways to reduce their consumption of aviation fuel, diesel and other hydrocarbon fuels.

As has been suggested before, the Indian military must focus on its organisational efficiency rather than on equipment modernisation and technology infusion. While the Services no doubt have to constantly enhance their fighting ability, it is a moot point whether technology alone provides all answers. Although India has an unresolved border dispute with its two major neighbours, neither India nor its adversaries are likely to fight a conventional war. What the Indian military therefore, needs to achieve is, the capacity to positively deter any adventurism. This may be possible only if India displays a stubborn resolve to give a befitting yet, proportionate and timely reply, to any mischief. At present, each Service makes its own assessments of the extant threat and somehow manages to convince the government, that to maintain its current size, it needs a certain minimum amount of money. The government then finds ways to provide the necessary funds. Since it is difficult to assess true intentions of the likely enemy and since no one wants to run the risk of losing a war, the Indian military continues to prepare for a major conventional war, while hoping that it can automatically tackle all other smaller threats. Although essentially localised, the 1999 Kargil intrusions, the more than a quarter century of proxy war and cross-border terrorism, have engendered a sense of general insecurity and hence, various decision-makers think that there exists the potential for sudden and unprovoked escalation. It is time India examined whether its current unimaginative approach to national security is the only way to deter potential threats. The Indian decision-maker claims to know that India cannot afford to get drawn into an open-ended arms race with China, but in reality its defence expenditure goes on spiralling upwards without really enhancing its security.

If current difficulties are anything to go by, the Indian military's planned modernisation is difficult to sustain in the long run. The Services must take the initiative to get out of the old 'conventional war' 'any time any where' mindset and find innovative ways to enhance security and yet avoid profligate expenditure. One reason for this is the oft-repeated statement that India faces the threat of a 'full spectrum' conflict. This means that the military has to be prepared to face any challenge; from a nuclear war to sub-conventional conflicts. This is ridiculous as no country can ever be ready for the worst-case scenario. In trying to do everything, India's armed forces end up doing nothing. The constant refrain that "we will fight with what we have" and undue emphasis on high technology are at the root of this problem. If we do not change our approach, we will never be able to meet our needs, whatever the budget. The other main reason is that there is little interest among the country's political leadership to evolve an efficient yet economical way to address India's security challenges because that would require sitting down with the military, which the politicians rarely do.

Many other departments of the government are equally inefficient and also indulge in wasteful expenditure but that cannot justify the ever-increasing defence budgets. The upshot of all this is, there is no system to assess the basic efficiency of the budgetary process, or what it actually delivers, in terms of military capability and operational readiness. So long as the demands of the Services appear *reasonable,* the government grants them. The Ministry of Finance is keen to ensure that the Services do not pay a high price for particular equipment and get value for money, but never questions *why the particular weapon or equipment* is needed in the first place. Acceptance of Necessity (AoN) is the most important step in the acquisition process and it is here that multi-disciplinary consultations are required. It is not known if any specific effort is made to determine if the IAF indeed needs 45 fighter squadrons, or the army actually requires 5,000 tanks. In the absence of a joint mission statement, it is not known how the three Services together would fight a future war and hence, the tendency is to never question the prevailing size and shape of the military.

The Tables in Appendix IV provide details of defence expenditure since 1950-51 when the process first began, but do not give any clear idea of the thinking behind the increases. It appears that the government, after much bargaining, finally succumbs to the wish-lists of the Service Headquarters. Most analyses of the budgetary allocations also appear to get bogged down in the nitty-gritty of BE, RE, surrenders and percentage shares of various services and departments. Most observers conveniently forget that the actual expenditure on India's defence and internal security is in fact much higher than that seen in the annual defence budgets. For example, in 2008-09, the defence budget was only Rs. 1,05,600 crore while the total expenditure on defence was 1,34,133 crore, which included Rs. 1,300 crore on nuclear forces; Rs. 7,632 crore on paramilitary forces; Rs. 555 crore on paramilitary housing; Rs. 608 on border fencing; Rs. 504 crore on border infrastructure; Rs. 15,564 crore on defence pensions and Rs. 2,307 crore on MoD (civil estimates).[17] According to the same source, close to one-third of the budget of the Department of Atomic Energy (DAE) is spent on nuclear warhead production and research. A sizeable amount is also spent by DRDO on missile tests and research. It is, therefore, safe to assume that over 30 per cent more than the publicly declared amount, is spent on defence and security. While some analysts and experts have expressed the need for performance or outcome budgeting, in place of input budgets, there is no movement in that direction. In any case, measuring the performance of the military is not easy since 'security' cannot be measured. The Kelkar Committee had recommended that defence expenditure be gradually reduced to no more than 1.6 per cent of the GDP.[18] The budget for 2013-14 brought it down to 1.79 per cent but it is not clear if this trend will continue. India has placed so many big-ticket orders and made such huge commitments, that it will be difficult to actually effect the necessary cuts, to keep the defence expenditure at 1.6 per cent of the GDP, unless the latter shows good growth. It is time the armed forces themselves came up with innovative ideas to right-size their strength, and revisit the existing force structures to bring them in closer congruence with the threat and current doctrine, and examine ways to keep the defence expenditure from spiralling out of control.

India's Defence Industry

At the time of independence, India had 26 Ordnance Factories (OFs) which made a variety of arms, guns and bombs including air delivered weapons. In the last 68 years, the number of these factories has gone up to 39. In addition, India has nine DPSUs capable of manufacturing a variety of tanks, guns, ships and aircraft but the Indian military continues to depend on foreign sources for nearly 70 per cent of its needs. The OFs and DPSUs function under the MoD where the Secretary, Defence Production, a senior Indian Administrative Service (IAS) officer is responsible for their smooth operation. An Ordnance Factory Board oversees the functioning all OFs and reports to the Secretary, Defence Production.

Even a cursory glance shows two main characteristics of the indigenous defence industry. First, although India liberalised its economy in 1991, its defence industry remains under government control and is unlikely to be privatised. Second, India has been spending increasingly large sums of money in foreign exchange on arms imports, but strangely has put a cap of 26 per cent on Foreign Direct Investment (FDI) in defence, which is also likely to remain relatively small. The MoD in its Defence Procurement Policy (DPP) that has been regularly updated since it was first announced in 2001, has laid down a mandatory offset clause of up to 50 per cent in all defence purchases exceeding Rs. 300 crore. The government had also opened up the defence sector to Indian private players but demand uncertainties and high initial investments have resulted in very few players entering the field. Some companies such as Larsen & Toubro (L&T), Mahindra and Tata have on occasion manufactured some defence equipment, but their participation has by and large been only a fraction of the huge defence requirement. Some of them such as Tata Advanced Systems (TAS), Mahindra Defence, and Reliance have recently entered into joint ventures with foreign defence companies, probably to derive some benefits from future offsets arrangements, but this is too recent to show any trends. Following the hike in FDI in defence from 26 per cent to 49 per cent, TAS has shown heightened interest in defence and had domestic orders worth Rs. 8,000 crore.[19] The development of the Light Combat Aircraft (LCA) had spawned some 300 Small and Medium Enterprises (SMEs) during its active phase but many of these have now ended their defence collaboration and moved on to other areas, and a few have been taken over by bigger companies. Some experts believe that consequently much valuable expertise might have been lost.

Another major reason for the slow and halting development of the defence industry is that the DRDO, under the control of the Scientific Adviser (SA) to the Defence Minister, until late 2014 wielded a virtual veto over buy/make decisions of the MoD and this often resulted in the private sector industry not enjoying a level playing field. The newly appointed Defence Minister Manohar Parrikar (November 2014) has, however, asked the DRDO and DPSUs to focus on core areas of defence and promised a new direction to the defence industry. Despite its size and long experience, Hindustan Aeronautics Limited (HAL), the only aviation giant in India, has not succeeded in winning the trust of its main customer, the IAF. Though it has been manufacturing a wide variety of aircraft under licence, its record of building its own aircraft is not encouraging. To be fair, the HT-2 and Kiran HJT-16 proved quite successful, but the Marut HF-24 and Ajeet did not, and for a variety of reasons, were prematurely withdrawn from service.

Although the IAF has been the recipient of a very large number of locally licence-produced aircraft such as the Vampire, Gnat, MiG-21, HJT-16 Kiran, Alouette SA-316, Cheetah and Chetak helicopters and the HS-748 AVRO, it has not been fully satisfied with HAL's performance. The armed forces, especially the IAF, have been ready and willing to support indigenisation of various arms and aircraft, but rightly feel that these programmes must not be linked with the 'current' requirements of the IAF, until these have reached a level of certainty. Issues related to quality assurance and long delays in production directly affect its operational readiness – the AJT and LCA are two cases in point.

The Intermediate Jet Trainer, Sitara, developed as a replacement for the Kiran, successfully completed its first flight in March 2003[20] but nearly 12 years later, it is nowhere near ready for entry into service, although it is only a modest subsonic low technology trainer aircraft. The LCA made its first flight on January 4, 2001, but over 14 years later it has barely received Initial Operational Clearance (IOC). Local products also do not always meet all the Air Staff Requirements (ASR). Very often, the product is delayed so long that the very requirements of the IAF change, because in the meantime technological advances have altered the very nature of the threat. The LCA, for example, was designed as a replacement for the Ajeet and MiG-21, a first/second generation fighter, but the LCA obviously cannot be accepted if its performance is well below that laid down in the ASR. According to knowledgeable sources, this is simply because in the changed and enhanced threat environment, the LCA might become a liability instead of an asset. Instead of its original planned weight of 5.5 tons, it now weighs 8.5 tons, and is powered by the same low thrust GE F-404 engine.

Although the DRDO has successfully – if somewhat belatedly – produced a variety of missiles including the Agni V, and tested an Anti-Ballistic Missile Defence System, its prowess in the design and development of modern aircraft is yet to be proved. A modern fighter involves millions of spares and moving parts, milled to exacting standards and tolerances and these have to perform millions of flawless cycles of operations with assured safety; not a simple 'one off' activity as in a missile. Aircraft and engine manufactures also require mastery over high-end metallurgy and alloy manufacture and unless strenuous efforts are made to develop such capacity, indigenisation cannot be successful. The Kaveri engine, whose production by the Gas Turbine Research Establishment (GTRE) began at about the same time as the LCA, in the early 1980s, has proved a failure. As a result, the first 40 LCA aircraft would be compelled to fly with the American GE F-404 engines for the next ten years or so. The proposed purchase of GE-414 engines is also likely to take time. Due to its lower performance, the indigenously produced Kaveri engine, is being considered only for possible marine applications, since its thrust is totally inadequate for the LCA.

Instead of trying to make everything, the defence industry must prioritise the essential products that the armed forces need. This is perhaps possible if the Defence Ministry consults with all major private sector players, along with representatives of the DRDO, the three Services and the scientific community, to decide exactly which technologies can easily and quickly be developed in-house; the equipment and products that the military needs in a specific timeframe; the likely financial outlay; an honest assessment of available expertise in skilled manpower; the possibility of joint ventures with foreign companies under various offset provisions; their export potential; and finally, a realistic assessment of success. Based on the outcome of such detailed consultations, selected private players can then be offered financial assurances, if not actual guarantees, that their products will in fact be purchased in the quantities and numbers envisaged, provided these meet quality requirements. It is equally important to examine the cost-benefit ratios and the minimum numbers/quantities necessary for ensuring economies of scale. The Indian politician also needs to be disabused of his inherent opposition to arms exports. Some minimal cooperation with one or possibly two technology partners would also be inescapable.[21] It may be noted that, S. Krishnaswamy, a former member of the Aeronautics Committee, had in 1969, concluded that, "the primary aircraft requirements of the Indian Air Force should be met by indigenous development and production." He also believed that the habit of importing complete aircraft was not a good policy, as with long-term planning, with the availability of skilled manpower, and teamwork with a common goal, technical assistance in selected fields and hard work, it should be possible for the country to build a self-supporting aircraft industry. Circumstances have no doubt radically changed in the last 45 years but the principle of self-reliance remains valid.[22]

The MoD would then have to devise mechanisms and project management teams that would continuously monitor and supervise the progress of these programmes. To begin with, the Stinger class of MANPADS, Night Vision Goggles (NVGs), UAVs/UCAVs (Drones), aerostats, light transportable radars, multipurpose missiles for use from a variety of platforms, such as helicopters, fighter aircraft and even tanks and vehicles, basic dual use trainer aircraft for the civilian and military sectors, air-to-air and air-to-ground missiles and Precision Guided Munitions (PGMs) with the associated avionics, could be attempted.

The MoD and the Services must also lay down a firm time schedule by which all of these items would have to be indigenised. Without such a stringent time-table, there is every chance that projects would slow down, or even derail, at the first sign of trouble. It is also vital to groom and nurture leaders and project managers for such a programme, or else they will be tempted to leave prematurely if interest flags, or when the programme no longer presents opportunities, challenges and the necessary sense of accomplishment.

It is also essential to form a high-level national aviation policy-making body, presided over by a senior union minister, that can promote civil, commercial and military aviation activity in complete synergy, since air power and national air space, after all, are indivisible and must not be divided along parochial lines. In fact, there is an urgent need for joint planning of all aviation activity to avoid costly duplication of effort. It is often said that India need not reinvent the wheel, but such banal statements must not result in a product with such high foreign content, that the very purpose of indigenisation is defeated. Finally, the designated competent authority must know when to *terminate* a project, so that more resources are not committed to a programme that has all but failed.

The FDI limit was increased from 26 per cent to 49 per cent only in 2014. This could be further raised to 60 or even 100 per cent in selected sectors such as aero-engine development and manufacture, as it might prove the long needed catalyst to jump-start this overdue activity. It should be possible to firmly lay down timelines by which selected/designated foreign equipment must be substituted with local products. Unless we steadfastly lay down a timeframe, there is every possibility that 15-20 years from now, the Indian military would once again find itself exactly where it is today: helplessly and totally dependent on foreign sources.

Defence Research and Development Organisation

No discussion on India's defence industry can be complete without assessing the capabilities and role of the DRDO, spread across the length of India. The DRDO, as it is known today, came into being in 1958 with the merger of the Technical Development Establishment (TDE) of the Indian Army, and the Directorate of Technical Development and Production (DTD&P) with the Defence Science Organisation. It had only about 10 laboratories and scientific establishments at the time, but has now grown into a country-wide network of 52 laboratories engaged in Research and Development (R&D) in the fields of armaments, aeronautics, avionics, electronics, missile technology and a host of associated technologies. It employs some 5,000 scientists and 25,000 other staff and is headed by the Secretary, Department of DRDO who is also the SA to the Defence Minister. "But according to a MoD audit, only 29 per cent of DRDO developed products have entered the defence services in the last 17 years."[23]

The DRDO's primary responsibility is to develop defence products, for production by other agencies in the country. The Aeronautical Development Establishment (ADE) was instrumental in developing the LCA with the help of HAL, and many other private and public sector companies, laboratories and academic institutions. Some 500 engineers from the HAL design bureau were deputed to the Aeronautical Development Agency (ADA) which was formed in 1985, for the Project Definition Phase of the LCA, to provide project management for the LCA programme. The immense complexity of the programme, intended to develop a state-of-the-art multi-role fighter, was well known to all participants. Knowing the difficulties involved, the IAF had wanted only a low-cost replacement for its Ajeet (which was also a locally developed version of the Folland Gnat but had not met the expectations of the IAF) and the MiG-21 by the mid-1990s. The decision to incorporate high technologies such as the Fly-by-Wire (FBW) Flight Control System, Multi-Mode Radar, composite materials for aircraft structures and microprocessor-controlled general systems, resulted in inordinate delays. According to Air Marshal P. Rajkumar (Retd.), the leader of the LCA Flight Test Programme for a decade, "The seeds for protracted programme delays and cost overruns were sown by these decisions."[24]

From the very beginning, the DRDO Directors, as SAs were closely associated with the country's Science and Technology (S&T) R&D programmes and enjoyed unique proximity and access to the highest levels of decision-making. Dr. Kothari's association with Nehru and later Dr. Raja Ramanna's with Mrs. Indira Gandhi, followed by Dr. V.S. Arunachalam's with Rajiv Gandhi and Dr. A.P.J. Abdul Kalam's with A.B. Vajpayee, and their close association with India's nuclear and missile delivery programme, are well known. Such close proximity gave them immense influence at the highest political levels. Whenever the government decided to indigenise a defence system, the DRDO was invariably given the right of first refusal, which meant that if DRDO *agreed* to develop and produce a particular piece of equipment, it would do so at its own pace, without any interference from the government, or competition from the private industry.

It is noteworthy that India took nearly a decade, after the first nuclear test in 1974, to start the Integrated Guided Missile Development Programme (IGMDP) in 1983, and fired the first Prithvi missile only in 1988, and the Agni in 1989. Compared to Pakistan, North Korea and Iran, which have all produced a variety of capable missiles (albeit with Chinese assistance) in a relatively short period of time, the achievements of the DRDO seem less remarkable. Another upshot of this association has also been the unduly excessive emphasis that the scientific community, and on their advice, the political leadership, places on the deterrent value of India's nuclear and missile capability, at the cost of conventional weapons. This misplaced dependence on nuclear weapons has apparently induced a kind of a lethargy and complacency in the minds of the defence and security elite, about India's conventional capabilities.[25]

This is perhaps one of the reasons for the painfully slow progress on both the procurement/acquisition and indigenisation front. The SA has so far been a scientist and not an engineer, and it is natural for him to take more interest in the development of India's missile technology. Recent successes such as the firing of a Brahmos from a submerged platform, Agni-V, plans to test a Multiple Independently Targetable Re-entry Vehicle (MIRV) missile, Ballistic Missile Defence and the like, easily hide the very poor and dismal progress in other fields such as aircraft, tanks and other usable technologies. The DRDO is presently developing no less than eight types of low to high-end UAVs/UCAVs, Air-to-Air-Missiles (AAMs), Beyond Visual Range Missiles (BVRMs) and the Akash SAM, but none of these barring the Akash, have actually reached the military and/or become fully operational. The Rustam UAV is said to be in the initial stage of induction. It is not clear why the DRDO needs Israeli help to produce the Short Range (SR)/Medium Range (MR) Surface-to-Air-Missile (SAM), when it has already operationalised the Akash SAM. Electronic Counter Measures (ECM) and Electronic Counter-Counter Measures (ECCM) suites such as the RWR, Tranquil, Tarang and Tempest have also been around for nearly two decades, but have been used only on the MiG-21 and 27 aircraft.

The DARIN III modified Jaguar completed its first flight in 2014, but if this modification involves structural changes to the nose of the aircraft, the IAF cannot expect such work to be done quickly. In other words, with the re-engine upgrade looming, the Jaguar fleet will be out of action for a considerable length of time. However laudable the DARIN III upgrade may be, it is certainly too late in the life cycle of the Jaguar, which entered the IAF in 1979.

One possible solution to accelerate the indigenisation of aircraft, armament and equipment for the IAF – the leader in technology among the three Services – could be to create a separate aircraft division, distinct from the missile division, under a separate Director General (DG) or General Manager (GM), to spur the manufacture of locally produced aircraft, armament and equipment that is urgently needed by the IAF. Such a GM or DG must be placed directly under a minister of aircraft production, a modern-day Lord Beaverbrook. On January 14, 2015, the Defence Minister terminated the three-year extension to the incumbent Director General, DRDO in order to appoint a relatively younger person, ostensibly to ensure focused and dynamic thinking. This move might also ultimately result in the separation of his/her responsibilities.[26]

Following widespread criticism in the print and electronic media, the United Progressive Alliance (UPA) II Government had appointed a DRDO Review Committee to 'suggest measures to improve the functioning of the DRDO' which submitted its report on March 5, 2008. The report has been under the scrutiny of the government for over five years, without being implemented. The then Defence Minister A.K. Antony in a written reply in the Rajya Sabha on April 23, 2008 said, "There had been delays due to genuine difficulties but despite many constraints DRDO had equipped the services with state-of-the-art technologies in many fields."[27] Such statements clearly show how the government routinely shields the DRDO. Given such a cosy arrangement, the DRDO is unlikely to deliver on its promises.

Military Reforms and Civil-Military Relations

The fragile state of civil-military relations (CMR) is perhaps the most enervating infirmity that afflicts India's national security and the armed forces. Despite numerous articles, comments, debates and discussions in think-tanks and TV, there is little progress.[28] For reasons which are by now well known, CMR in India have been strained for most of the 68 years since independence. Suggestions and recommendations offered on this vexed and intractable subject and the pleas of the military officers, mostly veterans, seem to have fallen on deaf ears. The recommendations of the Kargil Review Committee (KRC) headed by the respected K. Subrahmanyam were also not implemented in entirety, and the issues of appointment of a Chief of Defence Staff (CDS) and the merger of the three Service Headquarters with the MoD, have been kept in abeyance. There were reports that although the government of the day had circulated the KRC recommendations to all political parties, it had found that there was no consensus with regard to the appointment of the CDS. The more recently concluded Naresh Chandra-led Task Force on Military Reforms has also made many recommendations. Although the report is still not available in the public domain, one of its members has already declared that its outcome was disappointing. Other than recommending a Permanent Chairman of the Chief of Staff Committee, the task force achieved little. According to this member a radical change such as the appointment of a CDS, the creation of theatre commands, and the merger of the three Service Headquarters with the MoD as part of the Government of India, rather than remaining only as 'attached offices' would pose major problems, since at present we lack the necessary experience and trained and educated manpower for the job. The Service Chiefs themselves are also not particularly enthusiastic about all the recommendations.[29]

One of the main complaints of the military appears to be the lack of direct access to the highest levels of political leadership. There are, however, many instances of Generals Cariappa, Thimayya, Air Marshal Subroto Mukherjee and others meeting Nehru at a more informal level. Generals Manekshaw and K.V. Krishna Rao also did not seem to have much difficulty in meeting with, and putting across their views to Indira Gandhi when such a need arose.[30] General K. Sundarji also apparently enjoyed a friendly relationship with Arun Singh and Rajiv Gandhi at least up to the time of Exercise Brasstacks and Chequerboard.[31] During the Narasimha Rao Government, the Service Chiefs appeared somewhat unhappy with the way the government was dealing with the Pakistan-aided insurgency in Jammu and Kashmir, and for inadequate defence funding, which was needed to make up the shortfalls in ammunition and equipment, perhaps because they did not really know the dire straits in which the Indian economy was at that time.[32]

The year 1986-87 may have been a turning point of sorts in CMR in India, when Exercise Brasstacks, followed closely by Indian military intervention in Sri Lanka, apparently vitiated the equation between the military brass and the political leadership. Although the demand for a CDS, theatre commands and better access to the political leadership – particularly the Prime Minister – was also heard during the Vajpayee regime, it was not as shrill as in the recent past. The armed forces appear to be more concerned and hurt by this distant, if not strained relationship than the civilians.

There is a widely held belief that the bureaucrat rules the roost, while the politician is generally disinterested, or simply does not care until the chips are down. The political leaders are more comfortable with, and depend on, the civil servant on a daily basis and hence, prefer to take his advice on almost all matters. India's political leadership tends to avoid direct interaction with the armed forces, including the Service Chiefs, except on formal and ceremonial occasions. Jaswant Singh, K.C. Pant and Arun Singh, who held the defence portfolio at different times, may have been the only exceptions. Jaswant Singh, a former army officer, may have had a special bond with the Services. He has also written three highly readable books, in which he has cogently discussed the various problems related to India's security, but his contribution has been more intellectual than political. According to some unconfirmed reports this interaction has improved since the installation of the Bharatiya Janata Party (BJP) led National Democratic Alliance (NDA) Government in May 2014.

It is also believed that IAS officers do not like to work in the MoD; some even call it a punishment posting. They prefer other Ministries such as Finance, Commerce and the like. They take little interest in equipping themselves with specialist knowledge about national security, strategy or the defence services, and treat the services exactly as any other department of the government. It is widely accepted that generalists are ill-equipped to deal with issues of defence and national security.

To be fair, the Heads of Departments like All India Radio, Doordarshan,

Coal India, Air India, Director-General Civil Aviation (DGCA), Central Reserve Police Force, Border Security Force and other corporations, are also rarely allowed direct access to the Minister. Every request, suggestion or decision, invariably goes through the Secretary of the Department, and only then to the Minister, if need be. So why should the armed forces expect different treatment? The answer is simple. First, the three Service Chiefs enjoy the status and salaries equivalent to the Cabinet Secretary, but are placed above him in the Warrant of Precedence and hence, cannot be expected to report to the Defence Secretary, who is junior to them. Depending on the personality of the individuals concerned, the Service Chief, Defence Secretary and the Defence Minister usually work out a *modus vivendi*. It is not difficult for the civilian bureaucrat to get round a 'difficult' Service Chief by leveraging his position and proximity to the political leadership, and by virtue of him being the number one in the MoD.

In the January 8, 2013 incident of serious border violation, for example, the Defence Secretary and the National Security Adviser (NSA), and not the Chairman, Chiefs of Staff Committee (CoSC) reportedly briefed the Prime Minister. This was duly noted by the Services. In another incident of ceasefire violations, the GoI once again summoned the Army Chief and the Defence Secretary and not the Chairman, CoSC Air Chief Marshal N.A.K. Browne, clearly indicating the way the government undermines service institutions.

India's vast geographical expanse with long mountainous borders and equally long coastlines appear to confer on the country, a unique sense of security. Every Indian knows that it is not easy for any power to conquer India, nor is it easy to subdue the spirit of its people. Salami slicing or limited incursions across the borders might take place, but given the massive presence of the army along the frontier, the chances of such enemy action going unnoticed for long are rather remote, and hence no political leader loses his or her sleep over India's defence preparedness.

India's defence policy rests on a long-held and unshakeable belief that since India does not covet territory, nor wishes to export ideology, and will not be the first to initiate a war, there is little chance of a major conflict. Its armed forces have been charged with the task of defending every inch of its territory, an impossible and impractical demand; it is the military that will once again have to shoulder the blame should things go wrong. This raises many serious problems and severely restricts the options available to the armed forces. As seen during the 1999 Kargil War, the then government laid down that IAF aircraft will not cross the Line of Control (LoC). This restriction not only took away the initiative from the armed forces, but also cost India more lives, since the army had to resort to suicidal frontal assaults on entrenched enemy positions in the high mountains, where the enemy was nearly invulnerable to air or even artillery strikes. In hindsight, it is possible that the situation could have been handled differently, if the government had held detailed consultations about Standard Operating Procedures (SOPs) and Rules of Engagement, well in advance of the actual conflict.

According to MoD annual reports, while the armed forces are primarily responsible for ensuring the territorial integrity of the nation, under the relevant rules of procedure, it is the Defence Ministry that is charged with the responsibility of the 'Defence of India and every part thereof'. By virtue of being the seniormost civil servant in the MoD, in reality it is the Defence Secretary who exercises this function. The Defence Secretary neither commands any forces, nor is he even familiar with defence and security matters, except the cursory knowledge he gains by virtue of his short and often truncated tenure with the MoD. But he is virtually the master of all that goes on in the MoD.

The defence portfolio is typically held by a senior cabinet minister, who is usually too busy with parliamentary, party or constituency responsibilities, and in addition his/her own political survival. Worse, he need not necessarily be well informed or even interested in equipping himself with the knowledge and information necessary to exercise effective control, and to provide meaningful guidance and direction to the military. He is unavailable to the three Service Chiefs for regular and timely consultation; he does not hear the advice or apprehensions of the Service Chiefs first hand, and hence, is dependent on the civil servant for all advice. The Prime Minister likewise is too busy, and meets the military commanders only during the Annual Commanders' Conference, and on Independence Day and Republic Day, in a very formal and ceremonial atmosphere, where no serious discussion can obviously take place. In effect, therefore, the Defence Minister and the Prime Minister only receive the Defence Secretary's version of the military's views. Many former Chiefs have openly complained that a 'one-on-one meeting' with the Prime Minister is nearly impossible.[33] (Manohar Parrikar an Indian Institute of Technology (IIT) graduate is the first technologically qualified Indian Defence Minister in 68 years.) The military and the civilians also have differing perception of military threats, with the latter showing a strong tendency to underestimate or underplay it.

Sometime in 1991-92, the MoD unilaterally announced a downward revision of the Warrant of Precedence, which resulted in the three-star officers holding the post of a Principal Staff Officer (PSO) at the Service Headquarters, or the Commander-in-Chief being equated with full Secretaries to the GoI, but when in Delhi, the Secretary would take precedence. Although the author was then posted to the MoD Military Wing, the reason behind such a revision could never be ascertained. As a result, at the Annual Commanders' Conference, the first two rows are occupied mostly by civilians of all denominations. Such treatment irks the senior Service officer and he naturally sees it as blatant demonstration of civilian arrogance.

Another situation in which the Service member, mostly a soldier, relates with civilian government functionaries, is at the district and lower levels. The soldier, who is invariably away at far-off locations, comes home on leave or after retirement to find a plethora of problems: land grab, school admissions, intimidation by local thugs or politically connected anti-social elements. He then goes to the District Collector or Divisional Commissioner for help, where he is usually directed to the Secretary or even President of the Zilla Sainik Board, who pacifies him and sends him away with platitudes. The author has not known of a single civilian government functionary ever giving a patient hearing to a soldier's woes. Little wonder then, that the retired soldier is forced to fend for himself, by means fair and foul. The apathy and indifference of the local governments is so monumental, that it is hard to fully visualise the problems of a serving or retired Jawan. Such apathy is widespread in society, although the soldier commands genuine respect when the country is faced with a crisis.

The Armed Forces Special Powers Act (AFSPA) is another bone of contention between the civil and the military. It is often forgotten that when the army is called in aid of the civil administration, its personnel need special legal protection to conduct searches, arrest suspects, and take action to capture or stop anti-national elements from killing innocents. The police by the nature of their duties, and constitutional and legal provisions, already enjoy such legal protection, and hence, the provisions of the AFSPA can be diluted only at the cost of undermining the morale of the armed forces, especially the army. The army is, after all, employed at the express sanction of the Central Government, and to aid civil power under constitutional provisions and other provisions of the law, and hence, it is for the government to protect the interests of the soldier in such special circumstances. Of late, there is growing demand from civil society that all cases of rape, sexual assault and other crimes against women must be dealt with expeditiously, and the offending soldier handed over to civilian authority, without waiting for sanction from the central government. Although at first glance this appears a fair and justified demand, the armed forces would obviously like to protect their members from undue harassment caused by false cases and baseless allegations, by the kith and kin of militants and insurgents, especially in deeply alienated sections of our society. There is no gainsaying that it is also equally important for the military to expeditiously punish the guilty.

The main points of friction between the military and the government may be summarised as:

- The absence of an institutionalised mechanism for the Service Chiefs to candidly express their views to the highest civilian leadership.
- Need for clear and regularly updated operational directives and realistic threat assessments, and regular briefings and consultations, whenever new

Confidence Building Measures (CBMs) or diplomatic initiatives are planned.

- Expeditious clearance of modernisation and procurement projects, without undue delays in decision-making.
- If foreign policy is indeed intimately linked to defence and domestic policy, then a regular personal briefing by the Foreign Secretary and NSA to the three Chiefs is absolutely inescapable.

It is argued that the appointment of a CDS will automatically ensure greater synergy, greater jointness and integration, and a single point of advice to the civilian leadership. The CDS will be responsible for operations and look after the functioning of the Andaman and Nicobar tri-Service command, Strategic Forces Command (SFC), Cyber, Space and Special Forces Command when formed. The three Chiefs would be left only with training, discipline, morale, and recruitment and retention – largely administrative functions. The Chiefs are unlikely to accept this greatly diminished role, as they are after all, the role models for the soldier and officer. They are responsible for planning and executing a successful war, whereby the authority to send men to war, and the responsibility of winning it is not divided. The Chiefs may be burdened with far too many peacetime functions such as procurement, modernisation, budgeting and strategic plans, but they have a large enough staff to help them fulfil these tasks.

Lack of respect, and not being allowed to play a bigger role in the government's decision-making, are actually at the root of the problem of strained civil-military relations, but merely appointing a CDS may not solve these problems. The United States (US) or UK models have not eliminated all points of friction between the civil and the military. While the US has a separate Secretary (Minister) for each Service, the UK also has a Chief Scientific Adviser and a permanent Under-Secretary – a civil servant – at the same level as the CDS. It is thus incorrect to think that the CDS will automatically help diminish the role and importance of the civil servant. What if the politicians do not want the advice of a single uniformed person? What if they prefer more broad-based and multi-disciplinary advice? Collegiate advice might be preferable to single point advice. In any case, whether the Cabinet, Group of Ministers (GoM), Committee of Secretaries or Crisis Management Group actually perform their duties on the principle of collective responsibility and collegiate decision-making, is not known. These questions need serious consideration before imposing another tier, in the already slow defence decision-making process. The Naresh Chandra-led Task Force has reportedly recommended the appointment of a permanent Chairman Chiefs of Staff, which appears to be a compromise solution to the controversial CDS issue.[34]

There is widespread belief that the IAF does not favour a CDS and theatre commands because:

- It wants to retain its independence in decisions regarding effective employment and efficient use of air power.
- The assets of the IAF are too small to be divided up into penny packets. The IAF believes in the indivisibility of air power, and is always ready and willing to provide support to the army and navy, but prefers that its quantum and timing be decided through prior consultations and joint planning in peacetime.
- It expects that a joint mission plan be prepared, and that each Service understands and respects its special attributes, strengths and weaknesses.
- The IAF believes that three highly intelligent, experienced, mature and knowledgeable Service Chiefs do not need a supervisor or 'head-master' to ensure that they work together.
- The IAF, while believing that future wars need a joint approach, is of the opinion that every situation may not need equal contribution of each Service. Very often, air power will be the chosen instrument for immediate retaliation, since use of air power may be sufficient.

In these circumstances, there is a need to devise a mechanism that would address the above complaints of the Services, without radically changing and fundamentally disrupting the present set-up. India could opt for a mix of the systems currently prevailing in the US and UK.

This would require the appointment of a separate Minister of State (MoS) for the army, navy and the air force, assisted and supported by a civil servant of suitable seniority and other staff. Each Chief of Staff will be required to report to the MoS, but continue to attend CoSC meetings as at present. Each MoS may also be given additional responsibility such as aircraft production, procurement committee, approval, planning and overall supervision of exercises with friendly militaries and the like. This will give each Chief day-to-day access to the 'political authority', albeit at a junior level. In addition, the Defence Minister's Committee may be revived so that the Defence Minister, three MoS, the Service Chiefs, Defence Secretary, Secretary Defence Production, the SA to the Defence Minister, the three Secretary-level officers attached to each MoS and the Financial Advisor Defence Services (FADS) could meet every month, to review the progress since the last such meeting. While there is an urgent need to remove the existing disconnect between the military and civilian leadership, this must be achieved with the least disruption to the present system.

Ownership of Air Power

Compared to the army, the IAF is rather small and gets only about half the funding, but remains the most critical and agile instrument of national security. The IAF has since its formation in 1932, employed air power as an independent

Service, and has been the principal operator of national air power. Stemming from its long experience and participation, air power is its primary strength and not a part-time activity like in the other two Services. The navy and the army certainly have sizeable aviation assets, the former much more varied than the latter, but that only meets each Service's niche requirements, and works in concert with the IAF when such a need arises. Just as seafaring is the primary activity of the navy, and providing ground fighting prowess that of the army, flying is the core activity of the air force. Given that the IAF is charged with the primary responsibility of safeguarding the country's air space, it is imperative that aviation assets of both the army and navy come under control of the IAF when needed. Air space management will always be the responsibility of the IAF. It must also be made clear that the IAF has a role other than supporting surface operations.

The army has all along expressed a desire to have the air force under command and not merely in support, and that appears to be the fundamental reason for the army's demand for the control of attack helicopters. The IAF has maintained and manned the nearly two-squadron worth of attack helicopters, the Mi-25 and Mi-35 for over three decades, but that arrangement has not been found to be effective, as the army has not found it necessary to employ these potent combat assets in India's fight against cross-border terrorism and armed infiltration. The recent debate on the ownership of attack helicopters needs to be seen in light of these observations. It is for the reasons of economy and expertise that the IAF has opposed the handing over of assets other than those used for artillery observation and light communication duties. To be fair, the navy has a sizeable force of fixed as well as rotary wing assets, but barring a few communication aircraft like the AVRO HS-748 and Do-238, others are specialist aircraft and helicopters that carry out specific maritime duties.

It is said that in the early 1960s, the IAF purchased the An-12 transport aircraft from the army budget, since the aircraft was to be used mainly for air maintenance of troops in the forward areas. In the 1980s, the Mi-25 and later Mi-35 were also reportedly purchased from army funds, but were maintained and operated by the IAF. These units were manned by IAF personnel and the attack helicopters flown by IAF pilots. The arrangement was apparently to avoid duplication and to effect economies, but was not acceptable to the army due to the perceived reluctance of the IAF to use these helicopters for each and every minor border management operation. This arrangement continued even after November 1987, when Air Observation Post (Air OP) Squadrons equipped with Cheetah and Chetak helicopters and a few fixed-wing aircraft were handed over to the army.

The IAF also had serious reservations about the army's understanding of the need for airspace management to protect own assets from friendly fire and other accidents, since the army did not like the idea of the IAF controlling airspace.

IAF's argument is that, as the primary operator of the nation's air power assets, and more importantly due to its role in providing air defence to the country, it was logical for the IAF to control airspace. In September 1984 the author, then a Wing Commander, was deputed to attend an army seminar on Air Space Management at I Corps Headquarters at Mathura. Even after a long and detailed presentation by the then AD Artillery Brigade Commander, the Generals, especially those belonging to the Armoured Corps, refused to accept any restrictions on the movement of their helicopters in the Tactical Battle Area (TBA), because the helicopters were used primarily as flying staff cars. It is pertinent to note that the then Corps Commander and his Chief of Staff, an Air OP pilot, later rose to the position of Chief of the Army Staff.

When told that in a congested battlefield, with a plethora of organic Air Defence (AD) weapons such as the Soviet self-propelled (SP) AD missiles (inducted in 1979-80), long-range artillery gun-fire, and transiting air force fighters at ultra-low levels, it would be suicidal to venture into the air without proper permission from and in coordination with the local AD Commander, the Generals simply shrugged their shoulders, and said they were prepared to accept the risks involved. The IAF obviously did not want to jeopardise the safety of friendly aircraft. This discussion went on for many years without any conclusion, until a temporary arrangement was worked out to keep all airspace users, informed of each other's presence in the TBA.

India has mercifully not fought a major conventional war since 1971, and it can only be hoped that modern telecommunications and the so-called network-enabled operations would resolve this issue of airspace control in the near future. Even so, some restrictions on air movement will have to be accepted by all users. In light of this, the army would once again expect total operational control of its attack helicopters in peace and war. In the past there were also some demands that the country acquire special close air support (CAS) fixed wing aircraft, like the Soviet SU-25/39 or the American Fairchild A-10, for exclusive use in Offensive Air Support (OAS) and under the army's control. If acceded, the safety, control, efficiency and economy of air operations would be severely jeopardised. Significantly, the army has not asked for the control of the IAF's fixed and rotary wing transport assets that are routinely employed for air maintenance duties, perhaps because air maintenance remains a non-glamorous but back-breaking and thankless task, that the air force has cheerfully performed for over 60 years.

Although it is patently inefficient, unsafe and uneconomical to distribute costly combat assets to different arms of the military for niche activity, one good fallout of the ownership shifting to the army would perhaps be that the army would not ask the IAF to provide CAS, OAS or even Casualty-Evacuation (Cas-Evac). With this, the IAF would be left only with the task of providing tactical and strategic airlift to the army in war and peace. This will amount to additional expenditure and avoidable duplication, as logistics and maintenance activity would then have to be managed by the army. The US military has four separate aviation wings, viz. air force, army, navy and marine corps. These are often seen as a wasteful arrangement, and the arrangement has recently come under pressure to reduce these divisions to possibly two: the air force and the naval aviation.[35]

For the present, the MoD seems to have placated the army and has accepted that the 28 AH-64 Apache attack helicopters would be under army control, but has obviously not thought through the long-term implications of its decision.

The most undesirable outcome of yielding to the demands of the senior Service would be a fundamental rupture in the fragile jointness that is now under slow and difficult construction. A fragmented and duplicated approach to air power employment would be damaging to military effectiveness and the overall economy.

In 1986-87, when in command of a fighter squadron in the Eastern sector, the author found that the army was not ready to temporarily stop or even restrict its helicopter movement in the narrow Himalayan valleys, during an army-air force joint exercise that was ironically planned by the army. Repeated pleas to the BGS and Chief Of Staff (COS) of the corps failed to convince the army of the risks involved in air force fighters and army helicopters criss-crossing through the narrow valleys. A solution was, nevertheless, found through a quiet arrangement of time-sharing with the Air OP aviators of the army, without the BGS ever coming to know of it. Such issues are likely to become even more critical with the army and air force buying more and more UAVs and UCAVs without prior consultations on sharing of airspace. This will add to the confusion and the risk of 'friendly fire' accidents. It is time the army and the air force leaders sorted out these differences for the larger good of the country's security.

The Nuclear Dimension

Refuting H.J. Mackinder's theory of geopolitics that control of the Asian and European heartland meant world domination, Nehru says:

> But civilisation is no longer confined to oceanic fringes and tends to become universal in its scope and content. The growth of the Americas also does not fit in with a European heartland dominating the world. And air power has brought a new factor which has upset the balance between sea-power and land-power.[36]

Nehru wrote this while in prison in 1944, but air power became even more important after the atomic bombing of Japan in August 1945. Little wonder, then, that in 1948 he said, "The future belongs to those who produce atomic energy. That is going to be the chief national power of the future. Of course, defence is intimately concerned with this. Even political consequences are worthwhile," thus clearly indicating that it was worthwhile having nuclear weapons, even if it meant facing the wrath of the world. Later, however, he changed his mind. Writing after the 1962 border war with China, B.K. Nehru, the then Indian ambassador to the US says, "Nehru was an idealist removed in many ways from reality. He looked upon the Chinese aggression as a wicked, cruel and selfish act and it would break him." Nehru himself admitted in Parliament that he had "lived in an artificial world of our own creation." Yet, when the then Director of the Department of Atomic Energy (DAE) Homi J. Bhabha pressed Nehru for clearance to go ahead with India's nuclear weapon, he did not give his approval. "Nehru almost threw me out of his room" says Bhabha. While Nehru was vehemently against a test, he did tell Bhabha in that meeting to speed up efforts to develop the capability for a peaceful nuclear explosion."[37] Nehru encouraged nuclear research, held the DAE under his charge, and kept India's options open; perhaps for too long. He was in no hurry to develop a nuclear weapon. In 1962, sensing the imminence of a Chinese nuclear test, the US offered India an option to get nukes under the Senator McGhee Plan, but India refused. China carried out its first nuclear test on October 16, 1964. India complained, but did not accelerate its own nuclear programme. It was Indira Gandhi, who finally authorised the Peaceful Nuclear Explosion (PNE) in 1974. As was to be expected, the US imposed sanctions and India almost totally stopped work on nuclear weapons. The reasons for the reluctance to quickly weaponise this nascent capability, might have included political turmoil resulting in the imposition of Emergency, Indira Gandhi losing elections, and the strong opposition of Morarji Desai, who became the next Prime Minister in 1977, and only reluctantly allowed the continuation of nuclear research.

The Integrated Guided Missile Development Programme (IGMDP) began only in 1983, a full nine years after the first 'peaceful' nuclear test. The liquid-fuelled Prithvi was first tested in 1988 and the Agni on May 5, 1989, but Indira Gandhi did not live to see the tests. Although successive Prime Ministers kept the programme going and provided the necessary funding, there was little urgency. Events and incidents such as the 1987 Exercise Brasstacks and the 1990 nuclear scare caused by the thinly veiled nuclear threats from Pakistan, followed by Exercise Chequer Board and the Sumdorong Chu incident on the Chinese border, should have rekindled India's quest, but nothing of the sort happened. It is alleged that General K. Sundarji, the then Chief of Army Staff, thought that it was the last chance to sort out Pakistan before it acquired nuclear weapons, but India lost it, and in fact became even more concerned about Pakistan's possible irrational behaviour.

It is a moot point if Indian armour making 50-100-km-deep forays into Pakistan, as per Sundarji's plan, was a realistic option. No one seemed clear about the political aim, if any of Sundarji's offensive plans. The Indian Army had always thought, and continues to think even today, that capturing chunks of Pakistan's territory would be a major bargaining counter, little realising that such a strategy is not possible in today's nuclearised and globalised world. It is also debatable if Pakistan would have actually used a nuclear weapon in retaliation to the Indian Army's aggression, when in close proximity of its own ground forces. It is also not clear if Pakistan really possessed an air or missile deliverable atomic weapon in 1987. But it is safe to surmise that these events compelled India to take a harder and more serious view of the nuclear option.

It is generally believed that by the early 1990s, India had a rudimentary device ready for aircraft delivery. The IAF came into the loop because the Mirage-2000 was selected as the delivery aircraft but only the Chief of Air Staff knew. Pakistan already had the F-16 for nuclear delivery. In December 1988, the Rajiv Gandhi Government signed an agreement with Pakistan, prohibiting attacks on each other's nuclear sites. Strangely, there has been little discussion on this agreement and no one really knows why this step was taken in such haste. Did India fear a Pakistani air attack on its nuclear sites along the coastline in Maharashtra, targets well within the range of PAF F-16 aircraft? In 1990 again, there were widespread rumours of a nuclear face-off with Pakistan, when the US sent Robert Gates, the then Deputy National Security Adviser to diffuse the situation, but no one in India has ever acknowledged that a threat of war indeed existed. The IAF did make some efforts to update its 'arms and ammunition status' but little else happened. There was little commotion or activity in the IAF.

The Narasimha Rao Government also planned a test, but had to postpone its decision when the US came to know of it. The 1998 Shakti tests came only when India was being cornered into signing the Comprehensive Test Ban Treaty (CTBT), and faced the daunting prospect of losing its long-cherished option. The thermonuclear test was reportedly unsuccessful as per most scientists, but again and for obvious reasons, there is no official confirmation. Following the tests, India voluntarily gave up testing by declaring a self-imposed moratorium. There were angry reactions from the P-5, except France; P-5 members imposed economic and other sanctions. It was said that the Indian tests legitimised Pakistani nuclear weapons – strange logic, especially since the US knew that Pakistan already had nuclear capability. While India assured the world that its nuclear weapons were not aimed at any country, the then Defence Minister George Fernandes called China, India's enemy No. 1, and the then Indian Prime Minister Vajpayee's letter to the US President, allegedly naming China as the basic cause for the test, was leaked to the press.

In August 1999, India announced the 'draft' nuclear doctrine in which it clearly indicated its ambivalent attitude to nuclear weapons by adopting a 'No First Use' or NFU doctrine of Credible Minimum Deterrence. During the 1999 Kargil hostilities, Pakistan once again held out a nuclear threat. Although it is now widely believed that the Kargil intrusions were aimed at interdicting the

Srinagar-Leh highway, to force the Indian Army to vacate the Siachen heights, and to internationalise the Kashmir issue, a subsidiary unstated Pakistani aim might have been to assess the Indian reaction to Pakistan's highly advertised low nuclear threshold. By restricting the IAF on own side of the LoC, India perhaps unwittingly validated Pakistan's nuclear strategy of defeating India's conventional superiority.

The Indian nuclear doctrine rightly believes that nuclear weapons are not for war fighting, but only for deterrence against nuclear blackmail, and that a credible nuclear deterrent does not require the accumulation of a large stockpile of nuclear warheads and missiles. In 2003, India revised its 'draft' doctrine to include chemical and biological attacks on 'Indian troops anywhere', as one of the reasons for nuclear retaliation. There is no clarity on what forced the Indian decision-makers to make these amendments, which in fact were seen by many as a dilution of its NFU pledge.[38] There has been no public debate and the 2003 Nuclear Doctrine continues to be the guiding document for its nuclear strategy.

India formed the Strategic Forces Command (SFC) in 2003, but its ambit is restricted to management of India's nuclear arsenal, with the civilian government keeping a tight control (justifiably so) over the warheads and missiles, which are kept separately and away from each other, as a measure of safety against unauthorised and/or accidental use.

The DRDO has registered slow but steady progress, and built a variety of missiles such as Prithvi I and II, Agni I to V with impressively larger ranges and improved accuracy. The Agni V tested in June 2012, claims a 5,000-km range and the DRDO is also stated to be working on MIRVs.

India has leased a nuclear submarine from Russia to train the navy for operations of a nuclear submarine. On January 27, 2013, India's DRDO announced the successful launch of a Submarine Launched Ballistic Missile (SLBM), the B-15.[39] This was supposedly the 14th successive such launch in which "everything went as per plan" and India inched closer to operationalising the third leg of its nuclear triad. The B-15 or K-4 SLBM tested in January 2013, was rumoured to have received Russian assistance. On March 20, 2013, India also successfully test-fired the Brahmos cruise missile from a submerged platform in the Bay of Bengal, while the indigenous Arihant nuclear-powered submarine continues to be tested.

Of the three Services, the army is the most vulnerable to nuclear strikes, especially if during a future conventional conflict it advances into Pakistani territory. The army regularly exercises its troops for fighting in a nuclear, biological and chemical (NBC) environment. The IAF faces a medium threat, but a Chemical and Biological Warfare (CBW) attack can easily and quite comprehensively disrupt air operations. The Indian Navy is relatively safe and will soon fulfil the responsibility of activating the third leg of the nuclear triad.

There is little clarity on what India's political aims are, but India appears to rely on its rudimentary nuclear capability to deter the threat of nuclear blackmail. While India routinely declares its concern about Pakistani nuclear weapons, the Chinese nuclear threat appears to be of less concern, although China possesses a far bigger and more sophisticated nuclear arsenal, including tactical nuclear weapons. According to Bharat Karnad, a self-confessed nuclear hawk, India should quickly build a sizeable arsenal of megaton fusion bombs and Inter Continental Ballistic Missiles (ICBMs) capable of delivering these to all corners of the earth, but there is no clarity on what that minimum number should be.[40]

It is thus difficult to predict the size of India's arsenal in 2030. Indian weapons are apparently safe, and there is little chance of their unauthorised, accidental use. Widely prevalent nuclear theories and jargon are not applicable, even if some theorists continue to use them to describe Kashmir as the nuclear flashpoint in South Asia. Indian and foreign scholars can keep writing on the size of India's nuclear deterrent and try to provoke a response, but the government does not oblige. Paradoxically, the Indian nuclear elite somehow seem to readily accept the argument that Pakistan's nuclear threshold is indeed low, and shape their own 'use of force' options to this reality. India's non-retaliation to 26/11, and oft-repeated attempts at reconciliation with Pakistan, even when the latter refuses to initiate action against the perpetrators of the ghastly Mumbai attack, are a clear indication of this apprehension.

It is now a well-established fact that India will always be a reluctant nuclear power. The political leadership was always divided over the issue of nuclear testing and generally favoured an ambiguous stance even after the first test in 1974, but now that India has possessed a rudimentary deterrent since 1998, the government seems to be excessively sanguine about its rudimentary nuclear capability actually deterring its enemies. While it is difficult to prove this, in all probability, India is satisfied with the slow and steady pace at which its nuclear deterrent is being developed. This excessive dependence on nuclear weapons is perhaps the reason why the government is not unduly concerned with routine delays in the timely development of conventional weapons and platforms. India is slowly reaching a 'triad', but at least for the present and foreseeable future, it is based on borrowed technology, since the Arihant is yet to become fully operational.

While advocating total disarmament and the total abolition of nuclear weapons, India is unlikely to give up or roll back its programme or sign the Nuclear Non-Proliferation Treaty (NPT), the CTBT or the Fissile Material Cut-off Treaty (FMCT). The nuclear liability bill is likely to remain a major impediment for trade in civil nuclear technology and purchase of nuclear power reactors from other countries, especially the US. India is also unlikely to accept international inspections and may even accept delays in nuclear power production. India's credible minimum deterrent is meant to deter nuclear weapons, but implicitly also a conventional war. There is much pragmatism in this policy. With the US and the People's Republic of China (PRC) always enhancing Pakistan's power to balance India, it is impossible to push Pakistan into spending large amounts on its defence. Its benefactors will always bail it out and maintain a strategic balance in South Asia, so that India is never assured of an outright military victory over Pakistan. This, it seems, is at the root of India's self-imposed 'strategic restraint' strategy. But this hypothesis is difficult to prove in the absence of any open source material. There is as yet no consensus on how India should deal with Pakistan or China, or what it should do with its nuclear weapons, but a slow and steady increase in missile ranges and payloads seems to be under way, the Agni-V being the latest such example.

Barring a handful of IAF personnel trained for the purpose, no one really knows how and when India will be required to consider an aircraft-launched nuclear response, and why. While the advantages and vulnerabilities of aircraft over missiles are only too well known, there has been no public discussion on the size of the nuclear arsenal and delivery platforms. It is also rumoured that some of the 42 additional Su-30MKIs ordered in December 2012 are actually for nuclear weapons delivery. Some commentators have even referred to these as Super Sukhoi. In March 2010, the cost of this deal was reported to be US$ 2.73 billion, but in August 2010, it had gone up to US$ 4.3 billion, raising the unit cost of each aircraft to $102 million, which is comparable to the American F-35 JSF, the fifth generation stealth fighter.

All these issues must, however, be seen in light of India's undeclared national security posture, which has generally been characterised by a marked reluctance to use force. India will always try its utmost to find a peaceful and negotiated solution to every issue and problem, will avoid violence at almost any cost, and only if it becomes unavoidable and inevitable will India consider resort to use of force. If in the bargain, Indian armed forces have to fight a defensive war from a position of disadvantage, then that would have to be accepted. This, in fact, means that the national leadership may impose increasingly more restrictive rules of engagement, even when these militate against correct and time-tested military tactics. The armed forces continue to be totally clueless about India's nuclear policy and strategy, and play no role in the development of nuclear strategy, but simply remain loyal custodians of the missiles under their charge.

Understanding Doctrine

In his Foreword to the 2012 edition of the *Basic Doctrine of the IAF*, Air Chief Marshal N.A.K. Browne says:

> Recording the collective memory of core beliefs in the form of a doctrine enforces a discipline and clarity of thought that helps sustain this dynamic

process. Once recorded and periodically updated, the doctrine provides a common baseline for education and the dissemination of collective thought.

Doctrine it is said, is a set of fundamental principles and beliefs by which military forces guide their actions in support of objectives. It is also defined as the codification of beliefs or a body of teachings or instructions, even principles. It is a guide to action and a frame of reference, rather than strict rules or dogma. It is constantly refined and updated with time, and is authoritative, but does not bind its practitioner. The *Basic Doctrine of the IAF* states, "A doctrine provides a military commander with the framework to prepare and fight a war in a coordinated and controlled manner."[41]

The IAF is often seen as an open, democratic and forward-looking organisation and acknowledged as the least rigid among the three Services. It participated in the international Exercise Shiksha with the US and UK air forces in 1963. The IAF was also the first to publish its doctrine in 1995. This edition of the doctrine borrowed heavily from the American experience of the first Gulf War of 1991. In fact, it was widely seen as the endorsement of the US Air Force's role in that war, and an indication of how the IAF intended to fight its future wars.

As was expected, the publication provoked the army to publish its own doctrine, and once again highlighted the issue of the role of the 'air' in support of the army. Some unpleasant correspondence was exchanged between the two, on the question of 'time-critical targets', with the army insisting that the IAF must be available to it from day one, and not after a week of Counter Air Operations, as the IAF doctrine had indicated. As usually happens, there was no major war and no further discussion, but there was also no reaction or comment from the government. After the establishment of Headquarters Integrated Defence Staff, a number of doctrines on specific roles such as counter-insurgency, joint forces actions, out-of-area contingencies, anti-piracy and amphibious operations have been published, but remain classified, and hence are not available for comment. The Tri-Service Joint Command at Andaman and Nicobar Islands had also conducted a number of Tri-Shakti exercises in which all three Services took part. The Integrated Defence Staff also published a tri-Service joint doctrine, but it is not known if a joint army-air force mission doctrine exists.

The IAF again published an unclassified version of the *Basic Doctrine of the IAF* in September 2012, in an attempt to obtain the views of a larger cross-section of the public, academia, government departments, the two sister Services and paramilitary organisations. Not surprisingly, there has been no public discussion or debate, and one wonders if any senior government official in the MoD has even read it. None of these doctrines have been endorsed by the MoD or the

GoI, and hence remain, at best, a declaration of intent of the Services. In the absence of a government-declared national security strategy, the *Basic Doctrine of the IAF* relies on the relevant portions of the Indian Constitution, to lay down basic objectives of freedom, sovereignty and territorial integrity, reiterates India's desire for peaceful coexistence and emphasises that India does not have any extra-territorial ambitions.

Regarding the employment of air power, it restricts itself to the classical and traditional approach based mostly on wars fought by other countries and of course World War II. While it mentions the role of the IAF during Kargil operations, it does not make any specific reference to the future of war in high-altitude border areas of the country. It also does not offer innovative ideas on how the IAF can prosecute a Compellence, Punishment or Containment campaign, or operation in a limited war scenario, especially when the main adversary frequently holds out nuclear threats. To be fair, it mentions punitive action in passing but generally adheres to the traditional roles. It is after all only the *Basic Doctrine of the IAF*, and details of employment of air power in specific situations might be covered in Part II, the Operational Doctrine, which naturally remains classified. As suggested in a paper by the author published in 2003 titled "Air Power and Escalation Control",[42] it is essential to employ combat air power, comprising both manned and unmanned aircraft, in the way the Mongols, and later the Marathas used their cavalry to harass their enemy. After the attack, their cavalry disappeared before the enemy could even wake up to the raid.

Although the IAF published its doctrine in 1995, there was no effort to shape the thinking in the Service, nor was there any major effort to train its so-called 'Air Warriors' for specific situations that might arise in a future war. In short, the emphasis was once again on the employment of air power in a *conventional war scenario* or a traditional approach.

A doctrine normally plays a vital role in the force structure planning of a military organisation. As brought out earlier, the IAF structure was not influenced by its doctrine. Instead, it appears to have been shaped by (a) the perception of the threat, (b) affordability, and (c) a vague notion of a 'balanced air force'. Total dependence on arms imports, limited access to technology and more importantly, paucity of resources, seems to have been the reason for ad hoc planning. For example, the IAF obtained two Mirage-2000 squadrons in 1985, which remained a generation ahead of all its other combat aircraft for over a decade, until the entry of the Su-30MKI in the early years of the 21st century. There is no direct linkage of this choice of the Mirage-2000 to India's need for an assured nuclear weapon delivery platform.

In terms of doctrinal development, the IAF has maintained a close watch on air power trends in other countries. From 2004 onwards, making use of positive changes in the international political climate, IAF began its participation in many international exercises with the French, American, British and Singapore Air Forces, and derived much useful experience. But it is not clear if the lessons learnt through these exercises with the leading air forces of the world, were disseminated to personnel who had not taken part in the exercises, and if the relatively less advanced aircraft such as the MiG-21, 23, 27 and Jaguar were indeed able to adapt to the level of these fourth-generation aircraft. The IAF, no doubt, must make all efforts to expose as large and wide a cross-section of its personnel to best practices followed by the air forces of advanced countries.

Conclusion

Air power continues to be a very potent instrument of national power, especially suited to close control and finely calibrated application of force. It can also be useful when employed for political signalling, to indicate national intention and resolve, or to convey the limits of patience without even firing a shot, or actually causing any damage. It, therefore, makes escalation control easy yet positive.

Being offensive by its very nature, air power calls for mature and careful handling, with necessary tenacity and fortitude, and its application cannot be given up at the first sign of attrition, or international public outcry for caution and restraint. India's policy of utmost restraint is well known and highly appreciated across the globe. Its commitment to peaceful resolution of disputes is probably beyond doubt. The world, however, shows a marked tendency to take for granted India's demonstrated reluctance to use of force. India on its part also gives mixed signals through delayed reaction, and is sometimes blamed for over-reaction, as during Kargil, and again in the aftermath of the December 13, 2001 terrorist attack on its Parliament. It is time India devised a more calibrated response to these frequent provocations by its recalcitrant neighbours, instead of an overwhelming reaction such as the total mobilisation of its armed forces.

The former NSA, Shivshankar Menon in his tribute to K. Subrahmanyam, called the KRC the origin of modern Indian national security structure, and also said it was 'still work in progress'. He also alluded to the need for true 'jointness', not simply between the three branches of the military, but one that includes the various organs of the Indian State, its academia, intelligentsia, industry, in short, all elements of national power.[43] He also clearly warned the military to fundamentally change its thinking, to ensure its continued relevance to national security.

Such advice is equally applicable to the numerous civilian agencies and departments who show scant regard for, and utmost reluctance to engage the armed forces in a regular, formal and well-structured dialogue or consultative process, to throw up new and workable initiatives. The tendency to treat the military as 'security guards' to be called only when the threat has already materialised, must now be replaced with a more nuanced and thoroughly discussed and refined response mechanism. Whether or not it wants it, India is too important a power to be seen as somehow muddling through and must develop the necessary *strategic poise and posture* to address the multifarious security challenges that are likely to become even more complex. India has always placed a high value on strategic autonomy, but it must also show its readiness to exercise it when the need arises. For, as President Pranab Mukherjee said, when he was the External Affairs Minister, "The biggest challenge for our foreign policy, however, lies in changing our mindsets." These remarks were made at the Shangri La symposium on January 16, 2007.[44] The reader can judge if Indian policy has actually shown any significant change in the handling of its security challenges since then.

For some time now, India has absorbed the so-called peaceful rise of China with utmost forbearance and finesse. China, however, seems to show little concern for India's sensitivities and there is as yet no indication of how its new leadership will view its relations with a slowly rising India. China's all-round assistance to Pakistan emboldens it to continue its policy of cross-border terrorism to destabilise India. One wonders if India can go on bearing the economic, societal and political costs of this one-sided relationship, in which India makes all the concessions, while the other side makes no effort at accommodation. India's deep and sincere desire to normalise its relations with all its neighbours, especially Pakistan, is indeed laudable, but it will bear fruit only when Pakistan is made to realise that there will be costs to its wayward behaviour.

Merely increasing military assets and personnel strength has the inherent danger of entering an unsustainable arms race with powerful and prosperous neighbours and hence must be avoided, and yet, India must maintain a credible nuclear and conventional deterrent. In November 2003, the Centre for Air Power Studies, based in New Delhi, held an important seminar on Joint Warfare during which many air power experts including former Air Chiefs, propounded their views and offered some very important ideas that are valid and valuable even today. Marshal of the Air Force Arjan Singh was of the view that there were some serious problems with the way India handles its security. He also felt that cooperation between the Services was inadequate. Air Chief Marshal O.P. Mehra (Retd.) opined that each Service must learn to respect the other's strengths and special attributes, while at the same time being cognisant of inherent weaknesses. He felt that we can never achieve true 'jointmanship', unless we develop mutual trust in each other.

Air Chief Marshal S. Krishnaswamy, the then CAS, was the most forthright of all, when he said that he was simply too busy running the air force and had no time to find faults with others. He was of the firm opinion that his duty was to ensure that each of the air force members knew exactly what his duty and specific job was in the larger scheme of things, so that he as the Air Chief could assure the government of the readiness of his service for action. He said it was important to convince the government that the air force was capable of providing desired and timely outcomes, with the greatest economy of effort. He felt that without such an assurance, the government would hesitate to give the air force or the armed forces the task at hand, and would instead be forced to look for other less efficient alternatives, and that such an option would undermine our national security. His was a hands-on approach that concentrated on the job at hand. He indirectly said that the armed forces needed to introspect on their individual strengths and weaknesses and find new ways to offer the best joint options possible, and if that was not forthcoming, he would as the CAS, continue to work to enhance the efficiency and output of the IAF.[45] India's national security leadership must take note of these points and initiate urgent measures to close the existing gaps in perception of the various players and stakeholders in the military and civilian decision-makers, to provide comprehensive security to the country.

The foregoing clearly shows that India's military weakness lies not in numbers or sophistication of its weapons, but in its inability to send out clear and timely signals to pre-empt and prevent surprises. It is noteworthy that both the US and UK put in place necessary instrumentalities following catastrophic terror strikes, and have successfully prevented their repetition since September 9, 2001 and July 5, 2005 respectively, without resorting to unduly harsh measures or excessively draconian anti-terror laws.

NOTES

1. Air Marshal Y.V. Malse, interview with the author, July 12, 2000.
2. Interview with Air Marshal Randhir Singh (Retd.), January 5, 2012.
3. George Tanham and Marcy Agmon, *The Indian Air Force: Trends and Prospects*, RAND Monograph, Santa Monica, CA, 1995, p. 94.
4. Interview with a serving officer who prefers to remain anonymous.
5. The suggestions are based on the author's informal discussions with some serving and retired officers.
6. See http://www.pib.nic.in/newsite/erelease.aspx?relid=96129 (Accessed March 12, 2015). Also see, http://www.rediff.com/news/column/needed-urgently-the-indian-national-defence-university/20150119.htm (Accessed March 12, 2015).
7. Ajai Shukla, *Business Standard*, March 22, 2013.
8. Chris Smith, *India's Ad Hoc Arsenal: Direction or Drift in Defence Policy?*, SIPRI, Oxford University Press, 1994, p. 166.
9. Interview with Air Chief Marshal H. Moolgaonkar, July 12, 2000. Also see no. 2.
10. Indian Warbirds at Bharat Rakshak.com
11. Interview with Air Marshal S.G. Inamdar (Retd.) on January 4, 2001.
12. Rajat Pandit, *Times of India*, May 7, 2012.
13. Interview with Air Chief Marshal H. Moolgaonkar, no. 9.
14. Interview with Air Marshal A.P. Garud, DG, FS&I, IAF, *SP's Aviation*, (12), December 2012, emphasis added.
15. See http://in.reuters.com/article/2015/02/28/india-budget-defence-idINKBN0LW0BB20150228 (Accessed March 15, 2015).

16. Amiya Kumar Ghosh, "Review of the Defence Budget", *Air Power Journal*, 4 (3), July-September 2009, pp. 143-64.
17. Ajai Shukla, "How much is the defence budget?", *Business Standard*, March 11, 2008 as quoted in Laxman Behera, "Defence Budget Trend in the Past Two Decades", Paper presented at National Seminar on Defence Budget, IDSA, New Delhi, November 20, 2008.
18. See http://pib.nic.in/newsite/erelease.aspx?relid=8386 (Accessed November 15, 2014).
19. See http://www.moneycontrol.com/news/cnbc-tv18-comments/tata-bets-bigdefence-jvsfms-fdi-boost_1129397.html (Accessed March 26, 2015).
20. Ministry of Defence, Government of India at http://mod.nic.in/product&supp/welcome.html (Accessed March 20, 2013). Not surprisingly, some of the data on this official website of the MoD has been updated only to 2003-04.
21. On the lines of meetings held to discuss Air Staff Targets (AST) which are issued when a new product like an aircraft is to be produced in India or purchased from a foreign vendor.
22. S. Krishnaswamy, "Policy for Aircraft Production", *IDSA Journal*, 5, January-March 1969, pp. 75-81.
23. "India as a Great Power – Know Yourself", *Economist*, March 30, 2013, Delhi Print Edition.
24. Air Marshal Philip Rajkumar (Retd.), *The Tejas Story: The Light Combat Aircraft Project*, Manohar, New Delhi, 2008, p. 28.
25. This at first might appear as an unsubstantiated assertion, but the author's interactions with a large number of bureaucrats and scientists have been pretty convincing, with most of them dismissing the fact that there is any major military threat which India cannot take care of easily.
26. See http://www.telegraphindia.com/1150115/jsp/nation/story_8534.jsp#.VRZTXG2j IU (Accessed March 26, 2015).
27. Press Information Bureau, Recommendations of the P. Rama Rao Committee on DRDO, at http://pib.nic.in/newsite/erelease.aspx?relid=37794 (Accessed November 14, 2013).
28. A few samples are: P.V.R. Rao, "Government Machinery for the Evolution of National Defence Policy and the Higher Direction of War", *IDSA Journal*, 1 (1), July 1, 1968, pp. 1-11; K. Subrahmanyam, "Decision Making In Defence", *IDSA Journal*, 2 (4), April-June 1970, pp. 424-44; Air Cmde. R.V. Phadke (Retd.), "Tinkering with India's Higher Defence Control Organisation", *IDSA Journal*, July, 2000, at idsa.in/archives; Gen. V.P. Malik (Retd.) and Anit Mukherjee, "Do we need a chief of defence staff?", *Indian Express*, July 11, 2011; Anit Mukherjee, "The Future Is Now", *Times of India*, June 17, 2011; Air Marshal R.S. Bedi (Retd.), "Redefine civil-military relations", *Tribune*, Chandigarh, October 22, 2012.
29. Admiral Arun Prakash (Retd.), "National Security Reforms: Ten Years After the Kargil Committee Report", *USI Journal*, October-December 2012, pp. 504-23.
30. Raj Chengappa, *Weapons of Peace: The Secret Story of India's Quest to be a Nuclear Power*, HarperCollins, New Delhi, 2000, p. 253.
31. Ibid, pp. 321-25.
32. During 1991-94, the author was posted to the Military Wing of the MoD and saw at first hand the frustration of the Service Chiefs and the strong tendency on the part of the civilian bureaucrat to maintain a cold and almost condescending attitude towards the Services.
33. Interview with Gen. V.P. Malik, Chandigarh, January 12, 2012.
34. Rajneesh Singh, "Chairman Chiefs of Staff Committee: A Midway Solution", IDSA Comment, August 7, 2012 at http://www.idsa.in/node/9986/5744#comment-5744 (Accessed November 23, 2013).
35. Col. Chet Richards (USAF, ret), "Shattering Illusions: A National Security Strategy for 2009-2017", in Winslow T. Wheeler (ed.) *America's Defense Meltdown*, Stanford Security Studies, 2009, p. 30.
36. Jawaharlal Nehru, *The Discovery of India*, First published Signet Press, Calcutta 1946 (Reprint 2004, Penguin, New Delhi), p. 601.

37. Raj Chengappa, no. 30, pp. 71 and 86-89.
38. At the time of signing the Chemical Weapons Convention, in 1993, India had surprised the world by promising to destroy its existing stocks of chemical weapons, another well-kept secret. Many believed that these were actually left over from the World War II era. Whatever the truth, a peace-loving country had kept these under safe custody for decades in total secrecy.
39. Pallav Bagla, *Outlook*, February 11, 2013, pp. 10-11.
40. Bharat Karnad, "Nuclear Effects of Agni V", Security Wise, Bharat Karnad Blog, at http://bharatkarnad.com/2013/10/04/nuclear-effects-of-agni-v/, (Accessed October 10, 2013).
41. *Basic Doctrine of the IAF,* Unclassified version published on September 17, 2012, p. 25.
42. Air Cmde. R.V. Phadke (Retd.), "Air Power and Escalation Control" at www.stimson.org (Accessed March 2003).
43. Shivshankar Menon at the General K.M. Cariappa Memorial Lecture, October 5, 2011.
44. Prakash Nanda (ed.), *Rising India: Friends and Foes,* Lancer, New Delhi, 2007, p. xvii.
45. Jasjit Singh (ed.), *Air Power and Joint Operations,* Centre for Air Power Studies, New Delhi, 2003, pp. 269-72.

9

Findings and Recommendations

The last 68 years of India's security practice present a mixed picture of lost opportunities as well as bold moves. India's security decision-making has fluctuated between a strong urge to operate from a high moral position and the imperatives, and the immediacy of a looming crisis. In effect, India has responded to its security threats and challenges based on the 'merits of each case' or the prevailing circumstances and not according to any well planned defence strategy. India has shunned the option of adopting a publicly declared security strategy and has reportedly followed a vague and woolly strategy of defensive defence to 'deter' Pakistan and 'dissuade' China. To be fair, some commentators have also termed India's overall approach to national security as one of 'strategic restraint'.[1]

Although successive governments have been spending large sums of money on defence, much of it in precious foreign exchange, India's armed forces have often complained about inordinate delays and the questionable quality of arms, especially when received from indigenous sources.

According to Lorne J. Kavic:

> The raison d'etre of this defence programme was never made clear by the government on the grounds that it was not considered to be in the national interest to reveal information about such matters. The Indian public and the press were, in any case, generally apathetic and Parliament consistently passed by unanimous vote whatever defence estimates were placed before it.[2]

This was written in 1967 but is generally valid even today. In fact, with the parliamentary committee system in place since the late 1990s, there has been little open discussion on the demands for defence, with bills getting passed without much debate. Not more than a handful of Members of Parliament have any idea of what exactly the country's defence needs are, and even fewer bother to find out what the government plans to do, to meet various external and internal threats. Discussion on the adequacy or otherwise of defence is thus restricted to and monopolised by a very small elite comprising the Prime Minister's Office (PMO), Ministry of External Affairs (MEA) and Ministry of Defence (MoD) bureaucracy and lately the National Security Council (NSC). The so-called strategic community comprising retired government officials, some academics and military veterans continue to debate defence and security issues in the few think tanks and journals, but without any policy inputs from the government of the day. In fact, government officials rarely discuss defence issues with the think tanks and worse, never give their opinion on current or even past policies, nor share lessons with the general public. Never criticise past leaders and never admit past mistakes, seems to be the general rule.

A brief review of India's responses to the many security crises since its independence shows a strong tendency to wish away problems and failure to take defence and security programmes to their logical conclusion. The study has shown that when used with determination, even in cases where a crisis developed without much warning, air power, particularly the Indian Air Force (IAF), proved effective.

In 1947, it saved the Kashmir Valley from the Pakistani hordes and thwarted strong and concerted Pakistani attempts to gain control of Ladakh and Poonch. In October 1947, India sent troops to evict Pakistani raiders from Jammu and Kashmir (J&K) and used its nascent air power when the IAF possessed very limited air assets – a mere six and a half fighter squadrons of World War II vintage – but failed to fully resolve the Kashmir issue, by prematurely approaching the United Nations (UN). Indian leadership also permitted the British Governor General and his three British Service Chief appointees to unduly influence strategic and even tactical decision-making to Pakistan's advantage. India also failed to appreciate growing British interests in retaining a toehold in South Asia, based on the changed circumstances in the immediate aftermath of World War I, the fast-increasing salience of West Asia as the new supplier of oil, and the reach of air power. To be sure, India also learnt its lesson and did not take any other issue to the United Nations.

Based on this experience, India soon expanded its air force to some 15 squadrons, and in spite of serious economic constraints, purchased aircraft and equipment from Britain and France to raise the IAF strength to 25 squadrons by 1962. India, however, failed to use this potent and valuable asset in the short border war with China, and once again allowed outside advice, in this case the United States (US) Ambassador (J.K. Galbraith), to influence its decisions. Not using the IAF was a monumental blunder. At the time, the IAF had some two squadrons or nearly 40 Hunter Mk.56 fighter ground attack aircraft stationed in the Punjab. These aircraft were almost brand new with No. 7 squadron already practising 'nine-aircraft formation aerobatics' which shows that it had an adequate number of experienced pilots. The Aksai Chin area of Ladakh where fierce battles were fought with the Chinese, was well within the striking range of these Hunters at medium and high levels. Almost all battles from October 20 to 28, 1962 and again from November 18 to 21, were fought during daylight hours over barren hills with unlimited visibility.[3] Neither the attacking Chinese troops nor their logistics facilities had the advantage of natural forest cover or camouflage as in the Eastern theatre and could easily be engaged from the air, especially since the IAF had already deployed a few Forward Air Controllers (FACs) with the army. Galbraith's advice was based on his knowledge of Chinese tactics in the Korean war, which clearly did not apply in Aksai Chin. "At the highest level, Jawaharlal Nehru chose to appeal to the US President for aerial support without first ordering the Indian Air Force into battle."[4] The war left a lasting psychological scar on the country's psyche and seriously affected civil-military relations. It must, however, be reiterated that it was not a humiliating defeat for the Indian Army since only a fraction of its strength was actually deployed, and that too in a tactically unsound manner, in section and platoon strength, without mutual fire support. In retrospect, it is clear that employment of air power against the Chinese during October 20-28, 1962, would in all probability have ended the local skirmishes with radically different outcomes, and the enemy would not have repeated its attacks in November of that year. The bitter truth is that India failed to employ its sizeable air and ground forces in a systematic and well-thought-out fashion. The reasons for this historic blunder are not far to seek. It was the unhealthy civil-military relationship that was largely responsible for it. Had Menon and Nehru given a patient hearing to the views of the Service Chiefs, instead of depending entirely on their intuition, which was reinforced with the Intelligence Bureau Chief B.N. Mullick's advice, India's history would be different.

In North East Frontier Agency (NEFA), a handful of IAF helicopters, nevertheless saved a large number of hapless troops, by carrying out timely casualty evacuation and supply drops in the face of the enemy. In the aftermath of the Chinese aggression, India embarked on an ambitious defence expansion and modernisation programme, but allowed it to drag on and lose momentum. In an effort to deflect blame, India continued to harp on Chinese *perfidy* and not on its own inability to read Chinese political and diplomatic signalling. Mainly due to poor intelligence, both at the strategic and tactical level, India overestimated China's military, especially air power capabilities. Due mainly to a misplaced faith in India's importance in the international system (no doubt because of its role in Korea, Indochina, Congo and Gaza), Nehru continued to believe that a war with China would inevitably lead to a general world war. Although he later said, "We were living in an artificial world of our own creation", that did not fundamentally change India's thinking, which it seems was based on the belief that both the US and erstwhile Union of Soviet Socialist Republics (USSR) needed India more than it needed either, and that it could easily play one against the other.

The February 2012 *Nonalignment 2.0* report prepared by a group of influential writers and tacitly endorsed by the former National Security Adviser (NSA) shows that we have not really overcome our hubris. That "India's strength lies in its example," a conclusion drawn in the report, is a clear indication of how we continue to live in an artificial world of our own making. In a conference of South Asian countries held on October 29-30, 2013 at the Institute for Defence Studies and Analyses (IDSA), New Delhi, all of India's neighbours unanimously expressed the view that India was a bully.

The Indian Army has traditionally played a dominant role in India's defence, while expanding from a strength of a mere 220,000 in 1947, to 550,000 personnel in 1962, and 1.13 million in 2013. With the proposed raising of an additional mountain strike corps, the strength would rise by another 65,000. The IAF has also expanded to nearly 127,000 personnel but has seldom reached the sanctioned strength of 45 squadrons. The current sanctioned strength of the IAF is reportedly 39 and a half combat squadrons. After the 1962 debacle, the IAF was allowed to increase its trained manpower through accelerated recruitment but it took almost a decade for it to get adequate numbers of the much-publicised MiG-21 supersonic fighter. This sudden and ill-planned expansion resulted in what was popularly called the 'bulge', that skewed the career prospects of many capable officers and led to premature and avoidable in-service wastage.

In 1965, India had to face another aggression from Pakistan. Seeing India's slow pace of military build-up in the post-1962 era, Pakistan quickly launched an attack to gain control of Kashmir, but only after a probing attack to assess the Indian reaction in Kutch in April, and infiltrating tribal raiders into the Kashmir Valley in August 1965. This time again, India failed to read Pakistani intentions and woke up only when the Pakistan Army launched a concerted infantry thrust, supported with artillery and armour into Chhamb, with the aim of cutting off India's land access to Kashmir. Even though the new Defence Minister Y.B. Chavan had been holding 'daily meetings'[5] with the Chiefs of Staff and senior civilians in the MoD, India found itself ill-prepared, in fact, surprised by Pakistan's audacious action. This was not just an intelligence failure but also a failure of the army to take the IAF into confidence about the fast-emerging threat of war from across the western borders.

Mainly due to poor coordination between the army and the IAF and a general lack of firm guidance from the civilian government, the short, if intense 22-day war ended in a stalemate, with the Cabinet mostly busy trying to stave off a UNsponsored (and supported by major powers) ceasefire. The aim of the exercise, it seems, was to stop the invader in its tracks and bring the hostilities to a quick conclusion but without any clear idea of the desirable outcomes. As a result, the few chunks of enemy land won at heavy cost in men and material were returned, and Pakistan's military potential and its capacity to cause nuisance, was allowed to remain more or less intact.

The IAF wasted precious time before launching its first air offensive against the Sargodha airfield complex on September 7, and stopped it as abruptly as it began due to high attrition. Sadly, the support the IAF provided to the army remained unplanned, with more and more IAF fighters being sent out on 'search and destroy' missions and 'opportunity strikes' rather than against well-planned and briefed offensive air strikes. The result: More often than not, the Indian soldier saw more enemy fighter aircraft over his head than his own. The mighty Indian Army failed to gain a decisive victory over a relatively weak enemy. The Pakistan Air Force (PAF) destroyed many fighter aircraft on ground in a single raid at Pathankot. The IAF saw how a single F-86 Sabre PAF squadron based at Dhaka, could wreak havoc on its poorly defended bases at Kalaikunda, Barrackpore and Bagdogra.

In 1965, Indian air power again helped to stop the Pakistani Army from taking Akhnoor, even though the IAF was called only at the eleventh hour. Later, the IAF carried out some bold forays into Pakistan and could have done much better, if only it had been used as an integral part of the overall strategy. Lack of planning and consultation with the army and absence of a joint plan resulted in sub-optimal employment of air power.

The IAF certainly learned many lessons from this war and quickly built new forward airfields with concrete bomb shelters to avoid losing precious aircraft on ground. There was, however, no attempt to develop a more effective joint strategy to meet future challenges. India's military strategy could be summarised in a single sentence: Any attack on Kashmir will be considered an attack on India and India will be free to retaliate across the International Border in Punjab. India's preference to use only its army or ground forces and at the same time to restrict the scope of operations to avoid a 'full-scale war' is so deep rooted, that even today doctrines such as 'Cold Start' continue to enjoy pride of place in its 'conventional' or 'limited war' thinking.

The PAF was able to make full use of its marginal technological superiority, realistic training and aggressive spirit to take a heavy toll of IAF aircraft on ground, especially at Pathankot and Kalaikunda, due to poor air defence, absence of early warning, lack of bomb shelters and inadequate preparation. In spite of many examples of personal courage and ingenuity, the IAF was not successful in capitalising on its numerical superiority.

In the 1971 Bangladesh War, the IAF had learnt its lessons and quickly achieved complete air superiority over the Eastern theatre, took a heavy toll of the enemy and virtually crippled its mobility. The execution of a helicopter-lift to move a large body of troops across a river, a well-planned and executed drop of the para battalion and finally a four-aircraft fighter strike on the Government House in Dhaka on December 14, ensured the surrender of Lieutenant General A.A.K. Niazi's forces in a mere 14 days. It was probably the best example of army-air force joint operations.

In the west, the battle of Longewala, where a handful of Hunters stopped a regiment of Pakistani tanks and prevented the enemy from threatening the strategically important town of Jaisalmer, will forever remain a shining example of air power effectiveness. IAF attacks on Karachi, Sui Gas Plant and the Power House at Mangla Dam, and on the PAF airbase at Peshawar, caused considerable damage to the Pakistan economy and helped maintain pressure on the enemy, by forcing the PAF on the defensive, but the war ended well before these strikes had any real effect on the outcome of the war. On the western front, the Indian military's performance was not commensurate with its potential. India could not exploit its numerical superiority, even though its army had captured some 5,000 sq. km. of enemy territory probably due to international pressure to quickly stop hostilities.

India gained little from the Simla (now Shimla) Agreement reached in July 1972, but Pakistan's Prime Minister Z.A. Bhutto, managed to ecure the release of 90,000 Prisoners of War (POWs) on a verbal promise of working on the proposal to convert the Ceasefire Line (CFL) in J&K into a permanent international border. Implicit in this was the understanding that the Kashmir issue would be closed, maintaining the current status quo, but this was not to be. Bhutto changed his tune after the return of the POWs and threatened India with a thousand-year-long war and also began Pakistan's clandestine programme to acquire the atom bomb.

In 1971, the armed forces fared much better because Prime Minister Indira Gandhi gave General (later Field Marshal) S.H.F.J. Manekshaw, the necessary time of over six months, to prepare for the war which eventually came in December of that year. The IAF played a stellar role in the east. By quickly establishing total air superiority, it could devote all its air effort in support of the Indian Army's rapid advance to Dhaka. The December 14 air strike on the Government House at Dhaka proved a masterstroke of timely intelligence, combined with instantaneous yet accurate armament delivery, that culminated in Lieutenant General A.A.K. Niazi surrendering with his 90,000 strong army intact. Air power proved decisive in the east, but in the west the IAF and the army's performance could have been better. Here, the strategy of resorting to a mainly defensive posture and making limited forays into enemy territory proved costly yet ineffective. The

PAF generally remained on the defensive but took a heavy toll on IAF aircraft engaged in sporadic daylight counter air operations over PAF airfields. The Canberra proved far more effective in night attacks against the PAF airfields. Single aircraft night strikes by IAF Sukhoi (S-22) and MiG-21 fighters were a bold and innovative tactic and proved of some nuisance value but the IAF could not ascertain the degree of damage these strikes caused to PAF airfields and installations. The IAF lost a large number of Sukhoi (S-22) fighters in ground attacks to small arms fire, mainly due to the aircraft carrying out repeat dive attacks following a predictable pattern. Pakistani air defence (AD), including its anti-aircraft artillery with Chinese Quad Air Defence guns, seemed better organised and more lethal than its Indian counterpart. The IAF flew a number of 'offensive sweep' missions to entice the PAF into aerial combat but the enemy did not oblige. Instead, the IAF could have provided more intimate air defence cover for the ground battle. According to Lieutenant General J.F.R. Jacob, the Chief of Staff of the Indian Eastern Army Command, liberation of East Pakistan was not India's war objective from the start but became possible due to the audacious offensive strategy of the army, ably supported by the air force. The demoralised Pakistani Army was forced to retreat and to finally surrender to the Indian army.

Following the 1965 war, the only discussions in the IAF remained focused on improving its prowess in aerial combat. The addition of some six squadrons of S-22 Sukhoi fighter ground-attack aircraft in 1967-68, had undoubtedly increased the offensive potential of the IAF, but the programme for strengthening the country's AD by commissioning the string of six US-supplied high-powered radars took its own time and was only completed years later.[6] The IAF's re-equipment programme with the locally licence-produced MiG-21s also took a long time and by the time the 1971 war came, the IAF had managed to raise just eight squadrons with very limited ground attack capability.[7] This war again underscored the urgent need for a long-range fighter bomber capable of reaching Pakistan's depth areas, if meaningful deterrence was to be achieved. Accordingly, after much debate and delay, India acquired the Jaguar Deep Penetration Strike Aircraft (DPSA) only in 1979-80. There was, however, little change in India's overall military strategy with respect to its adversaries. In the much-publicised Simla Agreement which Pakistan refused to honour, India had tacitly accepted the status quo in J&K, implicitly 'abandoning' Pakistan-occupied Kashmir (PoK) and Gilgit-Baltistan areas under Pakistan's illegal occupation.

During the 1980s, the Indian leadership was preoccupied with the Punjab militancy and other domestic issues. The Government of India (GoI), however, embarked on a massive modernisation programme for the IAF. In 1987, Exercise Brasstacks nearly brought India and Pakistan to war, which also added for the first time, the nuclear dimension to the Indo-Pak confrontation. Pakistan had apparently succeeded in convincing India that it (Pakistan) already possessed an atom bomb. This spurred the effort to mate India's nuclear 'device' with a delivery platform; first a Jaguar and later the Mirage-2000 and the Prithvi missile. The exact date when India actually built a usable air-launched atomic bomb continues to be in the realm of conjecture. According to journalist Raj Chengappa, however, it was only with the successful test of the 2,000-km Agni II on April 11, 1999 that India for the first time possessed a fail-safe nuclear deterrent. The experience of Exercise Brasstacks in 1986-87 and the 1990 nuclear scare, clearly demonstrated India's vulnerability in the face of a nuclear-armed Pakistan.

This once again shows the slow and grinding pace of India's security decision-making. The 1987 crisis also highlighted the tenuous relationship between the civilian political masters and the military leadership and the yawning communication gap between the two. No effort, however, was made to bridge this chasm. In fact, the two became even more distant. Pakistan had during the period, raised the bogey of India planning to bomb the Kahuta nuclear facility with Israeli assistance, but there was little to substantiate such rumours. India was not able to exert enough pressure on the US and other influential members of the P-5 to prevent Pakistan from acquiring nuclear capability.

During the 1987-90 Sri Lanka operations, the IAF once again provided the badly needed mobility and logistics support to the Indian Peace Keeping Force (IPKF) but India's overall politico-military strategy remained tentative and confused. There was much avoidable bickering between the three Services. The political leadership was not in sync with the armed forces, even though the Army Chief and the Minister of State (MoS) for Defence enjoyed an unprecedented level of mutual trust and understanding.

In 1988, the IAF again flew troops of the Indian Army's parachute brigade to Male, when the Maldivian Presidency was threatened by a coup. The action of the Il-76 squadron and India's para brigade at Agra was commendable, but India was once again surprised by the sudden turn of events in its backyard.

The Pakistani intrusions in Kargil in 1999 once again came as a total surprise to the army, and indeed the central government in Delhi. The unnecessary delay in committing the combat elements of the IAF was again due to the absence of a joint politico-military strategy and not because of any inherent reluctance on the part of the IAF. Its belated entry, however, provided invaluable support to the troops in the high Himalayas. Although asked to restrict its operations to own side of the Line of Control, the IAF improvised its armament delivery techniques, effectively engaged the enemy and hastened its withdrawal. The commitment of the IAF also helped convey India's determination to evict the enemy at any cost. In this case too, India's defence policy-making apparatus moved into action at a grinding slow pace and remained reactive, with no attempt to shape the outcome or to wrest the initiative. Although India finally managed to win diplomatic support of major powers, it also had to go along with the American President's effort to allow a face-saver to Nawaz Sharif by halting offensive air operations in early July, and a safe passage to withdrawing Pakistani intruders.

The IAF was also used on numerous occasions to provide succour to the civilian population in times of natural calamity and other contingencies, in aid to civil power. Air power was successfully used to evacuate a very large number of stranded Indians from Kuwait in 1990 and from Lebanon in 2006. Its role in conjunction with the army, Indo-Tibetan Border Police (ITBP) and other government agencies during the June 2013 cloudburst over Kedarnath in north Uttarakhand was truly outstanding. Although less visible and hence, almost unknown to the general public, the IAF has also been continuously air maintaining civilians and army troops in the high Himalayan frontier areas for over 60 years.

Following the border incidents in 1986-87, India made concerted efforts to mend ties with China that culminated in the historic visit of the then Indian Prime Minister Rajiv Gandhi to Beijing from December 19 to 23, 1988. India also granted full statehood to Arunachal Pradesh, sending a clear signal to China that it was indeed an integral part of India. Sino-Indian relations went through some incremental improvements with the visit of P.V. Narasimha Rao and the signing of the accords in 1993 and 1996, for the maintenance of peace and tranquillity along the Line of Actual Control (LAC). The Confidence Building Measures (CBMs) indeed brought a sense of stability, but 20 years on, the LAC remains un-demarcated, with the Chinese becoming progressively more active and assertive. The October 2013 Border Defence Cooperation Agreement (BDCA) is expected to prevent unnecessary confrontation, but is also likely to severely constrain India's attempts to build its infrastructure and defence works along the LAC. Some Chinese troops again intruded into Indian areas in Ladakh during the visit of the Chinese President Xi Jinping in September 2014. This matter was peacefully resolved but only after the departure of the Chinese leader from India.[8]

India has for the first time since 1962, permanently based some truly offensive air power capability in the form of two Su-30MKI squadrons in the North-east, as a deterrent to Chinese adventurism. The army plans to raise a mountain strike corps to meet the Chinese threat. It is difficult to see how a force of some 65,000 personnel with its heavy artillery and armour will launch an offensive or defensive operation in the high Himalayas, with non-existent infrastructure, and extremely difficult logistics largely dependent on air supply, against an enemy enjoying the advantage of height. India, it seems, has once again failed to understand the importance of a joint air-army strategy based on lightly equipped forces, capable of instantaneous response. This emphasis on the 'army option' could be due to any or all of the following reasons:

- The strong if incorrect belief that air power is escalatory.

- The difficulty of executing precision air strikes in bad weather and at high altitude in the mountains.
- The dominant role of the army in almost routinely assisting the government fighting the numerous separatist, insurgent and terrorist threats.
- Raising of a mountain strike corps seen as an avenue for generating additional employment to a larger number of Indians from the backward regions of the North-east.
- The choice of Panagarh in West Bengal as the Headquarters of the proposed mountain strike corps, to create a countervailing force to the increasing Maoist challenge in the region, at a time when the army is justifiably reluctant to get involved in yet another counter-insurgency operation.

It is, however, still not too late to reconsider the decision to raise the mountain strike corps, simply because it will be prohibitively expensive to maintain over the long term, and will not be usable. Most countries, including China, are reducing the size of their ground forces. Unlike Israel, the US, the North Atlantic Treaty Organisation (NATO) (and indeed recently even Pakistan), who use air power with impunity, the Indian policy-maker continues to fight shy of relying on this eminently suitable and effective military instrument, especially now that the IAF has an array of sophisticated aircraft, Precision Guided Munitions (PGMs), support platforms like the Airborne Warning and Control System (AWACS) and Air-to-Air Refuelling (AAR) with modern avionics and communications.

In India's neighbourhood, both the PAF and People's Liberation Army Air Force (PLAAF) are fast developing into two truly modern air arms in sync with each other and hence, pose a formidable combined challenge. Pakistan is already reaping the benefits of its close all-weather relationship with China and its role as the prime non-NATO ally of the US. The PAF has already raised three squadrons equipped with JF-17 Thunder multi-role fighters. The PLAAF is currently adding a full regiment (70 aircraft) of J-10 type to its strength annually and is well on its way to field two 'fifth generation' fighters, such as the J-20 (First Flight on January 11, 2011) and J-31 in the near future. China's defence industry is at the threshold of building its own modern turbofan jet engine and is exporting a sizeable number of modern machines to many third world countries at competitive prices. The Chinese defence industry has derived immense benefits from its close collaboration with Moscow and made full use of its exposure to Western arms and equipment through a highly developed network of friends and business partners. The recent addition of an indigenously built aircraft carrier clearly shows the extent of self-sufficiency that China has achieved. Its forays into the military use of space, the Anti-Satellite Test (ASAT) (January 2007) and missile defence demonstration (January 2010) along with its prowess in the use of space for communication, navigation, surveillance and targeting have clearly demonstrated the trajectory of China's progress. Given its robust economic growth, its power differential with India is growing at a spectacular pace and demands a suitable yet calibrated and well-thought-out Indian response.

The foregoing clearly shows that air power continues to be the instrument of first choice in any crisis situation in war and peace. In the last six decades, the IAF has learnt many lessons and also enhanced its effectiveness in all its roles. Exercising with many foreign air forces since the turn of the century has given it added confidence to handle high technology. While it has won the respect of these advanced air forces, it still has a long way to go before becoming a truly modern air force as almost half its assets are nearing obsolescence. Its current motto of 'preserve, upgrade and acquire' can well be modified to read preserve, maintain, economise and innovate and finally, improve its flight safety record, as it has little option but to live with dwindling numbers, for at least 10-15 years.

The IAF also needs to make renewed efforts to develop a far closer and deeper understanding of the needs of the sister Services and engage with them to enhance their understanding of the strengths and limitations of India's air power, while assuring them of total and unconditional support at all times. The ground and maritime elements must also make a concerted effort to forge a truly joint solution to the country's security challenges, without falling prey to turf battles and budget wars.

A glaring anomaly with defence funding has been the persistent attempt to make an equitable or pro rata allocation between the three Services, with the army usually receiving the lion's share (about 50-60 per cent) mainly due to its enormous size and the role it plays in internal security operations, and not in conformity with the actual role that each Service would play in a future war. In the absence of a joint strategy, each Service continuously tries to get a bigger portion of the defence pie and promptly makes its private plans to fight a future war.

Today, the IAF has a mix of fourth generation fighters and modified second generation aircraft such as the Jaguar and even older MiG-21 but until the induction of the Rafale Medium Multi-Role Combat Aircraft (MMRCA) and the Fifth Generation Fighter Aircraft (FGFA), the IAF cannot become a truly modern air force. Given the current economic difficulties, that might not happen for the next decade or more. Until then the IAF must make plans to fight a limited war with available resources and more importantly be ready to take instantaneous punitive air action, if and when needed.

India must however, remember that a modern air force is both technology and capital-intensive and hence, demands frequent injections of heavy funding for regular technology upgrades. To reduce dependence on foreign sources India has no option but to quickly build a true indigenous capability to design, develop, build and maintain modern fighter, transport aircraft and helicopters, Unmanned Aerial Vehicles (UAVs)/Unmanned Combat Aerial Vehicles (UCAVs) and the variety of Precision Guided Munitions (PGMs) and air-delivered weapons. This is simply because such sophisticated armament and delivery systems have already entered India's neighbourhood.

Finally, despite an ever-increasing defence budget, the Indian military has not found an answer to Pakistan's strategy of inflicting repeated terrorist attacks under the so called nuclear shield. It is possible, even likely that another 26/11 type of catastrophic terror attack in the future, will again go unpunished. India also does not have an answer to the increasingly strong Sino-Pak joint strategy to keep India unbalanced.

Without restarting the guns versus ploughshare debate, it should suffice to say that a minimum level of security from internal and external threats is the first duty of the nation-state. India's self-image of a centuries-old civilisation, as a champion of peace, non-violence and mutual cooperation, has often come into conflict with the imperative of building its hard power or national military strength. As a result, the latter often fails to get single-minded and focused attention.

India's policy of non-alignment was designed to derive economic and other aid from all quarters without getting embroiled in an East-West confrontation; a policy that paid handsome dividends during the Cold War. According to K. Subrahmanyam and Shivshankar Menon, the former National Security Adviser (NSA), "Nonalignment was a strategy and never an ideology."[9] Yet, it was couched in highly moralistic and ideological terms, at least during the Nehru era. Nehru resisted attempts to form a non-aligned bloc during his lifetime, as he was against joining or forming any bloc. Nonalignment is perhaps valid and unexceptionable even today, but the habit of always cloaking India's security decisions in moral terms, robs it of its inherent strength. Despite its policy of maintaining equal distance from the two blocs, India has made few genuine and trusted friends and continues to shy away from forging a truly close relationship, even with smaller powers like Vietnam, Bangladesh, Myanmar and its smaller neighbours.

As K. Subrahmanyam has so clearly said, "Among the strategic challenges facing India are those relating to (1) defence policy, (2) nuclear strategy and (3) governance."[10] Although a relatively mild rebuke, he has clearly warned all Indians that many of India's security challenges are of their own making.

The civil-military disconnect, due perhaps to a highly exaggerated fear of militarism, continues to be the biggest stumbling block to devising a suitable, workable and universally acceptable defence policy for the 21st century. Although India's decision-makers claim that they are determined to avoid an arms race with China, the ever-rising defence spending, due mainly to the cost of maintaining a huge standing army, is simply prohibitive and unsustainable and therefore, a new and innovative approach is needed. The one-size-fits-all approach to meet every challenge from the sub-conventional to nuclear war, displays a lack of imagination.

The currently unhealthy civil-military equation and inter and intra-Service turf wars need to be addressed immediately. The Indian defence industry's indifferent performance continues to be a huge drain on the exchequer and without a firm direction from the GoI, and exemplary punishment for those responsible for failures, it will be difficult to expect major improvements. Modern air power is most affected by these policy failures, because to be effective, it requires tenacious thinking and dogged determination. While the chance of a conventional war may indeed be remote, it is not clear how India would respond to an unexpected major and combined border intrusion by its powerful adversaries, especially since Pakistan's doctrine of first or early use of nuclear weapons appears to inhibit Indian thinking.

As we saw, even after the 1962 politico-military debacle, national security did not become an electoral issue. Excessive secrecy and highly elitist close-circuit decision-making processes leave most educated and interested Indians totally ignorant, yet deeply worried about India's ability to face diverse security challenges. The decision-makers need to correct the impression that air power employment is costly or escalatory, if the government wishes to marshal true and wholehearted public support for a robust joint defence strategy.

Recommendations

Before making any specific recommendations, it might be useful to revisit some of the current thinking on the subject of defence and security and there is no better example than statements of the former Indian NSA and the former Indian Prime Minister. We will recall that the NSA had said:

> In other words, while domestic societies have evolved or are evolving towards rule of law, international society is still much closer to primeval anarchy, where to a very great extent the strong do as they will and the weak do as they must.[11]

He added elsewhere:

> [W]e have all heard the statement that 'war is diplomacy by other means' attributed to Clausewitz. The actual statement was more nuanced but this will serve for our present purpose. We are also familiar with the corollary that diplomacy is war by other means. Each contains enough truth to justify the cliché. That truth is that war and diplomacy, military force and international relations, are Siamese twins, joined together at birth for life.
>
> Militaries have always provided states with an instrument for effective

diplomacy, mainly through the threat of the use of force or, in the case of a militarily weaker state, the ability to withstand military attack or engage in attrition. The actual use of force in most, if not all cases demonstrates the failure of diplomacy.

[I]n today's age of technology and media, small powers and groups can create effects disproportionate to their physical scale or ostensible material power. In other words, we have to reckon with the changing nature of global power, as power itself is becoming much more diffused and fragmented. We need to develop the power to deal with weak states, terrorists and small groups and post-modern forms of power, a capability which is different from the conventional tasks that the military has been configured to achieve in the past.[12]

The above clearly demonstrates that there is no ambiguity in India's understanding of the real world challenges and the role that the military plays in international relations or in national security. In spite of such a clear-headed approach to this vital subject on which the very survival of the country depends, there are many gaps between theory and practice. To add to the inherent difficulties, India also faces renewed challenges to maintain high rates of economic growth.

Probably for the first time in recent years, even the former Prime Minister Manmohan Singh sounded a warning on this count. Addressing the Combined Commanders' Conference on November 22, 2013 at New Delhi, he directly referred to the US strategy of 'pivot' or rebalancing in Asia and the uncertainty attached to it. He also spoke of the global surveillance operation mounted by the US National Security Agency, the need to stop the interminable debate between private and public sector contribution to building India's defence industrial base, the current difficulties in maintaining a robust economic growth and finally, voiced his concerns about civil-military relations clearly and directly, cautioning military commanders and other decision-makers to urgently address these critical issues, without further waste of time. Above all, and in a welcome change, the former Prime Minister actually spoke of the need to build India's Comprehensive National Power. It is in light of these statements that the following recommendations are made. In an oblique way, the former Prime Minister told the commanders that the ongoing military modernisation programme would have to be reviewed and adjusted to make it sustainable.[13]

Some salient recommendations are given below:

- Civil-Military relations form the very basis on which the national security edifice is constructed and hence, India's Higher Defence Organisation (HDO) needs the most urgent and serious attention. The government must implement the relevant recommendations of the Kargil Review Committee, Group of Ministers and the Naresh Chandra-led Task Force on the subject.

The appointment of a permanent Chairman, Chiefs of Staff Committee may be seen as a half measure but is still better than the current status quo. As suggested in the previous chapter, the appointment of a MoS for each of the three Services in the MoD, to look after modernisation and day-to-day needs of the Service, and additionally, a specifically selected area such as aircraft production, may be considered. This would provide the long felt need for the Service Chiefs and Service Headquarters to become part of national security and defence decision-making. It will also address the critical issue of urgently developing India's defence industrial capacity, to reduce the country's dependence on foreign countries for aircraft, armament and other defence equipment, by direct and personal guidance and intervention. The three MoS will also provide the interface between the civilian political leadership and the military commanders, on whose shoulders rests the onerous responsibility of maintaining a high level of military readiness, to meet any contingency. Such close and daily interaction will also help in developing a truly joint strategy for use of force in a variety of complex security scenarios and avoid surprises and knee-jerk reactions.

- The establishment of the Indian National Defence University (INDU) has been under consideration by the GoI for over a decade, but its foundation stone was laid only in 2013. To ensure a steady supply of young, bright, knowledgeable and confident individuals to occupy important posts in the vital security areas of cyber security, high technology, MEA, MoD, Defence Public Sector Undertakings (DPSUs) and other related areas, the government must operationalise the INDU on a war footing. The INDU graduates after studying a wide variety of subjects related to military strategy, doctrine, modern warfare, Revolution in Military Affairs (RMA) and Network Centric Warfare (NCW) and 'stabilisation operations', military and international law, economics and the like, with synergies obtained from a truly joint approach, rooted in deep respect for and understanding of every relevant discipline, will obviously be intellectually and emotionally better equipped to meet the challenges of the new millennium.
- The government must consider establishing an apex national aviation council to oversee, anticipate and absorb emerging technologies to ensure their seamless adoption and operationalisation of civil, commercial and military aviation in a transparent, economical and efficient manner. Because air power is indivisible.
- Defence procurement must be given the importance it deserves, and dealt with as an independent charge by a senior and experienced minister, and not left to the vagaries of bureaucratic wrangling and financial audit. If need be, the GoI could form a holding company to handle the increasingly

complex issues of defence offsets, transfer of technology, price negotiation and value for money, but with a watchful eye on the timely delivery of the subject item to the user.

- It is high time India overhauled its career management and promotion policies for the defence services to ensure high morale, job satisfaction and a regular flow of high quality experienced and motivated leadership to meet future challenges. The world over, militaries are treated with immense respect for their commitment and readiness to make the supreme sacrifice in the service of the nation; without such intrinsic respect, there is a danger of the soldier losing confidence in his/her superiors and indeed the government. For some years, the IAF has been facing difficulties in getting the right kind of young and motivated professionals to handle the increasingly complex technologies related to modern aircraft, missiles and allied equipment.
- The government and the senior leadership of the IAF, army and navy must devote urgent attention to restructuring the basic organisation of the armed forces to effectively reduce expenditure, get value for money, reduce duplication, and ensure higher levels of efficiency and interoperability to make the armed forces more lean, agile, mobile and ready for rapid response to face emerging situations. A uniform, pro-rata distribution of government funding to keep each Service happy is neither sustainable nor efficient, and will also not meet the needs of future warfare.
- There must be a regular, sincere, structured and institutionalised consultation between the civilian and military leadership at fixed intervals, to further improve all-round understanding.
- At the Service level, the IAF needs to pay renewed and regular attention to conserving its precious assets, while simultaneously maintaining optimum training patterns and schedules at basic, advanced and operational levels.
- In the interest of flight safety – care, maintenance and upgrade of ageing aircraft and equipment must also get high priority, along with absorption of new technologies.
- The government must encourage innovative ideas to curtail expenditure in every field of activity. The routine and pro-forma promises of meeting the needs of the military sound hollow in the current climate of economic difficulties.
- Finally, India must formulate a national security strategy that is effective in peace and war. For it to be effective, it must be capable of generating asymmetry in our favour, shaping the strategic environment and creating opportunities for India to use its conventional military superiority and greater economic power, to defeat Pakistan's strategy of using jihadi terrorism

> under the nuclear shield. Air power must be given the necessary freedom to gain command of the air, at the earliest opportunity. With the proposed induction of the Rafale and the T-50 FGFA, the IAF will be endowed with extraordinary capabilities in air superiority and AD roles. The recent acquisition of the C-17, C-130J, AWACS and AAR tankers and the soon to be acquired AH-64 Apache and CH-47 Chinook will transform the IAF and offer amazing possibilities in strategic lift and power projection. While the IAF must make every effort to quickly absorb and operationalise these new technologies, the country must formulate effective strategies for their timely and intelligent utilisation.

To be able to achieve all these ambitious objectives, the government must show its readiness to include the military, especially the IAF, in all its security planning. As discussed earlier, the experience of exploiting the third dimension gives the air warrior a unique multi-dimensional situational awareness, which few other professions can match. The country must learn to use this outstanding attribute in the fulfilment of national security objectives, by constantly innovating and refining its air power employment doctrines and strategies.

NOTES

1. Shekhar Gupta, "The Man Who Got It Right: Poet Pragmatist, Always Political", *India Today*, April 6, 2015, pp. 20-21.
2. Lorne J. Kavic, *"India's Quest for Security: Defence Policies 1947-65"*, EBD Publishers& Distributing Co., Dehradun, 1967, p. 4.
3. P.J.S. Sandhu, "1962-War in the Western Sector (Ladakh): A View from Other Side of the Hill", *USI Journal*, July-September 2013, pp. 444-65.
4. K. Subrahmanyam, "That Night of November 19: On Nehru's Correspondence with JFK during the Chinese Aggression 18 November 2010", *Indian Express*, online version, February 3, 2011.
5. R.D. Pradhan, "*Debacle to Revival: Y.B. Chavan as Defence Minister, 1962-65*," Orient Longman, Hyderabad, 1998, p.18.
6. The 500 series of static high power radar units were established at Amritsar, Delhi, Lucknow in Uttar Pradesh, Singharsi in Bihar, Shillong in Meghalaya and Dinjan in Assam.
7. Nos. 1, 8, 29, 45, 47, and TACDE in the West and Nos. 4, 28 and 30 Squadrons in the East.
8. See http://www.forbes.com/sites/ericrmeyer/2014/09/23/who-sabotaged-xi-jinpings-india-visit/ (Accessed April 2, 2015).
9. Shivshankar Menon quoted in "China Playing a Waiting Game on Border Dispute: Former NSA", *The Hindu*, February 29, 2012.
10. K. Subrahmanyam, "India's Strategic Challenges", *Indian Express*, February 4, 2012.
11. Extracted from two lectures delivered by the NSA–first the K.M. Cariappa Memorial Lecture on the "Role of Militaries in International Relations", on October 5, 2011 and the Prem Bhatia Memorial Lecture on "India and the Global Scene", in New Delhi, in July 2011.
12. Ibid.
13. The Prime Minister's Address to the Combined Commanders' Conference in New Delhi on November 22, 2013 at http://pmindia.nic.in/speech-details.php?nodeid=1396 (Accessed November 25, 2013).

APPENDICES

Appendix I

Indian Air Force Squadrons and Units

Table 1: IAF Squadrons (Fighter, Bomber and Transport)

S. No.	Sqn. No.	Date Formed	Type	Remarks
1	1	April 1, 1933	Wapiti Mk IIA	First IAF Squadron.
2	2	April 1, 1941		First Squadron. of World War II
3	3	October 1, 1941		
4	4	February 1, 1942		
5	6	December 1, 1942		
6	8	December 7, 1942		
7	7	December 8, 1942		
8	9	November 13, 1943		
9	10	February 20, 1944		
10	12	December 1, 1945	Dakota DC-3	First Transport Squadron.

Notes 1: To avoid confusion with the Royal Air Force (RAF) No. 5 Squadron then operating in India, number '5' was not allotted to an IAF squadron. There were no further additions during World War II.

2: Air Headquarters Communication Squadron was formed on January 1, 1947 and Headquarters Western Air Command Communication Flight (HQ WAC COM Flight) on November 1, 1947.

3: Flying Instructors School (FIS) was formed in April 1948, at Tambaram near Madras (now Chennai).

Table 2: New IAF Squadrons formed between 1947 and 1962

S. No	Sqn. No.	Date Formed	Type	Remarks	Remarks
11	5	November 2, 1948			
12	101	May 1, 1949	Vampire Mk 55	Night Fighter	
13	14	August 15, 1951			
14	15	August 20, 1951		Second Transport Sqn.	
15	17	October 1, 1951			
16	11	November 1, 1951			
17	32	October 15, 1953			
18	16	September 15, 1954	Canberra B-58	Bomber/Interdictor	
19	42	1955 see note below	Il-14	Communication &Light Transport	USSR gifted the first Il-14 to India; IAF later acquired 29 Il-14 aircraft.
20	20	June 1, 1956	Hunter Mk 56		
21	23	October1, 1956			
22	27	February 15, 1957	Hunter Mk 56		
23	ASTE	April 15, 1957	Various Types	Earlier formed as Aircraft & Armament Testing Unit	Later moved to Bangalore
23	37	December 23, 1957	Hunter Mk 56		
24	43	January 1, 1958	Otter DHC-3		
25	41	March 1, 1958	Toofani		French Ouragon
26	29	March 10, 1958	Dakota DC-3		
27	35	August 1, 1958	Canberra B-58		

28	45	November 20, 1959	Otter DHC-3		
29	59	December 1, 1959	Vampire Mk 52		
30	47	December 18, 1959	Toofani		
31	JBCU	1959 (See Note 3 below		Jet Bomber Conversion Unit	At Agra
32	106	1959 (See Note 3 below)	Canberra PR	Strategic Recce	At Agra
33	49	February 2, 1960	Packet C-119	Transport	
34	48	February 5, 1960		Transport	
35	19	July 4, 1960			
36	PTS	Early 1950s (See Note 4 below)	Packet C-119	Paratroopers Training School	At Agra
37	44	March 31, 1961	An-12	Heavy Transport	Chandigarh
38	24	February 1962	Vampire Mk 52		

Notes 1: The exact date of the formation of No. 42 Squadron is not available. The IAF operated the Il-14 till 1979. No. 42 Squadron was later disbanded.

2: Transport Training Wing formed at Begumpet, Hyderabad on May 1, 1963, Navigation & Signal School on May 1, 1963.

3: Both the JBCU and 106 Strategic Reconnaissance Squadron were formed after the IAF inducted the three versions (medium bomber, interdictor and photo reconnaissance), of the English Electric Canberra between 1958 and 1960.

4: During World War II the Indian Army formed several Air Landing Schools for training Indian soldiers in para-trooping operations. One of these schools operated at Ambala and was later shifted to Agra in the early 1950s and renamed the Paratroopers Training School (PTS).

Table 3: Post 1962 Sino-Indian Conflict Expansion: IAF Squadrons formed between 1963 and 2012

S. No.	Sqn. No.	Date Formed	Type	Remarks
39	33	January 2, 1963	Canadair Caribou	
40	220	January 9, 1963	Vampire Mk 52	
41	221	February 2, 1963	Vampire Mk 52	
42	25	March 1, 1963	An-12	At Chandigarh
43	28	March 3, 1963	MiG-21 Type 74	First supersonic squadron
44	31	September 1, 1963	Mystere IVA	
45	18	April 15, 1965	Gnat Mk 1	
46				
47	21	October 16, 1965	Gnat Mk 1	
48	22	October 15, 1966	Gnat Mk 1	
49	26	January 1, 1968	S-22	
50	222	September 15, 1969	S-22	
51	30	November 1, 1969	MiG-21	
52	AFA	May 8, 1970	Harvard Mk II Vampire Mk 55/52	At Dundigal. Later Kiran HJT-16 replaced Vampire Mk 55/52
53	TACDE	January 2, 1971	MiG-21 & S-22	Ambala, later moved to Jamnagar and Gwalior
54	102	August 17, 1981	MiG-25 Trisonic	Strategic Recce
55	223	May 10, 1982	MiG-23 MF	
56	224	July 4, 1983	MiG-23 BN	
57	51	February 1, 1985	MiG-21	
58	52	January 1, 1986	MiG-21	

Notes 1: Thus the IAF has raised some 46 fighter/bomber and 12 transport squadrons and 25 helicopter units/squadrons in addition to training units/establishments for all types. Some 30 plus BAe Hawk trainers are now divided into two training squadrons at Air Force Station Bidar. Similarly TACDE and ASTE have fighters on their establishment.

2: In addition, the IAF raised a few squadrons of NATO codename 'Guideline' Sam II air defence missiles in 1963-64 and some 24 SAM-III Pechora missile units and still later, acquired a few OSA AK tracked/mobile missile batteries and shoulder fired Igla missiles.

Table 4: IAF Helicopter Units (HU)

S. No.	HU No.	Date Formed	Type	Remarks
1	104 HU	March 25, 1954	Sikorsky S55-C	First HU
2	105 HU	November 23, 1959		
3	107 HU	January 1, 1960		
4	109 HU	August 26, 1961		
5	110 HU	September 11, 1962		

Table 5: Post 1962 Sino-Indian Conflict Expansion

S. No	Sqn. No.	Date Formed	Type	Remarks
6	LSTU See Note 1	May 25, 1962	Bell-47G	Later Helicopter Training School (HTS)
7	111 HU	January 3, 1963		
8	112 HU		Alouette-III	
9	114 HU	April 1, 1964	Alouette-III	
10	115 HU 116 HU	April 1, 1967 July 27, 1967		
11	117 HU	February 1, 1971	Mi-8	
12	118 HU	November 14, 1971	Mi-8	
13	119 HU	March 3, 1972		
14	121 HF	December 15, 1972		
15	131 HU	August 1, 1974		
16	141 HU	August 1, 1974		
17	142 HU	August 1, 1974		
18	122 HF	December 12,1981		Bombay High
19	125 Hel Sqn.	November 1, 1983	Mi-25	Armed/Attack
20	127 HU	June 10, 1985	Mi-17	Hindan
21	128 HU	December 30, 1985	Mi-17	Hindan
22	132 HU	February 20, 1986	Mi-17	
23	133 HU	March 23, 1986	Mi-17	
24	126 HU	May 15, 1986	Mi-26	Heavy Lift Chandigarh
25	152 HU	June 27, 1988	Mi-17	During Op. Pawan
26	151 HU	June 1, 1989	Mi-17	During Op. Pawan

Notes 1: LSTU or Logistics Support Training Unit was re-christened as HTS or Helicopter Training School in the 1970s.

2: Mi-35 Improved Attack helicopter was inducted in 1990.

Appendix II

The Gnat Story

In the early 1950s, India set out on many exploratory missions to Britain and other European countries in search of a suitable fighter-bomber. As we have seen, the Indian Air Force (IAF) had already finalised the purchase of the British Hunter, Canberra and the French Mystere IVA but none of these could be licence-produced in India. By then, Hindustan Aeronautics Limited (HAL) was producing the Vampire under licence but it was no match to other contemporary fighters and was soon relegated to purely training tasks.

When a team led by Air Commodore P.C. Lal (later Chief of the Air Staff [CAS]), went to Britain, it noticed a very small fighter flying around at Chilbolten, the same airfield the Indian team was visiting. When the team found that the Supermarine Swift, then under development, was unsuitable for India's needs, Air Commodore Lal enquired about this unusually small fighter. Earlier called the Midge, it had been developed as a highly manoeuvrable but small and economical aircraft for Britain and its Western allies. At first, its designer, Professor W.E.W. Petter, was unwilling to sell it to India, which he thought was a Communist country. At lunch, he asked Lal if Indians played cricket and got an emphatically affirmative reply that clinched the deal. Two days later, he again called Lal and agreed to let him fly the Gnat. Lal and other members of the team were impressed with this 'excellent little aeroplane' and immediately recommended its manufacture at HAL. Lal writes, "The Gnat has been described as a single-seat fighter or fighter-bomber about one-third the size and about half the weight of a conventional jet fighter and in its time, was capable of out-climbing, out-turning and out-accelerating contemporary fighters."[1]

The Indian Government soon signed a contract with Folland for the airframe and with Bristol Aero-engines Ltd. for the manufacture of Orpheus engines in September 1956. Chris Smith talks of some reports of commission and other malpractices, with the French offering their expertise in quickly concluding negotiations, but that did not seem to influence IAF decisions.[2] The IAF received the first batch of 15 aircraft in knocked-down kit form for local assembly at HAL. The Gnat began to enter service with the IAF in 1959. A Gnat Handling Flight was formed at HAL Kanpur but the little aircraft had many teething troubles. Its hydraulic system that operated the undercarriage and flight controls and the Hobson Unit part of the longitudinal control were the main culprits. In trying to keep it light and small, the designer had resorted to many a novel arrangement. The undercarriage could be partially extended to work as air brake or speed brake, the aileron control surfaces automatically drooped by 22 degrees to act as landing flaps when the under carriage was fully extended.

With a wing span of just 22 feet and 1inch and length of 28 feet and 8 inches, the Gnat had very little space to accommodate a jet engine, other accessories and ammunition for the two fuselage-mounted 30mm Aden guns. As a result, access for maintenance was severely restricted. At just 4,500 pounds when empty, the aircraft was very light and could easily be turned around when a technician sat on its tail plane and another lifted the nose on his shoulder. The fuselage could be 'split' in just under an hour and the jet engine could then be worked upon. As mentioned earlier, the Aden guns suffered frequent stoppages as these were mounted 'upside down' to save space, and this entailed pulling the ammunition links against gravity. It had a small, almost primitive Radio Telephony (R/T) set with just 10 voice channels and a miniature standby with just two channels; no navigational aids worth the name and only a mechanically operated tail-chute (also called drag-chute) used to quickly arrest speed on the landing run.

In the 'clean', configuration, that is, without externally mounted under-wing fuel tanks, each with a capacity of 66 gallons, the Gnat enjoyed a thrust-to-weight ratio of almost one; rarely seen in any modern jet fighter of that period. The Gnat, however, was a transonic fighter – it could cross the speed of sound, but only in a steep dive at high altitudes. Its maximum speed was also limited to about 600 knots and although fast, it could not match the supersonic fighters such as the MiG-21 in their rate of climb, top speed and acceleration, and as a result, the F-104 class of fighters invariably managed to get away in combat. Without the external drop tanks, the Gnat could barely fly for 30 minutes at low/medium levels.

By 1965, the IAF had barely equipped three squadrons, Nos. 23, 2 and 9. The Gnat earned a name during the 1965 Indo-Pak war by shooting down many enemy Sabre F-86 fighters. Innovative tactics were developed to overcome its limited endurance and top speed, by initially flying at 10,000-15,000 feet and swooping down on the enemy. Soon after the war, the IAF raised four more Gnat squadrons and used them effectively during the 1971 Bangladesh war, when the Gnat again scored three victories against the Sabre over the eastern skies on

November 22, before the war actually started. The Gnats were used to provide offensive air support to the army in the Eastern theatre, once the IAF had attained complete air superiority. The Gnat was also used in the air defence role in the Western theatre. For defending the Srinagar airfield in the Kashmir Valley in a Gnat, Flying Officer Nirmal Jit Singh Sekhon posthumously earned India's highest gallantry award, the Param Vir Chakra (PVC).

In the 1970s, the Gnat also played an important role as an undeclared advanced jet trainer and was used as a lead-in fighter before young pilots were sent to more advanced aircraft such as the MiG-21, S-22, and in the 1980s, Jaguar and MiG-27. The Gnat was a delightful little aircraft to fly but had its own share of idiosyncrasies. Its hydraulic system, fuel transfer, electrical trimmer, flight controls and a host of other problems adversely affected its serviceability and sortie rate. Some 215 of these fighters were produced at HAL, which in the late 1970s also embarked on the manufacture of the Ajeet, of which some 50 units were produced. HAL also produced a two-seater trainer version of the Ajeet but it did not prove very successful due to the inherent limitations of its forerunner.

The Ajeet was similar in its external dimensions to the Gnat Mk1 since the only major change (the HAL called it an 'improvement'), was that the Ajeet had additional internal fuel tanks located in its wings. This, however, curtailed the size of the external drop tanks by almost half. There was thus no real increase in its Radius of Action (RoA). The aircraft became heavier and less manoeuvrable than the Gnat; suffered from endemic fuel leaks and poor serviceability and above all the gun-stoppage problem remained. The Gnat Mk. 1A, a modified version of the original was far superior to the Ajeet, and could well have met the operational training needs of the IAF, without it opting for the expense of producing the Ajeet. In early 1977, when the modified and more reliable Gnat Mk IA version was becoming available to the IAF, the author was attached to Air Headquarters to rework the RoA calculations of the proposed Ajeet but found that there was no increase. The then CAS Air Chief Marshal H. Moolgaonkar was very unhappy with HAL for pushing the IAF to accept the Ajeet, but did not succeed in stopping this wasteful venture, although it was once again touted as an *indigenous design* and hence, a feather in the cap of the Indian defence industry. Its operational usefulness had considerably diminished by about the late 1980s and it was finally phased out in 1991.[3] The IAF had at all times looked only at Pakistan as the major threat and its modernisation was therefore Pakistan Air Force-oriented. The People's Liberation Army Air Force (or the Chinese Air Force) posed no threat as most of its fighters and medium bombers (Il-28) at that time were antiquated and did not have the necessary range to reach Indian targets. There was not much interest or intelligence on its actual capability.

NOTES

1. P.C. Lal, *My Years with the IAF*, Lancer International, New Delhi, 1986, pp. 79-80.
2. Chris Smith, *India's Ad Hoc Arsenal: Direction or Drift in Defence Policy*?, SIPRI, Oxford University Press, 1994, pp. 159-69. Smith also mentions that the IAF seemed to favour the French Ouragan, probably because of 'consideration money' and even quotes Nehru's dismay at Indian officials and ministers wanting India to remain dependent on foreign sources for its defence needs, but there was no such talk about these allegations in later years in the IAF.
3. The author flew the Gnat from 1968 to 1975 and commanded an Ajeet squadron from 1986 to 1988.

Appendix III

The MiG-21 Story

Not unlike the venerable Dakota (DC-3) that proved to be a uniquely long lasting design, serving various air forces and civil/commercial organisations around the world, the MiG-21 was and is also without parallel in sheer longevity. It entered Indian Air Force (IAF) service in early 1965 and for over three decades, remained its mainstay, even though its flight safety record left much to be desired. In hindsight it seems clear that India would not have searched desperately for a supersonic fighter platform if Pakistan had not received a squadron of the 'supersonic' F-104 Starfighter from the United States (US) in 1960-61. The prospective entry of the F-104, then a frontline high-level interceptor designed specifically to meet the threat of the long range Soviet nuclear bomber, and equipped with the deadly Sidewinder air-to-air missile (AAM), caused a commotion of sorts in the Indian defence community. Thus began a clamour for India to acquire a supersonic fighter of its own to meet this emerging Pakistani threat. India was then negotiating a defence supply arrangement with the Soviets to meet the Chinese threat, and had already managed to get a squadron of An-12 transport and a few Mi-4 helicopters that were urgently needed for air supply operations in the mountains. In the politically charged atmosphere where the Soviet leadership was still trying to calm the Communist Chinese brothers and their non-aligned Indian friends, the offer of the MiG-21 to India was seen as a major Indian victory, since until then, the Soviets had not offered it even to the Chinese. To maintain a rough military balance or to appear even handed, however, the Soviets did not actually allow the export of MiG-21s until well after the 1962 Sino-Indian border war. The more notable advantage of the MiG-21 deal was that the Soviets also allowed its licensed production in India. Soon the Indians got busy selecting locations for MiG factories. The Indian Government decided that the engine factory would be located at Koraput in the tribal part of Orissa (now Odisha) and Ozar near Nashik in Maharashtra was chosen as the location for the aircraft/airframe factory. The instruments and avionics for the MiG-21 were to be manufactured at Hyderabad, and later at Korwa near Lucknow. These widely dispersed geographic locations also added to the difficulties in the manufacture of the MiG-21. HAL soon began the assembly of these aircraft and the IAF began equipping the Vampire, Toofani, Mystere and later the Gnat squadrons with first the MiG-21 FL (Type 77), followed by MiG-21M & MF (Type 96) and in 1976-77 the 'bis' which in the Russian language means the latest/last version, with almost half the IAF fighter fleet converting to these four versions of the MiG-21. While the Type 77 was generally used for air defence duties, the other types with more under-wing stations and hence greater armament carriage capacity were earmarked for Offensive Air Support (OAS) and armed recce tasks.

The earliest version of the MiG-21 to enter IAF inventory in 1963, was the MiG-21F-13, also called the Type 74, with two K13 AAMs, a single 37 mm NR-37 cannon, and a gyro gunsight (GGS) with radar ranging, to facilitate range estimation of the enemy target aircraft. It was not until early 1965 that the first IAF squadron, No. 28 Squadron was formed, and by that time, the Type 74 had been replaced by the MiG-21PF (Type 76), the first aircraft to be equipped with the R1L airborne radar. It was this version that saw action during the 1965 Indo-Pak War, during which the integral gun was sorely missed. The MiG-21 FL (Type 77) came in 1966 with the R2L radar which was only a slight improvement over the R1L, but the Type 76 and 77 had only the AAM, but no guns. These small numbers of Type 74 and 76 aircraft were phased out by 1968. A podded gun carried on the ventral station was provided by the Soviets before the 1971 war, but had only a PKI or fixed gunsight[1] in place of the earlier GGS. This fixed gunsight affected the accuracy of its guns, both in the air-to-air and air-to-ground mode. The plan to fit a modified gunsight, the GGS Mk 4, was given up, as it had to be fitted upside down, due to lack of space in the cockpit.

"The experience of 1971 convinced the decision makers at Air HQ that the MiG-21 had to have a gun with a predictor GGS, so a request was made for a gun armed version. In 1973, the Soviets made an offer of a MiG-21 M (Type 96) with GsH-23, a 23 mm integral gun with 300 rounds of ammunition, a GGS and an improved RP-21 AA Radar, and an improved ejection seat with 0/90 capability[2]. With a new engine R13-300 which was tested but rejected, as it gave little advantage, it also had a Radar Warning Receiver (RWR) and could carry 2x490 ltr. external drop tanks under wing and a 1×800 ltr. drop tank on the ventral station. The R13 engine certainly gave the MF version a slight advantage in the Supersonic regime over the M version, but since the R11 was already being manufactured at Koraput, the R13 was dropped on techno-economic grounds".[3] Numbers 7 and 37 squadrons were the only two units equipped with the Mig-21 MF. "In 1975, after many attempts to persuade us to buy the R13 engine, the Soviets offered us the MiG-21 'bis', fitted with the R25-300 engine with a second after-burner, and an improved AA Radar – the Almaz, which entered IAF service in mid-1976"[4] (Nos. 21, 23, 4, 15 and many other squadrons were equipped with the 'bis'. But Nos. 7, 8, 37, 29, and 30 squadrons continued with the older versions).

Hindustan Aeronautics Limited (HAL) also launched the MiG 'bis' modernisation project which included a vortex generator, a blown flap that went up at 700 kmph for manoeuvring, an enlarged saddle tank with additional 200 ltr. of fuel and Western avionics in place of Soviet instruments. The biggest drawback was that the 'bis' did not have a Nav-Attack system and navigation was done only with a map and stopwatch. Only dive attacks were possible for weapon delivery. Low Level Lay Down attacks with retarder weapons used mainly to avoid exposure to enemy anti-aircraft defences were equally difficult. In 1986, the IAF launched a serious search for a suitable Nav-Attack system but the effort did not fructify for a variety of reasons. The Russians offered the Kopyo AA radar, a Beyond Visual Range (BVR) missile and also the latest Close Combat missiles. In 1993, the MiG 'bis' upgrade programme was approved, which was officially called the Bison. Most of the flight test programmes were completed at Nizhny Novgorod in Russia during 1999-2002, at the end of which the Bison began entering service. The Bison was now equipped with Western avionics and lethal AA Missiles, but its airframe and engine did not see any modification and hence, some old problems of maintenance remained.

The MiG-21 FL (Type 77) did not have 'blown flaps' and this meant that the rate of descent on the landing approach, of nearly 1,000 metres per minute, which was nearly three times that of the Western aircraft like the Hunter and Gnat, caused considerable difficulty for inexperienced pilots. Air Chief Marshal A.Y. Tipnis, a highly experienced and respected MiG-21 pilot, readily acknowledges that the aircraft suffered from a large number of serious problems: limited range and endurance, simple instrumentation requiring careful engine handling, poor forward visibility, primitive weapon systems and above all, relatively difficult flying characteristics.[5] The IAF did not, however, have much choice, and this resulted in three squadrons of MiG-21FL or Type-77 aircraft being used for operational training of young pilots at MiG Flying Training Units (MOFTU), when the Hunter serviceability started to drop with age. The upshot of this decision was that the IAF was forced to use a difficult fighter for operational training, and a relatively easy-to-fly fighter such as the Jaguar and Mirage-200 for operational flying. For over three decades, from the 1970s to 2000 and even later, the MiG-21 remained the mainstay of the air force fighter fleet. Delayed decision-making, absence of a suitable indigenous aircraft, non-availability of suitable and affordable Western fighters, seriously constrained air force choices, contributed to accidents, and worse, their limited range, armament and obsolescent avionics affected military preparedness and deterrence. The army with its ever-increasing demands for immediate close air support was also unhappy because the air force simply could not assure the necessary combat punch.

NOTES

1. The fixed gun sight nevertheless served the purpose as proved by the successful rocket attack on the Government House at Dhaka.
2. 0/90 signifies a capability that allows the pilot to eject on ground at 0 altitude so long as the aircraft speed is more than 90 kmph.
3. These few paragraphs are based on Air Marshal Philip Rajkumar, "The MiG-21 Upgrade Story", *Vayu Aerospace & Defence Review*, 1, 2012, pp. 76-81, as well as the author's own experience.
4. Ibid.
5. Air Chief Marshal A.Y. Tipnis (Retd.), in an article he wrote when the MiG-21 was often referred to as the 'flying coffin' in the Indian media. See http://www.bharat-rakshak.com/IAF/Aircraft/Current/606-MiG-Tipnis.html (Accessed July 31, 2012). Also see, Air Marshal Philip Rajkumar, *The Tejas Story: The Light Combat Aircraft Project*, Manohar, New Delhi, 2008, pp. 55-56.

Appendix IV

Defence Budgets

Defence Budget (in Rs. Crores)

S.No.	Year	Army Share & %	Navy Share & %	AF Share & %	AF Revenue Share in %	AF Capital Share in %	Total Def. Exp. Actual + or –
A	B	C	D	E	F	G	H
1	1950-51	138 82%	09 05%	15 09%	10 66%	05 33%	168 -16
2	1951-52	145 80%	11 06%	16 09%	15 94%	01 06%	180 -17
3	1952-53	148 67%	15 07%	17 08%	15 87%	02 13%	222 +20
4	1953-54	141 71%	15 07%	29 15%	27 93%	02 07%	196 -14
5	1954-55	138 72%	19 09%	30 15%	28 94%	02 06%	195 -16
6	1955-56	127 67%	23 10%	31 16%	28 91%	03 09%	189 -16
7	1956-57	135 64%	26 11%	41 19%	37 91%	04 09%	211 -12
8	1957-58	165 60%	25 09%	72 26%	70 97%	02 03%	277 -13
9	1958-59	154 56%	29 10%	78 28%	75 98%	03 02%	277 -16
10	1959-60	151 57%	34 12%	62 23%	59 96%	03 04%	266 -13
11	1960-61	174 62%	32 11%	55 19%	51 93%	04 07%	281 -19
12	1961-62	211 68%	24 08%	58 19%	53 92%	05 08%	309 -19
13	1962-63	365 77%	25 05%	95 20%	78 82%	17 18%	474 -00

A	B	C	D	E	F	G	H
14	1963-64	606 74%	27 03%	169 20%	134 79%	35 21%	816 -08
15	1964-65	600 74%	28 03%	151 19%	126 83%	25 17%	806 -03
16	1965-66	645 73%	34 04%	171 19%	144 19%	27 21%	888 -03
17	1966-67	674 74%	40 04%	175 19%	147 18%	28 25%	942 -33
18	1967-68	691 71%	47 05%	175 18%	151 18%	24 23%	970 -02
19	1968-69	733 71%	57 06%	189 18%	169 18%	20 19%	1,033 -18
20	1969-70	745 67%	73 07%	212 19%	195 20%	17 13%	1,104 -03
21	1970-71	790 66%	95 08%	239 20%	222 19%	17 12%	1,199 +16
22	1971-72	1030 68%	113 07%	295 19%	271 18%	24 13%	1525 +114
23	1972-73	1110 67%	127 08%	321 19%	295 18%	26 11%	1652 +52
24	1973-74	1070 64%	149 09%	353 21%	327 19%	26 13%	1681 -72
25	1974-75	1374 65%	169 08%	437 21%	406 19%	31 16%	2,112 -45
26	1975-76	1603 65%	215 09%	496 20%	470 19%	26 12%	2,472 +62
27	1976-77	1644 64%	226 09%	525 20%	504 20%	21 10%	2,563 -52
28	1977-78	1663 63%	251 10%	535 20%	510 19%	25 10%	2,634 -117
29	1978-79	1746 61%	263 09%	644 22%	617 22%	27 11%	2,868 +23
30	1979-80	1953 58%	294 09%	866 26%	839 25%	27 10%	4,200 +927
31	1980-81	2234 58%	342 09%	953 25%	919 26%	34 10%	3,867 +67
32	1981-82	2,671 59%	530 12%	1,052 23%	1,005 24%	47 10%	4652 +52
33	1982-83	3,103 57%	566 10%	1,278 24%	1,226 25%	52 10%	5409 +59
34	1983-84	3,605 55%	750 11%	1,357 21%	1,295 22%	62 11%	6309 -41

A	B	C	D	E	F	G	H
35	1984-85	4,210 66%	813 13%	1,508 24%	1,437 25%	71 10%	6661 -514
36	1985-86	4,872 61%	1000 13%	1,860 23%	1,772 25%	88 09%	7987 +125
37	1986-87	6,527 62%	1311 13%	2,244 21%	2,141 23%	103 08%	10477 +284
38	1987-88	7,285 61%	1537 13%	2,764 23%	1,592 18%	1,172 38%	11967 -33
39	1988-89	8,060 60%	1799 13%	3,002 23%	1,735 18%	1,267 34%	13341 +141
40	1989-90	8,594 59%	1953 14%	3,325 23%	1,879 18%	1,446 34%	14416 -86
41	1990-91	9,273 60%	1963 13%	3,711 24%	2,078 19%	1,633 36%	15426 -313
42	1991-92	9,687 59%	2091 13%	4,107 25%	2,335 20%	1,772 36%	16347 -03
43	1992-93	10,040 57%	2,021 11%	5,174 29%	2,759 23%	2,415 44%	17,582 +82
44	1993-94	12,656 58%	2,705 13%	5,996 27%	3,364 22%	2,632 38%	21,844 +344
45	1994-95	13,346 57%	2,999 13%	6,430 28%	3,695 22%	2,735 38%	23,245 +01
46	1995-96	15,377 57%	3,800 14%	6,930 26%	3,907 21%	3,023 38%	26,856 -13
47	1996-97	16,916 57%	3,975 13%	7,490 25%	4,327 21%	3,163 37%	29,505 +33
48	1997-98	19895 56%	4,794 14%	9,126 25%	5164 57.0%	3,962 43.0%	35,278 -342
49	1998-99	24,169 61.0 %	6,016 15.0%	9,046 23.0%	5388 60.0%	3658 40.0%	39,898 -2102
50	1999-00	30014 64.0%	6,837 14.0%	10,243 22.0%	6019 59.0%	4,224 41.0%	47,071 +1,377
51	2000-01	30,650 62.00%	7,384 15.0%	10,611 21.0%	7,265 68.0%	3,346 32.0%	49,622 -8,965
52	2001-02	33,795 62.0%	8369 15.0%	11,784 22.0%	6,836 58.0%	4,948 41.0%	54,266 -7734
53	2002-03	32,482 58.0%	8156 15.0%	12,386 22.0%	7,369 59.0%	5,017 41.0%	55662 -9338
54	2003-04	33,521 56.0%	10109 17.0%	13,187 22.0%	7732 68.0%	5,455 42.0%	60,066 -5234
55	2004-05	35,603 47.0%	13,529 18.0%	23,036 30.0%	8,252 36.0%	14,784 64.0%	75,856 -1144

A	B	C	D	E	F	G	H
56	2005-06	39,792 49.0%	13,967 17.0%	21,704 27.0%	9,173 42.0%	12,531 54.0%	80,549 -2451
57	2006-07	39,903 47.0%	16,201 19.0%	24,275 30.0%	9,648 40.0%	14,627 60.0%	85,495 -3505
58	2007-08	46,128 50.0%	15,885 17.0%	23,594 26.0%	10,102 43.0%	13,492 57.0%	91,680 -4320
59	2008-09	58,142 50.0%	17,248 15.0%	29,271 26.0%	12,673 43.0%	16,598 57.0%	114,223 +8623
60	2009-10	77,540 55.0%	22,935 16%	33,259 23.0%	14,708 44.0%	18,551 56.0%	141,781 +78
61	2010-11	78,730 51.0%	27,119 18.0%	38,155 25.0%	14,551 38.0%	23,604 63.0%	154,117 +6783
62	2011-12	84740 50%	31,116 18 .0 %	45,585 27.0%	16,773 37.0%	28,812 63.0%	170913 +6498
63	2012-13	92,139 50.0%	29,594 19.2%	50,509 24.9%	17,529 35.0%	32,980 65.0%	181,776 -11631
64	2013-14	99,708 49%	36,343 18%	57,502 28%	20,455 BE	37,048 BE	203,499 -173

Notes 1: For no apparent reason, except in 1952-53, the actual expenditure was less than RE. Although the IAF strength had increased from 10 to about 25 squadrons by this time, this is not reflected in revenue/capital expenditure figures.

2: Once again, except in 1970-71, the actual expenditure was less than RE.

3: During six of the 10 years, the actual expenditure was well above the RE and in the remaining four years it was below RE, thus showing erratic utilisation probably due to uncertainty regarding acquisitions from abroad/delayed contracts.

4: In column H plus or minus sign indicates the under/over spent amount with respect to BE. All figures denote 'actual expenditure'. Until FY 1986-87 purchase of aircraft and aero-engines was under Revenue head.

5: This data is taken from various official publications; Dr. Laxman Kumar Behera's comments on annual defence budgets at the IDSA website; and also from the IDSA Statistical Digest compiled by Gp. Capt. Vinay Kaushal (Retd.) and Dr. Pankaj Jha; 'International Seminar on Defence Acquisition, July12-14, 2011'. Also see Vinod Misra, (ed.) *Core Concerns in Indian Defence and the Imperatives for Reforms*, Pentagon Press, New Delhi, 2015, at idsa.in/book/CoreConcernsinIndianDefence_vmisra.html (Accessed April 15, 2015).

6: The data on defence budgets from 1950 to 1997 was compiled and analysed by Late Shri Sreedhar Rao, former Senior Research Associate, IDSA who had kindly given me a copy in 2001. To the best of my knowledge this data has remained unpublished.

Appendix V

Air Maintaining the Indian Army and Civilians in the Himalayan Frontier Region

For over 50 years, every morning at the crack of dawn, a transport aircraft of the Indian Air Force (IAF) gets airborne from a forward airfield like Chandigarh, Jammu, Mohanbari, Dinjan and others, for what is known as 'weather recce'. Once in the air, its aircrews assess the weather en route and at the destination, and give a signal for others to follow. Each aircraft does at least two round trips of two-three hours each, every day. Indian air power is quietly at work, while the rest of the country goes about its daily routine. According to some estimates, the IAF airlifts some 40,000-60,000 tons of supplies every year for the troops and civilians living in the mountainous border area of the North and North-east. From the early 1950s, the IAF and before that, some intrepid civilian pilots of a few aviation companies, have been providing the necessary victuals to the tribals, civilians, army and border security forces and helping them survive harsh winter conditions.

Air supply or maintenance is done by either landing the aircraft or by para-dropping the supplies on open ground known as 'Dropping Zones' (DZs) that often look like the size of a postage stamp from the air. Strong winds, clouds and the rare atmosphere at heights above 12,000-15,000 feet increase the difficulties because even a slight error in the allowance for cross-wind can send the loads into the adjoining valley. Such is the unpredictability of weather in the high Himalayas that very often conditions become extremely difficult if not dangerous, in a matter of minutes. Some DZs have only one access route and others very narrow valleys, making it extremely difficult to turn the aircraft around. All air maintenance operations thus have to be completed by the early afternoon, as cloud build-up in the latter part of the day shuts down the valleys. Most landing sorties also carry passengers – soldiers proceeding to and from leave both ways – and are a vital link for them, especially in emergency situations.

Landing the aircraft poses its own problems as the Advanced Landing Grounds (ALGs) are usually a fraction of the length of normal runways, and are very often unpaved or covered with only a carpet of metal sheets or what are called Perforated Steel Plate (PSP) sheets. The ALGs are situated in remote valleys, where only a small contingent of air force personnel can be stationed. The same person sends out signals, carries out air traffic control duties, clears the aircraft for landing and also gives weather and other reports.

Even after 68 years, there are hardly any roads in the forward areas comprising all of Arunachal Pradesh and Ladakh. The Srinagar-Kargil-Leh highway that came under Pakistani artillery threat during the 1999 Kargil conflict is veritably the lifeline for our troops along the border. The relatively new Manali-Rohtang highway is another important road in the northern sector. These and roads are subject to landslides and heavy snowfall during winter, and are continuously maintained and cleared by the untiring efforts of the Border Roads Organisation (BRO), but very often prove to be inadequate.

Arunachal Pradesh is divided into five administrative sub-divisions – Kameng, Subansiri, Lohit, Siang and Tirap – and many more districts since it attained statehood in 1987 but there are no lateral roads between these sub-divisions. This means that if one wants to go from the north of Kameng to the adjoining Subansari division, one has to first travel all the way south to the Assam plains, and then once again enter the hills further east. These roads are still primitive. An Institute for Defence Studies and Analyses (IDSA) scholar on a road trip to the origin of the Siang River records that their SUV had to be ferried in a boat across the Siang, at the foot hills, before they could begin their journey along the mostly unpaved narrow road northwards.

As far back as 1951, a large contingent of the Indian Army was successfully para-dropped in Walong, at almost the extreme eastern edge of the NEFA (North-East Frontier Agency) border. Even today, road connectivity remains poor. Of late, a number of new road projects have been started but it will take a long time before reliable all-weather surface communications are established.

In the 1950s and 1960s, the IAF had to rely mostly on the DC-3 Dakota which barely carried 3,500 lb of load or about 20-22 passengers. The Fairchild C-119 Packet could carry more passengers and with its rear door, could also off load them or the loads more quickly. The Packet, a piston engine aircraft, was later fitted with a 'jet pack' or an additional jet engine that considerably improved its ability to fly over high altitudes. The IAF received the Soviet An-12, almost the same size as the US C-130 Hercules in 1961. Two squadrons, Nos. 25 and 44 were raised at Chandigarh and became the mainstay of IAF transport operations for over four decades, until being phased out in the 1990s.

Typical air supply loads included wheat flour, rice, tinned food, construction material, PSP sheets, meat-on-hoof or live goats and kerosene in jerry cans. Today, most of the work is done by the turbo-prop An-32 or the Il-76 transport aircraft which can carry far bigger loads than the venerable Dakota of the 1950s.

The IAF received the Canadian Caribou, capable of take-off and landing from short runways, as also the Otter that was used mostly for carrying 8-10 passengers. The induction of the C-130J Hercules transport is designed specifically for Special Operation Forces, but the IAF may be tempted to employ these aircraft in the traditional air maintenance role.

It is said that the An-32 costs some Rs. 2 lakh per hour in fuel alone. A two-ton load of kerosene from Chandigarh or Jammu to Leh; after a three-hour round flight, would cost Rs. 2 lakh when delivered at Leh. A litre of kerosene at Leh would thus cost a prohibitive Rs. 600. Both the IAF and the Ministry of Defence (MoD) know well, the prohibitively high costs of air maintaining our troops and civilians, but are unable to do very much in the absence of road connectivity to these remote areas. Some analysts believe that the Indian Government did not want to provoke the Chinese and hence, delayed road building. Others say that they feared giving easy access to an invading enemy if more roads were built. Both these arguments are fallacious and the true reason for such delays is probably our indifference, indecision and procrastination.

A major portion of all transport flying in the IAF is devoted to the task of air maintenance and hence, almost every young transport pilot begins his flying career in these forward air bases and learns from his seniors, the intricacies of flying over high mountains. They learn to interpret weather forecasts and the unpredictability of nature; learn to recognise safe and dangerous areas and navigate their unwieldy and difficult-to-manoeuvre heavily loaded aircraft to inaccessible areas of the frontier. Until the arrival of the pressurised An-32 in 1984, the aircrews and army supply corps loaders routinely operated in freezing conditions, with only a puff or two from oxygen cylinders. These aircraft often had to negotiate narrow valleys under extensive cloud cover when weather suddenly 'packed up'. The induction of the An-32 in the early 1980s eased the situation as these could now carry nearly six tons of load or 40 passengers.

Such was the pressure of demand that in the 1980s it was a common sight to see two young Flying Officers as Captain and Co-pilot of a spanking new An-32 being supervised by an experienced Wing Commander navigator. Personnel policies, recruitment, training, postings or regular rotation of these air and ground crews and availability of suitable aircraft together play a vital role in ensuring safe and efficient air maintenance operations. In addition, the IAF has also been flying weekly 'courier' flights from remote airfields in Ladakh and Assam to New Delhi and Bangalore, and other cities and railway stations in the plains, to help jawans posted in forward areas to visit their home towns. Without such regular courier flights it would become impossible for those posted in forward areas to attend to family emergencies or avail short casual leave.

Appendix VI

Air Defence of the Srinagar Valley – 1971

Number 18 Squadron was raised on April 15, 1965 at Ambala and equipped with Gnat Mk1 fighters. Many of its pilots took part in the 1965 Indo-Pak war, but with other squadrons based at Pathankot and Halwara, as the squadron was still in the process of raising when the war started. Located at Ambala, the oldest air force station in India, the squadron's operational task in any future war was to provide air defence to Srinagar airfield. Since on account of United Nations (UN) restrictions, India had not until then permanently stationed any fighter squadrons in the Valley, the squadron ran a detachment of six Gnats at Srinagar in October 1968 to assess its operational needs. Thereafter, the squadron operated three such detachments at Srinagar. By the time tensions began to rise in March 1971, the squadron was stationed more at Srinagar than at Ambala. It also operated a short detachment at Amritsar in Punjab in May-June 1971. All pilots were thus fully familiar with the air defence environment at Srinagar and Amritsar.

Although the Srinagar air base had by then a 3,500-yard-long runway and a parallel taxi track, it had only a few hardened concrete aircraft shelters called Blast Pens in the Indian Air Force (IAF). Consequently, a maximum of only four Gnats were allowed to be stationed at that base. Therefore, one or two aircraft would have to be flown and replacements brought back from Ambala, whenever an aircraft developed a problem or became due for servicing. Since the task was air defence (AD), the Gnats were parked at the southern end of the only runway near the 31 dumbbell. The Gnats being small fighters, these were housed in two open but well-camouflaged pens on the Operational Readiness Platform (ORP). So effective was this simple arrangement that not once did the enemy detect or specifically target the two Gnats in these open and totally unprotected pens. Being a mere 30 metres from a very small and often cramped underground aircrew room where we sat waiting for action, it took little time to run to the aircraft and start it. Once the war began, the squadron went on a two-minute standby alert which entailed that the pilot remain strapped inside the Gnat cockpit. Srinagar can get pretty cold in December and our feet used to become numb if we sat strapped for more than about three hours. So pilots did three-hour shifts, everyone hoping for action during the shift. Depending on the orders of the Station Commander or higher authorities, which were mainly based on 'hunch and intuition', a pair of Gnats would be scrambled to set up a Combat Air Patrol (CAP) overhead.

The base did not have any AD radar and hence, we had to depend on our eyes to spot an enemy aircraft. During winter months, visibility in the Valley is extremely poor due to mist/fog or smog. A chain of observation posts (OP) was set up along the crest of the hills on the western side of the Valley where a soldier, usually from the local Ack-Ack regiment (anti-aircraft gun regiment), was given a battery-operated radio communication set to report enemy aircraft sightings. A board in the Base Operations room depicted the exact location of these operations and gave an approximate direction and flying time to Srinagar airfield. We had all flown a number of practice missions to perfect this local warning system but finally it was only marginally useful. Very low temperatures on the top of the hills, frequently discharged batteries, poor visibility and above all close proximity to the airfield meant that very often the enemy would arrive with little or no warning. Two or three under-training operational (U/T ops) pilots were deputed as observers and CAP Controllers, and were located near the Air Traffic Control (ATC) dug-out on the eastern side of the runway. We used to live in the Badami Bagh Officers Mess located some 20 km from the airfield, where living conditions were also very primitive, due mainly to very low voltage, and small, dingy and very cold rooms. Every morning, a pair of two pilots used to come to the airfield at about 4:30 to 5:00 am as we were expected to be ready at least 30 minutes before sunrise. The big bus, called a coach in the air force language had most of its glass window panes missing, and we were almost frozen by the end of the 45-minute long trip.

Srinagar airfield was subjected to a total of 14 daylight attacks by the Pakistan Air Force (PAF). Given the easy access that the enemy enjoyed to the Valley, Pakistan intelligence had infiltrated an agent who used to inform the incoming PAF fighters on his radio, if the Gnats were airborne. On at least two or three occasions, the PAF attackers went back from near Baramulla or Pir Panjal Pass, two of the preferred entry points of the PAF. We had thought of mounting CAPs at a distance from the airfield to fool this agent but with total absence of radar cover and very poor in-flight visibility, it was well-nigh impossible to spot enemy intruders till they had come very close to the airfield. As a result of these constraints, only on three out of the 14 raids were the Gnats in fact airborne. The first time, on December 6, at about sunset, Flight Commander, Squadron Leader 'Pat' V.S. Pathania VrC, VM, a veteran of the 1965 Indo-Pak war, who had shot down a PAF Sabre, and Flight Lieutenant 'Bops' B.N. Bopaya were burning extra fuel prior to landing, when the PAF struck with four Sabres carrying two 500-lb bombs each and were spotted by Pat. Local Ack-Ack guns opened up even though their instructions were to hold fire when the Gnats were overhead, and this forced 'Bops' to abandon his attack, by which time the Sabres had dropped their bombs; some of which fell on or near the runway and caused some damage.

Here a slight digression is necessary. Strangely, the full-fledged 3,000-yard runway at Awantipura airfield just 15 km away to the south had been blocked with used oil drums to 'prevent' the enemy from landing para-troops. Our pleas to clear the drums and make that runway available as a diversionary airfield in case of emergency fell on deaf ears. The result was that we had to keep a larger emergency reserve of fuel to go all the way to Udhampur, the designated diversion for Srinagar. Given that the Gnat already had very little internal fuel, this was a huge penalty.

On spotting the enemy, Pat called Bops to retract his airbrakes and look out for the enemy ahead while he pursued another. Soon Pat got behind the now returning Sabre and opened fire from about 500 metres, but his aircraft guns jammed/suffered a gun-stoppage, an old and persistent problem with the Gnat. Pat followed the enemy and tried to call Bops for help but with low fuel and no radar the chase had to be abandoned. It was a lucky PAF pilot.

It was already getting dark and some portions of the runway were damaged. Wing Commander Parmarthi (Prince) Raina, the Commanding Officer (CO), made a quick trip in his jeep and guided the two pilots so that they could land on the undamaged side and slowly veer off to avoid the bomb craters. To add to the confusion, a bomb fell on a pile of runway repair material consisting mainly of large boulders that were neatly arranged a short distance from the runway edge; these were now randomly scattered on the runway. Landing a high-speed jet in darkness on such a runway became difficult. All aircrews and some technicians scrambled to light up the kerosene lamps, called 'goose necks' placed along the runway edge. Just when I was bent over a lamp, Bopaya's Gnat went over me, thankfully missing my head by a few inches. He had abandoned landing as he was not properly aligned with the runway. I still remember my thoughts, "Dying on the runway edge after a hit from a Gnat undercarriage would be the worst fate a fighter pilot could bargain for." We managed to light up a few more goose necks and Bopaya made a safe landing on his second attempt. It was my task to tow the Gnat that he had switched off in the middle of the runway. I connected the towing rod to a jeep and began the slow drive back, wondering how the Gnat had remained totally unscathed with so many large boulders strewn around on the runway. Fortunately, there were no casualties and the thought that there might have been an unexploded bomb in the near vicinity never crossed my mind.

Another big if sad event now awaited us in Srinagar. December 14, 1971 was to prove a fateful day. G'man', Flight Lieutenant Ghuman and 'Brother,' Flying

Officer N.J.S. Sekhon were on the ORP for the morning CAP mission. Inflight visibility was as usual very bad. They were scrambled but the warning was short. A six-aircraft Sabre formation, four plus two for top cover, was already arriving overhead. The ATC was asked to cancel the scramble orders but the CAP aircraft were on a different frequency. G'man' got airborne and turned left to set up CAP. Sekhon had barely got airborne when bombs fell behind him on the runway. Sabre Nos. 1 and 2 overshot Sekhon. Sekhon immediately followed them but when the Sabre leader saw the Gnat gaining on his No. 2, he warned him and both broke left, but by then Sabre Nos. 3 & 4 were ideally placed to *sandwich* Sekhon. All this was happening out of sight of the CAP controllers and other onlookers on the airfield. Sekhon first got into a circle of 'joy' or more correctly 'no joy' with two Sabres (a situation when neither pilot gains any advantage); it was at this stage that another Sabre watching these developments from the top swooped down and positioned itself behind Sekhon. Sekhon had called, "I am behind two Sabres. I won't let them get away." Sekhon had one Sabre ahead of him while another was apparently gaining an edge. A little later, a burst of 30 mm Gnat gunfire could be clearly heard. Flight Lieutenants Bopaya and Naliyan of 18 Squadron say they saw a Sabre with its right wing on fire. This was followed by a long burst from Sabre guns which sounded distinctly different from those of the Gnat. Then came the last Radio/Telephone call from Sekhon, "I think I am hit, G'man come." Sekhon had ejected but his parachute failed to open as he was too close to the ground. Sekhon lost his life fighting valiantly till the very end. He was killed but his memory will always remain alive.

Sekhon belonged to the 97th General Duties (Pilots') Course and was posted to 18 Squadron at Ambala in October 1968. He was affectionately called 'Brother' by his course mates and friends because he used to invariably start all his conversations with the word 'Brother'. Sekhon was rightly and most deservedly awarded the ParamVir Chakra, the nation's highest gallantry award, posthumously. He was a simple rustic, unaffected man who was determined to leave his mark on history; a mission he performed admirably.

A few days later, on December 15 at about lunchtime, we were caught again. We had just returned from Brother's funeral parade, the cremation having been carried out with full military honours on the edge of the airfield. This time most of us were out in the open chatting a few feet from the underground crew room next to the 31 ORP. We saw a formation of four plus two Sabres coming up from the shallow valley that ran along the western side of the airfield. Probably on being told by the ATC, a helicopter of the local unit had taken shelter in a narrow ravine; unknown to the crew, the Sabres saw it. One of the attacking Sabres then turned by just a few degrees to the left, fired a short burst with its six guns and quickly got back in the formation. The helicopter was severely damaged. One of the attackers came up from the left in a dive, all guns blazing. It is not very often that one sees the blue flashes of aircraft guns from up front. We jumped in the shallow drain that had been dug up for some pipe-laying work, hardly any protection. Some 50 shots were fired in our close vicinity with a few getting lodged in the doorframe of the crew room but miraculously none were injured. While on the ground, I had felt a heavy but blunt object hitting my neck and back of the head. I thought I was hit and the pain would follow soon, but when I looked up after the Sabre had passed, I saw a huge sheep dog crouching right behind, obviously a stray, scared of the din of strafing, but apparently also unhurt.

A similar thing had happened some years earlier when one had gone with a friend to a firing range as understudies to the Range Safety Officer (RSO). Standing one level lower than the top floor, we were watching four Hunters in a low-level front-gun strike. The one on the right had unfortunately misjudged the line of attack and opened fire from an angle to the actual dive direction, showering us with no less than 79 empties of a 30 mm round, each weighing almost half a kg. That time too we had come through 'unscathed'.

By then, i.e. the 14th of December 1971, we were angry and frustrated. What with the primitive AD warning set up and poor visibility, the enemy was elusive. To relieve the anger, we began flying a few strike and escort missions with the Vampires based at Srinagar. Two Gnats escorted a mission beyond Kargil but saw little action. With Flight Lieutenant Ghuman a.k.a. G'man I went on a mission to strike a Brigade Headquarters (Bde HQ) near Hajira not too far away, but on reaching there found little evidence of any army presence. Just as I was pulling out of the dive, I noticed the shining brass cover of a fire extinguisher that had been kept close to the entrance of a hut. No villager would keep a fire extinguisher outside his hut. I fired, but one of the guns stopped and the nose swerved viciously to the side. On coming back, one got a scolding from Pat because I had lost visual contact with G'man who was a few km ahead. More CAPs followed but with little gain.

Appendix VII

Author's Note

When I joined the Indian Air Force (IAF) on November 16, 1964, I was a little over 18 years old and the IAF 32. Following the drubbing India received at the hands of the Chinese in October 1962, the Indian leadership had embarked on a massive expansion of the armed forces. The Indian Army had begun a scheme of granting 'Emergency Commissions' to eligible candidates with a college degree. The IAF due to high costs of flying training, decided to grant only 'permanent' commissions to eligible males who had passed their Higher Secondary exams with physics and maths. The IAF had also begun a scholarship of 25 hours of free flying training at the various flying clubs, for identifying potential candidates for entry into the General Duties (Pilots) branch of the IAF. I was selected for the grant of the scholarship and was to begin my flying at the Madhya Pradesh Flying Club, Indore, but did not actually start flying as I was also selected to join the 97th Pilots' Course (PC).

Some 150 of us Direct Entry cadets reached Coimbatore on the morning of November 16, 1964 and were quickly bundled off the railway station by a stern-looking Warrant Officer, Coutinho, to the Initial Training Wing (ITW) of the Air Force Administrative College (AFAC) at Red Fields, Coimbatore, where our training began in right earnest. There were lectures on General Service Training (GST), Air Force Law, Administration, IAF History, Principles of Flight (P of F) or Aerodynamics, Airmanship, Navigation, Meteorology, and the like. In addition to daily drill, physical training and games, the cadets were also 'broken' into the Service way of life. We had to attend Dining-in-Nights on a weekly basis where we were taught how to eat 'properly' and drink a toast to the health of the President; the toast was drunk in special wine glasses but contained plain water. We were also taken on visits to some industries and saw for the first time a few fighter aircraft that were stored at No. 5 Base Repair Depot (BRD) at Sulur airfield, some 25 km from Coimbatore. Here we witnessed the French Mystere IVA single-seat, single-engine fly a demonstration sortie. The speed and sound of the fighter were truly awe-inspiring and not a cadet present that day at the top of the Air

Traffic Control (ATC) tower could have dreamt of becoming anything but a fighter pilot.

On completion of ground training in March 1965, we were divided into five lots and sent to the Civil Flying Clubs at Tambaram near Chennai, Nagpur, Kanpur, Delhi and Patiala where we were to do some 25 hours of basic flying on the Cessna, Piper Cub, Sentinel L-5 or the Pushpak made at Hindustan Aeronautics Limited (HAL), Bangalore.

At the time, entry to the flying branch of the IAF was through the National Defence Academy (NDA), which took three years of training after class X or Matriculation; National Cadet Corps (NCC) cadets who had successfully completed their C certificate exam; and also to a number of specially selected young airmen. Some 40 air force cadets of the 28th NDA course joined us in July 1965 at the various flying clubs. The civilian instructors at the flying clubs were assisted by a Wing Commander of the IAF who, besides being the Commanding Officer (CO) of the Elementary Flying Training Unit (EFTU), checked our progress regularly. Number 5 EFTU at Nagpur had Pushpak and L-5 aircraft but the air force cadets flew only the L-5 which was a tandem two-seat arrangement with a speaking tube for the instructor, who shouted his instructions above the din of the engine; very often such instructions could be heard on the ground when the aircraft came on the final approach to landing. The IAF had devised this simple training scheme to overcome the shortage of flying instructors and aircraft. It must be noted that the main aim was to dramatically increase the number of pilots available to man the 45 squadrons that the IAF was now authorised. The IAF however, took over ten years to get the additional aircraft, mostly MiG-21 and S-22 by which time many of these young pilots were wasted out. The civilian flying instructors were usually very sincere and conservative in their approach to flying training and did not take many short cuts. In the 25 or so hours allotted to each cadet, solo flying comprised just about three hours. I did my first solo in July 1965 and the sorties comprised only a circuit, approach, overshoot another circuit approach and landing, but it was a great feeling. For the first time ever, I flew alone. Later, when I became a flying instructor and sent numerous cadets on their first 'solo' trips, I used to tell them to savour every moment that they spent in the air alone.

The aim of putting the cadets through EFTUs was to weed out those who could not make the grade as military pilots, at relatively low costs and high safety, and in that the EFTUs were fairly successful. The IAF was in the throes of a major transition. Some of the early Pilots' Courses (85th to 89th) had managed to complete their flying training in as little as nine months, while others like mine took over 30 months.

We completed our initial flying training sometime in August 1965 when the Indo-Pak war intervened, and we were sent off on indefinite leave. Some of us who had already reached the next stage of training at the Pilot Training Establishment (PTE), Allahabad, were unable to commence our flying due to the huge backlog of flying training, and were asked to guard the airfield with lathis (bamboo sticks). Soon after the war ended in September 1965, we were recalled from leave and reached PTE, Allahabad, which was in shambles as there were many cadets from the previous courses. The train journey, however, was memorable as at every station ordinary people were enthusiastically distributing sweets and other goodies to 'soldiers and airmen' for having successfully fought a war. For the first time, we got a taste of adulation by a grateful nation and it was exhilarating.

The PTE at the time also had a helicopter training unit called the Logistics Support Training Unit (LSTU), which was then training some 15-20 cadets from the 94th Pilots' Course. The PTE was then housed in two buildings built for training civilians; it was the Civil Aviation Training Centre (CATC) premises that the IAF had taken over at Bamrauli air field that can truly be called one of the oldest in India. A railway line passed through the airfield neatly dividing it into two. The administrative wing, cadets mess, and playing fields were on one side, while the runway, dispersals and flying training squadrons were on the other side, with cadets cycling from one to the other end at all times of the day. So chaotic were the conditions at the PTE that very often cadets lived only on chicken or pudding. Missing classes was common and the NDA cadets who were more experienced and hardened compared to the Direct Entry variety had a good time, but to be fair, so did we.

Most instructors had five to six or even seven pupils, and that meant a long wait for the sorties, but it was fun too. This phase saw many cadets being suspended from flying and every day some cadet or the other was on the dreaded 'review board' for extension or suspension. It was tough as being sent home at the age of 18-19 was bad enough, but finding no place in the flying fraternity was even more painful. Many of those suspended were, however, recalled for navigation training and became outstanding navigators and logistics or administrative officers of the IAF.

At the PTE which was called the basic stage of training, cadets flew around 25-30 hours on the HT-2, an indigenously designed tail-wheeled trainer that was prone to 'swinging' on landing, especially after it had decelerated on the landing run, when the natural tendency for the cadet was to relax, and it was precisely at this time that the HT-2 would suddenly swing and veer off the runway. Mercifully, there were no injuries nor much damage to the aircraft but you could not be sent solo until you learnt to control the swing. The HT-2 was the first aircraft on which the cadets were taught aerobatics and 'spinning' or more correctly 'spin and recovery' which sometimes was a hair-raising experience if the aircraft proved reluctant to recover. The wild gyrations and rapid loss of height was somewhat discomfiting but we soon got used to it. If I remember right, some 20-25 per cent of the original lot of cadets had gone home by the time we finished this stage. The phrase 'survival of the fittest' had acquired a new meaning by the time our course left the PTE, Allahabad, in early 1966.

Next we went to the Air Force Flying College (AFFC) at Jodhpur by a special train in March 1966, which was a unique experience in itself. The train stopped at some unknown stations and had a schedule of its own, with food being served on the platform. Jodhpur had been on the Indian aviation map for a long time. Here, the erstwhile Maharaja had donated one of his sprawling properties to the air force, in which the officers'/cadets' mess was housed. The airfield has two parallel runways, one long and the other short, each supporting the flying training of two squadrons, a decidedly large station. Here, we flew the Harvard 2B or Texan T6G, with very little difference between the two. Like the Sentinel L-5 at the Nagpur Flying Club which was of World War II vintage, the ambulance and training aircraft, the Harvard/Texan were also American, and had been procured just after independence. The Texan as well as its twin the Harvard were delightful trainers, very easy to fly, although the big radial engine in the nose used to restrict forward view (visibility) on the ground. So confident did all of us become on this aircraft that very often cadets used to intentionally spin it to lose height, not a safe practice at the best of times. Here, we flew a total of 80 hours, some 30 of which were solo. We also learnt to fly by night. For the first time, the flying syllabus included a triangular cross-country route in which the cadet flew a solo trip to Jaipur. To civilian pilots who routinely fly to different places at a relatively early stage of their training, this might not be a big event, but for us in the air force, it was our first experience of landing at a new base and gave us immense confidence. Flying in close formation was another interesting exercise. Here, we also saw Vampire Mk. 52 aircraft of the Control and Reporting (C&R) School on routine flying sorties, which proved a great motivator and morale booster, as we were to fly the same aircraft during the final stage of our training at Hakimpet, Secunderabad.

At Jodhpur too, the suspension rate was very high, with one or two cadets packing their bags on an almost daily basis. It was disconcerting as no one was certain about his future. Jodhpur can get extremely hot in summer and we saw really frightening sandstorms that could envelope the airfield and the city in a matter of minutes. A visit to Mandor Gardens, specially maintained by the Maharaja, still stays in memory because the variety of lush green plants and trees was truly remarkable, especially in the middle of a desert. We were also taken to the Umaid Bhawan Palace, a beautiful and imposing structure in sandstone that the local king had made during a famine in the previous century, to create employment for his hapless subjects.

At the end of the 'Intermediate Stage' training at Jodhpur, the course was trifurcated into fighter, transport and helicopter streams with those selected for fighter training proceeding to Hakimpet at Secunderabad; those for transport to Begumpet at Hyderabad; and also to Yelahanka at Bangalore and the helicopter cadets to LSTU at Allahabad. (LSTU was later moved to Hakimpet and renamed Helicopter Training School (HTS). Secunderabad was a major city with many distractions. For small town boys like me, it was a new experience. We now had a choice of continental or Chinese cuisine, if only we could save some money for a weekend treat. Given that we were allowed an allowance of only Rs. 40 per month for our incidental expenses, we had to carefully plan these trips. Now the cadet gets a stipend of several thousand rupees during his training and so is relatively independent.

The Vampire Mk52 and its two-seat version, the Vampire Mk55, were in fact both in operational service when we began our training at Jet Training Wing (JTW), Hakimpet. The first jet that entered service with the Indian Air Force in 1948, it was relatively fast and it took us all some time to get used to the higher speed, thrust and agility. The first solo on the Mk52 was again a memorable experience, as for the first time we were flying a single-seat version that was quite different from the two-seat trainer. By the time one realised that the aircraft was airborne, the diminutive fighter had already reached 4,500 feet. Flying training in the 'Advanced Stage' progressed much faster at JTW, as we were by now more experienced, and the instructor/pupil/aircraft ratio was good. Until now my own flying training had proceeded without much difficulty and I had experienced only minor flight emergencies.

April 11, 1967 dawned as a normal day. Little did I know that the day was to prove very exciting. Our course was divided into two training squadrons of about 25 cadets each, and flying was in two shifts: first beginning at 0530 hours and the second at about 1130 hours. That day, our squadron was in the afternoon shift and I got airborne on a solo general handling sortie after lunch. Everything was fine until at about 7,500 feet, the engine just stopped. As per the procedure, I gained some height with the extra speed and put the aircraft in a gentle glide. I was facing away from the airfield after take-off and the first thing to do was to turn towards the base. At first, I thought that I might have to turn 180° and land on the opposite runway as my height was only about 6,000 feet Above Ground Level (AGL), but the aircraft was not losing as much height as we had been briefed during 'practice forced landing' procedures, which we had all regularly practised. Attempts at relight-restarting the engine were unsuccessful, and after consulting the ATC I decided to carry out a normal descending circuit, and land on the easterly runway from where I had taken off. I was still high when I came abeam the landing dumbbell, also known as 'low key' point in aviation training parlance, so I extended my downwind leg to lose a little more height, but that was not enough. It is after all not easy to deliberately lose more height, when gliding away from the runway with a dead engine. I was, therefore, high on the final approach and try as I might, the aircraft refused to lose height quickly enough, and hence, I touched down ahead of the first half of the runway. Fortunately for me, a new arrester barrier had been installed only a few weeks earlier, and I was the first to engage it. The aircraft came to a stop on the 'overshoot' area and I managed to jump out of it in a jiffy. Within seconds, the Station Commander's car, a black Ambassador with its flag fluttering, was alongside my aircraft, and I hitched a ride back to the squadron. Although I had not realised it in the air, the jet engine had in fact ceased and hence, it was not wind milling. That should normally have caused much drag and made gliding difficult. The hydraulic system had also shut down and the undercarriage came down, but the landing flaps did not, and hence, the overshooting approach. In my excitement, I had forgotten to check 'hand pump solid' – to ensure that the flaps had come down fully and locked with the available hydraulic fluid. Luckily the authorities did not take too serious a view of this lapse and I was allowed to continue my flying training.

All my course-mates were of course delighted to see me safe and sound and in one piece. After all, it is not often that one does a dead-stick landing with a 'seized' engine. I thanked the Lord for looking after my interests and sparing my life. I did not realise at the time that I had chosen a career where I would need 'His' assistance on many occasions throughout my life. Once while flying a Gnat I had a flame-out or engine failure at 7,000 feet but the engine relit in no time. The result was that no one would believe that the engine had in fact failed, until I proved it on ground after I had safely landed.

We were commissioned on June 4, 1967. The then Defence Minister Swaran Singh took the salute and pinned the wings on our chests swollen with pride, and we marched to the haunting melody of *Auld Lang Syne*. My parents witnessed the ceremony and I was justifiably proud and happy and so were they. Our first posting was to a Vampire Squadron at Poona (now Pune). Half of us went to No. 220 Squadron and the other half to No. 221 Squadron. Here we went through the 'Applied Phase' during which we were introduced to tactical flying and armament delivery. Although we barely flew 20-25 hours in six months, we were able to learn tactical flying and also carried out live firing of guns, rockets and bombs; we were getting there, though not yet 'Fully Operational' on any type of fighter. This short tenure was also most enjoyable as we were often sent on week-long Temporary Duty' or T/D moves to Bombay (now Mumbai). Since most of us had never been to this most famous metropolis, we looked forward to these moves. We also made new friends, since at the time, there were two Canberra light bomber squadrons, and a Super Constellation heavy transport squadron based at Pune; the latter with a small complement of World War II fame Liberator four-engine bombers, which were now also used for maritime reconnaissance duties. The Super Constellations had been with Air India, and flying these even as passengers was great fun. For the first time, we saw many veterans of the recent conflict with Pakistan and were both impressed and inspired by their stories of valour.

The next posting was to Operational Training Unit (OTU) at Jamnagar on the Gujarat coast. Course-mates who took longer to complete their Applied Phase training syllabus at Pune, were sent direct to Hunter Squadrons, mostly in the east. At that time, we did not know how lucky we were to be posted to OTU Jamnagar. Before starting our flying on the Hunter aircraft, we had to undergo a short theory course called Mobile Conversion Flight (MCF). As the name suggests, the Flight should normally have come to us, but in reality it did not move from its permanent location at 28 Wing, Hindon. This was once again a highly informative and educative trip as we were learning a lot about the aircraft, flying and the Service in general. Visiting the national capital in early 1968 was also an added bonus. We soon realised, that the Hunter was a complex aircraft compared to the Vampire, and also much faster. Its flying controls were hydraulically operated and hence, were very light and sensitive to the touch. Until he gained some proficiency, it was common to see a novice unintentionally waggling his wings after take-off.

The IAF station at Jamnagar was and is still called Armament Training Wing (ATW), where all fighter squadrons of the IAF carried out annual live air-to-air firing over the sea. There was and still is a major IAF Air-to-Ground Firing Range at Jamnagar. As a result, it is an extremely busy station with squadrons coming and going all the time. The officers' mess, especially the bar, was always over-crowded. On Saturday afternoons when officers are allowed to have beer, the crowd used to be six-deep around the bar counter and getting to the barman was well-nigh impossible. It was nearly the end of August by the time we completed our training syllabus of some 35 hours. Unfortunately, the minimum experience on a power-controlled aircraft needed to fly the Gnat Mk1 was then 40 hours, but we did not know about this requirement, and had to cool our heels for a few months when we were posted to our first operational squadrons in the north. We also did not know then that the IAF was fast entering a phase of low aircraft serviceability and it was difficult to train the extra pilots commissioned in the post-1962 expansion. The fighter squadrons in the east were worse off compared to those in the west. Transport and helicopter units that routinely carried out air-maintenance tasks for our troops in the high Himalayas were always busy, but could not spare aircraft and instructors to convert the newly commissioned pilots. There were rumours that the COs of some of these squadrons did not even know the names of their pilots and navigators. Many of our course-mates languished in these units in the first four or five years of their service, when in fact they should have flown the maximum in the prime of their service life. Little did we know that the conditions would get worse before they eventually got better. Poor serviceability was, however, a very uneven phenomenon, with some squadrons flying far more than the others. A lot depended on personalities, squadron ethos and reputation of the CO and one's luck.

Before long, I had somehow managed to do the 'five' hours on a Hunter and had begun flying the Gnat Mk1 at Ambala, which at the time had two Gnat and two Mystere IVA Squadrons. The first few sorties on the Gnat were also very challenging because there was no two-seat Gnat trainer. We were shown an 'approximate' glide path on a Hunter Trainer and as in the Vampire Mk 52, once again, someone sat on the tail of the Gnat to raise the nose to show the correct take-off 'attitude' or angle. The student was expected to remember it. Primitive as it might sound, the arrangement worked quite well, and I do not know of a case where a pilot had difficulty landing the really fast and diminutive Gnat on his first solo flight. So small was the aircraft that the pilot simply raised himself with his arms on the side of the cockpit and jumped into it. The Gnat also held a record of getting airborne in less than a minute, when on air defence alert. Those who saw the little fighter for the first time did not believe that it was the real aircraft they were looking at and not a model. The Gnat had already gained much fame during the 1965 Indo-Pak war and was known as the Sabre Slayer for having shot down a number of enemy fighters by that name.

Soon we were to learn that keeping this aircraft in the air was not easy as maintenance and spares support from its manufacturer Hindustan Aeronautics Limited (HAL) were often well short of expected. It was also prone to many problems such as engine surge, hydraulic system and control malfunctions, Radio Telephony (R/T) failure and very frequent gun stoppages. Most of these problems arose from the miniaturisation of the components fitted in the Gnat. The Orpheus engine, a de-rated version of which still powers the Kiran Mk2 aircraft, had a very narrow surge boundary and often misbehaved, or even failed, if and when the pilot was a little harsh with throttle opening, especially at heights above 20,000 feet.

These regular 'snags', however, made all Gnat pilots very cautious and alert and greatly improved their situational awareness. I think we genuinely respected the machine and allowed for its idiosyncrasies. One felt part of it. As an old pilot appropriately put it, "Flying the Gnat was like strapping it on your back." A somewhat plump pilot was asked how he got into the little Gnat. The answer was, "With a shoe-horn!" He also had the presence of mind to say, "But I do not need a can opener to get out of it." In spite of the best efforts, it took over two years to become Fully Operational (F/Ops) on the Gnat. Almost the first course that a fighter pilot then did and does even today, is the locally run 'cadre' for Forward Air Controller (FAC) where he is trained to direct fighter strikes on ground targets that the army wants destroyed. This is the first time that a pilot learns about the army's philosophy of war fighting. From early on, this kind of training was termed army co-operation, and contrary to popular belief, supporting the army has always been and will continue to be one of the most important tasks that the IAF performs. Some of us also got the opportunity to spend a few days with the army units and in turn, invited the young counterparts to visit our air force stations to familiarise themselves with our daily routine. Those of us who flew as supernumerary crew in transport aircraft to 'earn' flying bounty, also got an opportunity to visit forward areas in Ladakh and Jammu and Kashmir, and actually saw for the first time that there was so much more of India beyond Leh or Srinagar. We were also impressed by the difficult flying environment in which our transport counterparts routinely flew.

By the early part of 1970, the situation in the region had begun deteriorating, and by the end of the year, it was widely believed that the probability of another war with Pakistan was very high. Number 18 Squadron to which I was posted, was earmarked for the air defence of Srinagar, and we had begun visiting the Kashmir Valley from late 1968 onwards. Srinagar was far more beautiful, quiet and peaceful than one imagined, even if the locals sometimes let us know that we, the visitors, were from India.

Well before the third Indo-Pak war began in December 1971, the squadron was in place at Srinagar. Due to there being no aircraft shelters at the Srinagar airfield, the squadron was allowed to keep a maximum of only four Gnats with only one more stand-by, for the air defence of the Valley. Frequent 'unserviceabilities' or technical snags meant many trips to Ambala to get a replacement. The visibility in winters used to be pretty bad sometimes, making it impossible to spot another aircraft in the air. The absence of an air defence or airfield surveillance radar meant that we had to rely on our eyes. Some 'observer posts' were located on the mountain tops on the western side of the Valley, for giving us warning about the approach of enemy fighters. This was far from a reliable procedure, as very often, the observer only heard the sound of a jet but could/did not see it. At other times, the batteries of his R/T set ran low and could not be recharged. To add to the difficulties, some Pakistani spies or sympathisers in the Valley warned the approaching PAF aircraft in advance, if a Gnat patrol was already in the air. In spite of these difficulties, the squadron saw some 14 daylight air attacks but only three encounters in the air, in one of which Flying Officer N.J.S. Sekhon went down fighting the enemy, and was awarded the highest gallantry award, the Param Vir Chakra.

Soon after the War, I was posted to another Gnat squadron at Bagdogra near Siliguri in West Bengal. I spent a total of seven years in Gnat, and two more years in Ajeet Squadrons. In 1980, I was posted to a MiG-21MF Squadron, by which time I had completed the Air Staff Course at Defence Services Staff College (DSSC), Wellington, the Qualified Flying Instructors (QFI) Course at Tambaram,

Madras (now Chennai) and a two-year tenure as a flying instructor at the Air Force Academy (AFA) Dundigal near Secunderabad. After about two years in No. 7 Squadron then based at Chandigarh, I was selected for deputation to the Government of Iraq, as India had been sending QFIs to that country from the late 1960s. As one wit put it, "Mao and Zhou gave us a job, and Saddam Hussein pulled us above the poverty line." This is how he described those of us recruited in the post-1962 air force expansion. Later, the IAF found it difficult to manage the careers and promotions of these officers and called it the 'bulge' in the pyramid, conveniently forgetting that for over a decade in the late 1970s and 1980s, most of the 'appointments' where real work was done, were manned by these officers. A very large number of these pilots did not get a fair deal and lost out on promotions for no fault of theirs and were prematurely wasted out despite some efforts by Air Headquarters such as 'deep selection' promotion policy to allow officers a fair chance of promotion to the rank of Wing Commander.

The Iraq experience was unique and an eye-opener for those of us brought up in a free-for-all democracy, where the citizen could get away with almost anything. The long Iran-Iraq war was on when we reached Baghdad in June 1982, but there was neither any blackout, anxiety nor any other indication that the country was at war. Our base, the Air Force College at Tikrit, Saddam Hussein's home town, in fact, a small village, was equally quiet. Only when we started flying to the east of the river Tigris were we sometimes called back to land. The Iraqi authorities never told us that an air defence alert was underway or that an enemy attack was imminent. The Indian Embassy library was well stocked, and one read some memorable books. Most of us were busy shopping, as Iraq's import-oriented economy was full of foreign white goods. Very often, items of daily consumption like butter, onions and chicken became 'makoo' or Arabic for unavailable, if imports were delayed. For an Indian used to plenty at the worst of times, this was a major shock. Iraqi paranoia for their leader's safety and the workings of a dictatorship, albeit a popular one, were some of the other shocks to our Indian minds. Back home in India, Khalistani separatists had been creating serious problems for the Central Government. Operation Blue Star of June 1984, had its backlash in Indira Gandhi's assassination at the hands of her bodyguards in October 1984, that was followed by mayhem in Delhi and elsewhere, in which over 3,000 Sikhs were massacred.

Soon after my return from Iraq in August 1984, with a brand new Volkswagen Passat hatch-back, which was the cynosure of friends and foes alike, I found myself on the faculty of the DSSC at Wellington, in the salubrious Nilgiri hills of Tamil Nadu. This was considered a prestigious appointment and a necessary step in the promotion ladder, or so it was generally thought. After a nearly two-year-long tenure, during which I broke my back in a horse-riding accident, but miraculously regained A1G1,the medical category essential to fly any fighter aircraft, thanks to help from some highly qualified aviation medicine specialists, I was posted to take over command of a fighter squadron, a goal that every self-respecting pilot has in his mind. Number 22 Squadron, then equipped with the Ajeet, was based at Bagdogra. Since this was my second tour of Bagdogra, the landscape was familiar, the job demanding but professionally immensely satisfying. There were the usual trips for firing practice to another station in West Bengal, at Kalai Kunda near Kharagpur. Given the limited endurance of the Ajeet – like all fighters of that generation, and poor serviceability – it was extremely difficult to complete the government authorised task of 240 hours per month, but during the two years, the squadron made a record of sorts, by regularly flying 250-300 sorties every month. So busy was the routine, that before I realised it, the two-year tenure was over, with almost every young pilot of the squadron achieving his F/Ops status and night flying qualification, so that all of them could be posted out to either Jaguar or MiG-27 units. The squadron also won the Flight Safety Trophy for that year.

I soon found myself, much against my wishes, on the personal staff of the Air-Officer-Commanding-in-Chief (AOC-in-C) Eastern Air Command (EAC) at its Headquarters at Shillong in Meghalaya, further east. In fact, I was very keen to go to Gwalior, Pune, Jodhpur or Ambala where some of the new fighters like the Mirage-2000, MiG-29, MiG-27 and Jaguar were based. I had spent too many years with the Gnat, Hunter and MiG-21. It took me some time to come to terms with my new job, which I must admit, proved very interesting, educative and demanding. I got to see how a senior Air Marshal thought and worked. During this period Rajiv Gandhi, the young Prime Minister, made a landmark visit to China, to bring about a thaw in Sino-Indian relations, and calm the atmosphere that had got tense following the Sum Durong Chu incident of 1986, in which Chinese and Indian troops had nearly clashed on the border. I remember a case of a Chinese fighter violating Indian airspace that India did not openly protest about.

At the end of a year and a half, I became a Group Captain and left Headquarters EAC, to command the newly raised mini-wing No. 43 co-located with No. 5 BRD at Sulur, near Coimbatore in Tamil Nadu. This too was an interesting stint, as I first had two Mi-8 helicopter units under me with a Mi-17 and a Mi-25 unit on long attachment, for operations in Sri Lanka. Later an An-32 Squadron joined us. Funnily, the CO of this squadron was at least four courses senior to me, and it is to his credit that we got along very well. Not once did he let me feel the difference in our seniority. I visited my units at Jaffna, Vavunia, and Trincomalee in Sri Lanka and learnt of their problems and needs first-hand. This was my second command assignment.

About a year and nine months later, I was posted to Delhi as part of the Joint Planning Staff (JPS) in the Military Wing of the Cabinet Secretariat. Our offices were located on the ground floor of the imposing and majestic South Block, but were as dusty and unkempt as any *sarkari* office. Since the JPS was part of the Chiefs of Staff Committee (CoSC), we used to attend the CoSC meetings every Monday afternoon. This was a great opportunity to see the highest commanders of our armed forces at close quarters.

In 1993, I took command of a Forward Base Support Unit (FBSU) at Uttarlai, near Barmer in Rajasthan. Known as a punishment posting in the IAF, I found that the people in small remote bases form a far more cohesive group and work better. Uttarlai was notorious for brackish water, very high temperatures in summer, poor drainage due to a sub-soil layer of gypsum and rock, malaria and fluorosis. Health issues affected other areas too. There was an acute shortage of qualified teachers in our Central School as most of those posted to Uttarlai, simply used to take leave without pay and not report for duty. This tenure was both challenging and satisfying, as we were able to do some useful work for the uplift of the villagers of Uttarlai.

After a short stint of just over a year at Air Headquarters, as the Director, Personnel Planning (DPP), I was once again transferred, this time to take over command of a very large and busy airbase at Kalai Kunda near Kharagpur in West Bengal. This base like ATW, Jamnagar, was used for air-to-air firing practice over the sea, off the coast of Odisha. At any time, there was at least one visiting squadron (in addition to the two MiG-27 and one Hunter Target Towing Unit permanently based at Kalai Kunda) which meant an extremely busy schedule for all station personnel. At the end of 1997, the IAF went through very serious turmoil, due to unprecedented protests by a section of disaffected technical personnel, unhappy about changes made to the then prevailing grade structure of airmen. Some engineering officers also were affected by rumours of disproportionate pay rise recommended for the Flying Branch personnel, to the Fifth Pay Commission. Visiting squadrons from all over India brought with them all kind of news, and at times unfounded rumours, that were to play a major role during those unfortunate and troubled times that affected the normal working of many air force bases. It was a harrowing time, and it was only with tact and sincere persuasion that the situation was brought under control. In retrospect, the real reason for this widespread unhappiness was that the higher authorities at Delhi, had planned to make changes to the trade structure, without first consulting people in the field. Incidents of tool-down strikes and other such disruptions were widely reported in the national print and electronic media, further alienating large sections of air force personnel. A few culprits and rabble rousers were ultimately brought to book but the damage was done. In my personal opinion, the agitation severely affected inter- and intra-branch relations in the air force, and it will be a long time before the wounds are completely healed.

At the end of one year, I was posted out to Pune as AOC Advance

Headquarters, South Western Air Command. It seemed that I had paid the price for someone else's mistakes.

Each of the Army Commanders in India is responsible for conducting army/ ground operations in the area of his responsibility. To do this job effectively, an air force officer of the rank of Air Commodore is established to command a small element of air force personnel that is co-located with the army command. The AOC Advance Headquarters is essentially meant to advise the Army Commander on all issues related to employment of air power, to assist him in executing his army's plans and also to direct the Tactical Air Centre (TAC) Commanders co-located with the Army's Corps Headquarters, under the control of the Army Command. At the time, the jurisdiction of the Southern Army Command, based at Pune, extended from Jodhpur in the north to the southernmost limits of the Indian Peninsula. The Army Commander was thus required to liaise with Headquarters South-Western Air Command (SWAC) and Southern Air Command (SAC) IAF, and also with the Western and Southern Commands of the Navy.

Soon after reaching Pune, I visited the Tactical Air Centres (TACs) at Bhopal and Jodhpur and familiarised myself with their operational plans. In late November-December 1998, a huge Command-level army-air force exercise was planned in the Rajasthan desert, in which more than 30,000 troops participated. The tasks allotted to the IAF were executed in time and the army elements were provided with adequate air support. The exercise was a complete success.

I feel that while the contribution of the IAF was laudable, the effects of air power were not adequately factored into the overall assessment by the umpires; as such, the lessons drawn from such a massive exercise were incomplete. A more thorough process of joint planning from the very conception of the exercise would have been far more beneficial. As brought out before, from its very inception in 1932, when its strength was a few handful of aircraft, and also during World War II, when its strength gradually increased to 10 squadrons, and again, immediately after independence in the nearly 14-month war in Jammu and Kashmir, the IAF did little else but to act in direct support of the army. Despite this record, the army has always complained that the IAF did not adequately support land operations. Instead of planning an operation with the IAF, the army tends to use air power as a bonus, and is loath to discuss the details, and the army's concept of operations and objectives. The army simply demands that a particular minimum number of aircraft/sorties be allocated to it, and that the army then be allowed to use the earmarked assets as it pleases. The IAF on the other hand, wants to be included in the planning of the operation from the very beginning, and expects to be allowed to suggest ways to use available air power to achieve a certain 'effect'. The IAF is then ready to employ even larger numbers of aircraft if need be, to achieve the stated objective. It is unfair to simply expect the IAF to be ready at the army's beck and call without including it in joint planning. Worse, the army very often draws wrong lessons from an exercise or actual operation, when it fails to critically evaluate IAF's contribution.

At the end of a short period of eight months, I was posted as Member, Air Force and Senior Fellow, on deputation to the Institute for Defence Studies and Analyses (IDSA), a Ministry of Defence-funded think tank in Delhi. I retired from the IAF after spending a little over three years in this position on August 31, 2002, thus bringing to a close a 35-year fruitful yet challenging and enjoyable career with the IAF.

Select Bibliography

Primary Sources – Official Publications

Annual Report 2011-2012, Ministry of Defence, Government of India.

Basic Doctrine of the IAF, Air Headquarters, New Delhi, September 7, 2012.

Basic Doctrine of the Indian Army, Air Headquarters, New Delhi, 1999.

British Air and Space Doctrine, AP 3000, Fourth Edition, Air Staff, Ministry of Defence, Government of the United Kingdom, London.

British Defence Doctrine, Fourth Edition, Headquarters, Royal Air Force, UK, 2006.

India's Nuclear Doctrine: Draft Report of National Security Advisory Board, (Released by Government of India on August 7, 1999 and amended January 2003).

Interviews with Retired and Serving Military Officers

Air Vice Marshal H.S. Ahluwalia (Retd.)

Air Marshal S.G. Inamdar (Retd.)

Air Marshal Bharat Kumar (Retd.)

General V.P. Malik (Retd.)

Air Marshal Y.V. Malse (Retd.)

Air Marshal M. Matheswaran

Air Marshal N. Menon (Retd.)

Air Chief Marshal H. Moolgaonkar (Retd.)

Air Marshal S.C. Mukul (Retd.)

Air Marshal B.K. Pandey (Retd.)

Air Marshal R. Raghu Rajan (Retd.)

Air Marshal P. Rajkumar (Retd.)

Air Marshal Randhir Singh (Retd.)

Air Chief Marshal S.P. Tyagi (Retd.)
Several Unnamed Serving Officers

Secondary Sources

Abdullah, Sheikh Mohammad, *Flames of the Chinar: An Autobiography*, Viking, New Delhi, 1993.

Alagappa, Muthiah (ed.), *Asian Security Practice: Material and Ideational Influences*, Stanford University Press, Stanford, 1998.

Alexander, P.C., *Through the Corridors of Power: An Insider's Story*, HarperCollins, New Delhi, 2004.

Burles, Mark and Abram N. Shulsky, *Patterns in China's Use of Force: Evidence from History and Doctrinal Writings*, RAND, Santa Monica, 2000.

Campbell-Johnson, Alan, *Mission with Mountbatten*, Robert Hale, London, 1951.

Chaturvedi, M.S., *History of the Indian Air Force,* Vikas, New Delhi, 1978.

Chengappa, Raj, *Weapons of Peace: The Secret Story of India's Quest to be a Nuclear Power*, HarperCollins, New Delhi, 2000.

Cohen, Stephen P. and Sunil Dasgupta, *Arming Without Aiming: India's Military Modernisation*, Viking, New Delhi, 2010.

Dahiya, Rumel, Namrata Goswami, Ajey Lele, (eds.), *Asia 2030: The Unfolding Future*, Lancer, New Delhi, 2010.

Dalvi, J.P., *Himalayan Blunder*, Thacker & Company Limited, Bombay, 1969.

Das, Durga, *India from Curzon to Nehru and After*, Rupa & Co., Delhi, 1969 (Reprinted 1974).

Dasgupta, C., *War and Diplomacy in Kashmir 1947-48*, Sage, New Delhi, 2002.

Fischer, Louis, *The Life of Mahatma Gandhi*, Bharatiya Vidya Bhawan, Mumbai, 1995.

Galbraith, John Kenneth, *Ambassador's Journal*, Hamish Hamilton, London, 1969.

Gandhi, Rajmohan, *Patel: A Life*, Navjivan Press, Ahmedabad, 1991 (Reprint 2008).

Garver, John W., *Protracted Contest: Sino-Indian Rivalry in the Twentieth Century*, University of Washington Press, Seattle, Washington, 2001.

Hodson, H.V., *The Great Indian Divide: Britain-India-Pakistan*, Hutchinson, London, 1969.

Jalan, Bimal, *The Future of India*, Viking, New Delhi, 2005.

Jha, Prem Shankar. *The Origins of a Dispute: Kashmir 1947*, Oxford University Press, New Delhi, 2003.

Kalyanaraman, S., "The Indian Military Response to Threats from Pakistan, 1949-

2010", Paper presented at the IDSA Fellows Seminar, July 8, 2011 (Unpublished).

Kaul, B.M., *The Untold Story*, Allied Publishers, New Delhi, 1967.

Kavic, Lorne J., *India's Quest for Security: Defence Policies 1947-1965*, EBD Publishing and Distributing Co., Dehradun, 1967. Also, University of California Press, Berkeley & Los Angeles, 1967.

Khan, M. Akbar, *Raiders in Kashmir*, Second Edition, National Book Foundation, Islamabad, 1975.

Khilnani, Sunil, *The Idea of India*, Hamish Hamilton, London, 1997.

____, Kumar, Rajiv, Pratap Bhanu Mehta, Prakash Menon, Nandan Nilekani, Srinath Raghavan, Shyam Saran, Siddharth Vardarajan, *Non-alignment 2.0: A Foreign and Strategic Policy for India in the Twenty First Century*, New Delhi, Centre for Policy Research, February 28, 2012.

Khullar, Darshan, *When Generals Failed: The Chinese Invasion*, Manas Publications, New Delhi, 1999.

Kumar, Bharat, *An Incredible War: Indian Air Force in Kashmir War 1947-48*, Knowledge World, New Delhi, 2007.

Lal, P.C., *My Years with the IAF*, Lancer International, New Delhi, 1986.

Lele, Ajey, *Strategic Technologies for the Military*, Sage, New Delhi, 2009.

Lewis, John Wilson and Xue Litai, *China's Strategic Sea Power: The Politics of Force Modernization in the Nuclear Age*, Stanford University Press, Stanford, 1994.

____ and Xue Litai, 'China's Search for a Modern Air Force', *International Security*, Summer 1999, 24 (1), pp. 64-94.

Malik, S.K., *The Quranic Concept of War*, Associate Printers, Lahore, 1979.

Malik, V.P., *Kargil: From Surprise to Victory*, Harper Collins, New Delhi, 2006.

Mankekar, D.R., *The Guilty Men of 1962*, Tulsi Shah, Mumbai, 1968.

____, *Twenty Two Fateful Days: Pakistan Cut to Size*, Maniktalas, Mumbai,1966.

Maxwell, Neville, *India's China War*, Jonathan Cape, London, 1970.

Mac Farquhar, Roderick, *The Origins of the Cultural Revolution: Volume 3, The Coming of the Cataclysm 1961-1966*, Columbia University Press, 1987.

Menon, V.P., *The Story of the Integration of Indian States*, Longman Green, London, 1956.

Mullik, B.N., *My Years with Nehru: The Chinese Betrayal*, Allied Publishers, New Delhi, 1971.

Morgenthau, Hans J., *Politics Among Nations: The Struggle for Power and Peace*, (Third Edition), Scientific Book Agency, Kolkata, 1966.

Nanda, Prakash (ed.) *Rising India: Friends and Foes*, Lancer, New Delhi, 2007.

Nehru, Jawaharlal, *The Discovery of India* (First published Signet Press, Calcutta 1946, Reprint 2004, Penguin, New Delhi).

Palit, D.K., *War in the High Himalayas: Indian Army in Crisis, 1962,* Hurst & Co., London, 1991.

Pape, Robert A., "The True Worth of Air Power", *Foreign Affairs* 83 (2), March-April 2004, pp. 116-27.

Paret, Peter (ed.), *Makers of Modern Strategy: From Machiavelli to Modern Age*, Princeton University Press, New Jersey, 1986.

Phadke, R.V., *PLAAF: Shifting Air Power Balance*, Occasional Paper, CISAC, Stanford, February 2002.

____, *Air Power and Escalation Control*, Stimson Center, Washington DC, May 2003.

____, *China's Power Projection*, Manas Publications, New Delhi, 2005.

Prasad, S.N. and Dharm Pal, *Operations in Jammu & Kashmir, 1947-48*, History Division, Ministry of Defence, Government of India, New Delhi, 2005.

Pradhan, R.D., *Debacle to Revival: Y.B. Chavan as Defence Minister, 1962-65*, Orient Longman, Hyderabad, 1998.

____, *The 1965 War: The Inside Story, Defence Minister Y.B. Chavan's Diary of India-Pakistan War*, Atlantic Publishers, New Delhi, 2007.

Raghavan, Srinath, *War and Peace in Modern India: A Strategic History of the Nehru Years*, Permanent Black, Ranikhet, 2010.

Rajkumar, Philip, *The Tejas Story: The Light Combat Aircraft Project*, Manohar, New Delhi, 2008.

Rashid, Ahmed, *Descent into Chaos*, Viking, London, 2008.

Saigal A.L. (ed.), *Birth of an Air Force: The Memoirs of Air Vice-Marshal Harjinder Singh*, Palit and Palit Publishers, New Delhi, 1977.

Sachdev, A.K., *Space Age Gladiators*, Knowledge World, New Delhi, December 2000.

Saksena, K.P., *The United Nations and Collective Security,* D.K. Publishing House, New Delhi, 1974.

Sarila, Narendra Singh, *The Shadow of the Great Game: The Untold Story of India's Partition*, Constable, London, 2006.

Singh, Jasjit (ed.) *Nuclear India,* Knowledge World, New Delhi, July 1998.

____ (ed.) *Pakistan Occupied Kashmir: Under the Jackboot*, Siddhi Books, New Delhi, 1995.

Sisodia, N.S. and Kalyanaraman, S. (eds.), *The Future of War and Peace in Asia*, Magnum Books, New Delhi, 2010.

Sisodia, N.S. and Sujit Dutta, (eds.) *India and the World, Vol. 1 – Strategic Thought: The Formative Years,* Promilla and Co., New Delhi, 2005.

Smith, Chris, *India's Ad Hoc Arsenal: Direction or Drift in Defence Policy*?, SIPRI, Oxford University Press, 1994.

Smith, David, *The Dragon and the Elephant: China, India and the New World Order*, Profile Books, London, 2007.

Swaine, Michael D. and Ashley J. Tellis, *Interpreting China's Grand Strategy: Past, Present and Future*, Project Air Force, RAND, Santa Monica, 2000.

Tanham, George K. and Marcy Agmon, *The Indian Air Force: Trends and Prospects*, RAND Monograph, Santa Monica, 1995.

Thorat, S.P.P., From *Reveille to Retreat*, Allied Publishers, New Delhi, 1986.

Vallance, Andrew G.B., *The Air Weapon: Doctrines of Air Power Strategy and Operational Art*, St. Martin's Press, London, 1996.

Magazines and Journals

Air Power Journal, USAF Air University, Alabama, USA.

Journal of Defence Studies, Bloomsbury, New Delhi.

Jane's Defence Weekly, IHS, UK.

Strategic Analysis, Routledge, UK.

Index